ECDL

with Microsoft Office 2000 and Windows 2000

A Self-Paced Training Course for ECDL Using
Microsoft Windows 2000, Microsoft Office 2000 and
Microsoft Internet Explorer 5

ECDL Approved Courseware
Syllabus Version 3.0

Published by
GTSLearning International Limited

© *GTSLearning International Ltd 2001*
ISBN 1 84005 281 3

First edition published 2001 (ISBN 1 84005 280 5)
Second (revised) edition published 2001

P/N AXIS 001

Author	**James Pengelly**
Editor	Jane Cooper

Publisher and Distributor

This courseware is owned and distributed internationally by **GTSLearning International Ltd**, the market-leading Education Services Provider, supplying a portfolio of courseware for IT skills and certifications to more than 500 **gtspartner** sites in more than 50 countries.

ECDL Approved Courseware
Syllabus Version 3.0

Table of Contents

Using the Computer and Managing Files

Word Processing

Spreadsheets

Database

Presentation

Information and Communication

<u>Appendices</u>

How This Book Works

Understand the course's learning objectives and how the book is organised

---

Introduction

(**Learning outcomes**) ☐
(About the **ECDL**) ☐
(How to **work through** the lessons) ☐
(Using the **mouse** and **keyboard** conventions) ☐
(About **notes** and **tips** while working) ☐
(Using the **data CD**) ☐
(**Different ways** to complete the course) ☐

Who Can Use This Course?

This training course is designed to help you to obtain a **European Computer Driving Licence**, an internationally accepted validation of your proficiency with **computers** and common **software applications**. It is also an ideal course if you simply want to learn the **basics** of using a computer or if you want to consolidate some **previous experience** with computers and Office software.

This is a **self-paced** training course, which means it teaches you through simple instructions and step-by-step examples that you can work through as often as required and at your own pace. You can use this course to study **on your own** at **home** or at **work**, to study with the support of a **tutor** or to study as part of a **distance learning** program.

The ECDL is a **vendor-neutral** qualification, which means that it is not designed for any particular brand of software. This course demonstrates the use of the Microsoft products **Windows 2000, Office 2000 (Word, Excel, Access, PowerPoint** and **Outlook)** and **Internet Explorer 5**. Other courses are available for different software.

No previous experience of using a computer or any software application is required.

> **Note** You could also use this course if you are using the **Windows Millennium** operating system and/or if you prefer to use **Outlook Express 5** for the Communication module. Features of these programs are dealt with in the appendices. You should also be able to work through the practical exercises, though the step-by-step instructions will not apply to these applications exactly.

Learning Outcomes

This course will help you to achieve the following goals:

♦ Obtain a **European Computer Driving Licence** (the ECDL qualification is described in more detail below).

♦ Recognise the role of **Information Technology** in society.

♦ Understand the basics of how a **computer** works.

♦ Use an **operating system** to manage the computer and data files.

♦ Use the main features of **Office software** (a word processor, spreadsheet, database and presentation graphics).

♦ Browse the **world wide web** and send **electronic mail**.

More detailed learning objectives are given at the start of each **module** and each **lesson**.

On completion of this course, you may wish to go on to learn about more advanced features of Office applications. For details of other books in the **Learn** range, please refer to page 744.

About the ECDL

> The European Computer Driving Licence (ECDL) certifies that the holder has knowledge of the basic concepts of Information Technology (IT) and is able to use a personal computer and common computer applications at a basic level of competence.
>
> *The ECDL Syllabus*

The ECDL is an internationally-recognised certificate designed to assure employers that job applicants have proven competence in using a computer.

> **Tip** Outside the European Union, the ECDL is referred to as the ICDL (International Computer Driving Licence). The two qualifications are identical.

The ECDL/ICDL syllabus (the set of learning objectives) is developed and maintained by the ECDL Foundation (ECDL-F). ECDL-F license organisations to operate the qualification in each country.

ECDL Syllabus

The ECDL Syllabus is organised into seven **modules**.

◆ **Basic Concepts of Information Technology** - use of a personal computer and awareness of the application of IT in society.

◆ **Using the Computer and Managing Files** - use of an operating system to manage a computer and organise data files.

◆ **Word Processing** - use of word processing software to create, format and distribute documents, such as a letter, report or brochure.

◆ **Spreadsheets** - use a spreadsheet application to manage, format, calculate and distribute numerical data.

◆ **Database** - use a database application to store and retrieve data.

◆ **Presentation** - use software to create, format and distribute a slide show to accompany business presentations, or produce drawings.

◆ **Information and Communication** - use a web browser to browse the world wide web and send, receive and manage electronic mail.

Software

The ECDL is a **vendor-neutral** qualification, that is, the syllabus is not tied to specific features in software of any one brand. However, to learn features and to take the ECDL tests you will use specific products.

Most vendors update their software every 2-3 years. Each new release of the software is given a **version number**. You should note that the design of software can vary from version to version.

This training course is designed for the product versions listed on page 1. Other courses are available for different products and product versions.

You should ensure that the tests you take are designed for the same versions of the products you are training with.

When you have completed your ECDL, you should be able to **apply** your knowledge of one product or version to use another one successfully.

Test Centres

To obtain an ECDL, you must complete a test for each of the seven modules. You can take a test at an ECDL Approved Test Centre.

If you have not found a test centre already, contact the organisation administering the ECDL in your country. In the UK, this is the **British Computer Society** (www.ecdl.co.uk).

A pass mark of 70-80% is expected for each module. Tests can be evaluated manually (by test centre staff) or automatically (using a software test tool).

There are generally two types of test:

♦ **Question-based** - where you have to complete a series of questions (usually multiple-choice).

♦ **Task-oriented** - where you have to perform a series of tasks using the appropriate software.

If you have a preference for either type of test, find out which the test centre uses. If the test is automated, you might want to ask if it is possible to complete a "mock" test, to familiarise yourself with the software used for testing.

Courseware

This training course will demonstrate all the knowledge, features and actions you need to pass the ECDL tests. The course has been approved by the ECDL-F for use as ECDL training material.

You can use this course with or without a tutor or further support.

Course Organisation

The course is organised into seven main chapters, matching the seven **ECDL modules**. There are also appendices containing some useful tools and information.

Each chapter is divided into a series of **lessons**. A lesson is designed to cover related **topics** or **tasks**. Please note that the order of the lessons does not follow the order of ECDL syllabus items. The lesson order has been designed to give the best possible path into each module for a complete novice.

Tip	If you want to follow the ECDL objectives in syllabus order, refer to the Appendix on page 691 for a list of page references to each syllabus objective.

Choosing How to Study

As well as meeting the needs of **beginners**, this course has been designed to adapt to the **different ways** a more experienced user might want to study. You can follow the lessons in almost any order you choose, to take account of your previous experience or task requirements in your job. For example, you might need to learn how to use presentation graphics software before learning about the spreadsheet application Excel.

Some suggestions for different ways of following the lessons are given under "Learning Paths" on page 10.

When and Where to Study

This book is designed to be used **at your computer**, so that you can follow the practice examples as you learn about each topic. You can use a PC at **home** or in the **workplace**. It is assumed that the computer hardware and applications you will use have been installed and setup for you already.

If you are following the course **without tutor support**, work through each lesson in one study session. If you want to complete more than one lesson in a study session, take a 15-minute break between each lesson.

Use each lesson as many times as you want, until **you** feel confident that you can move on. Use the appendix to keep careful track of which **ECDL syllabus** points you have learned and identify topics needing further practice.

> **Note** If you cannot complete a lesson in one go, you will usually be able to save the file you are working on and start again later.

If you are studying **with a tutor**, try working back through a lesson in your own time if you feel that a study session has moved to quickly for you.

Working Through Each Lesson

Learning objectives

At the beginning of each module and each lesson there is a list of learning objectives, showing which topics and features will be covered by the lesson. It is important to have a clear idea of what you want to achieve in each session and to be able to check that you have covered everything required by the syllabus.

You can use the appendix on page 691 to keep track of which items you have practised and highlight any areas you want to review.

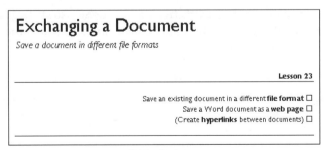

Exchanging a Document
Save a document in different file formats

Lesson 23

Save an existing document in a different **file format** ☐
Save a Word document as a **web page** ☐
(Create **hyperlinks** between documents) ☐

Start of a lesson

Any points not directly required by the ECDL syllabus are shown in brackets. These topics can be omitted if you wish.

Topics

Each topic starts with a brief description of the use and benefits of the task or tool, followed by hands-on examples of how to use it.

In most cases, you will be given explicit instructions to follow, using the example data files provided.

Instructions to follow

The instructions to follow are shown with a black circle bullet point.

Some more complex topics, where there are many alternatives, are described generically (the steps to follow in any situation). These topics appear with the ⑨ icon next to the heading and use white circle bullet points.

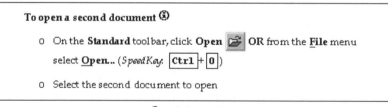

Generic instructions

They are often followed by a **Practice** topic to demonstrate by example. Practice topics are also used to reinforce learning and where there is plenty of scope for you to experiment with a feature.

In some lessons, you will also find **review questions** to test what you have learned. Answers to review questions are given at the end of the module.

As you progress, you will find that instructions for common tasks get less detailed. If you find yourself struggling to follow the instructions, review previous lessons to get more confidence.

Mouse and Keyboard Conventions

Software can be operated using both the mouse and keyboard. This course tries to show you alternative ways of completing a task. These are given in the order:

♦ Toolbar button

♦ Menu command/shortcut menu - including underlined menu access keys

♦ SpeedKey (keyboard shortcut)

Different options for selecting a command

You can use whichever method you prefer, but note that for some types of ECDL test, you may need to know **each way** of choosing a command.

Mouse terms

You will get to practice use of the mouse during the course. The following terms are used throughout the course to describe common mouse actions:

Term	Meaning
Point	Move the mouse pointer over the object or item required.
Click/ Right-click	Point to the item you want to select then press and release the mouse button.
Double-click	Point to the item then press and release the mouse button twice in quick succession.
Click-and-drag	Point to the item or area you want then press the left mouse button and hold it down whilst pointing to another area of the screen. Release the mouse button.

Note If you are **left-handed**, the mouse buttons are reversed, so "click" means press the **right** mouse button; "right-click" means press the **left** mouse button. If your mouse is not setup for left-handed use, refer to page 168 to find out how to do so.

Keyboard terms

As well as using the mouse, you can issue commands from the keyboard. You also use the keyboard to type text into documents.

When you are instructed to press a key on the keyboard, the key is illustrated as: F1 or Caps Lock. If you are not familiar with a PC keyboard, use the table below to help recognise keys without text labels.

Key	Appearance on Keyboard
Tab	
Shift	
Backspace	
Enter	

Note The Enter key is also referred to as the Return key.

To operate software, you often need to use a combination of keys at the same time. In the lessons, two keys shown with a plus sign (+) between them means you should press both keys together. So, Alt+F4 means "Hold down the Alt key while you press F4 then release both keys".

You will also use certain keys in combination with the mouse. For example, Ctrl+click means hold down the Ctrl key while you click different items with the mouse.

When you are asked to type text, numbers or letters, the text appears in a different typeface from the instructions. For example:

• Type This text is in a different typeface

You would be expected to type "This text is in a different typeface".

Notes, Tips and Warnings

Notes and tips are given throughout each lesson.

Notes give additional information about the current topic. Always read the note before completing the task.

> **Note** Selecting or de-selecting the **Menus show recently used commands first** check box will affect every Office 2000 application on your PC.

Note

Tips provide alternative ways of carrying out a task.

> **Tip** When you start Word, a new document is created automatically. To create another new document, on the **Standard** toolbar, click **New** ☐ (*SpeedKey* `Ctrl` + `N`).

Tip

You may also see the **Warning** message. This means that you must pay careful attention to the text before proceeding.

Finally, the **ECDL** box indicates that a topic is not specifically required by the syllabus. These topics have been included because they are considered important for general use of an application.

Index, Glossary and Syllabus

At the back of the book you will find an **index** of the topics and features covered in the course, a **glossary** of computer terms and jargon and a copy of the **ECDL syllabus**, with cross-references to the page(s) in the book where each learning objective is described.

The Data CD

The CD-ROM attached to the back cover of this book contains sample data files for use during the lessons.

You will load the data files onto your computer during the lessons.

If you are a more experienced user, and want to get started with a particular lesson straight away, there are also instructions for installing the files in the CD's **ReadMe** file.

Hardware and Software Setup

This course assumes that the PC hardware and software you are using has been installed and setup already.

As well as a PC, a printer and floppy disk are required to complete some exercises.

Modern software is very easy to customise. Where possible, the examples in this course use the default settings when the software is installed. However, you may find that some features referred to are missing or do not look the same as on your own computer.

If software is setup differently to the way the course describes, you should contact your IT support person for help. Please do not change the setup of a computer at work without your employer's permission.

If you are working from home, there is a basic guide to setting up software in the appendix on page 687.

Learning Paths

If you have some previous experience of computers, you may want to study the lessons in a different order.

Remember that you can use the appendix on page 691 to keep track of your progress against the ECDL syllabus.

To get started with software applications quickly

The first module is mostly knowledge-based, with few practical examples.

If you are a complete beginner, the first practical lesson is on page 101. If you have used a computer before, you could start with "Word Processing" on page 181.

To get started with a specific application

You can start the course on any module. Some common features of applications (such as customising toolbars and getting help) are only described in detail for Word Processing, so if you are completely new to Office software, start on page 181.

To get started if you have some basic experience

If you have used Office software before, you should be able to omit the first lesson for each module. Alternative starting points are given below.

To get started with the internet

The lesson on using a web browser starts on page 599. You can also learn more about what the internet is on page 60. If you have never used a computer before, you should learn to use Windows (page 101) before starting on the internet.

To learn good practices

If you are a casual PC user, you may not have learned best practices when working with data. Use the lesson on "Security, Copyright and the Law" on page 81 to learn about backup, viruses and other potential problems.

To learn a specific feature

If you want to review a specific feature, use the table of contents and index to locate the correct page reference. You can use the instructions in this book to complete a task when working on your own data files, as well as the practice ones.

Enjoy the course!

Notes

_____

_____

_____

_____

_____

_____

_____

_____

_____

_____

_____

_____

Basic Concepts of Information Technology

Basic Concepts of Information Technology

Understand the basic concepts of IT, hardware and software

Lesson 1

Understand the terms **hardware**, **software** and **Information Technology** □
Understand and distinguish between **different types** of **computer** □

Understanding the Basic Concepts of IT

An **Information Technology** (IT) system is one that processes, stores and/or transfers information. Information can take many different forms: words, numbers, pictures, sound or video).

An IT system could use computers, the telecommunications network and other programmable electronic devices.

♦ Because it involves many different and often highly specialist areas, IT is often seen as a very daunting subject. However, the basis of IT is simply to help us to improve the way we deal with information in all areas of our lives.

♦ IT is **used** in business, industry, government, education and health care. It is also an important part of everyday home and social life.

♦ Computers enable us to process information and perform specific tasks much more **quickly** than we could do ourselves.

♦ IT systems are very **flexible** and can be made to perform a wide variety of different tasks.

♦ IT **networks**, such as the global **internet**, allow us to distribute and share information very quickly.

♦ Although many developments in IT are designed to make our lives easier, people's **expectations** of what they (and others) can achieve are often increased. This can lead to unrealistic demands being placed on people and the technology around them.

We live in an "Information Society". The **effective** use of information is regarded as the defining element of the 20th-21st centuries, as important as the industrial revolution before it.

What is a Computer?

A **computer** is a device that manipulates data according to a set of instructions. Nearly all computers are based on the use of **electronic** circuits, although a computer does not **have** to be electronic.

♦ The pieces of equipment that make up a computer system are called **hardware**. These are the parts you can touch. Many parts are contained within the computer's **case**. Other parts are connected to the computer. These usually allow information (or **data**) to be entered (**input**) and retrieved (**output**).

♦ The **instructions** that a computer follows come from **software** (or **computer programs**). Operating systems, spreadsheet programs and payroll programs are examples of software. Software means that the same hardware can be put to a variety of uses.

Types of Computer

The type of computer most often used in the office and the home is known as a **Personal Computer (PC)**. However, not all computers are PCs.

Mainframe

A **mainframe** is a large, powerful computer capable of serving large numbers of users at the same time.

♦ Users do not sit down in front of the mainframe computer itself. They connect to it using another smaller computer (or **dumb terminal**), which consists simply of a keyboard and screen to enter and display information. A dumb terminal does not process or store any data itself, that is, it is not **intelligent**.

♦ Because mainframes need to process and store information for many different users at once, they require much more **processing power** and **storage capacity** than other computers; that is, they need to be **faster** and have more **memory**. The result is that they tend to be very expensive.

♦ Large corporate and government data processing departments, where many users need access to large amounts of information, often use mainframes. They allow information to be centrally stored and controlled. They also offer more power and require less maintenance than clusters of smaller computers.

♦ An automatic cash dispenser at a bank is an example of a dumb terminal. It is used to access a central mainframe computer, which stores information about your account and processes your request.

Minicomputer

A **minicomputer** is a smaller, less powerful version of a mainframe. Lower processing power and storage capacity mean that a minicomputer is cheaper than a mainframe but is not able to serve as many users at once.

♦ As with a mainframe, users do not sit down in front of the minicomputer itself. They connect to it using another smaller computer or a dumb terminal.

♦ Minicomputers are often used by small and medium-sized companies, or departments in larger organisation, to provide a centralised store of information and computer programs.

Personal Computer (PC)

The PC is the most common type of computer used in the office and in many homes.

Typical PC setup

♦ Usually, only one user accesses a PC at any one time. The user sits in front of the PC and works with it directly, rather than connecting to it using another computer.

♦ Because a PC only has to serve one user at a time, it requires far less processing power and storage capacity than either a mainframe or a minicomputer. This in turn means that a PC is much cheaper.

◆ All PCs have a similar basic **design** but are produced by a large number of manufacturers with different **specifications** and **components**. PCs can vary quite widely in terms of performance and the sort of tasks they are suitable for.

◆ The term "PC" is usually used to refer to desktop computers running the Microsoft Windows operating system. However, there are other types of personal computer, such as the **Apple Macintosh**. These require different versions of software to "PCs".

◆ A PC is often used as an **intelligent terminal** to connect to a mainframe or a minicomputer. The advantage of this over using a dumb terminal is that users can process and store some information locally. This reduces the burden on the central computer.

◆ The main reason why the PC is so popular is that it is a versatile tool that can be used for a wide range of applications.

Network Computer (NC)

A **Network Computer (NC)** is a low-cost version of the PC.

◆ It is designed to connect to and be managed by a central computer (for example a mainframe or a minicomputer). Each time the Network Computer is switched on, it retrieves the latest version of the software it needs from the central computer. This means that components used to install and upgrade software (such as a disk drive or CD-ROM drive) are not required.

◆ Network Computers tend to have slightly less processing power and storage capacity than PCs. This coupled with the lack of other components makes them substantially less expensive. However, a Network Computer is of no use unless it is connected to a central computer, whereas a PC can operate on its own.

◆ Network Computers tend to be used in call centres, help desks and data processing departments where users do not require the flexibility of a PC, but need to access centralised software and information. The main advantage is that when software needs to be upgraded, support staff can do this on the central computer without having to update each individual machine.

Portable Computers (laptops, notebooks and palmtops)

A **laptop** computer (often called a **notebook**) is a portable computer designed to fit inside a briefcase. Most laptops are approximately 12" (30 cm.) wide by 9" (23 cm.) deep by 2" (5 cm.) high.

Sony laptop computer

A **palmtop** computer is a hand-held device around 6" (15 cm) wide by 3" (8 cm) deep and ¾" (2 cm) high.

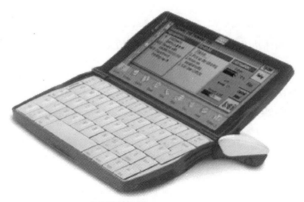

A PSION palmtop computer

♦ **Laptops** have most of the features and components available on PCs, and offer the same level of flexibility in performing a wide range of tasks. However, the size of a laptop makes it more difficult and costly to manufacture, so a laptop will usually cost more than a PC with a similar specification.

♦ **Palmtops** do not have the same features and components as PCs. They are used mostly as personal organisers to store contact information, to store lists, and also for email and internet access.

♦ The advantage of portable computers is that they can be used almost anywhere. Portables can be carried around because they have a built-in screen and keyboard. The screen is usually a **Liquid Crystal Display (LCD)** less than 1" (2.5 cm) thick. They also have a battery, which means that they can be used without access to mains power for several hours. Some laptops are designed for use in extreme conditions, such as underwater or in the freezing cold.

♦ Portable computers tend to be used by people who do a lot of travelling in their job, and need to be able to process and store information wherever they are (and whether or not they have a power source available). Examples are sales representatives, consultants, support engineers and scientists.

Practice

Q1. Identify a suitable type of computer to perform the following tasks:

a) Make a sales presentation at a client's office

_____

b) Create a company newsletter

_____

c) Store a sales database for six regional offices

_____

d) Give 1500 staff access to the sales database plus a word processing application for creating letters

_____

Answers on page 94

Hardware

Know the main parts of a personal computer

(Understand the function of the **motherboard**) ☐
Know what the **Central Processing Unit** does and how its **speed** is measured ☐
Recognise different types of **input devices** and what they can be **used for** ☐
Recognise different types of **output devices** and what they can be **used for** ☐

Components of a PC

Computers are made up of many **components**. Most of these are internal, that is they are located inside the computer case. However, some are connected externally, using **ports**. A port is a kind of plug, usually located at the back of the computer.

PS/2 Port (Keyboard and Mouse)

Parallel Port (Printer)

Serial Port (Mouse)

Graphics Adapter (Monitor)

Network Card Connector

Disk Drives

Memory

CPU

Motherboard

Inside a PC

Because they use components, PCs are **customisable**. You can add components for specific tasks, such as playing sound, and choose more powerful and expensive parts to make a **high-end** PC. Conversely, you can specify less powerful, cheaper components for a basic office PC.

This means that PCs vary quite widely in terms of performance (the **speed** at which a PC performs different tasks), cost and the sort of **applications** (**software**) that they can run.

PC components can be divided into the following categories:

◆ **Microprocessors** process instructions and perform calculations.

◆ **Storage** devices (**memory** and **disks**) hold data.

◆ **Input** devices (**mouse** and **keyboard**) let the user enter data.

◆ **Output** devices (**monitor, speakers** and **printer**) (dis)play data.

◆ **Network** devices (**network card, modem**) allow PCs to connect to other computers.

The Motherboard

A **motherboard** is a large printed circuit board with **connections** for all the other components in the PC. The motherboard allows the components to **exchange** data. It also houses the **power supply**.

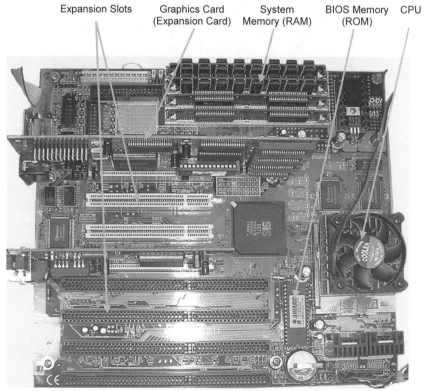

Components on the motherboard

♦ The type of motherboard determines the types of **CPU**, **memory** and **hard disk** that can be installed in the PC.

♦ The motherboard contains several slots that allow you to plug **expansion cards** into your PC. A motherboard will have 5-7 expansion slots of different kinds.

Slot Type	Use
ISA	Used on older PCs. Not commonly found on new PCs except to support "legacy" cards when upgrading.
PCI	Standard expansion slot for new PCs.
AGP	New expansion slot for high-performance graphics cards.

The Central Processing Unit

The **Central Processing Unit (CPU)** is the part of the computer that **processes** and **calculates** data. You can think of the CPU as the "brains" of the computer.

Intel Pentium III CPU

♦ The CPU is an advanced **microprocessor**. A microprocessor performs **calculations** on data and determines what to do with the results of those calculations (**logic control**).

♦ The CPU is sent **instructions** by the computer's **software**. The CPU processes many millions of instructions per second and passes the results to other components of the PC. The speed at which the CPU works is the main factor influencing the **performance** of the PC.

♦ The CPU's activities are co-ordinated by a **clock**, which is used to synchronise all the internal processes within it. The unit of time for each movement of data within the CPU is called a **cycle**. Clock speed is measured in **megahertz (MHz)**. One megahertz equals one million cycles per second.

♦ The three main manufacturers of CPUs are **Intel** (Pentium and Celeron CPUs), **AMD** (K6, Athlon and Duron CPUs) and **Motorola** (who make CPUs for **Apple Macintosh** computers). These manufacturers release faster CPUs fairly often. At the time of writing, CPUs on sale range from 500MHz to over 1000 MHz. Most Office software requires a CPU of at least 166MHz to run efficiently.

♦ Special **design features** in some processors enable them to perform certain tasks more quickly. Given two different processors running at the same clock speed, you may find that one is faster when searching a database, while the other is faster when displaying complex graphics.

♦ Because the CPU runs much more quickly than other components, the performance of the system can be affected if it cannot get instructions to and from the CPU efficiently. **Immediate access memory** (or **cache** - see page 35) is often incorporated into the CPU or motherboard to maintain a consistent flow of data to and from the CPU.

♦ The CPU also requires a fan to keep it cool while the computer is switched on.

The CPU is assisted by many other microprocessors in other components. For example, an advanced microprocessor is often used on the graphics card, enabling the PC to display complex and realistic 3D graphics.

Input Devices

An input device is any device that is used to supply information to a computer. A few examples of input devices are given below.

Keyboard

The most common input device is the keyboard, which is used for text-based data input and for selecting commands.

Keyboards usually have the following:

♦ Keys for the letters of the alphabet.

♦ Keys for punctuation symbols.

♦ Numbered keys or a numeric keypad (or both).

Standard keyboard

♦ Keys to move the typing cursor and other text controls, such as `Tab`, `Insert`, `Delete`, `Backspace`, `Enter`, and so on.

♦ Keys which change the function of other keys, such as `Shift`, `Caps Lock`, `Alt` and `Ctrl`.

♦ Function keys numbered from `F1` to `F12`. The function of these keys is set by whichever program is running.

Practice

Find the following keys on your own keyboard:

- `Tab`

- `Caps Lock`

- `Shift` - *you should find two* `Shift` *keys*

- `Enter`

- `Alt`

- `Esc`

- `Ctrl` - *you should find two* `Ctrl` *keys*

Mouse

PCs are usually operated through a **graphical user interface**. This means that the user selects commands from the computer's screen display by moving a pointer and clicking a button.

A mouse is the device usually used to control the movement of the pointer on the screen.

Microsoft mouse

♦ A mouse is used by moving it across a mouse mat or other flat surface. This moves a ball on the bottom of the mouse. The movement of the ball sends a signal to the computer. Software will then interpret this signal and perform an operation, such as moving a cursor or drawing a line.

♦ A mouse has two or more buttons on top of it, the function of which depend upon the software being used.

Trackball

♦ A **trackball** can be used as an alternative to a mouse. It has buttons, like a mouse, but the pointer is moved using a rotating ball set into the top of the device (basically an upside-down mouse).

♦ Some people find a trackball easier to use than a mouse. One advantage is that it does not need a flat area to use it. For this reason, trackballs are often included on laptop computers.

Touch Pad

♦ A **touch pad** is another device for moving the pointer. In this case you use your finger or a pen-like instrument (or stylus) on a sensitive pad to move the screen pointer.

♦ Because a touch pad is flat and does not require the user to push down a specific key (as with a keyboard) or grasp it (as with a mouse), it is often used as an input device for people with particular disabilities. Touch pads are also used on laptops and palmtop computers.

♦ Another form of touch pad is the **graphics tablet**. This enables the user to create an image on the computer by drawing on the pad with a specially designed pen. Graphics tablets are used by graphic design artists and for children's drawing software.

Light Pen

- A **light pen** is a hand-held device (very similar to a standard ballpoint pen) that has a device at the tip, which either emits light **or** is light sensitive. The user is able to send information to the computer by touching the pen onto certain areas of a specially designed screen.

- Light pens are not widely used because they require a lot of arm movement, making them tiring and uncomfortable to use.

- Possible uses include engineering production lines and science laboratories where dirt or other environmental factors make the use of a keyboard or mouse impractical.

Joystick

- A **joystick** consists of a base and a stick perpendicular to the base. The stick can be moved in any direction, enabling the user to move an object around the computer screen. A joystick can perform a similar function to a mouse or trackball, but is only commonly used for playing games.

Scanner

Scanners are input devices used to detect patterns on paper (pictures or text) and then translate them into computer data.

- **Hand-held** scanners are dragged across the paper to scan it.

- **Flatbed** scanners have the paper placed on top of them, in a similar way to a photocopier. These are more expensive than hand-held scanners but they are usually able to produce higher resolution images.

- Companies needing to store paper records can transfer them to **microfilm**. A microfilm is a series of page images, miniaturised onto 35mm film. Special scanners are available to prepare and read microfilm using a PC.

- If a scanner is used to scan a page of text, Optical Character Recognition (OCR) software can be used to convert the scanned image into text data.

Digital Cameras

- Digital cameras work in much the same way as normal cameras, except that the exposure from the subject is recorded onto light sensitive diodes not photographic paper. The image is saved to disk and can be displayed on-screen and printed.

- There are also devices to capture moving images. Web Cams can record low resolution video images. High resolution digital video cameras are available, but are still quite expensive. Some filmmakers are starting to record motion pictures entirely on digital video.

Output Devices

Output devices (dis)play information from the PC to the user.

Practice

- *Before reading on, try to think of **three** ways in which a computer can output data and see if you can name three types of device that might be used*

_____

_____

_____

_____

_____

Graphics Display

With modern software, the screen display is the most important interface the user has with a PC. All commands are issued using a mouse or keyboard to select elements of a **Graphical User Interface** (see page 45) such as menus and toolbars.

Displaying data on-screen requires two components:

- The **Graphics Card** is connected to an expansion slot (**PCI** or **AGP**) on the motherboard. Many graphics cards are optimised to display 3D graphics effects. They often incorporate sophisticated microprocessors and have their own memory so that the screen display can be kept updated as smoothly as possible.

- The **Visual Display Unit** (**VDU**) takes the signal from the computer's graphics card and converts it into an image to display on a screen.

Most PCs use a **Cathode Ray Tube (CRT) monitor** to display an image (CRTs are also used in television sets).

Liquid Crystal Display (LCD) screens are flat panel displays, which take up a lot less space, but do not generally give as sharp a picture. LCDs are most commonly used as the display screen on laptops and palmtops.

CRT monitors have screen sizes ranging from 14" to 21" (30 - 60 cm). A larger screen can display images at high **resolution** (see below) more comfortably. A large monitor is also easier to work with and so more productive (though a large monitor requires a fairly powerful CPU and graphics card).

CRT Monitor

The screen image is made up of **pixels** (a pixel being the smallest area of the image that the computer can change). The maximum number of pixels that the computer can display horizontally and vertically on the screen gives the **screen resolution**. An example of a screen resolution is 800 x 600 pixels. Software on your computer usually enables you to select the resolution you want to use from a set of pre-defined alternatives.

The higher the screen resolution you use, the more you will be able to fit on the screen, and the smaller each object on the screen will look. For example, an image that is 10 pixels square will look much smaller at a screen resolution of 1280 x 1024 than it will at 800 x 600, because each pixel will be smaller. Monitors capable of very high resolutions are often used for tasks like CAD (Computer Aided Design) to ensure the accurate representation of lines and curves.

An example of a very low-resolution screen display is a Teletext page, where you can clearly see each of the pixels that make up the image on the TV screen.

A monitor should also have a sufficient **refresh rate** at the selected resolution. The **refresh rate** is the frequency with which an image is redrawn. If the refresh rate is too low (below **70 hertz**), the image will appear to flicker, causing eye strain and headaches.

LEDs

The PC case will also have several **Light Emitting Diodes** (LEDs). These are used to indicate the status of the PC (whether it is turned on) and disks (whether the disks are being accessed).

LEDs show whether the power is on and if the hard disk is being accessed

Printers

A printer allows the user to print out on paper a copy of the data that is being processed by the computer. Modern printers can print text and pictures.

Printers are available in both colour and black and white. Colour printers are more expensive than black and white printers.

There are several types of printer. The most commonly-used types are **inkjet**, **bubble-jet** and **laser**.

◆ Inkjet and Bubble-jet Printers

Inkjet and bubble-jet printers form images from a series of dots by firing tiny droplets of ink at the paper from a print head that moves horizontally across the page.

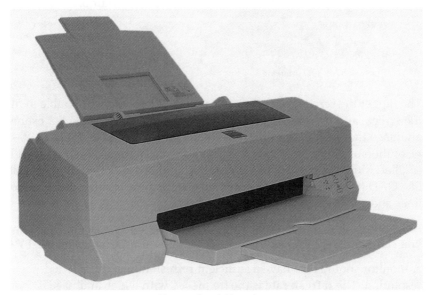

Epson colour inkjet printer

They are sometimes known as **line printers** because they print each page one line at a time.

Inkjet and bubble-jet printers are reasonably fast and produce good quality print. Most new inkjet and bubble-jet printers are able to print in colour. Special photographic paper is available for printing high-quality images. They are also relatively inexpensive, which has made them popular for home use.

♦ **Laser Printers**

Laser printers combine a very narrow beam of light and a light sensitive drum to fuse particles of **toner** (a fine powder) onto the paper.

Laser printers are sometimes known as **page printers** because they print the whole of each page in one go.

They produce very high quality print and are generally quieter and faster than inkjet or bubble-jet printers. However, they are usually much more expensive, especially if colour printing is required. For these reasons, laser printers tend to be more suited to business use.

Plotter

A **plotter** works by drawing lines onto a piece of paper, using pens held in a mechanical arm.

They are often used for scientific work. They can also be used for computer-aided design work.

Sound card and speakers

Many computers, especially home PCs, are equipped with **speakers**. Speakers take the signal generated by a **sound card** and convert it into sound.

If your computer has speakers, you can listen to music CDs or hear sound effects generated by software. This capability is often used by educational software and computer games.

Speech Synthesiser

A speech synthesiser receives the output from a computer and turns it into speech, played through the speakers.

♦ A speech synthesiser can be used as an output device, enabling a user with a visual disability to operate a PC.

♦ A **microphone** can be attached to a sound card to provide audio **input**. With suitable software, a microphone can also be used to issue commands and create files.

Practice

Q2. Identify the following pieces of equipment:

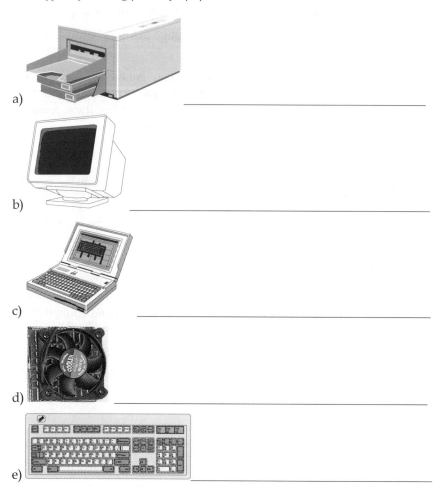

a) _____

b) _____

c) _____

d) _____

e) _____

Answers on page 94

Storage

Recognise the components used to store data

Understand how computer memory is **measured** □
Understand the types of **storage device** used in a computer and how to **compare** them □
Understand different types of computer **memory** □
Identify different **disk storage devices** □
Evaluate the factors that impact on a computer's **performance** □

Measuring Data and Storage

A PC processes **digital data**. When you use an input device, the signals from the device are converted into a stream of **bits**, the smallest component of computer data. Each bit can be in one of two states **1** or **0**, with the 1 standing for **On** and the 0 standing for **Off**.

Memory and **disks** are the components used to store data for processing.

The units used to measure data (and therefore the **capacity** of memory and disks) are **bits**, **bytes**, **megabytes** and **gigabytes**.

♦ Bits are combined in sets of **eight** to form **characters**, such as letters from the alphabet. For example, 01000001 is used to represent the letter A in binary code. This group of eight bits makes a **byte**.

> **Tip** You may see hardware and software described as being a certain number of bits. This refers to how much information the hardware or software can process at any one time. For example, CPUs are 32-bit processors, which means that they can process 32 bits of data in each clock cycle.

♦ A **kilobyte** (KB) is 1024 bytes. The size of a data file is often measured in kilobytes.

♦ A **megabyte** (MB) is often used to measure the storage capacity of a disk or the amount of main memory. A megabyte is 1,048,576 bytes (1024 kilobytes). 1 MB is about as much data as 500 pages of double-spaced text.

♦ A **gigabyte** (GB) is equivalent to 1,024 MB. The memory capacity of many larger storage devices, such as hard drives, is measured in gigabytes.

Types of Storage

The PC has three storage requirements when handling data:

Read Only Memory (ROM)

ROM stores the data necessary to start the PC and identify its components.

Random Access Memory (RAM)

RAM stores data while it is being processed. For example, RAM is required to run software while the computer is switched on.

Storage disks

Disks are used to preserve data when the computer is turned off and to move and backup data.

Memory

The two main types of memory are **Read-Only Memory (ROM)** and **Random Access Memory (RAM)**.

Read Only Memory

♦ **ROM** holds **permanent** information, such as the BIOS software that enables the components in your computer to communicate with each other. It cannot usually be deleted or overwritten in the course of normal computer operations. Only a small amount of ROM is required.

Random Access Memory

♦ RAM is a **temporary** memory store. Data held in RAM is only stored while the computer is switched on. For example, when you create a document (such as a letter), the document is stored in your computer's RAM until you save it to disk.

♦ RAM holds data required by the CPU, which cannot store large amounts of data itself. RAM is important because it enables the CPU to get data quickly. For example, when a software application is started, the data needed to run the program is copied from the main **disk** into RAM, where the CPU can access it.

♦ There are two principle uses of RAM in a computer: for **main memory** and as **cache**.

Main memory

Main memory (or **system memory**) is the largest amount of RAM installed on the motherboard. RAM is used to run software applications and temporarily store data being entered by the user.

♦ Every piece of software needs a certain amount of main memory to operate efficiently. The exact amount varies from one piece of software to another. Modern software usually requires more main memory than older software, so the amount of main memory installed in new computers is increasing all the time (at time of writing a new PC would be sold with 64-128 MB of system RAM).

♦ Having an adequate amount of memory is a very important factor in determining the PC's performance. As well as optimising the overall speed of the computer, having more memory enables you to run more software applications at the same time and allows you to work with larger files.

Cache

Cache is a very fast type of RAM directly attached to particular components such as the CPU, hard disk or graphics card. It enables a certain amount of data to be copied from the main memory so the component can access it more quickly.

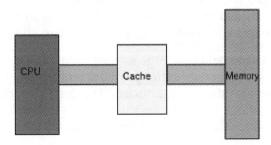

♦ Cache is important because it balances the ability of relatively slow components, such as disk drives, to keep fast components, such as the CPU and memory, supplied with a constant stream of data. Cache makes the computer's performance more efficient.

Disk Storage Devices

Disk drives of various kinds are used to **store** and **transfer** data **files**. When data is entered into a computer, it must be **saved** as a file to preserve it when the computer is switched off. Also, software applications need to **install** files on the main disk drive in the computer in order to run.

The most important type of drive in your PC is the **hard disk**, which is used to store the software and data on which the PC runs.

Most PCs will also have **removable** disk drives to **install** software and **backup** data files.

Disk **performance** is principally a question of capacity: how much data can be stored on the disk? Other factors that influence disk performance are the **seek time** (the time it takes to find data on the drive) and the **transfer rate** (the speed at which data can be moved to and from a disk).

Hard Disk

The **hard disk** is usually a device fixed inside the computer. It stores large volumes of data, which can be accessed and retrieved quickly. The seek time of a hard disk is much **lower** and the transfer rate much **higher** than any other type of disk drive.

♦ Hard disks consist of a number of rigid magnetic disks in a protective casing. Data is recorded magnetically onto concentric circular tracks, each one divided into a number of sectors. Data is accessed by an arm moving over the surface of the disk.

♦ Hard disks can hold very large amounts of data (equivalent to hundreds or thousands of **floppy disks**) and are usually very fast in comparison to other storage devices. They vary considerably in terms of price, depending on their speed and capacity. Hard disks on sale at the time of writing vary in capacity from 8 GB to 30 GB.

♦ When you install software, the setup instructions indicate the amount of **free** disk space required for the software to run effectively. Applications typically take up 50-200 MB each, though multimedia applications and games can require far more.

♦ Most hard disks are fixed inside the computer. Removable hard disks (which can be inserted into and removed from a special bay without opening the computer case) are available, but tend to be much more expensive.

Floppy Disks

Floppy disks are flexible magnetic disks held in a protective plastic jacket. They are sometimes known as **diskettes**. As with hard disks, data is recorded onto concentric circular tracks, divided into sectors.

♦ Floppy disks can only hold a small amount of data and are also relatively slow (accessing data on a floppy disk will take much longer than accessing data on a hard disk). However, floppy disks are very cheap, as is the drive needed to use them. They are also very **portable**. Because most computers have a floppy disk drive, you can rely on being able to use a floppy disk to transfer a file from one computer to another. Thus, floppy disks have remained popular despite their lack of speed and capacity.

♦ The standard size for a floppy disk is 3½". The floppy disks used with PCs usually have a capacity of 1.44 MB. 120 MB floppy disks are available, but they are more expensive and a special type of drive is required to use them.

Other Magnetic Disks

Other magnetic disk devices, such as Iomega **Zip** and **Jaz** disks, cover the middle ground between floppy disks and hard disks, in terms of both speed and capacity.

Iomega Zip disk and drive

♦ These disks tend to offer much less capacity than a hard disk (although much more than a floppy disk). The cost of **media** (buying each disk) can also be quite expensive.

♦ The main advantage is that the disks can be removed and transferred elsewhere. Also, because you can have as many disks as you want, overall capacity is not limited (except by the cost of the disks and your budget).

CD-ROM/DVD-ROM Drive

CD-ROM (Compact Disc - Read Only Memory) drives are common in modern PCs. A CD-ROM - which looks just like an audio CD - can hold 650 MB of data. Compared to floppy disks, this is quite a lot of information. For example, the Microsoft Encarta CD not only contains the entire text of a 27-volume encyclopaedia but also over one hundred video and audio clips.

♦ In the past, applications were distributed on floppy disks. As new programs got larger and larger, manufacturers started to use CDs as the preferred media. By putting the program, help files and documentation onto a single CD, the software company can reduce the cost and size of the package. For users it is also far easier to install the program from a single CD than from tens of disks. For these reasons, CD-ROMs are almost as essential as hard disks in new PCs.

♦ Because of the increased use of PCs as leisure and games machines, even CDs do not have enough capacity to satisfy the demands of video and multimedia applications. A standard DVD (which stands for **Digital Versatile Disc** but is sometimes referred to as **Digital Video Disc**) drive can store **17 gigabytes** of data (133 minutes of video with stereo sound) making them usable outside of the IT industry as a replacement for videocassettes. On new PCs, DVD drives are usually installed instead of CD-ROMs, as a DVD drive can **also** read ordinary CD-ROMs.

♦ **CD-R** and **CD-RW** drives are ones that can **write** data to special CD-R and CD-RW discs. As CD drives are commonly found on PCs, CD-R has become a popular way of **backing up** data. A CD-RW disc is different from a CD-R because data can be deleted and overwritten. This makes the discs more expensive.

Tape Drives

Tape drives (or **cartridge** drives) can be used to store large amounts of data. Retrieving information from a tape drive is slower than for some other storage devices because the tape drive has to work its way through the tape to access the relevant information.

♦ Like floppy disks, Zip disks and CD-Rs, magnetic tape **cartridges** are removable and easy to transport. Many can store far more data than other removable storage devices, with some cartridges able to store more data than the largest hard disks.

♦ The price of tape drives varies more than any other storage device. Some drives are about the same price as a mid-range hard drive, while others are many times the price. The tape cartridges themselves tend to be relatively inexpensive.

♦ Tape drives are mainly used to backup data on computer **networks** and/or to backup large **databases**.

PC Performance and Evaluation

Practice

- *As we have already covered the main factors affecting performance, before you read this summary, think back and write down at least five things that will influence the speed of a PC*

_____

_____

_____

_____

_____

_____

_____

_____

_____

_____

_____

_____

_____

_____

_____

_____

_____

_____

_____

_____

_____

_____

_____

_____

_____

_____

_____

_____

Performance (Speed)

The operating speed of a computer system depends on the time taken for hardware and software to receive input, process data and display output. If one or more parts of a computer system operate slowly, the entire system can be slowed down.

Below is a summary of the main factors that influence a computer's speed:

♦ The **clock speed** of the CPU is one of the most important influences on the speed of a computer. A higher clock speed means more units of data can be processed each second. Remember, the clock speed of a CPU is measured in megahertz (MHz).

♦ Although the clock speed of the CPU is very important, and a good indicator of a computer's speed, the **type** of CPU must also be considered. Different CPUs may be designed to process larger amounts of data at a time or process certain types of data more efficiently. When comparing different processors, the design may be as important as the clock speed. For example, an Intel Pentium processor running at 233MHz will not be as fast as a Pentium II processor running at the same clock speed. This is because the Pentium II has a more efficient design. In some cases though, design improvements are only realised if the PC is running **software** that has been designed to take advantage of the improvements.

♦ A computer's **main memory** is another important consideration. If there is not enough main memory, the computer will have to rely more on accessing data from the hard disk, which is relatively slow. Therefore, the amount of main memory fitted in a computer will have a significant effect on its performance.

♦ The amount of **cache RAM** installed on components such as the CPU, motherboard and hard disk will affect the speed of the computer. Data stored in a component's cache can be accessed and manipulated far more quickly than data stored elsewhere. Therefore, the more cache RAM each component has, the faster it will be able to manipulate data. This enables the system as a whole to perform more efficiently, as it is less likely that the CPU will be sitting idle, while the hard disk is frantically trying to load the data required.

♦ Several other factors affect system speed. An advanced graphics card, with its own processor and memory, can be important, especially if a high resolution display is required. Some types of hard disk are faster than others. Many newer models include design features that reduce the time taken to access or move data on the disk. Finally, using a faster CD-ROM or DVD-ROM drive reduces the time taken to read or copy data from CD-ROMs or DVD-ROMs, which is important if software needs the disc in the drive to run.

Capacity

As well as speed, the **storage capacity** of a computer is also important.

♦ Computers usually store most of the files that make up programs and data on a hard disk. The larger the storage capacity of the disk, the more programs and data can be stored. Once the disk is full, no more programs or data can be added.

♦ A computer used for simple tasks such as word processing and email would not usually need a very large storage capacity. A computer used for working with advanced multimedia software requires more storage space for programs and files.

♦ Computers often use a small amount of hard disk space to supplement their main memory. If the amount of free (or unused) space on the hard disk becomes low, supplementing the main memory in this way can become much less efficient. Therefore the capacity of the hard disk (or more precisely, the free space available on it) can also affect the computer's speed.

Usability

Another factor in PC performance is the system's ease of use. Most usability issues with PCs occur through the design of the software, but the design of the PC's peripheral devices can also have a big impact on performance. If the PC is physically tiring to work at, having the fastest CPU in the world will not count for much.

♦ The size and resolution of the screen is an important factor in making a PC easier and quicker to use.

♦ The accuracy and comfort of input devices, mouse or keyboard or touch pad on a laptop, also affects performance.

Note The user's working environment can have a big impact on performance and on health and safety. This topic is discussed on page 76.

Hardware requirements

Software applications set out a list of **hardware requirements**, usually printed on the outside of the box, which the PC must meet in order for the software to run. These will include **minimum** and **recommended** CPU speeds and storage requirements, and a list of peripherals required.

Tip	Generally speaking, a PC should meet the **recommended** requirements to get adequate performance from the application.

Practice

- *You should now have a good understanding of the different parts that make up a personal computer.*

- *To consolidate what you have learned, write a letter to a relative who wants to get your advice on buying a personal computer.*

- *They want to use the PC for internet access, to write letters and to keep track of household accounts.*

- *Summarise the main components of a PC for them and how they will affect the use of the PC. If you have any computer magazines to hand, look through the adverts and identify suitable systems.*

- *You could use Microsoft Word to write the letter on your computer - see page 181 to learn how to use a word processor.*

Software

Recognise different types of software

Lesson 4

Recognise the difference between **operating systems** and **applications** software ☐
Understand the **functions** of an **operating system** ☐
Know what a **Graphical User Interface** is ☐
List some common **software applications** and their **uses** ☐
Recognise the main stages of **systems development** ☐

Operating Systems and Applications Software

Software enables the PC's hardware to perform useful tasks, such as creating, displaying and printing a letter.

Software can be divided into two important classes: **operating systems** and **applications**.

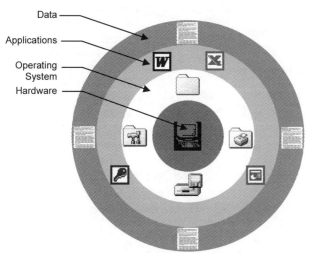

Users enter **data** into an **application** software package. The application gives the user a set of commands to work with (an **interface**). The application then translates those commands into instructions, which are passed to the PC's **operating system** software. The operating system sends instructions to the hardware, which processes and calculates the data and passes the results back up the chain.

The **operating system** provides a **common environment** for different software applications to work in. It controls the PC's hardware. It also provides its own **interface** to allow the **user** to configure the PC's components and to organise the storage of data.

You will learn more about **MS Windows**, the operating system used on most PCs, in Module 2 - Using the Computer and Managing Files.

What are Directories and Files?

To preserve data entered into a PC, it must be saved onto a disk as a **file**. **Directories** are used to divide a disk into different areas, so that files can be kept organised.

Directories

To help organise the data on a disk, it is stored in discrete areas, rather like folders in a filing cabinet. One important function of directories is to keep the files required for a software application to work in the same place.

Tip In Microsoft Windows, directories are referred to as **folders**.

Directories are stored in a hierarchy. It is possible for directories to have subdirectories, which in turn may have subdirectories of their own.

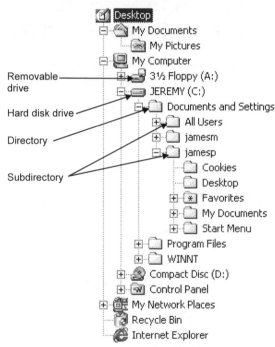

Directories in Microsoft Windows

Files

A file is data saved on disk. Most applications use a file of a particular **type**.

Notepad Document   Bitmap Picture   Word Document   Web Page

As well as data the user enters and saves, files are **installed** onto a PC to run software applications. These files are often referred to as **program** or **system** files.

Graphical User Interfaces

A **user interface** provides a way for the user to interact with the computer. Early IBM-compatible computers used **DOS** (Disk Operating System), which has a **command line** interface (the user enters text-based instructions using a keyboard).

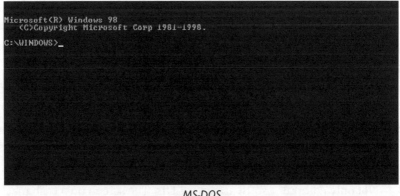

MS-DOS

One of the most significant developments in personal computing was the **graphical user interface** (GUI). A GUI uses the screen to display **windows**, **menus** and **icons**, which represent applications, commands and files.

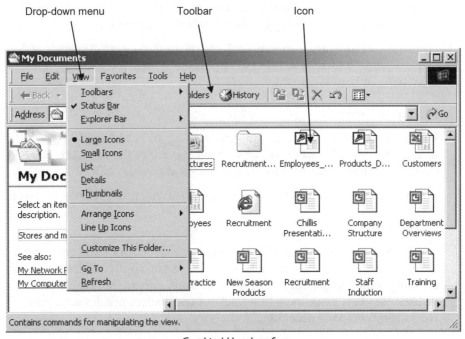

Graphical User Interface

♦ Because the user does not have to remember or type in complex commands, operating GUI software is much easier. Also the display of data is much more comprehensive and accurate. For example, **What You See Is What You Get** (WYSIWYG) applications can display data on-screen as it will appear when printed.

♦ In a GUI, a **window** represents a software application. A window can contain objects used to access the application's commands, such as **toolbars** and **menus**. The position, size and shape of these objects can often be changed, so the user can set the layout of the interface to suit their own needs.

♦ The user can select and move what is displayed on-screen using a pointing device, such as a mouse. The keyboard is used to enter data, and can be used to issue commands and move around the screen as well.

♦ Business software applications running in the MS Windows operating system tend to have a similar window layout to each other. Games and leisure software may have very different interfaces.

♦ Not only computer software uses GUIs. The screen on a cash machine is a GUI - you select commands by pointing at them.

Common Software Applications

As we have seen, an **operating system** controls the computer and provides an interface so that the user can interact with the computer.

Applications software, on the other hand, is used to perform specific tasks. The list below shows some types of applications, their use and examples from popular manufacturers.

Word Processing

Word processing means originating, formatting and checking text documents. Most "word processors" can also perform the functions of desktop publishing, incorporating graphics and page layout.

Examples include Microsoft Word, Lotus WordPro and Corel WordPerfect.

Spreadsheets

A spreadsheet consists of a table containing rows, columns and cells. When numbers are entered into the cells, formulae can be applied to them, enabling complex calculations to be carried out. Spreadsheet packages can be used for many tasks including tracking and analysing sales data, and working on company accounts.

Examples include Microsoft Excel, Lotus 1-2-3 and Corel QuattroPro.

Database

Database packages enable you to store, organise and retrieve information. Databases can search through thousands of records very quickly and display data in a format specified by the user. They can be used to store many different types of information, such as timetables, customer details and patient records.

Examples include Microsoft Access, Lotus Approach and Corel Paradox.

Presentation

Presentation graphics software enables you to create sophisticated business presentations that can be displayed as an on-screen slide show or printed onto overhead projector transparencies. Pictures, company logos, graphs and text can be added to the slides, together with a variety of animations. Examples include Microsoft PowerPoint, Lotus Freelance Graphics and Corel Presentations.

Communication

Communications software allows you to send and receive faxes and email and to browse the internet. Examples of email programs include Microsoft Outlook, Microsoft Outlook Express and Lotus Notes. Examples of internet browsers include Microsoft Internet Explorer and Netscape Navigator.

Accountancy/Payroll

There are many examples of predesigned databases to perform common functions, such as keeping accounts (Sage Line50) or managing staff (Simply Personnel). These database applications also come with functions for working out tax liabilities, NI contributions, pension payments and so on.

Desktop Publishing/Graphics/Design

Desktop Publishing applications control page layout in documents. They generally require other applications to supply the content (text and graphics). Products for home and small business use include Microsoft Publisher and Serif PagePlus and Adobe PageMaker. Professional products include Quark Xpress and Adobe InDesign.

Graphics programs can perform a wide range of functions: editing bitmaps, drawing and painting, technical drawing, 3D graphics, animation, video, multimedia and web design. A few examples are Adobe Photoshop, Corel DRAW, AutoCAD, Adobe Premiere and Macromedia Dreamweaver.

Multimedia

Multimedia applications incorporate text, graphics, sound, video and animation. Games and educational software are good examples.

Systems Development

IT systems design is a complex process requiring careful planning and management.

The process of systems development is a cycle of analysis, design, programming, testing and implementation. This can be depicted in the form of a flow diagram.

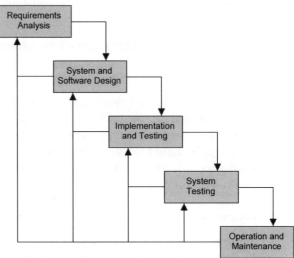

As the development of a new system progresses, problems or alternative solutions can sometimes become apparent. This may mean that a previous stage of the development process must be revisited.

Stage One - Requirements Analysis

◆ During this stage, the problem(s) that the new computer system should solve must be defined. The current system (whether computerised or not) is analysed and observed in operation. Existing users are interviewed to get their views on existing problems and what they would like the new system to do.

◆ This stage usually ends with the production of a feasibility report, which defines the requirements of the new system and recommends whether or not these requirements can realistically be met. The report may also suggest alternatives, such as a reduced system that meets some of the requirements, but also leaves some of the existing system in place.

Stage Two - Systems and Software Design

◆ Once the requirements of the new system have been agreed, the next stage is to design a system that will meet these requirements.

◆ There are two parts to the design stage. Firstly, the requirements are split into two main groups: those that require new hardware systems (for example computers, networks, input and output devices, and so on) and those that require new software systems. This process is known as **systems design**.

♦ Once the systems design process is complete, one or more computer programs are designed to meet the software requirements that have been identified. This is known as **software design**.

♦ The design for a new computer program must provide a detailed description of what the program will do, how it will work and what the main user interface will be. It should also describe how the program will interact with other parts of the system, such as other new and existing software, and the hardware around which the system will be based.

♦ It is important to take the skills of the existing users into account when designing a new system.

Stage Three - Implementation and Testing

♦ The design specifications created in stage two are made into software applications, written with a **programming language** (such as, C++ or Java).

♦ These programs are then tested to see if they meet their specification. Any errors in the program are found and corrected (a process known as debugging).

♦ End-users are often involved in the testing process to ensure that each program is suitable and that the user interface is understandable and easy to use.

♦ If testing uncovers any problems with the original design specification, the design must be amended and the program rewritten to meet the new specification.

Stage Four - System Testing

♦ Individual programs are combined and tested as a complete system to ensure that they work correctly together and that all the software requirements have been met.

♦ End-users are again involved in testing the whole system to ensure it meets their requirements and resolves the problems that were identified in the old system.

♦ Once testing is complete and any amendments have been made, the new system can be delivered to the client.

Stage Five - Operation and Maintenance

♦ This is usually the longest stage of the lifecycle. The new system (including hardware and software) is installed and put into practical use. Data from the old system may also need to be converted for use in the new system.

♦ Once the system is being used, feedback is obtained from users to find out where problems exist and to get ideas about improvements that could be made. This is known as **system maintenance** and is an on-going process.

Practice

Q3. *Answer the following questions on software development:*

a) *List the main stages of software development as outlined in this course.*

_____

_____

_____

_____

b) *Give a brief description of requirements analysis.*

_____

_____

_____

_____

_____

_____

c) *In terms of software development, what is usually involved in system testing?*

_____

_____

_____

_____

d) *What is usually the longest stage of software development? What happens during this stage?*

_____

_____

_____

_____

_____

Answers on page 94

Information Networks

Understand the type and functions of different networks

Lesson 5

Understand the terms **LAN**, **WAN** and **workgroup computing** ☐
Understand the use of the **telephone network** in computing ☐
Know what **email** is and understand what is required to send and receive it ☐
Know what the **internet** is and about some of the **services** available on it ☐

What is a Network?

In terms of information technology, a **network** is a series of devices connected by one or more **communication paths**, which could be network data cables, the telephone system or satellite communications.

Workgroup Computing

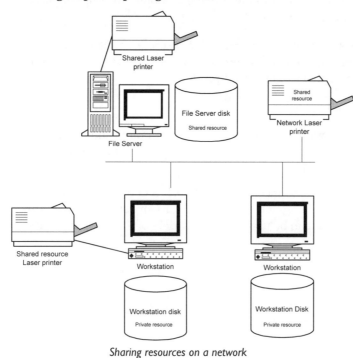

A **workgroup** is a group of computers on a network that can share **data** (folders and files) and **resources**, such as printers, modems and other hardware.

Sharing resources on a network

Advantages of workgroups

♦ Many different workgroups can be setup on a network, meaning that resources can be dedicated to specific groups of computers, instead of being made available to everyone. For example, different departments within an organisation can each have their own workgroup with their own set of resources.

♦ Access to resources can be protected by making users logon with a **user name** and **password**.

♦ Many software packages are now designed for workgroup computing, with a network server holding shared information. As the software does not have to be installed on each individual computer, it easier to manage and update.

♦ All the computers in the workgroup can share a single store of data so that information is available to everyone and duplication of data is reduced.

♦ Computers are not limited to particular tasks. Because data and resources are shared, any computer in the workgroup can be used to work on any task. This provides greater flexibility in assigning tasks and distributing the workload.

♦ Sharing resources can reduce costs. For example, instead of having printers connected to every computer in a department, a workgroup can be setup with a single shared printer.

Local Area Network

A **Local Area Network** (LAN) is a network of computers and other devices based at a **single site**. In general, there is no more than 1km between any two extremities of a LAN.

An individual computer connected to a network is known as a **workstation**. A LAN workstation will often be a PC running Microsoft Windows as an operating system, and can be used to run a variety of different applications.

Components of a LAN

♦ A **network card** (NIC) must be installed in the PC workstation.

A network adapter card

• A high-speed cable runs from the network card to another computer, such as powerful PC or minicomputer, called a **server**.

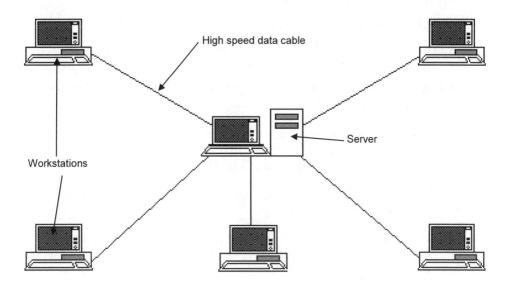

A **server** often runs a purpose designed **network operating system** such as **Microsoft Windows NT Server**. It is used to provide a number of different services to the network, such as a shared data store, access to a collection of software (a file/applications server) and communications services, such as email, fax and internet access (a communications server).

Dell Power Edge server

The LAN environment is usually setup so that users can access any part of the network as if it were a part of their computer. The network may simply appear to the user as a number of extra disk drives, printers and other devices shown on their computer.

Wide Area Network

A **Wide Area Network** (WAN) is a network used to connect large numbers of computers and terminals over long distances.

A WAN works in a similar way to a LAN. The major differences between the two are as follows:

♦   The geographical area covered by a WAN is larger and may encompass **several sites** in different parts of the country, or even different countries. A LAN is confined to a single site.

♦   WANs are usually much larger with more computers and servers connected to the network.

♦   WANs will often use very powerful computers as servers, such as mainframes or minicomputers. LANs tend to use powerful PCs for this purpose.

♦   WANs will use **telecommunications** links (for example telephone lines) or even radio or satellite communications to send and receive data. LANs use direct cable connections.

WANs are often **groups** of individual LANs spread over a number of sites and connected using either radio, satellite or telecommunications links.

Practice

Q4. *Answer the following questions on computer networks:*

a) *What is a workgroup?*

_____

_____

_____

b) *What are the main advantages of being part of a workgroup?*

_____

_____

_____

_____

_____

_____

c) *What is a LAN?*

_____

_____

_____

d) *What is a workstation?*

_____

_____

_____

e) *What is a file server and what is its function?*

_____

_____

_____

f) *What is a WAN and how does it differ from a LAN?*

_____

_____

_____

_____

Answers on page 95

Telecommunications in Computing

Telecommunication networks are often used to transmit data between computers and networks. Below are some examples of where telecommunications networks are used:

♦ To connect computers and servers on a wide area network.

♦ To link the various networks that make up the internet.

♦ To enable users to connect to the internet, retrieve information and send messages.

♦ To enable users to logon to a LAN or WAN from another location (**Remote Access**).

A number of different telecommunications networks can be used to transmit computer data. Two of the most commonly used are the **Public Switched Telephone Network** (PSTN) and the **Integrated Services Digital Network** (ISDN).

Public Switched Telephone Network (PSTN)

PSTN is the standard telephone network. It was originally designed to transmit audio signals (mainly speech of course) and is relatively slow in transmitting computer data. However, because it is cheap and readily available in most homes and offices, it is still the way in which most home and small business users connect to external networks, such as the internet.

PSTN is primarily an **analogue** network. This means that data is transmitted as a series of electronic signals with varying frequencies and amplitudes (equivalent to the pitch and volume of sounds). This is suitable for the transmission of audio signals, but is not the most efficient or reliable way to send more complex data, such as that sent from a computer.

Integrated Services Digital Network (ISDN)

ISDN is a **digital** telephone network. This means that data is transmitted as a series of **bits**. Digital signals are more efficient and reliable than analogue signals. The result is that up to twice as much data can be sent at a time using an ISDN line, making it up to twice as fast as a standard telephone line.

> **Note** The speed at which data can be transmitted across a network is known as its **baud rate** and is measured in **bits per second (bps)**. Currently, a standard telephone line (that is a PSTN line) can transmit data at a rate equivalent to 56,000 bps. An ISDN line, on the other hand, can transmit data at up to 128,000 bps.

Microwave and Satellite Communications

Both PSTN and ISDN rely on a network of underground and overhead wires to transmit data. Other telecommunication technologies, such as satellite and microwave communications (for example mobile phone networks) can also be used. Both of these rely on the use of **digital radio signals** to transmit data.

Microwave communications work by sending a radio signal via a series of land based transmitters. The principle for satellite communications is very similar, except that the radio signal is sent between two transmitters via a **satellite** in orbit above the earth.

A combination of these two technologies can enable us to send radio signals (and therefore data) anywhere in the world. So-called **wireless** access to networks is an increasingly important technology.

Fax

Fax (or facsimile) enables you to send and receive exact copies of documents over a telephone line.

The original document is inserted into a fax machine, which scans the document and converts it into an electronic signal that can be transmitted using a telephone connection. The recipient's fax machine interprets the signal being sent and prints a copy of the document.

Tip A PC with a **Fax Modem** (see below) can send documents to a fax machine without the need for scanning.

Telex

Telex is another way in which you can send and receive printed messages over a telephone line.

Unlike fax messages, which can be sent and received by anyone with a telephone line and a fax machine, telex messages can only be sent and received by individuals and companies who have subscribed to a telex service and have their own telex equipment and code number.

Telex can only be used to transmit messages with basic alphanumeric characters. Fax messages can contain anything that can be written or drawn on a page. The advantage of telex is the fact that users must subscribe to the service, making it more **secure**.

Modem (modulator/demodulator)

A basic modem converts digital signals from your computer into analogue signals for transmission over a standard telephone line. This process is called **modulation**. The modem then converts the phone line's analogue signals into digital signals that your computer can use. This process is called **demodulation**.

Hayes modem

A modem can consist of an expansion card installed inside the PC case (**internal** modem) or a box attached to a port (**external** modem).

Many modems can also transmit **fax** and **voice** data, allowing you to send and receive telephone calls and faxes through your PC.

There are different types of modem for connecting to different types of network. Examples include ISDN and cable modems.

Practice

Q5. Answer these questions on telecommunications technology:

a) In computing, what might a telephone network be used for?

_____

_____

_____

b) What does PSTN stand for? Give a brief description of what it is.

_____

_____

_____

_____

_____

Answers on page 95

Electronic Mail

Electronic mail (or **email**) enables you to send and receive electronic messages over a computer network. A basic email consists of a simple text message. However, you can also send formatted text and file attachments (any type of data file) via email.

Email is often available in a computer **workgroup**, enabling members of the workgroup to send messages to one another instantaneously.

Internet email enables you to exchange messages with anyone else on the internet with a **mailbox** (an electronic address to which email can be sent). Email is the most popular internet service.

Sending an email message is much cheaper than making a long distance telephone call or sending a document by fax and the recipient receives the email message much more quickly than a conventional letter. It is also easier to distribute an email to a large number of people.

What is needed to send and receive email?

♦ Connection to a network (either to a workgroup or over the internet).

♦ An email **client** program, such as Microsoft Outlook or Lotus Notes, installed on your computer. These programs enable you to create, read and manage email messages.

♦ An email **server** program to deliver email to your **mailbox**. Whether you are connected to the internet, a LAN or a WAN, your incoming email will usually be stored in a **POP (Post Office Protocol) mailbox**. In order for your email **client** software to collect any messages that are waiting for you, you must tell it the **name** of the **server** that holds your POP mailbox, your **account name** and **password**.

♦ An email **server** program to deliver email that you send to other people. **Simple Mail Transfer Protocol (SMTP)** is the protocol (or set of rules) used to send email messages from one computer to another. While POP is the protocol used to retrieve incoming email from your mailbox, SMTP is used to **send** outgoing email. In order for your email client software to send email messages, you must tell it the name of the SMTP server that handles your outgoing email.

♦ An email **address**. You need an email address yourself so that people can send email to you and you need to know other people's addresses to send them mail. An email address identifies which **mailbox** email is to be sent to. You can have more than one email address.

Practice

Q6. What advantages does email have over fax and postal mail?

_____

_____

_____

_____

_____

_____

Answer on page 96

The Internet

The **Internet** grew out of academic research into computer network technologies. The founding vision of the research was the ability to share data and programs quickly anywhere in the world.

The term **Internet** describes a global network of computer file servers spanning over 250 countries. Computers and networks are connected to the internet using a variety of telecommunications equipment and dedicated high-speed, high-capacity data lines. Different types of computers and networks can transfer data because they all use the same **protocol (TCP/IP)**.

Any one computer or network connected to the internet is usually only connected to a few other computers. However, these computers, in turn, connect to still more computers and so on, forming what is often described as a web of computers and computer networks. Each network allows data to pass through its servers on the way to its final destination.

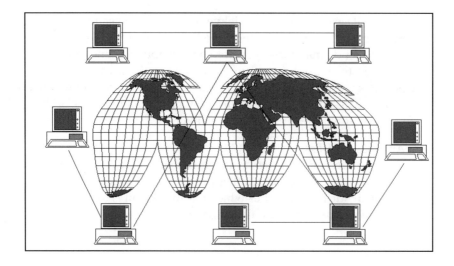

Removing or adding a computer or network does not disrupt the other networks or the internet itself. This flexibility means that the internet is always there and always available.

The idea that the internet forms a web of connections spanning the globe often means that people *wrongly* refer to it as "The World Wide Web" or more simply "The Web". In fact, the world wide web is just one of the **services** available on the internet, not the internet itself.

Services on the internet

The internet has as many uses as anyone can think to put it to. For example, the spare computing power of ordinary desktop PCs connected to the internet is being used to search for extraterrestrial life (www.seti.org)!

From its beginnings, the internet has been used as a tool for exchanging and distributing knowledge, and is an important tool for academic research. Since the internet was opened up to commerce in the early 1990's, many new facilities have been developed and business has seized the opportunity to use the internet for communications, marketing, advertising and selling.

Some of the better-known internet services are described below. Most of these services are free to use. Apart from actually buying products and services online, the only charges made for internet use are those made by your Internet Service Provider (see below) and the cost of connection (usually telephone charges).

The World Wide Web

The **World Wide Web** is the fastest growing service on the internet. The web is a vast collection of hyperlinked **files** *published* on the internet. These files are viewed using a **browser**. A **hyperlink** is simply a shortcut to a file. When you click a hyperlink, the file is opened in the browser.

The web is popular with businesses and consumers alike because it is flexible enough to display text, graphics, sound and video and to allow interaction (online ordering, playing games and so on).

Search Engines

Search engines help you to find information on the internet. You can enter words and phrases relating to the information you are looking for and the search engine will display a list of relevant hyperlinks from its database.

Internet email

Internet email is an electronic postal system through which all kinds of data can be sent to other users of the internet. This data includes documents, pictures, sounds, spreadsheets and programs. Internet email is one of the cheapest and most flexible forms of communication.

Newsgroups

Newsgroups allow users to exchange emails on a particular topic. The emails (or **posts**) can be viewed by all **subscribers** to the newsgroup. There are thousands of newsgroups covering any topic you care to imagine.

Chat

Chat rooms and **discussion groups** enable you to take part in **real-time** discussions on a variety of topics. You take part in a discussion by typing messages that can be read by other people in the group and replied to immediately. You can also view all the other conversations in the group.

File Transfer Protocol

FTP (File Transfer Protocol) sites contain millions of shareware and freeware files (see page 88), which you can download to evaluate or use.

Hardware and Software Needed for Internet Access

Internet access from the home requires the following:

♦ A **client computer** (usually a PC or an Apple MAC). You do not need a particularly powerful computer to connect to the internet.

♦ A **modem** (modulator/demodulator) and a **telephone connection** from the computer to the service provider. This could be a standard telephone line with a modem or a high-speed digital connection, such as an ISDN line. ISDN lines are more expensive than standard telephone lines, but they can transmit data considerably faster.

♦ An **Internet Service Provider (ISP)** - a company that provides customers with internet access.

♦ **Client software** that enables your computer to connect to a server and retrieve information, such as web pages and email messages. Microsoft Internet Explorer is an example of a web client (or browser) and Microsoft Outlook is an example of an email client.

Note Depending on the speed of connection you require and the amount of time you expect to spend connected to the internet, the cost of internet access can vary considerably. If you connect to the internet via a standard telephone line and a modem, it is best to use the fastest modem possible in order to reduce the connection time and consequently the cost.

> **Tip** As the internet grows more popular, the range of devices available for connecting to it is growing. You can already use video games consoles and digital television sets to browse online services. There is also more emphasis on **mobile** connection to the internet, using mobile phones and palmtop computers.

Practice

Q7. Answer these questions on the internet:

a) What is the internet?

_____

_____

b) Name three services available on the internet.

_____

_____

_____

_____

c) What is the world wide web?

_____

_____

_____

d) What do you need to connect to the internet from a home PC?

_____

_____

_____

_____

_____

_____

Answers on page 96

Computers in Everyday Life

Know some of the applications of IT at home, in business and in everyday life

Lesson 6

Know some of the uses of the PC **at home** ☐
Know some of the uses of IT in **business**, **industry**, **government** and **education** ☐
Recognise some of the uses of computers in **daily life** ☐
Understand some of the **benefits** and **limitations** of computers ☐

Computers are in common use today because they can process large amounts of data in a short time. Processes that today can be achieved in a few minutes would previously have consumed far greater resources in terms of manpower and time. Most areas of modern society take advantage of computing power.

Computers in the Home

♦ Word processing software can be used for letter writing and for children's homework.

♦ A spreadsheet or home accounting system can be used to work out household budgets, mortgage repayments, utility bills, and so on.

♦ Presentation graphics can be used for homework, or for creating things such as party invitations.

♦ Time-management/personal organiser packages can store contact details and remind you of meetings, birthdays, anniversaries, and so on.

♦ Computer games range from simple puzzles to complex strategies and adventure games. Leisure software is available for a wide variety of interests, including genealogy, cookery, gardening, music...

♦ Educational software can provide interactive, multimedia learning over all topics and age groups.

♦ The internet is an important tool for communication (via email, chat forums and newsgroups), information, shopping and home finance.

♦ More and more people are able to work from home thanks to modern communications technology. A computer with a modem can send and receive faxes, emails and other computer files so there is less need for people to travel to work every day.

Computers in Business

Commercial systems are those used by companies selling products and services. Most companies use IT for administration. Also, some businesses use computers to design and produce their products.

Office Applications

Applications software (as described on page 46) allows businesses to process data more efficiently and to create more sophisticated and professional-looking documents for marketing and internal communications, staff development and so on.

Bespoke Software

Many businesses depend entirely on IT to produce and market their products. Businesses may have specially written software (**bespoke software**) to assist in their design process. It is also common for businesses to have customised **database** applications, for example to implement a booking system that displays up-to-date information across a range of business premises and computer systems.

Payroll Processing

Computers are especially good at number crunching, so most companies use them for calculating salaries, PAYE and National Insurance contributions. There are a number of software packages designed specifically for this purpose.

Data Communications

Business benefits from IT communications, such as the internet and email.

Computers in Industry and Government

As well as the business systems described above, examples of industrial systems include photographic processing, speed trap cameras, washing machines, and so on. In addition, industrial systems control manufacturing processes, such as papermaking and car assembly.

- ◆ **Computer-Aided Design (CAD)** - using a computer means that technical drawings and schematics are easier to produce and revise. Drawings can be rotated or viewed in 3D and easily transmitted to a client for feedback. CAD is often linked to Computer-Aided Manufacturing (CAM), which enables the data produced in CAD drawings to be loaded into a machine, which then manufactures the part concerned.

♦ **Robotics** - industrial robots are used to carry out tasks that would be difficult or dangerous for a human to undertake. They have programmed "arms" which enable them to manipulate items.

♦ **Environment Monitoring and Control** - central heating systems and thermostatically controlled fan heaters are examples of environmental control. They keep the environment at a steady temperature determined by the operator. Other types of computerised monitoring systems include those for weather stations, pollution levels and river levels.

♦ **Traffic Control** - traffic lights work via a small sensor pointing at the road. If the sensor does not detect any traffic, it sends a message to the controlling computer telling it that the way is clear and that it can change to red and allow traffic from the other direction to pass. The traffic lights in a city are usually connected to a central computer which is able to co-ordinate them to allow a smoother flow of traffic.

Computers in Education

There are many educational software products on the market.

♦ Some of these products are referred to as **Computer-Based Training** (CBT). CBT consists of interactive multimedia tutorials and exercises. Using CBT can assist children in learning English, maths, geography, and so on. Adults can use CBT to learn how to type, use application software packages, speak foreign languages, and so on.

♦ Encyclopaedias, which may have been prohibitively expensive and bulky for many people in book form, are available on CD/DVD-ROM, and often include audio and video clips as well as animated sequences.

♦ Access to the internet presents a wealth of educational opportunities, from searching for information in online encyclopaedias to reading international newspapers and magazines. A few college courses can be taken online.

encarta.msn.com - an online encyclopaedia

Computers in Daily Life

Almost everywhere we go in our day-to-day lives we will encounter computers, although we have become so used to them that we may not always notice. Here are some examples of how computers are used to ensure the smooth running of our lives.

Electronic Funds Transfer (EFT), Electronic Point of Sale (EPOS) and EFTPOS

EFT is used to transfer money from one bank account to another using communications technology and without any paper transactions. For example, EFT is used to pay wages, by transferring an amount from the company's bank account to the employee's bank account.

Bar codes are sets of parallel lines of varying thickness, each of which represents a number. The numbers represent information, such as details about a product. To obtain this information, the bar code reader scans the bar code using a laser and sends the data contained in the bar code to a computer.

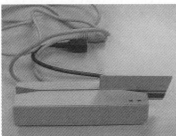
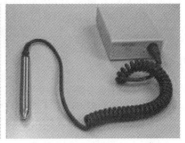

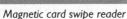

Magnetic card swipe reader   *Bar Code wand and reader unit.*

An **EPOS** system scans the barcode on a product when it is taken to a store's checkout and passes the information to a central computer, which adjusts the stock levels accordingly, calculates all sales and compares the number of sales to the quantity of stock. When stock runs out, or falls below a predetermined number, it is automatically reordered.

An **EFTPOS** system takes payment for goods from credit/debit cards and transfers it directly from the credit agency's account into the shop's bank account. The purchaser then receives a bill from the credit agency for the amount they have spent.

When a credit card is swiped, the shop's computer telephones the credit agency's computer to ensure that the card is valid. It may also be able to check whether the purchaser is still within their credit limit. Bank debit cards (for example Switch and Delta) work in a similar way, except payment is transferred directly from the purchaser's bank account.

Automatic Telling Machine (ATM)

A cash-dispenser is connected to a bank or building society's main computer. Not only can it issue money to customers, it can perform a number of other routine tasks such as displaying the balance of a customer's account.

To use an ATM (or cash machine), you insert a self-service card, which has information about your identity and account details stored in a magnetic strip on the back. You then need to key in a PIN (Personal Identification Number) before you can withdraw cash or obtain other services.

Barcode/Magnetic Strip Cards and Smart Cards

Identity cards of different kinds are widely used to provide access to libraries, leisure facilities, supermarket loyalty schemes and so on. These cards work in much the same way as the EPOS system. The bar code or magnetic strip on the card identifies you in a computer database and is used to update details of your "account" (for example, which library books you have out).

A **smart card**, also the size of a credit card, contains a small microprocessor, which can actually store data, rather than just identify the user to a central database. Smart cards have a huge range of potential applications but are not in widespread use.

Medicine

Doctors are moving toward using computer databases for **patient records**. In fact, it is likely that in the future people will carry their medical records with them, in the form of a file stored on the internet or on a smart card.

A doctor's surgery may also have a computer system to help with **diagnosis**. Information about a patient's symptoms is fed into the computer and it provides suggested causes to the doctor. Such systems are also used over the internet, to provide help and advice to the public and to relieve the pressure on GPs.

In hospitals, computers form part of, or are used to monitor, all kinds of clinical and diagnostic **equipment**.

Film, TV and leisure

Most films, TV programs, magazines and books are **produced** and **edited** with the aid of computers.

Also, much media is now **distributed** using computer technology. Music has been distributed digitally since the 1980s (on CD), film is now sold on DVD, TV is broadcast using digital signals and the most up-to-date cinemas use digital projectors.

The Benefits and Limitations of Computers

To understand the benefits and limitations of computers, you need to look at the way they operate. A computer is a complex calculating device. It receives instructions from programs (software) and performs calculations on these instructions. The results of the calculations can be output to different kinds of electronic devices.

While computers can operate very quickly, they can only perform tasks based on the information and instructions they are given.

Practice

- *Before reading this summary, try to identify three benefits and three limitations of computer systems (compared to people)*

_____

_____

_____

_____

_____

_____

_____

_____

_____

_____

_____

_____

_____

_____

_____

_____

_____

_____

_____

_____

_____

_____

_____

Main benefits of computers

♦ Many of the advantages of computers stem from the fact that they can handle and manipulate vast quantities of data. They can handle data so quickly that it would it be impractical for people to do the same work.

♦ Computers are electrical machines so by sending electrical signals they are able to communicate at extremely high speeds with other electrical machines. Computers are therefore ideally suited to control a wide range of electrical devices from robotic assembly lines to telephone systems.

♦ Computers do not get tired or bored and do not make mistakes (though unexpected circumstances can cause errors).

♦ A huge range of software has been written for computers, which means that they can be used in a variety of roles.

♦ For a business, a computer is usually cheaper than an employee. Also the company physically owns the computer.

♦ A computer can be made to work 24 hours a day/7 days a week. Computers do break down, but they do not take as many sick days as employees.

Main limitations of computers

♦ It is very difficult to make a computer act correctly in all situations since a computer cannot be truly intuitive. Without supervision, computers will operate poorly when dealing with unexpected circumstances, such as information or instructions that are incorrect or incomplete.

♦ Many people still prefer to deal with a person rather than a computer. For example, voice mail and automatic telephone answering machines sound impersonal, and it can be frustrating hanging on a telephone line without being able to talk to another person.

♦ It is very debatable whether computers can be truly creative. Although computers are often used to help with the design process, they are not capable of original thought.

♦ If the software being used on a computer is poorly written or the user has not been trained to use the software or the computer correctly, it can become a hindrance rather than a help.

Important Points

From looking at the major benefits and limitations of computers, it is easy to see where a computer may or may not be more appropriate than a person.

♦ Computers are ideal for tasks such as performing complex calculations on large amounts of data or searching through large databases to find information.

♦ They are also very good at controlling other electrical devices. For example, part of a car production line may involve welding two parts of a car body together. A computer can be used to control one or more robotic arms to perform this task over and over again with a constant level of quality and precision.

♦ Computers are not suitable where some level of intuition, original thought or imagination is involved. If a situation arises that the computer has not been programmed to deal with, it will not be able to consider the options available and devise an appropriate course of action.

♦ They are also unsuitable in situations where emotions may be involved or an element of discretion may be required. For example, when dealing with customer complaints, a person can weigh up the seriousness of the complaint, the mood of the customer and whether any special circumstances need to be taken into account. A computer would not be able to do this.

IT and Society

Understand the impact of information technology on society

Lesson 7

Know what is meant by the terms **Information Society** and **Information Superhighway** ☐
Know about the **Year 2000 Problem** ☐
Understand the concept of **e-commerce** ☐
Understand the requirements for a **good working environment** ☐
Be aware of some of the main **health and safety** regulations and guidelines related to the use of computer equipment ☐
(Understand the proper **use** and **care** of computer equipment) ☐

A Changing World

During the second half of the 20th century information technology advanced from the first working electronic computers in the 1940's to being vital to commerce and an important part of many people's lives:

◆ Electronic circuitry is now used in many everyday appliances such as cookers, washing machines and heating systems. Modern cars make use of computers to control parts ranging from the engine to the braking system (for example, antilock brakes). The dramatic increase in PC sales in the 1980's and 1990's has spread the use of computers into every part of life.

◆ Computers have gradually become more powerful and user-friendly. This has meant that people can use computers for a much wider range of tasks without having to understand how they work (at least not in detail). Since the 1980's computers have been used for tasks such as word processing, publishing, accounting and graphic design. The use of computers to store information has also become widespread, with computerised databases replacing old card-file systems.

◆ In addition to the changes in our working and domestic lives, computers have also affected the way we pay for goods and services. More and more transactions are undertaken without paper money, through the use of debit cards like Switch and Delta and credit cards such as VISA and MasterCard.

◆ One of the most important developments in IT in the 1990's was the spread of the internet, linking millions of people and organisations throughout the world.

♦ The advances in communications technology (faxes, email, the internet, and so on) have meant that many more people are able to work from home, giving opportunities to those unable to go out to work or for those who require more flexible working hours than 9am-5pm. These advances have also enabled companies with sites that are distant from one another to operate more closely through the sharing of information.

Work and Employment

The introduction of information technology has affected many people in the workplace. Fewer people are needed as computers can perform repetitive tasks both quickly and accurately. Most firms have computerised many of their operations in order to remain competitive.

♦ Typing pools are a thing of the past, along with banks of operators at telephone exchanges, which are now fully automated. In addition, the onset of desktop publishing and digital printing methods has dramatically changed the printing industry.

♦ A very large industry has grown up around IT, which employs a great many people, including hardware designers, engineers, system analysts, application programmers, trainers, computer consultants, Internet Service Providers, graphic designers and website designers.

The "Information Society"

Our society is often referred to as the "Information Society". This partly reflects the fact that much more of what we do at work involves the creation, manipulation and distribution of information. However, it also reflects the fact that information has become one of the most important factors in our social and domestic lives. The amount of information held about us, the amount of information we have access to and the speed at which we can exchange information regardless of distance have all had a marked effect on the importance we place on it.

♦ Information is now extremely valuable and can be distributed almost instantly to anyone, anywhere. From a commercial point of view, the amount and the quality of information a company has about its customers (and potential customers) will play a key role in determining whether or not the company is successful. Thus, accurate up-to-date information can command a high price.

♦ The ease with which computer databases can be created, accessed and maintained means that they are now an essential business tool. Most companies, regardless of their size, will have a database of customers and other important information. Using, maintaining and updating this database will be a core part of the company's operation.

♦ There has been a huge increase in the amount of information available to people, who are now more adept than ever at using information efficiently. People now need the ability to sift and filter relevant information from the mass available.

The "Information Superhighway"

The internet is sometimes referred to as the "Information Superhighway". This simply reflects the fact that it enables us to transport vast amounts of information almost anywhere in the world.

♦ We can think of the internet as the electronic equivalent of a high-speed road network spanning the globe. In the same way that a road network links us together by providing a means of transportation, the internet links us through the ability to share and exchange information, regardless of geographic location.

Electronic Commerce

Electronic commerce (or **e-commerce**) refers to the use of the internet (particularly the world wide web) for commercial activities. Many companies now use the internet to provide 24-hour access to information about their products and services.

♦ Companies market and sell products and services directly from a website. The nature of the web means that a company can make a large amount of information about a product directly available to the customer. Trading in this way enables companies to sell 24-hours a day, seven days a week to almost anywhere in the world. However, consumers can quickly compare products, companies and prices around the world, so competition is more intense.

♦ The internet can also be used to provide after-sales support using internet chat forums, newsgroups, email and interactive web pages.

♦ There are many online services, notably bank accounts, where you can operate your account over the internet rather than visiting a branch. As the infrastructure of the internet improves, further services such as software or video rental or pay-per-view sporting events will become widespread.

♦ The activities listed above are called **B2C** (**Business-to-Consumer**). Of equal importance is the use of the internet to trade with other companies (**B2B** or **Business-to-Business**). The internet can be used to auction sales and supply contracts, recruit staff, gather market intelligence and so on.

There are however still some limitations to e-commerce.

- If a company is selling actual goods, there is the problem of **distribution** (getting the goods to the customer on time). This particularly affects companies selling products internationally. Issues such as different sales taxes (VAT in Europe) can also be problematic.

- **Availability** is another issue. If a company is offering a wide range of products, possibly from different suppliers, they need an efficient stock system to ensure that they can actually deliver the goods advertised and that they can cope with demand. Also, if a new site becomes popular very quickly, the numbers of people visiting it can cause it to crash (stop working).

- As with any business, **confidence** in the brand is also important, but perhaps more so because a new technology is involved. People can be wary about placing an order with a company they know little about or with whom they have had no direct contact. It can also be more difficult to investigate fraud or poor practice on the internet if the laws of different countries are involved.

- Finally people often have concerns about the **security** of sending sensitive information such as credit card details over the internet.

The Year 2000 Problem - the "Millennium Bug"

During the 1990's, people began to recognise an inherent problem in some of the computer systems and software we use. It became known as the "Year 2000 Problem" or the "Millennium Bug" because the problem related to the change of the year date figure from 1999 to 2000.

- The problem exists in computers and programs that store date information using a two-digit number for the year, for example 96 for the year 1996. When the date changed from December 31st 1999 to January 1st 2000, computers and programs that store the date in this way were not able to recognise that the century number had changed from 19 to 20. This means that in some cases they would no longer be able to return the correct date.

- The problem arose because some computer systems and programs have remained in use far longer than anyone ever intended. When they were developed in the 1970's and 80's, no one imagined that these systems would still be in use at the start of the next century; so storing the date using a two-digit number for the year was not seen as a potential problem.

- The Millennium Bug seemed to pose many challenges to the structure of IT systems around the world. It was feared that data would become unreliable and that some electronic systems could break down, with implications for the health and safety of employees and consumers and the possibility of legal action against faulty or dangerous goods.

As it turned out, there was no widespread disruption of IT systems. Despite concerns lasting up until 4 January 2000, most major organisations had assessed their computer systems and taken appropriate action and the impact on other electronic systems had been over-estimated.

Nonetheless, the Millennium Bug did affect some systems and could potentially still cause problems with older software and files. Most importantly though, it demonstrated the way IT is crucial to the way society functions.

A Good Working Environment

Ergonomics is the study of factors affecting the performance of people at work. It is well established that a bad working environment can cause certain health problems.

Eyestrain and Headaches

♦ Looking at a monitor for long periods of time without a break can make your eyes tired and cause headaches.

♦ Using a good quality monitor that produces a clear image on the screen may help reduce this problem. The rate at which the monitor renews (refreshes) this image is also important. Higher image refresh rates are often more comfortable than lower ones because they reduce visible flicker on the screen.

 ## Working with VDU's

Introduction

This leaflet is a guide for people who work with visual display units (VDUs), and their employers. It:

☐ answers questions that are most often asked about VDUs and health;

☐ gives a summary of the law on VDU work (the Health and Safety (Display Screen Equipment) Regulations 1992), and outlines what employers and employees should do to comply;

☐ suggests some simple adjustments that users can make to workstations and screens to make them more comfortable and easy to use; and

---

Information about working with monitors from the Health and Safety Executive

♦ Adequate lighting should be provided. If the ambient lighting level is too low, you will experience increased glare from the monitor screen. If it is too high, you will experience glare from the lighting itself. Also, no light should be reflected from the screen.

♦ Filters that reduce glare from the screen are available. However, these are not a substitute for adequate lighting.

Repetitive Strain Injury (RSI)

♦ RSI is a complaint that occurs when the same task is carried out repeatedly for a long period of time, making use of the same muscles continuously.

♦ RSI has been linked with the use of keyboards and mice.

♦ Ergonomically designed, angled keyboards and moulded mice are designed to reduce the risk of strain injury.

Back Pain

♦ Sitting at a desk in a poor position can cause lower back pain. This is especially true if you sit for long periods of time without getting up.

♦ To help prevent back pain, monitors and workstations should be positioned at the correct height for the user and chairs that provide support for the user's back and neck should be used.

♦ You should be able to sit up straight with the screen at slightly below eye level. You should be able to rest your feet on the floor comfortably. Your wrists should be supported as you type with your forearms parallel with your legs

Ventilation

Adequate ventilation is also important when using computer equipment. Computers and monitors give off a lot of heat and make the surrounding air very dry. This can cause your eyes and throat to become dry and uncomfortable if there is an insufficient supply of fresh air.

Also, some printers and photocopiers give off toxic fumes, so good ventilation is essential if these are kept in the room where you are working.

Practice

- *Look around your workplace*
- *Make a list of any ergonomic or health and safety issues that may have a bad effect on your work*
- *If there are problems, find out what can be done to correct them*

Health and Safety at Work

Health and Safety Regulations

The Health and Safety (Display Screen Equipment) Regulations 1992 require employers to analyse computer equipment used by employees and assess and reduce risks. Some of the key points are:

♦ Monitors should normally have adjustable brightness and contrast controls.

♦ Employees who regularly use display screen equipment have the right to ask their employer to pay for regular eye tests and pay for special spectacles **if they are required for the job**.

♦ Employees who regularly use display screen equipment should be allowed to take breaks periodically.

Some Health and Safety Guidelines

♦ When spending a long time using a computer, look after your eyes by taking a break every 40 minutes.

♦ Adjust your chair and screen to find the most comfortable working position. As a guide, your forearms should be roughly horizontal, and your eyes should be at the same height as the top of your screen.

♦ Using a mouse or a keyboard has been linked to repetitive strain injury (RSI). Take regular breaks from using them.

♦ When sitting down for long periods, make sure that your back is well supported in order to avoid damaging it. Avoid sitting in the same position for long periods - adjust your posture as often as is practical.

♦ Avoid repeatedly having to stretch to reach things you need. If this happens, rearrange your workspace.

♦ Make sure that power points are not overloaded. Overloaded power points are a fire risk.

♦ Make sure that any computer equipment you work with is positioned securely. All devices should be placed away from the edges of desks and should not obstruct people walking through the office.

♦ Make sure that all cables are secured safely at the back of your workstation where they cannot be tripped over or pulled out of your computer by accident.

Use and Care of Computer Equipment

Many organisations have an IT support department to take responsibility for the management of computer systems and the training of users. If something goes wrong with computer hardware or software, you should usually contact them in the first instance.

Remember to supply details of the problem, including any error messages or codes that are displayed on the screen and exactly what you were doing with the system at the time of the error.

Taking care of your computer

♦   **Never** move the computer when it is switched on.

♦   **Never** obstruct the ventilation holes in the monitor or the computer's case.

♦   **Never** eat or drink near the computer.

♦   **Never** store floppy disks near magnetic fields, which are created by monitors, speakers, microwaves and other electrical devices.

♦   **Always** keep your computer in a clean, dry, cool and dust free place.

♦   **Always** keep your computer away from radiators or hot lamps.

♦   If you are taking delivery of a new computer system, let it warm up to room temperature if it is delivered on a cold day so that any condensation dissipates before the power is turned on.

Taking care of the monitor

The monitor's screen surface should be cleaned using a suitable cleaning agent and cloth or wipe. These should be:

♦   **Anti-static** to prevent the attraction of dust and fabric particles onto the screen surface. This attraction reduces the visible contrast and brightness of the display.

♦   **Non-smear** to reduce reflections and residue film left on the screen surface by the cleaning fluid. Excess cleaning fluid should evaporate without leaving a residue.

♦   Any cloth used should be **cotton** to prevent scratching of the screen surface, and minimise the deposit of lint/fluff.

Screen cleaning kit

What is screen burnout?

Screen burnout describes damage caused to the inside surface of the screen display. The inner surface of the screen is coated in a phosphorous material that emits light when struck by an electron beam. If a screen display is static, the electron beam continually strikes the same place on the screen surface, and eventually *burns a hole* (or wears away) in the phosphorous coating. This might take several days or weeks to occur.

Screen burnout is avoided by following common sense principles.

♦ Turn down the screen brightness if leaving the machine unattended.

♦ Use a **screen saver** program (see 172).

♦ Switch the monitor off over longer periods.

♦ Use an **Energy Star** compliant monitor with power saving enabled.

Cleaning the keyboard

The surface of the keyboard is cleaned in much the same manner as the screen display.

♦ Care should be taken to prevent excess downward pressure on the keys whilst cleaning.

♦ Avoid the use of abrasive or corrosive fluids that might scratch the letters of the keys.

♦ Dust is removed by use of a portable vacuum cleaner, or little brush with an air pump attachment.

Switching Off a PC

Switching off your computer without shutting it down properly may damage any files that are still in use. To switch off your computer correctly:

♦ Save any files you are working on. If you switch off your computer without saving these files, you will lose any changes you have made since the last time you saved them.

♦ Exit from any application software you are using.

♦ Shut down your operating system.

See page 118 for instructions on how to shut down Windows properly.

Security, Copyright and the Law

Know about securing data and complying with the law when using computers

Lesson 8

Understand the effects of a **power cut** on computers and data ☐
Know the purpose and value of **backing store** ☐
Know how to **protect** a computer and data from **intrusion** ☐
Understand what a **computer virus** is and how a PC can be **infected** ☐
Recognise the implications of software **copyright** and **licensing** ☐
Understand what is meant by **freeware** and **shareware** ☐
Know the implications of the **Data Protection Act** ☐

Power Cuts

If there is a power cut, the effect is the same as turning off your computer without shutting down the operating system. **You will lose any unsaved data.**

♦   When the power comes back on, a tool may run automatically to check the system for errors (for example **Scandisk** in Windows). **If errors are found, you should seek help from an experienced user or your IT support department.**

♦   Most applications have a facility which enables the user to specify that the file they are working on is automatically saved after a given time interval, for example every 10 minutes. If there is a power loss the application will display **recovered** files and give you the opportunity to save them normally.

♦   An **Uninterruptible Power Supply** (UPS) is a battery-powered device attached to your computer that protects against power cuts. If there is a power cut, the UPS continues to supply power to the computer so that you can shut it down properly without losing any data or causing any damage to the hard disk.

Backing Store

A **backing store** (or simply **backup**) is a copy of files stored away from the computer, usually saved on a removable disk or tape cartridge. A backup is often kept **offsite**, to protect from loss of data through theft or fire. Backup may also be used to store data when there is no room on the main storage device(s) installed in the computer.

♦ If important data is stored on your computer, you should backup that data regularly. If the computer is damaged, if there is a fire, flood or even a simple user error, your data could be permanently lost if you do not have any backup copies away from the computer.

♦ Backups are often made to a timetable. An **incremental** backup may be made every day to store changed data. A **full** backup (of all data files) may be made weekly. It is quite common to retain backup tapes for a few months, so that **previous** versions can be restored (for example, if a document becomes infected with a virus at some point, it may be necessary to go back past the last backup made).

♦ When making a backup, it is vital to test that the data can be **restored** successfully. The backup needs to be tested to see that the correct data is being stored and that backup devices and media are working properly.

♦ A variety of different storage devices can be used as a backing store. Removable media such as Zip disks, Jaz disks and tape cartridges can be removed from their respective drives and replaced with new empty media of the same type.

♦ Alternatively, if the computer is on a network, a fixed hard disk in another computer could be used as a backing store. Many organisations encourage their users to save data to a network folder, where it will be backed up by the IT department automatically. Increasing use is also being made of the **internet** to store and manage data.

Security

Sensitive or valuable information is often stored on computers. Therefore, it is important to protect computer data from unauthorised access.

Passwords

Password protection can be used to restrict access to the computer or some of the files on it to authorised users:

♦ Most **operating systems** will allow you to set passwords to access the computer when it is turned on or to access resources on the network.

♦ **Screen savers** and many **applications** can also be password protected.

♦ Many programs will allow you to password protect **files**.

Tips Ideally, passwords should be a mixture of characters and numbers, which are difficult to guess, but easy for the user to remember.
Try to avoid passwords that are obvious, for example your name or your date of birth.
Do not store your password on your PC (for example by typing it into a document). If software has the ability to **remember** passwords, it is best to turn this feature off.

Encryption of data

Encrypting data means **encoding** it so that it cannot be read by anyone without the appropriate **decoder** and **key**.

♦ An encryption program is used to "scramble" the data. A decryption program and the correct encryption key are needed to unscramble it.

♦ Encryption, when used well, usually offers a better level of protection than a password.

♦ It can also be combined with a password so that even if someone has the appropriate decryption program, they cannot decode the data without first entering the correct password.

Security on a network

Because a network consists of a number of computers connected to each other, it can be relatively easy to copy or move information from one machine to another.

♦ It is the job of the Network Administrator to set passwords for each network user, and to allow or limit access to various parts of the network.

♦ Each user on the network has the responsibility of keeping their password secure and logging off from network resources properly.

♦ The internet is a particular problem since it is possible to get information from any other computer connected to the internet. Software called a **firewall** is used to protect internal network folders from access through the internet.

Hacking

Hacking is an attempt to overcome security measures and gain unauthorised access to information held on a computer system.

♦ Hacking is a criminal offence in most countries. In the UK it contravenes The Computer Misuse Act 1990.

♦ The use of passwords and encryption only offers limited protection against hackers. While the techniques used in protecting data are sophisticated and gradually increasing in sophistication, so are the techniques used in hacking.

Theft

♦ Computers (and especially laptops) are a popular target for thieves. Data can be stolen along with the actual computer it is stored on.

♦ There are several measures to take against theft, including devices for securing a PC to the desk and special marking sprays or pens, which identify ownership of the case and internal components so that they can be traced.

Computer Viruses

A computer **virus** is a program designed to spread itself by first infecting **executable** files or the **system areas** of hard and floppy disks and then making copies of itself in other files and/or disks. Viruses usually operate without the knowledge or desire of the computer user.

Viruses have the potential to infect any type of executable code, not just the files that are commonly called **program files**. For example, a **macro** virus can infect word processing and spreadsheet documents that use macros. It is possible for web pages containing JavaScript, ActiveX or other types of executable code to spread viruses or other malicious code.

How do viruses spread?

Files **containing** a virus may be downloaded from the internet, attached to an email or found on bootleg software disks. However, just because a file contains a virus does not mean that it has infected your system.

A virus is only activated when you **open** the file (or run an application) that contains it. When this happens, the virus code will also run and try to infect other files on the same computer and other computers connected to it over a network. The newly infected files will try to infect yet more files when opened.

If your computer is infected with a **boot sector** virus, the virus tries to write copies of itself to the system areas of floppy disks and hard disks. Then the infected floppy disks may infect other computers that boot from them, and the virus copy on the hard disk will try to infect still more floppies.

Some viruses, known as **multipartite** viruses, can spread both by infecting files and by infecting the boot areas of floppy disks.

Some viruses can use the computer's email system to send themselves to other computers as an email attachment.

What do viruses do to computers?

Viruses are software programs, and they can do the same things as any other programs running on a computer. The actual effects of any particular virus depend on how it was programmed.

Some viruses are deliberately designed to damage files or otherwise interfere with your computer's operation. Others do not do anything but try to spread themselves around or display silly messages. Others may try to steal information from your computer. Such viruses may try not to give away their presence.

> **Note** Viruses cannot do any damage to hardware: they will not melt down your CPU, burn out your hard drive or cause your monitor to explode.

What is a Trojan Horse program?

A **Trojan Horse** is a program (often harmful) that pretends to be something else.

For example, you might download what you think is a new game, but when you run it, it deletes files on your hard drive; or the third time you start the game, the program emails your saved passwords to another person.

Can I get viruses from email or from downloading files?

In almost all cases, simply downloading a file to your computer (or opening a web page) will not activate a virus or Trojan Horse - you have to execute the code (by **opening** the file in Windows itself) to trigger it. See page 620 for more information about downloading files.

You cannot get a virus just by reading a plain text email message.

What can I do to reduce the chance of getting viruses?

◆ Install **anti-virus software** from a well-known, reputable company, **update** it regularly, and **use** it regularly. New viruses come out every single day; an anti-virus program that has not been updated for several weeks will not provide much protection against current viruses.

◆ Look for anti-virus software that scans **on access**. This will protect your system by checking for viruses each time your computer accesses an executable file or downloads email.

◆ Scan any new files before you run or open them, no matter where they come from. There have been cases of commercially distributed floppy disks and CD-ROMs spreading virus infections.

◆ If your email software or web browser has the ability to automatically execute JavaScript, Word macros or other executable code, it is strongly recommended that you disable this feature - ask your IT support person to do this.

◆ Be extremely careful about accepting programs or other files during **online chat** sessions. If any other family members (especially younger ones) use the computer, make sure they know not to accept any files while using chat.

◆ Do not open any email file attachments that you were not expecting to receive. Some viruses can email themselves, and so will appear in a message that seems to be from someone you know. Simply delete the message and empty the email program's mail bin.

◆ Perform regular **backups**. Some viruses and Trojan Horse programs will erase or corrupt files on your hard drive, and a recent backup may be the only way to recover your data.

How can I remove a virus?

If you do get infected by a virus, follow the directions in your anti-virus program for cleaning it. If you have backup copies of the infected files, use those to restore the files. Check the files you restore to make sure your backups are not infected.

For assistance, check the website and support services for your anti-virus software.

What is the best anti-virus software available?

The following websites have sections with reviews of various anti-virus programs:

www.zdnet.com/products - search for "antivirus" reviews

www.virusbtn.com/100

Application Security

Modern software applications and operating systems are enormously complicated. Despite extensive testing by the manufacturers, problems (often called **bugs** or **security breaches**) can occur that can allow hackers access to private data files on a PC or computer network.

♦ Some of these breaches mean that the security of your data is at risk **regardless of the anti-virus measures** that you take. It is important to monitor the information that the manufacturer posts on their website.

♦ Most security breaches are only ever **theoretical**. That is, they are discovered "in the lab" by computer security researchers and not exploited by hackers. Fixes for the problem (often called **patches**) are then made available from the manufacturer's website. Also, most breaches affect the **server software** rather than **user** applications such as **web browsers** and **email clients**.

♦ Security issues affecting Microsoft products are summarised at:

www.microsoft.com/security/bulletins

Software Copyright and Licensing

Most software is **copyrighted**, which means that the right to make copies lies only with its producer. The same law applies to a number of different products, such as pre-recorded videotapes and music CDs. It is illegal to copy, share or lend copyrighted material without permission.

♦ The law of copyright is respected internationally. In the UK, software is treated in the same way as books, videos and CDs. Copying software is contrary to The Copyright, Designs and Patents Act 1988.

♦ It is illegal to use unauthorised copies of software (**pirate copies**). Pirated software often contains errors and viruses as well.

♦ Files published on the internet (graphics, music, video or text) are subject to copyright too. You cannot use such material without the copyright holder's permission.

Software Licences

When you buy software, you must accept the **licence** governing its use. The terms of the licence will vary according to the use of the software, but the basic restriction is that the software may only be installed on **one** computer.

♦ A company may have hundreds of employees who need the same software on their computers. Software manufacturers do not expect such companies to buy individual copies of the software for each employee. Instead, they will issue a licence for **multiple users**, which means that the company can install the software on an agreed number of computers for their employees to use.

♦ If a site has a large number of computers, these computers are often networked. This means that software bought under licence can be installed onto a network server so that all authorised users can access it without it being installed on each individual computer.

Shareware and Freeware

Shareware and freeware are different ways of distributing applications.

Shareware

Shareware is software you can install free of charge so that you can evaluate it for a limited period of time. If you decide to continue using the software after this period, you must register it, usually for a fee. When you register the software you often become entitled to extra features and support.

Freeware

Freeware is software that is available free of charge. Popular examples include the web browsers **Microsoft Internet Explorer** and **Netscape Navigator**.

> **Note** Even if software is distributed as shareware or freeware, the copyright is still held by the publisher or designer. Use of both shareware and freeware may still be governed by a licence, which may restrict its use (for example, to prevent commercial use of the product or to redistribute or resell it).

Data Protection and Privacy

The right to privacy is one expected by citizens of most states. However the right to privacy has to be balanced against the need for the companies we work for and shop with to receive and process (and in some cases store) information about us.

For example, a mail order company needs to know your address in order to deliver goods to you. When you tell them your address, you might expect them to use it only for the purpose of delivering goods that you have ordered and not to use it to contact you about other products or to pass it to another company without your permission.

People's right to privacy in respect of information stored about them (**data protection**) is being implemented in law in many countries around the world. It is defined for citizens of the European Community by **EC Directive 95/46/EC.** Each member state must implement this directive by passing legislation in its own parliament.

In the United Kingdom, the directive is implemented by the **Data Protection Act 1998**. In the UK, you can find out more about how the Act is applied and enforced from the Data Protection Commissioner (The commissioner's **website** is at www.dataprotection.gov.uk).

Principles of data protection

The UK Data Protection Act sets out eight principles that **Data Controllers** (anyone who **processes personal data**) must comply with.

♦ **Personal data** means both **facts** (for example, a birth date or an address) and **opinions** (for example, marketing information or work appraisals) about an individual and any information about the data controller's **intentions** toward the individual.

♦ **Processing** means **obtaining, holding** and **disclosing** information. The act applies as much to paper records as to computer ones, though there are exemptions.

♦ Generally speaking, data controllers must **notify** the Data Protection Registrar that they are processing personal data, though again there are exemptions.

The basic principles of the UK Act are summarised as follows:

♦ **Personal data shall be processed fairly and lawfully.**
The subject (the person the data is about) must have given **consent** to their data being processed and the processing must be **necessary** to comply with a contract or legal obligation or to protecting the vital interests of the subject. Where the data is **sensitive** (if the data contains information as to physical or mental health, racial or ethnic origin, political or religious beliefs or membership of a trade union) further conditions must be met.

♦ **Data shall be obtained only for the specified and lawful purpose(s).**

♦ **Data shall be adequate, relevant and not excessive.**

♦ **Data shall be accurate and up-to-date.**

♦ **Data shall not be retained for longer than is necessary.**

♦ **Data shall be processed in accordance with the rights of the data subject under the Act.**
The Act grants data subjects the right to inquire about what information is held about them and to have it changed or deleted if it is inaccurate. Data subjects are also entitled to claim compensation through the courts if damage is caused to them through the loss, destruction or disclosure of data or because data held about them is inaccurate.

♦ **Measures shall be taken against unlawful processing of, or damage to personal data.**
This means that data must be stored securely.

♦ **Data shall not be transferred to a territory outside the European Economic Area unless the territory ensures an adequate level of protection for the rights and freedoms of data subjects in relation to processing personal data.**

Practice

Q8. Answer these questions on security, copyright and the law:

a) What happens to any unsaved data when there is a power cut?

_____

_____

_____

b) What does UPS stand for, and what is it?

_____

_____

_____

c) Why is it a good idea to have backup copies of important files? Why are removable media useful for storing backups?

_____

_____

_____

_____

_____

_____

d) Why is security particularly important on a network?

_____

_____

_____

_____

e) What does encryption mean?

_____

_____

_____

f) What is hacking?

_____

_____

_____

_____

g) What is a computer virus, and how can a virus travel between computers?

_____

_____

_____

_____

h) What is a software licence?

_____

_____

_____

i) What is the difference between shareware and freeware?

_____

_____

_____

j) What basic considerations must a Data Controller make when processing personal data in the UK?

_____

_____

_____

_____

_____

_____

k) What rights does an individual have under the Data Protection Act?

_____

_____

_____

Answers on page 96

Review of Basic Concepts

Review the topics covered during the module and identify areas for further practice and goals for the future

(Check **objectives**) ☐
(Complete **consolidation** exercise) ☐
(Identify topics for **further** study) ☐
(**Answers** to practice questions) ☐

Check Objectives

Congratulations on completing the lessons for ECDL Module 1 "Basic Concepts of IT".

You have learned to:

♦ Understand the basic concepts of **IT, hardware** and **software**.

♦ Know the main **parts** of a personal computer.

♦ Recognise the components used to **store data**.

♦ Recognise different types of **software**.

♦ Understand the type and functions of different **networks**.

♦ Know some of the **applications** of IT at **home**, in **business** and in **everyday life**.

♦ Understand the impact of information technology on **society**.

♦ Know about **securing** data and complying with the **law** when using computers.

Make sure you have checked off each syllabus item and identified any areas you do not fully understand or remember.

Consolidation and Going Further

Tests for Module 1 can take the format of exam-style question papers or multiple-choice questions. There are no practical tests to complete, so the material must simply be learned and remembered.

There are further test-style questions for you to try on the CD in the folder **ECDL Tests\1 Basic Concepts**

Print the document **Basic Concepts Questions** and try to complete the test unaided. Mark your own work using the **Answers** document.

Note These questions are provided as a consolidation exercise. They do not make up an approved ECDL test. See page 689 for more information about the extra tests.

Going further

While Module 1 is theory-based, there are many practical uses of the ideas discussed. You can get further training in any of the practical applications of IT, such as building and maintaining PC and network hardware or software design and project management.

Practice Answers

Q1. Identify the most suitable type of computer to perform tasks

(a) Laptop (b) PC (c) Mainframe (d) Network Computer

Q2. Identify the pieces of equipment:

(a) Printer (b) CRT Monitor (c) Portable Computer/Laptop (d) CPU
(e) Keyboard

Q3. Answer questions on software development

a) Requirements analysis, System and software design, Implementation and testing, System training, Operation and Maintenance

b) The current system is analysed and observed in operation.
Existing users are interviewed to get their views on existing problems and what they would like the new system to do.
A feasibility report, which defines the requirements of the new system and recommends whether or not these requirements can realistically be met, is produced.

c) Individual programs are combined and tested as a complete system to ensure that they work correctly together and that all the software requirements have been met.

d) Operation and Maintenance. The new system (including hardware and software) is installed and put into practical use. Feedback is obtained from users to find out about problems and possible improvements.

Q4. Answer questions on computer networks

a) A workgroup is a group of computers on a network that can share data and resources, such as printers, modems and other hardware.

b) Resources can be dedicated to specific groups of computers, instead of being made available to everyone.
Computers in the workgroup can share a single store of data so that information is available to everyone and duplication of data is reduced. Because computers are not limited to particular tasks, sharing resources can reduce costs.

c) A Local Area Network (LAN) is a network of computers and other devices based at a single site. In general, there is no more than 1km between any two extremities of a LAN.

d) A workstation is an individual computer connected to a network.

e) A file server is a computer providing a shared data store for workstations on the network and in some cases, access to software.

f) A Wide Area Network (WAN) is a network used to connect large numbers of computers and terminals over long distances.
WANs can cover any geographical area and often consist of multiple sites. WANs are usually much larger with more computers and servers connected to the network.
WANs will often use larger servers, such as mainframes or minicomputers, whereas LANs tend to use powerful PCs as servers. WANs use telecommunication links (for example telephone lines) or even radio or satellite communications to send and receive data between sites. LANs use direct cable connections.

Q5. Answer questions on telecommunications technology

a) Telephone networks are often used to transmit data between computers and networks.

b) PSTN stands for Public Switched Telephone Network. PSTN is the standard telephone network, designed to transmit audio signals.
It is relatively slow in transmitting computer data, but because it is cheap and readily available in most homes and offices, it is still the way in which most home and small business users connect to external networks, such as the internet.

Q6. What advantages does email have over fax and postal mail

Cheaper; Usually quicker; Easier to address to multiple recipients; Can include data files

Q7. Answer questions on the internet

a) The internet is the global network of networks.

b) World Wide Web, Search Engines, Email, Chat forums, Discussion groups, FTP (File Transfer Protocol Sites), Newsgroups

c) The World Wide Web is the collection of hyperlinked files published on the internet. The web allows publication of diverse material using a variety of different media all of which can be viewed using a browser.

d) Client computer, Modem, Telephone Connection, Internet Service Provider, Client software

Q8. Answer questions on security, copyright and the law

a) You will lose any unsaved data.

b) An Uninterruptible Power Supply provides power to a computer for a short time after a power cut, allowing you to save data and shut down the computer normally.

c) An organisation's data is one of its most valuable assets. If a computer is damaged, if there is a fire, flood or even a simple user error, your data could be permanently lost if you do not have any backup copies away from the computer.
Removable media are extremely useful for storing backup copies of files because they can easily be stored away from where the computer is located. If there is a fire or a flood, it is no use having the computer and the backup data stored in the same location as both could be destroyed.

d) Access to one machine can be used to gain access to the entire network.

e) Encrypting data means encoding it so that it cannot be read by anyone without the appropriate decoder.

f) Hacking is an attempt to overcome security measures and gain unauthorised access to information held on a computer system.

g) A computer virus is a program designed to spread itself by first infecting executable files or the system areas of hard and floppy disks and then making copies of itself.
Different viruses travel in different ways: through infecting executable files, through the boot sector of storage disks or by emailing themselves as attachments.

h) When you buy software, you are acquiring a licence to install and use the software.

Companies that need to install software for multiple users can buy a licence to make the software available to those users. This means that the manufacturer does not have to distribute so many installation disks.

i) Shareware is made available to install for a trial evaluation period, after which a licence must be bought.

Freeware is distributed without requiring a licence (though a voluntary fee may be made and there may be restrictions on its use and distribution).

j) Data Controllers must register with the Data Protection Commissioner and comply with the Data Protection Act. The main points to consider are:

Data must only be retained and used with consent and for the purpose stated and not kept longer than is necessary.

The data stored should be adequate, relevant and not excessive, accurate and up-to-date.

Data must be stored securely.

Data should be processed in accordance with the rights of the data subject under the Act. It cannot be transferred to another territory in an attempt to avoid the terms of the Act.

k) Individuals have the right to inquire about what information is held about them and to have it changed or deleted if it is inaccurate. They are also entitled to claim compensation through the courts if damage is caused to them through the loss, destruction or disclosure of data or because data held about them is inaccurate.

Notes

Using the Computer and
Managing Files

Getting Started with MS Windows

Use basic features of MS Windows

Lesson 9

Start, **restart** and **shut down** a PC ☐
Recognise, select, move and open Desktop **icons** ☐
(Use the **mouse** and **keyboard**) ☐
(Use the **Taskbar** and **Start Menu**) ☐
Recognise the different parts of a **window** ☐
Move, **resize** and **close** a window ☐
Scroll around in a window ☐
Move between open windows ☐
Use application **help** functions ☐

The MS Windows Operating System

MS Windows is a PC **operating system**. An operating system:

♦ Provides a **Graphical User Interface** to PC **hardware components** (such as the hard disk, floppy disk, CD drive or modem).

♦ Allows different PC **software applications** (word processors such as MS Word or spreadsheets such as MS Excel) to work together in a common environment.

♦ Manages the **data files** you create when using applications.

A graphical user interface (GUI - pronounced "gooey") means that commands are selected from **icons** and **menus** on-screen using the **keyboard** and the **mouse**. Applications run in **windows** on the screen. You can open several windows at once and switch between them, allowing you to use several applications at the same time.

> **Note** This course is based on use of **Microsoft Windows 2000**. You could also use it with **Windows Millennium**. However, you will find that some exercises do not work.
> There is an appendix discussing some of the major differences between Windows 2000 and Windows Me on page 683.

Start the Computer

If you are using the computer for the first time, make sure you have read the instruction manual for your PC carefully before turning it on. You should ensure that all the necessary leads and cables are securely plugged into the correct sockets. You should also be familiar with the layout of the controls on the front of the PC.

PCs are built differently depending on the manufacturer, but most should contain the basic controls shown to the right.

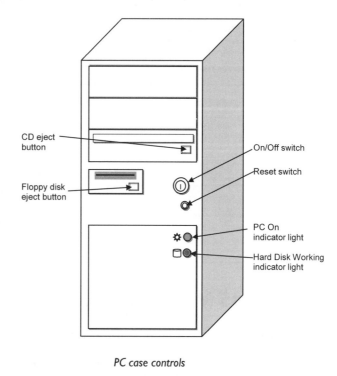

PC case controls

To switch on your PC

- Ensure that the PC is plugged in and that the floppy disk drive does not contain a disk

- Press the **On/Off** switch

Wait for a few seconds. The PC should beep and the monitor should turn itself on.

- If the monitor does not switch on, press the **On** switch **on the monitor case**

Some text will be displayed on-screen while the PC starts up. After a minute or so the **Welcome to Windows** dialogue box is displayed.

Logon to Windows

Windows 2000 is usually configured as a **secure** operating system. You need to **logon** to Windows with a **user name** and a **password** in order to access folders, files and applications on your PC.

If your PC is part of a **computer network**, logging on will also give you access to **network resources**, such as shared folders and printers.

Your IT systems administrator will have given you a **user name** and **password**. This is your **logon ID**, the means by which you are recognised as a registered user of the computer.

> **Note** There are many different ways that Windows 2000 can be setup, so some or all of the following steps may not apply to your own PC.

To logon to Windows

- If the **Welcome to Windows** dialogue box is displayed, press the following keys at the same time: `Ctrl` + `Alt` + `Delete` as instructed

The **Log On to Windows** dialogue box is displayed. This dialogue box allows you to enter your user name and password. Your user name will automatically appear if you were the last person to use the PC.

- In the **User name:** box, type your user name if necessary

- Press `Tab`

OR

- Move the mouse to position the cursor over the **Password** box and click the left mouse button once

- Type your password

The password that you type will not be displayed on the screen - you will see asterisks.

- Point to the **OK** button and click once **OR** press `Enter`

Windows will start and the **Desktop** is displayed.

> **Tip** If you click the **Options >>** button, the dialogue box extends to give you a choice of **domains** to logon to. Normally there will be a choice between logging onto the PC and logging onto the PC and the network.
> Ask your IT department for advice about which domain to logon to.

The Desktop

The Windows Desktop is a space for storing **shortcut icons** to commonly used software applications and files. The icons you can see in the screenshot represent some of the basic tools needed to use Windows. You may see more icons on your Desktop, depending on which software applications are installed.

A shortcut icon is a picture representing a **software application**, **file** or **folder**. When you double-click the icon, the application, file or folder will open.

At the bottom of the screen, there is a grey bar. This is called the **Taskbar**. The Taskbar provides you with access to your programs, data, documents, accessories and computer resources via the **Start** button **Start**.

To work with icons

- Using the screenshot below, identify the icons on your own Desktop

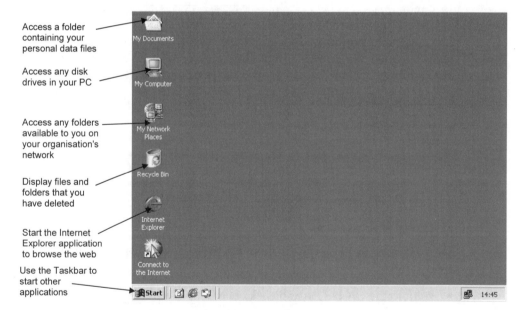

Access a folder containing your personal data files

Access any disk drives in your PC

Access any folders available to you on your organisation's network

Display files and folders that you have deleted

Start the Internet Explorer application to browse the web

Use the Taskbar to start other applications

Windows Desktop

- Move the mouse pointer over the **My Computer** icon
  - what happens?

If the icon changes colour, ignore the next instruction.

- If nothing happens, click the left mouse button once

The icon changes colour. You have **selected** the icon. Selecting is an important part of using Windows, since you generally have to select something to do anything with it.

Windows has two different ways of working, called **Desktop Styles**.

♦ **Classic Style** - if you are using Classic style, you have to click the left mouse button to **select** objects.

♦ **Web Style** - if you are using Web style, simply moving the mouse pointer **over** an icon selects it.

- Which Desktop Style are you using?_____

Tip	If you prefer using the keyboard, pressing the arrow keys ▲, ▼, ◄ and ► also lets you select different icons.

Use a Mouse

The function of the mouse is to move a **pointer** around the screen. You use the mouse to highlight areas of the screen, make selections and execute commands.

As you move the mouse on its pad, the pointer makes the same movement on the screen.

Tip	Using a mouse pad rather than the surface of the desk both protects the mouse from damage and makes the action of the mouse smoother.

The mouse pointer takes on up to 20 different shapes (or **cursors**) . The type of cursor indicates what actions can be performed at that point.

Pointer	Action	Pointer	Action
⬉ *Normal*	You can point to and select icons and commands	I *Insertion Point*	You can position a typing cursor on the screen
+ *Select*	You can select a group of objects	✎ *Handwriting*	You can draw on the screen
⬉? *Help Select*	You can select an object to get help on	↕ *Vertical Resize* ↔ *Horizontal Resize*	You can change the height **or** width of an object
⧖ *Busy*	The system is busy and cannot accept any input	⬉⬊ *Diagonal Resize*	You can change the height **and** width of an object
⬉⧖ *Working*	The system is working in the background, but you can still use the mouse	✛ *Move*	You can move an object
⊘ *Unavailable*	You cannot perform the action you were attempting	☝ *Link*	You can open a file or document by clicking the mouse button

A mouse has at least two buttons on it. The **left** mouse button is used for **pointing** and **selecting**.

The **right** mouse button is used to display **shortcut menus** and **context sensitive help**.

Note If you are **left-handed**, the *right* mouse button can be used for selecting and the left mouse button is used for shortcut menus. If your mouse has not been setup for left-handed use, refer to page 168 to find out how to do so.

Mouse Terminology

Remember that the following terms are used to describe common mouse actions:

♦ **Point** - move the mouse pointer over the object or item required.

♦ **Click** - point to the item you want to select then press and release the mouse button

♦ **Double-click** – point to the item then press and release the mouse button twice in quick succession. If this proves difficult the mouse clicking speed may be changed using the Control Panel (see page 169).

♦ **Click-and-drag** - point to the item or area you want then press the left mouse button and hold it down whilst pointing to another area of the screen. Release the mouse button.

To move an icon

You can move icons around the screen to make them more accessible.

- **Click-and-drag** the **My Computer** icon into the middle of the screen

If the icon does not go where you dragged it, the **Auto Arrange** option is probably activated. This option keeps your icons in orderly columns.

- **Right**-click an empty area of the **Desktop**

A shortcut menu is displayed.

Desktop shortcut menu

- Move the mouse pointer down to the **Arrange Icons** item

When the item is highlighted, a **submenu** appears.

- Move the mouse over to the submenu then down, until the **A**uto **Arrange** option is highlighted

If you could not move your Desktop icon, this option should have a tick next to it.

- Click the left mouse button once over the **A**uto **Arrange** option

This activates the menu item. The **A**uto **Arrange** item is turned off (or on if it was not ticked already).

Tip   If you prefer using the keyboard, pressing the shortcut menu key (below the right-hand ⌜Shift⌝ key) displays the shortcut menu. You can use the arrow keys ⬆, ⬇, ⬅ and ➡ to move around the menu or press the underlined letter on the menu option to select that command.

Practice

- *Practise moving icons around the screen and using the mouse or keyboard*

- *Experiment with the other options in the **Arrange Icons** menu*

To open an icon

Opening an icon opens the software application, file or folder that the icon points to. The **My Computer** icon opens a window that lets you view disks, folders and files on your PC.

- Point to the **My Computer** icon

- If you are using Classic Style Desktop, **double-click** the left mouse button

OR

- If you are using Web style, click the left mouse button **once**

A **Desktop Window** opens.

Tip   If nothing happens when you double-click, make sure the mouse pointer is still positioned over the **My Computer** icon. Try pressing the mouse button more rapidly.

Tip   You can use the ⌜Enter⌝ key to open an icon when the icon is selected.

Desktop Windows

When you open an icon, its contents appear in a **window**. To master MS Windows you need to become proficient in manipulating windows, as every application runs in one.

The window you have opened is called **My Computer**, which is used to look at (**browse**) files and folders on your PC.

The window is comprised of several elements. The area called the **Title** bar is most important in controlling the window itself.

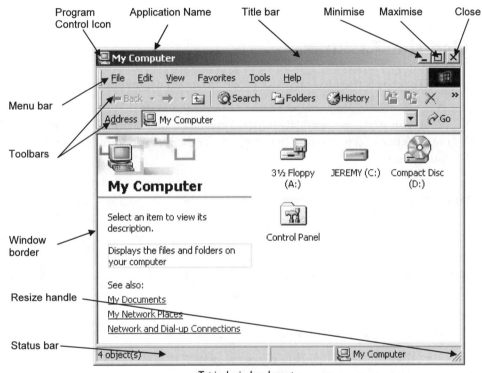

Typical window layout

- Look at the window on your screen. Can you see all the elements referred to in the screenshot above? In this workbook, tick each element when you have found it on the screen

> **Note** Do not worry if you cannot see every element. Windows can be customised to look quite different and elements of the screen can be turned on and off.

In the top-left corner of all windows there is the **Application Title**. In the above example, the **My Computer** application is shown. The area surrounding the application title is the **Title bar**.

In the top-right corner of the Title bar are three small **icon buttons** ▬□✕ . These icons perform the following functions: **Minimise** ▬ , **Maximise** □, **Restore** 卪 and **Close** ✕ windows.

- Move the mouse over the **Minimise** icon ▬ and click the left mouse button

The window seems to disappear into the bottom of the screen. The window has been minimised onto the **Taskbar**.

Use the Taskbar

The **Taskbar** is used to reactivate programs, open documents and switch between windows.

When you start a program, its button appears on the **Taskbar**. You can click the **Taskbar** icon to activate the program. The active program is shown "pushed-in".

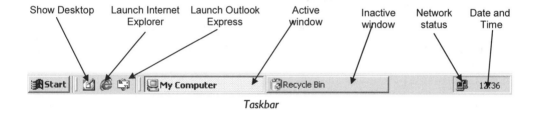

Taskbar

To reduce, enlarge and resize a Desktop window

- Can you see a Taskbar on your screen? If not, move the mouse pointer down to the bottom of the screen

- Point to the **My Computer** Taskbar icon and click

The window reappears.

- Look at the middle control icon - what shape is drawn on it □ or 卪?

If the icon is **Restore** 卪 then the window will also be filling the whole area of the screen.

- Click the middle icon □/卪

The window changes size.

- Leave the window so that the **Maximise** icon □ is displayed

---

When the window is not maximised, you can change its width and height to any size you want by using **click-and-drag** on the window's borders or by using the resize handle.

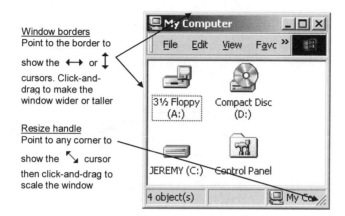

Window borders
Point to the border to
show the ⟷ or ↕
cursors. Click-and-drag to make the window wider or taller

Resize handle
Point to any corner to
show the ↘ cursor
then click-and-drag to scale the window

- Point to the resize handle in the bottom right-hand corner of the window

- Click the left mouse button and keep it depressed while dragging down and to the right

- When you reach the edge of the screen, release the mouse button

The window is resized.

- Click-and-drag on the window's bottom border to make it fill just a quarter of the screen

Other parts of the Taskbar

> **Tip** The **Quick Launch** section, next to the **Start** button, contains shortcuts to using Internet Explorer and Outlook Express. It also contains a Desktop toggle button [icon] to switch between the Desktop and the active window.

> **Tip** The **System Tray** on the far right of the Taskbar displays the current time. If you point to the time, the date is displayed as a ScreenTip. If you are connected to a network, the **Network Status** icon is also displayed.
> Other icons may indicate background programs, which operate without a window (a virus checker for example. You can usually disable the application by clicking the icon and selecting the **Disable** or **Exit** option from the menu displayed.

Scroll Around a Window

When you make a window smaller, its contents may no longer be visible. When this happens, scroll bars are displayed to let you move around the window to see different parts of it.

A scroll button indicates your current position in the window. The size of the scroll button indicates how much of the window is not displayed - if the button almost fills the scroll bar then there is not much left to see.

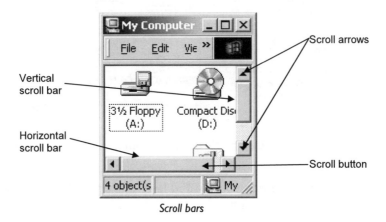

Scroll bars

To scroll around a window

- If you cannot see the scroll bars in your window, make the window smaller

- Click the scroll down arrow on the vertical scroll bar once to move one step then click the scroll up arrow to move back again

- Click the scroll down arrow and hold down the mouse button to move continually

If the window contains a lot of hidden data you can also:

- Click-and-drag the scroll button to move a large amount

OR

- Click a blank area of the scroll bar to move the scroll button to that point

Tip If you have a **wheel** on your mouse, you can use that to scroll up and down in windows.

Use the Start Menu

The **Start** button ![Start] on the **Taskbar** is used to access the **Start Menu**. The Start Menu contains more **shortcuts** to your applications.

Menus are used in all Windows applications to select commands.

Start Menu

To start an application from the Start Menu

- Move the mouse pointer to the bottom of the screen

The **Taskbar** appears if it was not visible already.

- On the **Taskbar**, click the **Start** button ![Start]
  (*SpeedKey:* `Ctrl`+`Esc`)

The **Start Menu** is displayed.

Tip   If you have a Windows-compatible keyboard, you can also press the key with the Windows icon ⊞ on it to display the Start Menu.

- Move the mouse pointer up the menu until the **Help** item is selected (turns blue) (*SpeedKey:* Press `↑` and `↓` to move from one menu item to another)

- Click the mouse button (*SpeedKey:* `Enter`)

The menu command is selected and the **Help** application window is opened.

Reposition and Move Between Windows

You can only work in the **active** window. When a window is active, the **Title** bar is blue and the Taskbar icon appears "pushed-in".

To switch between windows

- On the Taskbar, click the icon for the **My Computer** window

The window is brought to the front of the screen and made **active**.

- Press-and-hold down the $\boxed{\text{Alt}}$ key then press the $\boxed{\text{Tab}}$ key - a panel appears showing the two window icons

- Keeping the $\boxed{\text{Alt}}$ key held down, press $\boxed{\text{Tab}}$ - each time you press $\boxed{\text{Tab}}$ a different icon is selected

- Select the **Help** icon then release both keys

- Now switch back to the My Computer window

To move a window

- Point to a blank area in the **Title** bar of the **My Computer** window

- Click-and-drag the window to the left

Initially only the outline of the window will change position, when you release the mouse, the window is redrawn in the new position.

- Click the **Help** window - it is made active

Practice

---

*Working with the **My Computer** and **Help** windows, continue to practise the following techniques until you are confident using them:*

- *Minimise and maximise windows*

- *Resize and scale windows*

- *Scroll around in windows*

- *Move windows around the screen*

- *Switch between windows*

- *Select the Help window when you have finished*

Use Windows Help

Windows contains an extensive online **Help** feature. The help is indexed and searchable so that you can lookup keywords to get assistance on a particular topic.

Help works like a web page. Each topic acts like a hyperlink. When you click the topic name in the left-hand panel, the topic is displayed in the right-hand panel.

To browse help contents for Windows

- Click the book icon next to **Introducing Windows 2000** - a list of help **subtopics** is displayed.

- Click the book icon next to **How to Use Help**

- Click the topic icon [?] next to **Find a Help topic**

The help topic is displayed in the right-hand panel.

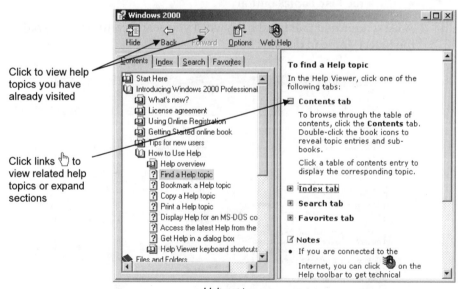

Help topics

The help topic pane may contain expandable subsections and further topics of interest. These links make the mouse pointer turns into a hand.

- Click the link to open it

- Explore the help topic for a while, following all the links and using the **Back** button and **Forward** buttons to review the topics you have already visited

To search for help

If you cannot see the topic you are looking for in the **Contents**, there are two ways to search for a particular topic.

◆   Use the **Index** tab to look up a word in the index.

◆   Use the **Search** tab to look for a word or phrase in all help topics.

To look up a topic in the Index

- Click the **Index** tab then enter a word to search for in the **Type in the keyword to find** box (type shut down)

The list of indexed topics scrolls to the nearest match for your keyword.

- Select the topic or subtopic you want to view and click **Display**

To search all of help for a keyword

- Click the **Search** tab then enter a word to search for in the **Type in the keyword to find** box (type restart)

- Click the **List Topics** button

A list of topics containing the keyword you searched for is displayed in the **Select Topic to display:** box.

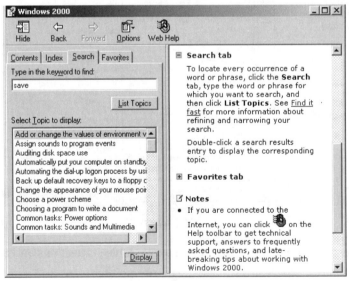

Windows Help Search tab

- Select the topic or subtopic you want to view and click **Display**

Close a Window

Closing a window will **exit** the application. You may be uncertain when to exit an application and when to minimise it. You will come to have your own preference, based on the way you work and the PC you are using.

◆ Exiting an application makes more **resources** (CPU time and memory) available to other programs.

◆ Minimising an application leaves it **running** in memory, so it is quick to access. Most PCs can work quite quickly with three or four applications running at the same time.

◆ You will probably find yourself keeping applications such as **word processors** and **email** running all the time and opening and closing other applications, such as **databases**, **spreadsheets** and **web browsers**, as and when they are needed.

To close a window

- Select the **Help** window
- On the **Title** bar, click the **Close** button ☒

To close a minimised window

- Minimise the **My Computer** window
- Move the mouse over its **Taskbar** icon and click the **right** mouse button

A shortcut menu is displayed.

Taskbar icon shortcut menu

- Select **C̲lose** (*SpeedKey:* `Alt` + `F4`)

Shut Down and Restart

When you have finished using your PC, you should never simply turn it off. Doing so could cause damage to Windows and the loss of data. The **Shut Down...** menu option provides you with a safe and orderly way to turn off your computer knowing that all your applications and data files have been closed and saved.

In some cases you may only want to turn off your computer temporarily. You might have to do this when **installing** an application or because a program has stopped working properly.

> **Note** Shut Down closes all your application windows automatically. However, for reasons that will become clear later, it is best to close each window manually **before** selecting Shut Down.

To shut down the computer properly and restart the computer

- From the **Start Menu**, select **Shut Down...**

The **Shut Down Windows** dialogue box is displayed.

Shut Down Windows dialogue box

- If you have finished using the PC, from the **What do you want the computer to do?** list box, click the down arrow and select **Shut down** (This option may already be displayed) then click **OK**

OR

- If you are going to start the next lesson straight away, select **Restart** then click **OK**

- If you chose **Shut Down**, wait for the "It is now safe for you to turn off your computer" message to appear then turn off your computer

If you chose **Restart**, Windows will shut down and then the PC will restart automatically, displaying the **Welcome to Windows** dialogue box. You **do not** need to turn the PC off.

> **Note** Some PCs may switch off automatically a few seconds after shutting down.

Using an Application

Create text files using the applications included with MS Windows

---

Lesson 10

Recognise parts of an **application** window ☐
Launch a word processing application and create a **file** ☐
(Use **menus**, **toolbars** and **dialogue boxes**) ☐
Save the file onto hard disk and floppy disk ☐

Application Windows

All applications run in a window, like **My Computer**. Different applications will have different window elements, but most will include:

♦ Title bar, Program Control and Window Control icons (▬, ▢/▣, ✕)

♦ Menu bar

♦ Toolbar(s)

♦ Status bar

♦ Scroll bars

The techniques for working with application windows are the same as for **My Computer**.

Note You will need a blank floppy disk to complete one of the exercises in this lesson.

Launch an Editing Application and Create a File

Windows contains several simple applications to create text and graphics files. There is also a **Calculator** and several **Games**.

WordPad is a **word processing** application. You can use it to create documents with **formatted** text. Text formatting means using different font styles, sizes and attributes. You can also change the appearance of lines and paragraphs, adjusting how they are spaced and aligned. Finally, you can include pictures in a word processing document as well as text.

To use WordPad

All your software applications (or programs), such as word processors, spreadsheets or databases, are accessed via the **Programs** menu.

In the Start Menu, many items contain submenus, which themselves may contain further submenus.

In the Programs menu, these submenus are called **Program Groups**, because they contain shortcuts to related applications. Software manufacturers usually install their software so that it all appears in one Program Group in the Start Menu.

- Click the **Start** button ![Start] then move the mouse up to the **Programs** menu item (there is no need to click)

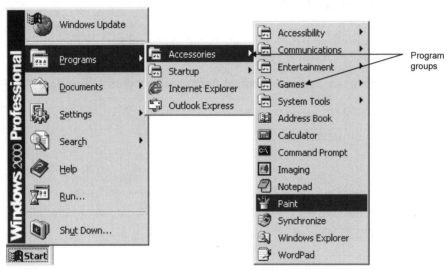

Programs menu and program groups

- Move the mouse pointer to the **Accessories** program group

- Guide the mouse pointer to the **WordPad** ![WordPad] WordPad item then click it

> **Note** Windows **hides** menu options that you do not use very often, so if you cannot see the **WordPad** item, click the chevron arrows at the bottom of the menu [⌄] to see the full list of commands.

The **WordPad** window is displayed. It contains the same basic elements as other windows plus some extra features particular to this application.

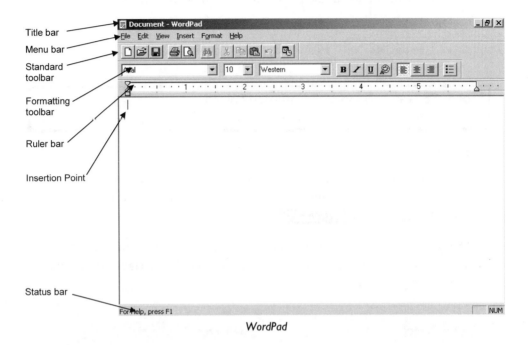

Title bar
Menu bar
Standard toolbar
Formatting toolbar
Ruler bar
Insertion Point
Status bar

WordPad

To enter and edit text

The black bar on the screen is the **insertion point**. The insertion point shows you where text will appear when you type using the keyboard.

- Type the text below shown in the box below

- Hold down the `Shift` key to type capital letters

- Use the `Enter` key to start a new **paragraph** at the points marked **<Enter>**

WordPad**<Enter>**
WordPad is a basic word processing application, for creating, formatting and printing text documents. Simply type text onto the page then save the document as a file.**<Enter>**
You can re-open the file at any time to edit it or print it or send it to someone else.**<Enter>**
WordPad has several tools for formatting your document. You can use different font styles, sizes and effects and align paragraphs in different ways.**<Enter>**

Note The text you type will not have the same line breaks as the example above.

To move the insertion point

- Click the mouse at the point you want to position the insertion point

OR

- Use the ◄, ►, ▲ and ▼ keys to move around

> **Note** You can only move the insertion point around existing text. You cannot move it to a blank area of the window.

To select text

As in any word processing package it is important that when you want to change text in any way it must be selected. Selected text appears in white with a blue background `This is selected text`.

The **selection area** is the area to the left of the text, close to the left edge of the screen. The mouse pointer will change to point to the right ⤢ when it is in the selection area.

To Select	Do This
Single word	Double-click the word.
Single line	Point to a line from the selection area and click.
Paragraph	Point to a paragraph from the selection area and double-click.
The whole document	Point into the selection area and click while holding down the `Ctrl` key.

You can also select any amount of text

- Click-and-drag across some characters with the mouse (drag down to select further lines)

OR

- Hold down `Shift` and press the ◄, ►, ▲ and ▼ keys

To delete text ①

- o To delete characters to the left of the insertion point, press the `Backspace` key; to delete characters to the right of the insertion point, press the `Delete` key

- o To delete selected text, press the `Backspace` or `Delete` key

Menus and Dialogue Boxes

Commands are displayed on drop-down menus that appear below menu headings. When selecting a command from a menu you can use the mouse or the keyboard.

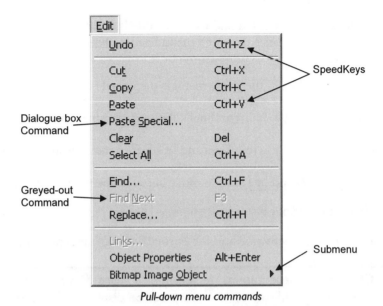

Pull-down menu commands

SpeedKeys are shortcuts for frequently used menu options. You will see these represented next to some of the menu items.

Menu commands that are "greyed out" (or appear faded) are unavailable for use at that particular time.

Many commands have additional commands and actions associated with them. These are grouped into submenus to make locating and using them easier. Commands with an arrow beside them indicate a submenu.

Commands followed by an ellipse (...) require further data, which is supplied using a **dialogue box**.

To select a menu command using the mouse

- Move the mouse pointer over the menu heading **Edit** - the heading appears raised

- Click the mouse button once - the menu is displayed

- Move the mouse pointer down until the **Select All** command is highlighted then click again

The command is applied - all the text is selected.

To select a menu command using the keyboard

Menu commands and options in a dialogue box can be activated using **menu access keys**. Each option in a menu has one letter underlined – pressing this letter activates the option.

- Press the [Alt] key

The **Menu** bar is activated and the word **File** is highlighted, but the menu is not displayed. Notice that each menu heading has one letter underlined.

- Press the [V] key - the **View** menu is displayed

- Press the [T] key - the **Toolbars** submenu is displayed

You can also use the arrow keys and [Enter] to move around a menu.

- Press the [↓] and [↑] keys to move between the items in the submenu

- Select the **Format Bar** item then press [Enter]

The command is activated and the **Formatting** toolbar is hidden.

Tip   Clicking on different items (for example a chart, data table, column or row header) with the **right** mouse button displays a **shortcut** menu, which contains commands relating to the selected item.

To deselect a menu

If you open a menu accidentally, it can be deselected without choosing a command.

- Select the **View** menu again

- Click the mouse once anywhere off the menu

OR

- Press [Esc] to cancel the menu, leaving the Menu bar active then press [Esc] again to deactivate the Menu bar

Personalised menus

Menus in some Microsoft products, such as Windows itself and the Office 2000 suite are **personalised** for you. This means that commands you do not use are hidden, making the commands you do use easier to select.

You will learn more about using personalised menus in the first lesson on Microsoft Word, on page 188.

Dialogue boxes

Some menu commands appear with three dots beside them, for example, **New**... on the **File** menu. When you select these menu commands a **dialogue box** is displayed. A dialogue box is used to provide the information necessary for a command to be carried out.

When you open a dialogue box, you must close it again before you can continue editing your document. If a dialogue box is open, the PC will beep if you try to click outside it (though you can use **other** applications normally).

To select commands in a dialogue box

- From the **File** menu, select **Print**... - the **Print** dialogue box is displayed

Dialogue boxes often have a series of **tabs** (or **pages**) to group related commands.

- Click the **Layout** tab

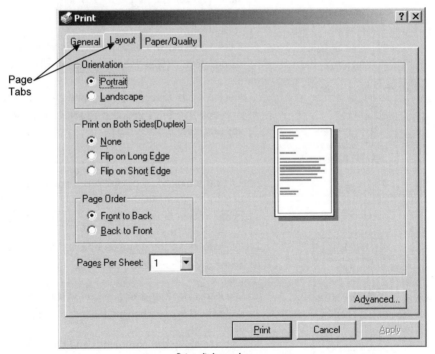

Print dialogue box

A dialogue box consists of a number of **controls**. You can select these controls by clicking with the mouse or by pressing ⎡Tab⎤ to advance to the next control or ⎡Shift⎤+⎡Tab⎤ to move to the previous control.

There are several different types of control, as explained below.

Dialogue box controls

Control	Use
1-65535 *Text Box*	Type and edit text using the keyboard.
Add Printer COLOURDEV on DEVELOP... HP LaserJet 55i *List Box*	Select an item from the list, using the scroll bar if necessary (*SpeedKeys:* [↑] and [↓]). You can also type text directly. Often you can only enter an item that is on the list though.
1 ▼ *Drop-Down List Box*	Click the arrow (*SpeedKey:* [Ctrl]+[↓]) to display a list of items to pick from. You can also type text directly. Often you can only enter an item that is on the list though.
1 ▲▼ *Spin Box*	Click the arrows to increment or decrement the value (*SpeedKeys:* [↑] and [↓]). You can also type a value directly.
☐ Print to file *Check Box*	Click to select the option (appears with a tick) or to deselect it (*SpeedKey:* [Space Bar]).
Page Range ◉ All ○ Selection ○ Current Page ○ Pages: 1-65535 *Option Buttons*	Click a circle (*SpeedKeys:* [↑] and [↓]) to select one option from a group (the selected option appears with a black dot).
Advanced... *Command Button*	Click the button to perform the command - usually to open another dialogue box (*SpeedKey:* [Tab] to the button and press [Space Bar]).
OK *OK*	Click to close the dialogue box and apply the commands (*SpeedKey:* [Enter]).
Cancel *Cancel*	Click to close the dialogue box without applying any selections or changes (*SpeedKey:* [Esc]).
Apply *Apply*	Click to apply the commands and changes selected so far **without** closing the dialogue box.

- Identify an example of each of the controls above in the **Print** dialogue box

- Practise using different dialogue box controls but do not press [Enter] or click **OK** or **Apply** - click **Cancel** to exit the dialogue box

Keyboard Shortcuts

As you become more proficient with software applications, it is often easier to use keys instead of the mouse to carry out a command.

Most of the major commands have keyboard shortcuts (referred to as *SpeedKeys* in this book) that are displayed beside the command name on the menu. Many SpeedKeys are the same in different applications. For example, to open a file the SpeedKey is always `Ctrl`+`O`.

Sometimes there is more than one SpeedKey option. For example you can also open a file with `Ctrl`+`F12` (Control and Function Key 12).

Save a File

In order to keep the data that you type into an application, you must save it. You should save documents regularly (every 10 minutes). If the computer crashes (stops working) or loses power, any unsaved data will be lost and you will have to retype it.

When you save a document for the first time, you need to give it a file name and choose a location to save it into. When you save the document subsequently, the changes are written to the same file automatically. You can save files to a **folder** on the hard disk in your PC, to a **floppy disk** or to a **network** folder.

To save a file to a folder

- On the **Standard** toolbar, click **Save** 🖫 OR from the **File** menu, select **Save** (*SpeedKey:* `Ctrl`+`S`)

The **Save As** dialogue box is displayed.

This dialogue box seems quite complex, but you only need to follow a few simple steps to save the file.

Select a drive in which to store the file here

Open icons in the window to save the file in a subfolder

Type a name here to identify the file

Click the Save button to complete the operation and save the file

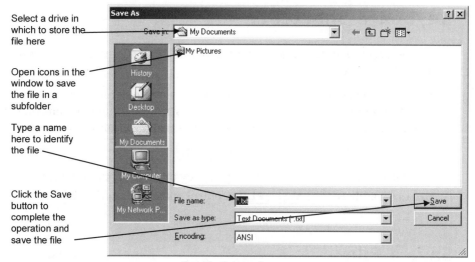

Save As dialogue box

The **My Documents** folder should be selected in the **Save in:** box already. If it is not, click the large **My Documents** icon in the left-hand bar.

- Click in the **File name:** box and delete any existing text - you can select and edit text in the box just as you did to create the document

- Type a name for the file WordPad

Note The **File name:** box may or may not already contain the **file extension** for the type of file. You can overtype this if you like. You do not need to type the file extension yourself, as Windows adds this to files automatically.
See page 141 for more information on naming files.

- Click **Save** to create the file

Notice that the **Hard Disk** light flickers and your PC makes noises while the file is being saved.

Subsequently, select the **Save** command or button 🖫 to update the file with any changes you make.

To save a copy of a file (onto a floppy disk)

You can use the **Save As** command to save another copy of the file to another location, such as a floppy disk. You will need a blank floppy disk to complete this lesson. If you do not have one to hand, simply read through the instructions.

- Take the floppy disk and push it into the slot on the floppy disk drive, with the label side facing up

The disk should click into place. If there is any resistance, the disk is probably the wrong way up. Remove it and try again.

- From the **File** menu, select **Save As...**

This displays the **Save As** dialogue box, so that you can save the file in another location and/or with a different name.

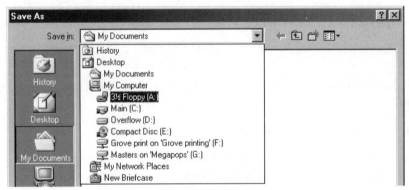

Saving to a floppy disk

- Click the down arrow on the **Save in:** box - a list of drives available on your PC is displayed

- Select **3½ Floppy (A:)** from the **Save in:** list box

- Enter the **File name:** WordPad (Backup) then click **Save**

The save is complete when the floppy disk LED goes out.

Close an Application

You can use the **Close** button **X** on the **Title** bar to close WordPad. However, there are other ways to exit a window.

To close an application

- From the **File** menu, select **Exit** (*SpeedKey:* Alt + F4)

- Press the eject button on the floppy disk drive and remove the disk

Organising Files

Understand the structure of drives and directories (folders) and to create folders and subfolders

Lesson 11

Understand the **hierarchy** of disks and folders in Windows ☐
Browse folders on your **PC** and on a **network** ☐
View the **attributes** of folders and files ☐
Create folders and **subfolders** ☐
Select single and multiple files and folders ☐
Move, copy, delete and **rename** files and folders ☐
Format a **floppy disk** and use it to **backup** files ☐
(**Undo** file and folder operations) ☐
Use the **Find** tool to locate files and folders by **name, date created/modified** and **type** ☐

Before starting this lesson, let's review how data is stored and accessed on a PC.

♦   All data you enter into a PC must be saved in a **file**.

♦   A file must be stored on a **disk drive**: either the PC's hard disk, a network folder or a removable disk, such as a floppy disk.

♦   **Folders** and **subfolders** are used to organise a disk into discrete areas and to store related files.

♦   Disks, folders and files are represented by **icons**.

♦   You can view the contents of drives and folders from the Desktop icons **My Computer, My Documents** and **My Network Neighborhood**.

Folder Structure in Windows

Disks and folders are located in a hierarchy. The top level of the hierarchy is the Desktop. The Desktop contains the main system objects: **My Documents, My Computer, My Network Places, Recycle Bin** and **Internet Explorer**.

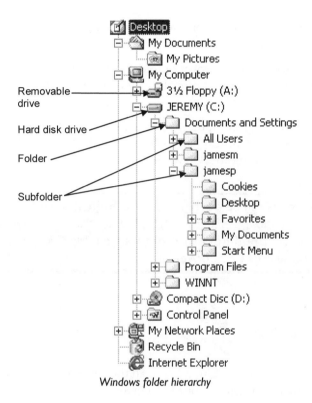

Windows folder hierarchy

The main system objects contain the drives, folders and subfolders where data files are actually stored.

Tip   If you have **Briefcase** installed, this also appears on the Desktop. Briefcase is used for transferring files between a portable computer or removable disk and your Desktop PC.

My Computer
My Computer

My Computer contains all the **local drives** available on your PC. These can include the **floppy disk, hard disk(s)**, a **CD-Drive** and other **removable** drives.

Each drive is assigned a letter. The floppy drive is usually **A.** The main hard disk drive is usually **C.**

Each disk can contain a number of folders. Each folder can also contain subfolders. Any files stored directly on the drive (not in a folder) are said to be stored in the **root folder**.

At the bottom of My Computer, you can see several folders with icons on them (for example, **Control Panel**). These are shortcuts to special **system folders**, used to configure Windows.

Tip   Hard disks can be **partitioned** into **logical drives**. If this is the case, each partition gets its own drive letter. Also, you may be able to access **mapped network folders** from My Computer. These appear as extra disk drives.

My Network Places
My Network
Places

My Network Places contains a list of all the computers, servers, printers and folders available to you on your PC network.

Recycle Bin
Recycle Bin

The **Recycle Bin** stores files and folders that you have deleted from your local hard disk(s) - usually the C drive. This allows you to undelete a file if you erased it by accident.

Internet Explorer
Internet
Explorer

The Desktop also contains a shortcut to the web browser Internet Explorer.

My Documents
My Documents

There are two classes of files and folders on your PC: those that you create yourself and those that are created by applications. It is a good idea to store all your own data in one place. This will make it easier to find and work with. It is also safer to store the data files that you create away from the ones used by applications. If you change or delete application files, the software could stop working properly.

My Documents is a special folder designed to store the data files you create. The My Documents icon on the Desktop is a **shortcut link** to the actual folder where the files are stored. Each user of the PC has their own **My Documents** folder, so the actual location of the files you save to My Documents depends on your logon identity. By default, this is **C:\Documents and Settings***username***My Documents** but your IT systems administrator might have changed this.

My Documents is the **default location** for saving files in all Microsoft Office products and for applications from many other software manufacturers.

> **Note** Your IT department may have assigned you a user folder other than **My Documents**, in which case you should store all your data there.

Path Names

A **path** is the location of a folder or file. A path is made up of the following elements:

C:\My Documents\Courses\Windows.doc

Drive letter   Folder   Subfolder   File name   File extension

◆ **Drive letter** - the disk on which the folder is stored. This is always followed by the characters **:**

◆ **Folder** - the name of the first folder in the hierarchy. Note however, that a file can be stored directly on a drive, in which case it is said to be stored in the **root folder** of the drive (for example, **C:\Windows.doc**).

◆ **Subfolders** - the rest of the folder hierarchy. Each folder is separated by a backslash ****

◆ **File name** and **extension** - if the path points to a file not a folder, the file name and extension appear at the end.

- Look at the screenshot of the Windows hierarchy on page 131

- Imagine that a file called **Windows.doc** is stored in **davidm's My Documents** folder

- Write down the full path to the file

Answer on page 178

To recognise drive and folder icons

There are several different types of drive and folder as shown in the table below.

Icon	Drive
	Hard Drive - the main disk drive inside your PC. You may have more than one hard disk and/or a hard disk may be partitioned into more than one drive. In this case you will see several hard drive icons.
	Removable Drive - this is usually a floppy disk though this icon could also indicate a backup device such as a tape drive. Many backup drives also have their own custom icons.
	CD-ROM Drive - for running CD-ROMs. You cannot normally save data onto CDs, but you can copy files from them.
	Network Drive - a folder on the network connected to your PC (**mapped**) so that you can use is as if it were a drive.
	Folder - a folder can be created on any drive. A folder can store files and other folders.
	System Folder - folders with icons on them are special system objects, such as **My Documents** and **Control Panel**.

Browse Drives and Folders

The Desktop icons **My Computer** and **My Documents** give you quick access to drives, files and folders on your PC. Another application, **Windows Explorer**, also lets you view the drives, folders and files on your PC and network.

To see what is on your computer using Windows Explorer

- From the **Start Menu**, select **Programs** then **Accessories** then **Windows Explorer**

The left-hand directory tree (called the **Explorer bar**) shows the hierarchy of objects available from the Desktop.

Click the minus icons to hide all folders that the item contains

Click the plus icons to view subfolders

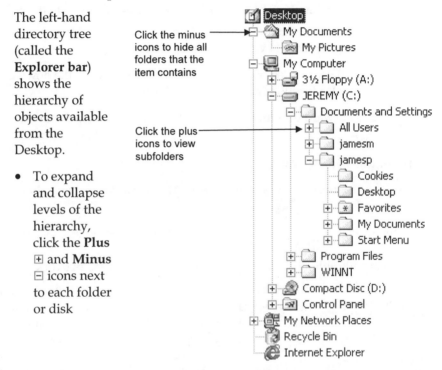

- To expand and collapse levels of the hierarchy, click the **Plus** ⊞ and **Minus** ⊟ icons next to each folder or disk

---

Tip The Explorer bar only shows drives and folders - not files.

- To view the contents of a folder, click it **once**

Any folders and files within the folder are shown in the right-hand pane.

Your current location (the path or object name) is shown in the **Address** bar.

- If the **Address** bar is not displayed, from the **View** menu, select **Toolbars** then **Address Bar**

Tip If you know the path or object name of the folder you want to look at, type it into the **Address** box then click **Go** 🔗 Go *(SpeedKey:* Enter *).*

To use the toolbar browse buttons

The toolbar contains three browsing buttons to help you navigate between folders.

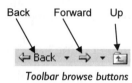

Toolbar browse buttons

- Click **Up One Level** 🔼 (*SpeedKey:* `Backspace`) to go to the next level up in the hierarchy (for example, if you are in **My Computer** clicking **Up One Level** takes you to the **Desktop**)

- Click **Back** to open the last folder you visited or click the down arrow and pick a location from the list displayed

- Use **Forward** to return to folders after clicking the **Back** button

To browse network folders

If you are connected to a computer network, the Desktop object **My Network Places** ![My Network Places] contains a list of all the computers, servers, printers and folders available to you (**shared**) on your PC network.

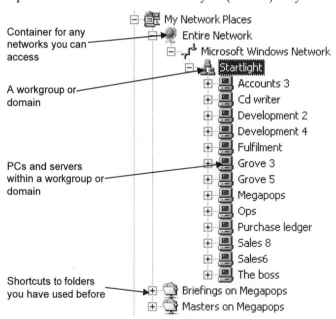

Container for any networks you can access

A workgroup or domain

PCs and servers within a workgroup or domain

Shortcuts to folders you have used before

Your logon ID determines what you can see and use on the network. For example, you might have permission to view files in a certain folder but not to change or copy them.

- In **Windows Explorer**, select **My Network Places**

- Navigate through the folders and system objects as you would on your PC

Network resources are grouped under **domains** or **workgroups** .

Within each domain there will be one or more computers and, on some networks, printers too. Computers on the network will usually be **servers**, which are computers designed to provide shared access to many users at once.

- Open a computer icon to view the folders and files available to you

> **Tip** When you open a file on a shared folder, a **shortcut** to the folder is automatically added to **My Network Places** so that you can access that folder again quickly.

View Folder and File Attributes

Windows stores various attributes about files, folders and disks. You can view the capacity and free space of a disk, the date a file was modified or the size of a file. You can also see previews of graphics files.

To change the appearance of items in a folder

- In **Windows Explorer**, select the **View** menu

- Click each of the following commands in turn: **Large Icons**, **Small Icons**, **List**, **Details** and **Thumbnails**

Large icon view

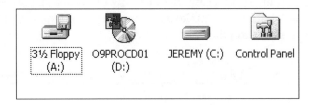

Small icon view

List view

List view displays objects as small icons in columns. You cannot drag icons around the screen in List view.

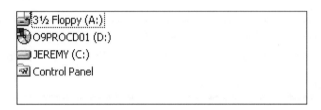

Details view

Details view is like List view but also displays information about each object.

Name	Type △	Total Size	Free Space
3½ Floppy (A:)	3½-Inch Floppy ...		
O9PROCD01 (D:)	Compact Disc	501 MB	0 bytes
JEREMY (C:)	Local Disk	1.62 GB	720 MB
Control Panel	System Folder		

From the Details view you can see the time and date that the folder or file was last modified. You can also **sort** how items are displayed by clicking on the view buttons. To make a column larger or smaller, point to the border of the button then click-and-drag.

Name	Type △	Total Size	Free Space

View buttons in Detail view

Tip   You can also select these options in any view from the **View,
Arrange Icons** menu.

Thumbnails view

Thumbnails view displays a preview image of files in the folder.

Sample   Shed in Field   Smokey Light

To use the toolbar view buttons

If you have the toolbar displayed, you can select different views using buttons.

- If the toolbar is not displayed, from the **View** menu, select **Toolbars** then **Standard Buttons**

- Click the drop-down arrow on the **View** button

View options on toolbar

- Select **Large Icons**

Tip   In **Large Icons** and **Small Icons** view, when you move and copy icons the window can become untidy and cluttered. To keep the icons in orderly rows, from the **View** menu, select **Arrange Icons** then **Auto Arrange**.

Tip   Web Page View is an optional panel in My Computer or Explorer that displays useful information about the selected icon. To activate Web Page View, from the **Tools** menu, select **Folder Options**. In the **Web View** panel, select **Enable Web content in folders** and click **OK**. For further options on changing the way folders appear, see page 174.

Create a Folder and Subfolder

As mentioned above, you should generally use one location (such as **My Documents**) to store the data files that you create. This makes it easier to find and maintain your work.

You should make use of subfolders to organise your work within this folder. For example, you would create a subfolder to store all files relating to one particular project.

If you are working on a network, you might already have folders setup for you to use, in which case you should use the folder(s) allocated to you.

To create a new folder

- In the **Windows Explorer** window, open the **My Documents**

  My Documents

  system folder from the Explorer bar

> **Note** You can create folders on hard and floppy disks, within other folders and in network places (if your logon ID gives you permission).

- From the **File** menu, select **New**
- Select **Folder** from the submenu

The new folder appears with a temporary name.

New Folder

- Type a name for the new folder `Training`
- Press the `Enter` key

> **Note** Folder names can be between 1-215 characters. Use a name that identifies the purpose of the folder accurately. Note that the following characters are **not allowed** in folder names:
>
> $$" * : \backslash \mid / ? < >$$
>
> Windows will not let you give the same name to two folders within the same folder.

To create a subfolder

- Open the new folder you created

- Right-click a blank area of the window, then from the shortcut menu, select **New** then click **Folder**

- Enter the folder name Word Processing

- Press the Enter key

The subfolder is created.

- Write down the full path to the **Word Processing** folder

Understanding Files

The term **file** refers to the documents, spreadsheets, records or other data you enter into your PC. The more you work with your PC the more files you will create. Frequently you will want to go back to files created earlier to amend them, add to them or print them out. So that you can find them again you need to organise your files into folders and give them meaningful names.

File Names

File names can contain from 1 to 215 characters. You can use spaces, but not as the first character. You can also use a mix of upper and lower case characters. For example:

File Name 20-December-2000

File name

Certain characters are not allowed: **" * : \ | / ? < >**. If you use one of these characters you will get a warning message and be unable to save the file. Remove the offending character and save again.

Even though you *could* use up to 215 characters in Windows, some software will not recognise very long names. Keep to around 8 to 50 characters (there are 26 characters in the example above).

> **Note** Some old computer systems can only read file names that are **eight** characters long. Long file names will be truncated to eight characters on these systems. For example: a file called **monthlyreport** would become **monthl~1**.

File Extensions and Types

Files are divided into different **types** according to which **application** is used to create and edit them. There are three ways to identify a file's type:

♦ Look at the file in **Details** view (**View**, **Details**) or with web page view enabled.

In Details view, the **Type** column tells you what application the file belongs to or what type of file it is. In web page view, the panel tells you what type of file is selected.

♦ Look at the **icon** on the file.

Each type of file has its own icon. For example, the icon for a **Microsoft Word document** looks like this: .

♦ Look at the **file extension**.

Each type of file has a unique three-character file extension, which Windows adds to the end of the file name you enter. The extension is separated from the file name by a period (.). For example, the full name of a Word document you call "My Document" is **My Document.DOC**.

> **Note** By default, Windows hides file name extensions from view. This is so that you do not accidentally damage a file if you rename it. To view file extensions, from the **Tools** menu, select **Folder Options** then click the **View** tab. Deselect **Hide file extensions for known file types** and click **OK**.

Common file types

Some common file types are described in the table below.

Type	Example	Icon	Description
Word Processing	Microsoft Word (DOC)		A document with formatted text (and often pictures) created in a word processor application.
Spreadsheet	Microsoft Excel (XLS)		A document divided into columns and rows using formulae to calculate and store data.
Presentation Graphics	Microsoft PowerPoint (PPT)		A set of slides containing formatted text and graphics for display on an overhead projector.
Database	Microsoft Access (MDB)		A file for storing and viewing data.

Type	Example	Icon	Description
Rich Text	RTF		Rich text files are a standard for using formatted text in applications from different manufacturers.
Text	TXT CSV		Text files contain unformatted text. Text files can also be used in MS Notepad or a word processor or in spreadsheet and database applications if the text is in a standard layout.
Image	JPG GIF BMP TIF WMF	GIF BMP	There are many different graphics file formats. The standard used by Windows is Bitmap (BMP). Graphics used on the world wide web are either JPEG (JPG) or GIFs. Image files can be created in applications such as MS Paint. Most graphics files can be used in a wide range of different applications, from Word Processors to Databases The choice of file format depends on how it will be used. Different graphics file types offer different methods of compression (making the file size smaller), different levels of image quality and different degrees of compatibility between programs.
Web Page	HTML HTM		A formatted document for display on the world wide web. Web pages are **viewed** using a Web Browser, such as Internet Explorer or Netscape Navigator. Web pages can be **created** in a variety of different applications.
Application	EXE		An application file runs the actual software program.
Shortcut	LNK		A link that opens another file. A shortcut is indicated by an arrow on top of the usual icon. You can delete a shortcut without affecting the original file.
Zipped File	ZIP		A zipped file contains file(s) that have been compressed. This is useful if you want to fit it onto a floppy disk or send it by email. You need to extract the file(s) using an extractor, such as WinZip or PKZip.

Note The icon used can depend on what **version** of an application is installed. For example, Word documents have a different icon depending on whether Word 97 or 2000 is installed.

File Size and Disk Space

When you are creating, moving and copying files you need to be aware of the amount of space they take up on disk.

When you examine a folder in **Details** view, you will see a column called **Size**. This column shows how large a file is - how much space it is taking up on the disk.

The fundamental unit of storage for PCs is the **bit**. A bit represents either a 1 or a 0 (A computer is a digital machine - everything you see and do on a PC is ultimately represented as a series of 1s and 0s). As a bit does not represent any kind of significant amount of data, more meaningful units are used (Just as centimetres not millimetres are used to measure clothes). File size is measured in kilobytes (KB) and megabytes (MB).

♦ 8 bits make up a **byte**.

♦ 1024 bytes make up a **kilobyte** (KB).

♦ 1024 kilobytes make up a **megabyte** (MB).

♦ 1024 megabytes make up a **gigabyte** (GB).

The capacity of a hard disk can vary enormously from around 500 MB to many gigabytes. The capacity of a standard floppy disk is 1.44 MB. Once a disk is full, no more data can be copied or saved to it. If a disk is filled in the process of saving or copying a file, Windows will display a warning message. **The file will not have been saved properly**. You must use a new disk or delete existing files.

To view the capacity of the hard disk

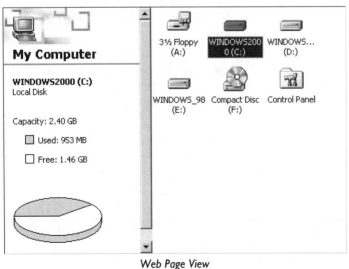

Web Page View

- In **Windows Explorer**, open the **My Computer** object

- If web page view is enabled, see details about each drive in the left-hand pane by selecting the drive icon

OR

- From the <u>V</u>iew menu, select <u>D</u>etails

The **Total Size** column shows the capacity of the disk. The **Free Space** column shows how much room is left for more data files.

- Write down the capacity _____ and free space _____ of your hard disk

> **Note** The main hard disk should not be filled completely. Windows usually requires at least 50-100 MB free disk space to work with optimum efficiency.

The following topics give you the basic steps to follow to rename, copy and move files and folders. A practice exercise follows on page 150.

Rename a File

> **Note** The following notes refer to files but the same operations can be applied to folders too.

To change the name of a file ①

- o In **Windows Explorer**, select the icon of the file you want to rename (Do not open it!)
- o From the <u>F</u>ile menu, select **Rena<u>m</u>e**

OR

- o Right-click the icon and from the shortcut menu, select **Rena<u>m</u>e**

OR

- o Click on the **name** of the file you want to change (Be sure to click the name of the file and not its icon)

> **Note** The last method does not work if you are using Web Style Desktop.

- o Type the new name, and then press [Enter]

Select and Open a File

You can select several files at once.

To select multiple files

- o Hold down the `Ctrl` key and then click each file you want to select

---

Tip Remember that if you are using **Web Style Desktop** you only point to select a file.

To select a group of files that are next to each other

- o Select the first file in the block then hold down `Shift` and select the last file

OR

- o Hold down the mouse button and drag a rectangle around the files you want to select

Using the mouse to select a group of folders

To select all the files in the window

- o From the **Edit** menu, select **Select All** (*SpeedKey:* `Ctrl`+`A`)

To open a file

As with Desktop icons, opening a file depends on whether Windows is in Classic or Web Style mode.

- o To open a file in Classic Style, double-click the file icon
- o To open a file in **Web Style**, click the file icon **once**

Move and Copy a File

You can copy a file from one location to another since files with the same name are allowed provided they are not stored in the same folder.

Note You *can* make a duplicate copy of a file or subfolder within the same folder but the file/subfolder will be renamed **Copy of *file name***.

There are several ways to copy and move files. You can use whichever one you prefer.

To copy/move a file using Cut, Copy and Paste ①

    o In **Windows Explorer**, select the file you want to move or copy

    o To copy the file, from the **Edit** menu, select **Copy** (*SpeedKey*: $\boxed{\text{Ctrl}}$+$\boxed{\text{C}}$)

OR

    o To move the file, from the **Edit** menu, select **Cut** (*SpeedKey*: $\boxed{\text{Ctrl}}$+$\boxed{\text{X}}$)

The file is stored in a temporary location called the **Clipboard** until you paste it.

    o Open the folder or disk where you want to put the copy

    o From the **Edit** menu, select **Paste** (*SpeedKey*: $\boxed{\text{Ctrl}}$+$\boxed{\text{V}}$)

Tip If you **copied** a file you can go on to paste it in another location. If you selected Cut you can only paste the file once.

To move/copy a file using drag-and-drop ①

Drag-and-drop lets you move and copy objects without selecting any commands. To use drag-and-drop effectively, you need to be using the Explorer bar or Windows Explorer.

    o In **Windows Explorer**, expand the tree view so that you can see the destination folder or drive

    o Select the file you want to move or copy from the right-hand pane

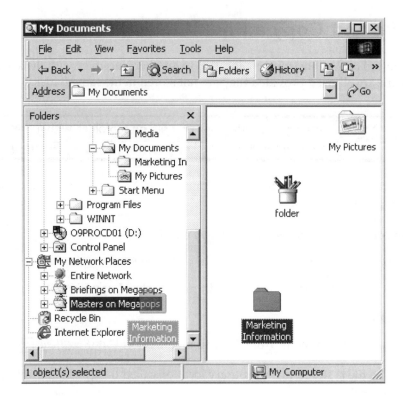

o Drag the file to the required destination (folder or drive)

Tip If you cannot get the destination folder visible on-screen **and** be able to select the file you want to move, hovering the dragged file over the top and bottom of the Explorer bar makes it scroll up and down. Also, hovering over a plus sign makes the subfolders within an object visible.

By default, if you drag a file to a new destination on the **same** disk, it will be **moved**. If you drag it to **another** disk, it will be **copied**.

If you hold down a key while dragging, you can change the actions as follows:

o To move a file, use `Shift`

o To copy a file, use `Ctrl`

o To create a shortcut, use `Ctrl`+`Shift`

Note When you hold down a key in conjunction with drag-and-drop, you must keep the key depressed until you release the mouse button.

To move/copy a file using Move To Folder or Copy To Folder ☉

The **Move/Copy To** command lets you browse for a folder in a dialogue box. You can also use it to **create** folders in which to move or copy files.

- o In **My Computer** or **Windows Explorer**, select the file you want to move or copy

- o On the **Standard** toolbar, click **Move To Folder** 📂 or **Copy To Folder** 📑

OR

- o From the **Edit** menu, select **Move To Folder...** or **Copy To Folder...**

The **Browse For Folder** dialogue box is displayed.

- o Select a folder from the tree view and click **OK**

OR

- o To copy to a new folder, select a location in which to create the new folder then click **New Folder**

- o Enter a folder name and click **OK**

Undo

Most Windows programs, including **My Computer** and **Windows Explorer**, have an **Undo** feature. Undo lets you reverse the last action you made. For example, if you delete a file, using Undo immediately afterwards will restore the file.

Note that some actions cannot be undone. In Windows for example, actions performed on a removable or network drive cannot be undone.

> **ECDL** Using Undo in Windows is not part of the ECDL syllabus, but it is a useful tool, and you need to know how to use it in every other application.

(To undo an action) ☉

- o From the **Edit** menu, select **Undo**

Practice

This exercise will give you some practice in renaming, moving and copying files. You will also setup the data files for use during the rest of the course.

Copying files from a CD

- *Press the Eject button on your CD-ROM drive*

- *Put the CD from the back of the book onto the CD tray with the label side facing up then press the Eject button again to close the drive*

The CD will start spinning in the drive. You need to wait for 20-30 seconds for the drive to get ready.

- *In **Windows Explorer**, locate your CD-Drive icon: it will probably be drive letter **D:** and have the following icon*

- *Click the icon to see the contents of the CD then in the main window, locate the folder **ECDL2000** and open it*

- *Select all the files (for example, click-and-drag a box around them or press* Ctrl + A *)*

- *On the **Standard** toolbar, click **Copy To Folder** OR from the **Edit** menu, select **Copy to Folder***

- *The **My Documents** icon should already be selected so click **OK***

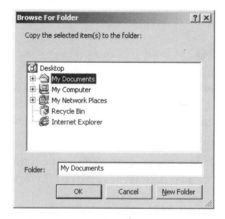

A message box is displayed while the files are being copied.

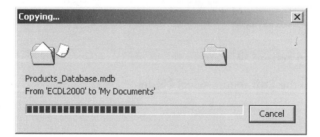

- *When the files have finished copying, you can remove the CD and put it somewhere safe*

Read-only files

*When files are copied from a CD, they are made **read-only**. This means that you cannot make changes to them. However, it is easy to make the files editable again.*

- *Open the **My Documents** folder and select all the files in it (not the subfolders)*

Tip   One way to do this is to switch to **Details** view, select the first file then hold down `Shift` and select the last file

---

- *From the **File** menu, select **Properties***

- *In the **Attributes** panel, click the **Read-only** check box to remove the tick*

- *Click **OK***

Selecting, moving and copying files

- *Select the file named **chilli logo***

- *From the **Edit** menu, select **Cut** (SpeedKey: `Ctrl` + `X`)*

- *Open the **My Pictures** folder then from the **Edit** menu, select **Paste** (SpeedKey: `Ctrl` + `V`)*

- *Move back to the **My Documents** folder*

- *Select all the files in **My Documents** (do not include the subfolders)*

- *Use `Ctrl` +drag-and-drop to **copy** the files into the **Training** folder*

- *Open the **Training** folder and select all the **Microsoft Word Document** type files*

- *Move the files into the **Word Processing** folder*

- *Create a new subfolder of the **Training** folder called **Spreadsheets***

- *Move the **Microsoft Excel Workbook** type files into the **Spreadsheets** folder*

- *Rename the **Spreadsheets** folder* Workbooks

Format a Floppy Disk

Floppy disk drives are a type of **removable** drive. Removable drives are used to transfer data between computers and to make backup copies of important files.

A floppy disk can usually store up to 1.44 MB of data, which is suitable for basic word processing documents and spreadsheets. Files containing large graphics or a very large amount of data are unlikely to fit. You can create folders on a floppy disk in the same way you create folders on a hard disk and copy more than one file to a disk, provided there is enough room.

Before you can use a floppy disk it needs to be **formatted** (prepared to receive data). Most disks are now supplied formatted by the manufacturer, but it is useful to know how to format a disk just in case.

You can reformat a formatted disk - you might be able to recover a damaged disk by doing this - but note that formatting a disk **removes** any data files already stored on the disk.

You will need a floppy disk to complete this exercise. You can reuse the one you used for the "Using an Application" lesson if you like.

To format a floppy disk

- Push the floppy disk into the A:\ drive label side up until it clicks into place

- In **Windows Explorer**, select the **My Computer** icon from the Explorer bar

- In the main part of the window, select the **Floppy Drive** 3½ Floppy (A:) icon (Do not open it)

- From the **File** menu, select **Format...**

The **Format** dialogue box is displayed.

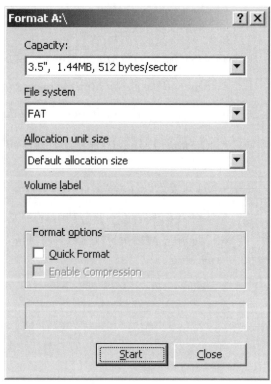

Format dialogue box

- Type a **Volume label** of up to 11 characters to identify the disk by:
  `courseware`

- Click **Start**

Warning   **Formatting will take up to a minute. Do not remove the floppy disk while it is being formatted. You will probably destroy the disk and may damage the drive as well.**

- Click **Close** when the format is complete

Once the disk is formatted, you can move and copy files to and from it in the normal way.

- Press the **Eject** button on the floppy drive to retrieve the disk

Backup a File with a Floppy Disk

You can use floppy disks to transfer files between PCs and to store your work. Creating a **backup** of data files is an important part of using a PC effectively. Make sure you backup your files on a regular basis and store the backup disks safely.

Floppy disks are quite fragile. Ideally they should be stored in a plastic container or box. When in use, disks should be kept away from dust and dirt, heat, direct sunlight and magnetic sources (such as a monitor).

To copy a file to a floppy disk

- Push the floppy disk into the A:\ drive label side up until it clicks into place

- In **Windows Explorer** or **My Computer**, select the **Word Document** type files in **My Documents**

- Look at the **Status** bar - the total size of the selected files should be displayed

---

Tip   If you cannot see the total size of the selected files, maximise the window.

If the size of the selected files is over 1.4 MB they will not fit on a standard floppy disk. You can select fewer files, use a different type of disk or use a file compression utility such as PKZip or WinZip.

- From the **Edit**
  menu, select **Copy**

- In **Windows
  Explorer** navigate
  to the **3½ Floppy
  (A:)** drive

Floppy disk is
found in My
Computer

```
☑ Desktop
⊟—🗀 My Documents
       🗀 My Pictures
⊟—💻 My Computer
      ⊞—💾 3½ Floppy (A:)
      ⊟—💾 JEREMY (C:)
            ⊟—🗀 Documents and Settings
                  ⊞—🗀 All Users
```

- From the **Edit** menu, select **Paste**

Note You can use any of the various methods to move and copy files and
folders to a floppy disk (menu or toolbar command, drag-and-drop or
Move/Copy to Folder). Note that if you use drag-and-drop, the file is
copied by default, not moved. To move the file, hold down `Shift`.

The files are copied to the disk. This may take some time - the copy is
fully complete when the LED on the floppy disk drive stops flickering.

Reverse the above procedure to copy files from a floppy disk onto a PC.

- Remove the disk from the PC by pressing the **Eject** button on the case

---

Note Always remove disks when you have finished with them. Leaving a
floppy disk in the PC can interfere with the Startup process.

Delete and Restore a File

You can delete files and folders in the same way. If you delete a folder, any
files and subfolders within the folder are also deleted.

To delete a file

- In **Windows Explorer**, open the **Training** folder

- Select all the files (but not the subfolders)

- On the **Standard** toolbar, click **Delete** ✕ **OR** from the **File** menu, select
  Delete (*SpeedKey:* `Delete`) **OR** right-click the folder and select **Delete**

The **Confirm Folder Delete** dialogue box is displayed.

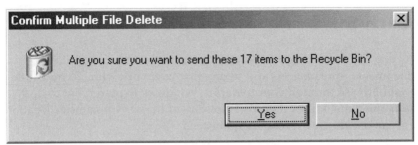

Confirm File Delete dialogue box

- Click **Yes** to move the files to the Recycle Bin

- Move up one folder then delete the **Training** folder itself - all its contents are deleted too

To restore a file

If you delete a file by accident you can retrieve it at any time from the **Recycle Bin**. A retrieved file will be placed back in the folder it came from and can be used in exactly the same way as if it had not been deleted in the first place.

ECDL Using the Recycle Bin is not a syllabus requirement, but you will find it invaluable.

- Minimise **Windows Explorer** to the **Taskbar**

- On the **Desktop**, open the **Recycle Bin** icon

Recycle Bin

The **Recycle Bin** and its contents are displayed.

- Select the **Training** folder

Tip To retrieve several files, hold down the Ctrl key while clicking each one.

- From the **File** menu, select **Restore OR** if Web Page view is enabled, click the **Restore** button in the left-hand pane

- Close the **Recycle Bin** window

- Maximise the Windows Explorer window and view the folder, subfolders and files that have now been restored back to their original positions

- Delete the **Training** folder again

Search for a File

As you use your computer you will increase the number of files -
documents, spreadsheets and so on - that you work with. To find a file you
could browse through your folders in Windows Explorer, but to find
something quickly, or if you are not sure of the correct name or location, you
are can use the **Search** command instead.

The **Search** command allows you to search for files by name, location, date,
type, size, or for those containing specific text. Found files are displayed in
Explorer and can be opened, moved, copied and renamed as usual.

To search for a file or folder

- In **Windows Explorer**, on the **Standard** toolbar, click **Search**
  Search   OR from the **View** menu, select **Explorer Bar** then **Search**
  (*SpeedKey:* `Ctrl` + `E`)

The **Search** bar is displayed in Windows Explorer.

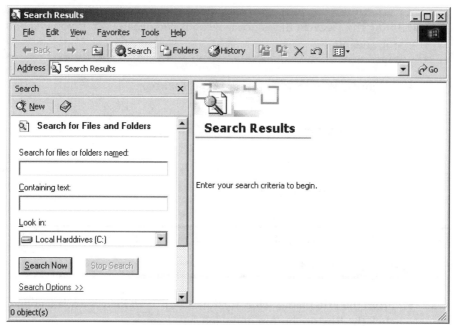

Search bar

> **Tip**   If Explorer is not already open, you can start a search from the Start
> Menu. Select **Search** then **For Files or Folders** (*SpeedKey:* `F3`).

- In the **Search for files or folders named** box, enter the file name or part of the file name to search for - type `readme`

- Click the down arrow to the right of the **Look in:** box, and select **Browse**

The **Browse for Folder** dialogue box is displayed.

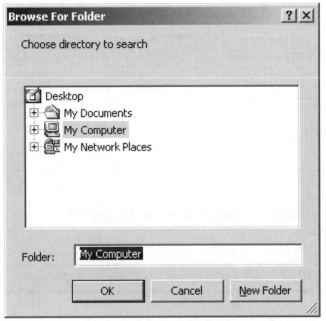

Browse For Folder dialogue box

- Select the **My Computer** icon to search for the files in all local drives

- Click **OK**

Tip   Selecting **Desktop, My Computer** or **My Network Places** means the search will be thorough but will also take a long time. Selecting a smaller area makes the search quicker. This is one example of why it is a good idea to store all your data files in one folder (**My Documents** for example).

- Back in the **Search** bar, click the **Search Now** button

The results of your search will be displayed in the right-hand window pane. Every file and folder with the search text "readme" in its file name is displayed.

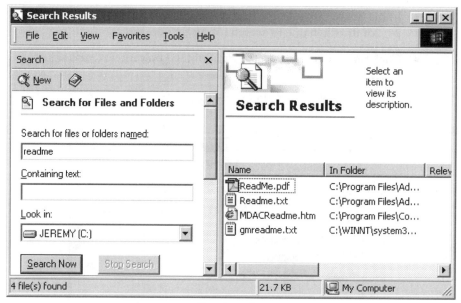

Search results

- Open a file icon (select one of the .TXT files) in the normal way then close it

Tip   You can **Rename**, **Copy** and **Cut** files from the search results pane.

To use other options to find a file or folder

The other options on the **Search** bar allow you to enter further **criteria** for finding files. For example, the time that a file was created or last modified is stored as a property of the file. You can use this to search for files that you have been working on recently or to find files that were used over a particular period. You can also look for files of a certain type.

You can combine different criteria (modified date, file name and file type for example) to create very precise searches.

- Click **New** ◌ **New** to clear the settings and results of the old search

- Select the location to search in as described above (select **My Documents**)

- You can enter text to search for in the **Search for files or folders named** box or in the **Containing text:** box, but leave these blank for this exercise

The **Containing Text** option checks the **contents** of each file for the search text. If you use this option, try to limit the search to one or two folders, as checking a lot of files will take a long time.

Tip   When you do not enter any text, the Search operation will find any file based on the other criteria you specify.

- Click **Search Options >>**

A panel is displayed allowing you to enter further criteria.

- Click the check boxes to set different types of criteria

Option	Action	
Date	Use the list box to look for date modified, created or accessed, then enter the range of time to search for.	
Type	Click the list box to select from a range of file types.	
Size	Choose At Least or At Most from the list box and enter a size in the spin box.	
Advanced Options	Search Subfolders - check subfolders within the folder chosen in the Look in box. Case sensitive - match the exact case of the search text. Search slow files - if this is unchecked, the Search will ignore files on slow drives, such as tape backup drives.	

- Click the **Type** box then select the file type **Microsoft Word Document** from the list

- Click the **Search Now** button

Tip   For help on settings in the **Search** bar, click [icon].

To close the Search panel

- Click the **Close** button `Search` `×` **OR** on the **Standard** toolbar, click `🔍 Search` again (*SpeedKey:* `Ctrl`+`E`)

Practice

- *Display the Search bar again*
- *Answer the following questions by searching for the relevant file*
- *How many 1KB files are there in the C:\WINNT folder?*

- *How many JPEG files are there on your C:\ drive?*

- *What type of graphics file is the Prairie Wind file?*

- *How many files have been modified in the last 15 days?*

- *What is the file size of the largest file on your C:\ drive?*

- *How many Access database files on your computer have the word "database" in them?*

- *Close the Search bar*
- *Close any open windows*

Printing

Print files, select different printers and manage the print queue

---

Lesson 12

Change the **default** printer □
Print a file from Windows or from an application □
Use the **print queue** to monitor and change the **status** of a print job □
(Set the default **print preferences**) □

Change the Default Printer

The **Printers** folder 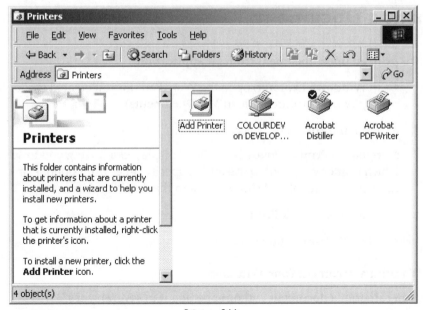 provides a way of adding new printers,
configuring existing printers and managing print jobs.

To view the Printers folder

- From the **Start Menu**, select **Settings** then **Printers**

The **Printers** folder is displayed.

Printers folder

The icons that may be displayed in the Printers folder are as follows:

Icon	Means
Add Printer	Open this icon to start the **Add Printer Wizard**, which guides you through the process of installing a new printer.
	A local printer attached to your PC.
	The default printer. All documents will print to this printer unless you specify otherwise.
	A shared network printer, attached to another PC or to a Print Server.

- Close the **Printers** window

To set a printer as the default printer ⑨

o In the **Printers** folder, select the icon for the printer you want to use as the default printer

o From the **File** menu, select **Set as Default Printer**

Print a Document

To print an open document from an application

- In **Windows Explorer**, open the **WordPad** file you created earlier (or any **Word Document** file in **My Documents**)

- From the **File** menu, select **Print**

Normally, a **Print** dialogue box will be displayed allowing you to select which printer you want to use and to specify other print options. In some cases the document will simply print to the default printer.

- If necessary, click **Print**

- Close the application window

To print a document from Windows

You can print a document without opening it in several ways.

- Right-click another file and from the shortcut menu, select **Print**

The document will be printed on the default printer.

OR

- Open the **Printers** folder

- Open the **My Documents** folder and the **Printers** folder and arrange them on the screen

- Drag a document icon (**Employee Handbook**) onto the icon of the printer that you want to print to

> **Tip** While a document is printing, a **Printer** icon 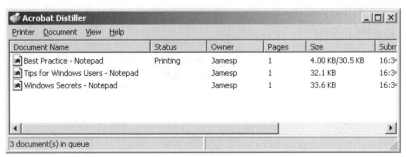 appears next to the clock on the Taskbar. When this icon disappears, your document has finished printing.

View the Print Queue

A document sent to a printer is called a **print job**. Each printer has a **print queue** showing which jobs it has to process. If a printer is shared, it might have a large number of jobs in the queue.

You can view the print queue in order to keep track of when your document will be printed.

To view printing status

- From the **Printers** folder, open the icon for your default printer

The **Print Queue** is displayed. The **Employee Handbook** document may still appear in it. If you share your printer with other users, there may be more print jobs.

Document Name	Status	Owner	Pages	Size	Subm
Best Practice - Notepad	Printing	Jamesp	1	4.00 KB/30.5 KB	16:3
Tips for Windows Users - Notepad		Jamesp	1	32.1 KB	16:3
Windows Secrets - Notepad		Jamesp	1	33.6 KB	16:3

3 document(s) in queue

Print queue

- Close the **Print Queue** window

> **Tip** If a printer is busy, you can also open the queue from the **Taskbar** - double-click the **Printer** icon.

To change the status of a printer ①

In some circumstances you might want to pause a printer (for example, to change the paper).

o   In the **Print Queue** window, from the <u>P</u>rinter menu, select **P<u>a</u>use Printing**

o   To resume printing, click the **P<u>a</u>use** command again

Printing Preferences

Printing preferences allow you to setup things like the default number of copies, paper type, print quality, colour and watermarks.

> **ECDL** Changing the print preferences is not a syllabus requirement.

To change printer settings

- From the **Printers** folder, select a printer icon then from the <u>F</u>ile menu, select **Pr<u>i</u>nting Preferences**

The printer's **Printing Preferences** dialogue box is displayed.

The settings you can change depend on the type of printer you have.

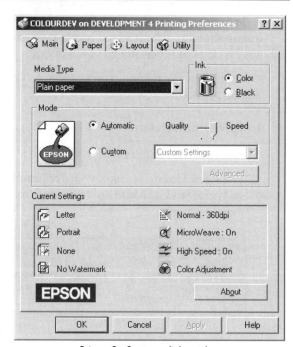

Printer Preferences dialogue box

> **Tip**   Changing the printer properties will change them for **all** documents you print on this printer. To change these settings for one document, select the **Print Setup** or **Print Properties** command in the application you are using.

- Click **Cancel** to exit the dialogue box then close any open windows

Customising the Desktop

Change the appearance of the Desktop and alter some system settings

---

Lesson 13

View the computer's basic **system information** ☐
View the computer's **Desktop configuration** ☐
(**Change** Desktop settings, such as screen and sound options) ☐
(Customise the appearance of **folders** and the **Taskbar**) ☐
Create a Desktop **shortcut** icon ☐

Windows can be customised to suit your individual needs. For example, you can choose which icons you want to appear on the Desktop or change the way the mouse pointer appears on the screen and setup a screen saver.

Custom settings are stored under your user logon ID, so any changes you make will not affect people logging onto the same computer with a different user name. Also, if you use a computer network, your custom settings may be available on any Windows 2000 computer on the network (depending on how the network is setup).

ECDL From the point of view of the syllabus, you only need to be able to view these settings. However, you are likely to need to customise the way folders appear and the operation of the mouse and keyboard too.

The Control Panel

The **Control Panel** 🗔 is a single location for all commands, controls and functions associated with configuring and customising Windows. You should use the commands found here with caution, as changing some settings could cause the computer to stop working properly.

Note You may not be able to access many of the icons in the Control Panel or even the Control Panel itself if your Windows logon ID does not have the correct **permissions**. In this case, inform your IT department of the changes you wish to make.

To open the Control Panel

- From the **Start Menu**, select **S̲ettings** then select **C̲ontrol Panel**

System Information

It is often useful to be able to find out about the hardware components on your system. The **System** applet contains such information.

To view information about your PC

- From **Control Panel**, open the **System** icon to display the
System

  System Properties dialogue box

Under **System:** the exact version of Windows is displayed.

Under **Computer:** the type of **processor** and the amount of system memory (RAM) is displayed.

- Click **OK**

Tip Alternatively, you can display a more comprehensive report by starting **System Information** from **Programs, Accessories, System Tools** on the **Start Menu**.

Regional Options

Windows defines a set of default formats for things like currency, numbers, dates and so on. Most software applications make use of these defaults to determine how they display these things too.

Windows contains many schemes for regional formats for different parts of the world. You can view the settings made and make changes to them through the Control Panel.

To view Regional Options

- From **Control Panel**, open the **Regional Options** icon

  Regional
  Options

From the **Your locale** list box, you can select the region whose settings you want to use or browse the tabs to view and change individual settings.

- Click **Cancel** to exit without applying any changes

View the Date/Time

A small battery inside the PC keeps track of the time even when the PC is switched off, so there should be no real need to adjust the date or time manually. However, if you do find that your PC is showing the wrong date or time, you can set it using the Control Panel.

To change your computer's date and time

- From **Control Panel**, open the **Date/Time** icon 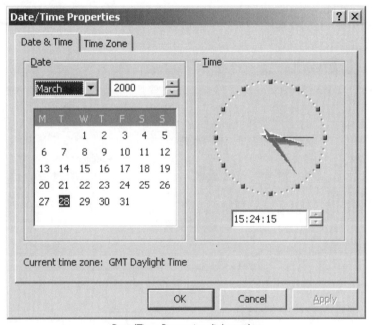 OR double-click the clock on the right-hand side of the Taskbar

The **Date/Time Properties** dialogue box is displayed.

Date/Time Properties dialogue box

- If the clock happens to be wrong, in the **Date** area, click the correct month, year, and day

- In the **Time** area, click in the box and type the time or use the spin arrows to adjust the time up or down

> **Note** Windows uses the date setting to identify when files are created or modified.

- Click **Cancel** to exit, unless you corrected the clock in which case click **OK**

Mouse Properties

You can setup a mouse for left-handed use and change the speed at which you use double-click and move the mouse. You can also select a new scheme of mouse pointers if you wish.

To change basic mouse properties

- From **Control Panel**, open the **Mouse** icon

The **Mouse Properties** dialogue box is displayed.

Note The options in this dialogue will vary depending on the type of mouse you have.

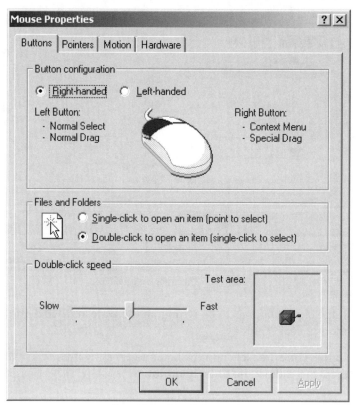

Mouse Properties dialogue box

- Under **Button configuration**, select **Right-handed** or **Left-handed** as appropriate

- Set the **Double-click speed** by clicking on the pointer and dragging it towards the desired speed

- Test your clicking skills by double-clicking the **Jack in the Box**

- You can also choose to use the **Single-click** or **Double-click** mode of opening icons

To change the appearance of your mouse pointer

- Click the **Pointers** tab

- Change all your pointers at one time by selecting a predefined set in the **Scheme** list

OR

- Change each pointer individually by clicking it, clicking **Browse...** and selecting the name of the pointer you want to use

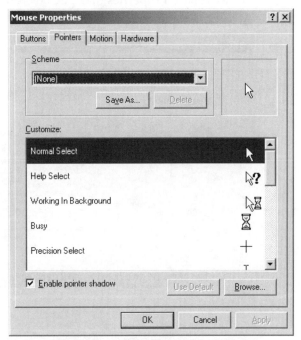

Mouse Properties dialogue box - Pointers tab

Tip   Customise as many pointers as you want then save them as a new scheme by clicking **Save As**.

To change the mouse speed

- Use the sliders on the **Motion** tab to control how fast the mouse moves across the screen

- Click **OK**

Keyboard Properties

If you find the keyboard responds too quickly or slowly you can adjust the repeat rate (the time taken for a character to repeat when you press a key).

To change the repeat rate of the keyboard

- From **Control Panel**, open the **Keyboard** icon

The **Keyboard Properties** dialogue box is displayed.

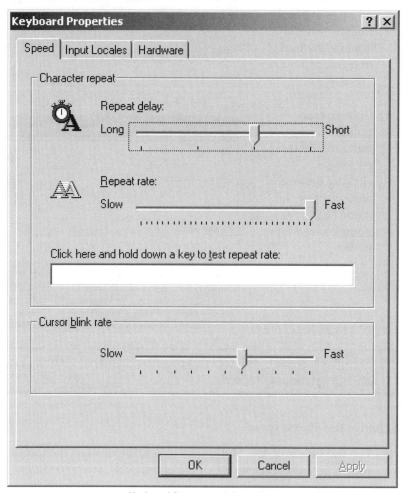

Keyboard Properties dialogue box

- Drag the sliders to adjust the repeat rate and test out the changes in the text box

- Click **OK**

ECDL with MS Office 2000

Display Properties

You can customise the display to make working as comfortable as possible. You can change the appearance of the Desktop by selecting a picture or web page to display or by selecting from a range of patterns. If you do not like the plain vanilla windows used in Windows you can customise them with your own colour scheme. You can also setup a screen saver, which protects your monitor from damage.

To change the background of your Desktop

- From **Control Panel**, open the **Display** icon

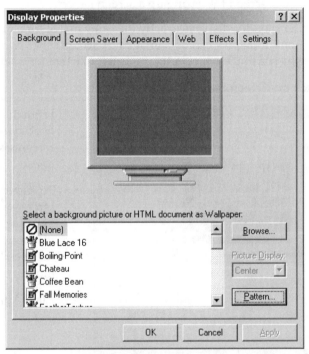

Display Properties dialogue box

- In the **Select a background** list, click the wallpaper you want to use

OR

- Click **Browse...** to use a different **Bitmap** or **HTML** file

- From the **Picture Display** list box, select **Center** (to display the image in the middle of the screen), **Tile** (to repeat the image until it fills the screen) or **Stretch** (to enlarge the image so that it fills the screen)

The effects of your choice are previewed on the screen above. You can also apply a pattern that will fill up any blank space around the wallpaper.

- Click **Pattern...** then from the **Pattern:** list box, select a pattern

- Click **OK** then click **Apply**

Your choices are applied to the actual Desktop.

Tip   You can use patterns and wallpaper simultaneously. However, if wallpaper covers your entire screen, you will not see the pattern.

To protect your screen by setting up a screen saver

If a computer monitor displays exactly the same image for a long period of time, the monitor display can be damaged. A screen saver prevents this from happening by starting whenever the PC is left inactive for a set amount of time.

- Click the **Screen Saver** tab

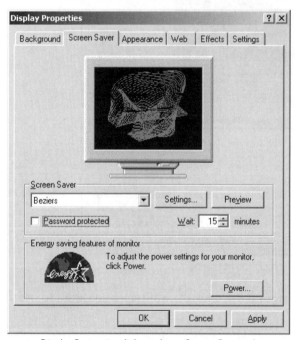

- From the **Screen Saver** list box, select the screen saver you want to use

- To customise the screen saver (for example, to edit text displayed or change the speed at which it moves) click **Settings**

- Click **Apply**

Display Properties dialogue box - Screen Saver tab

Tip   The screen saver starts if your computer is idle for the number of minutes specified in the **Wait** box. To clear the screen saver after it has started, move your mouse or press any key.

To change the appearance of windows

- Click the **Appearance** tab

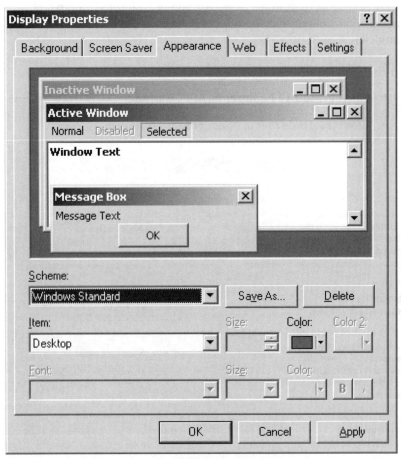

Display Properties dialogue box - Appearance tab

- To change the appearance of all screen elements simultaneously, select a **Scheme:** from the list box

OR

- If you want to change the appearance - colour, font and so on - of individual screen elements, select it from the **Item:** drop-down list box, then change the settings for size, colour and font

- Click **Apply** then click **OK**

- Close the **Control Panel** window

Folder Properties

You can customise folders in Windows to look more or less like web pages. There is a range of options, from displaying an information panel, which shows details about selected objects, to setting the method of opening icons (single-click or double-click).

To customise folder options

- Open **Windows Explorer** or **My Computer**

- From the **Tools** menu, select **Folder Options...**

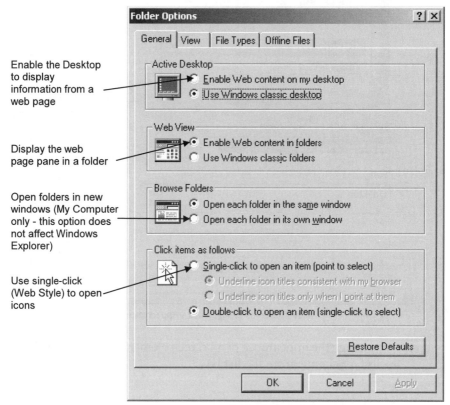

Folder Options dialogue box

- Set whichever options you prefer then click **OK**

Taskbar Properties

Various options can be set to customise the way the **Taskbar** and **Start Menu** work.

To move the Taskbar

The **Taskbar** can be moved to the top, left or right edge of the screen. You can also make the Taskbar larger by clicking-and-dragging its border.

Note It is possible to hide the Taskbar by dragging its border down. If the Taskbar disappears, it may be that you have done this by accident. Move the pointer to the edge of the screen so that it changes to the resize arrow ↕ then click-and-drag upward.

To set Taskbar properties

- From the **Start** menu, select **Settings** then **Taskbar and Start Menu...** OR right-click the **Taskbar** and select **Properties**

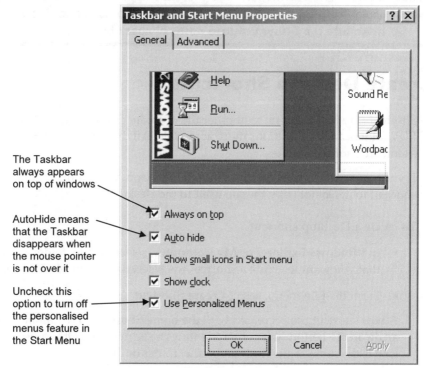

The Taskbar always appears on top of windows

AutoHide means that the Taskbar disappears when the mouse pointer is not over it

Uncheck this option to turn off the personalised menus feature in the Start Menu

Taskbar and Start Menu Properties

- Experiment with the different options to find out which you prefer

---

Control Volume and Sounds

If you have a sound card and speakers on your PC, you may need to lower the volume at which Windows plays sounds. You can adjust the volume quickly from the Taskbar or mute your PC entirely.

To change volume settings from the Taskbar

- On the right-hand side of the **Taskbar**, click the **Volume** icon

The **Volume** slider is displayed.

- Click-and-drag the slider to control the volume

- Click the **Mute** check box to silence your PC

- Click away from the volume slider to close it

Volume slider

Note If there is no volume icon in the Taskbar, open the **Multimedia** applet from the Control Panel. On the **Audio** tab, under **Playback**, make sure the **Show volume control** check box is ticked.

Create Desktop Shortcuts

Shortcuts are files that link to another file or folder. They are used to make files, folders and applications more accessible. All the icons in the Start Menu are shortcuts to files.

If you want a file to be accessible from the Desktop, you should create a shortcut to it. Do not copy the file itself to the Desktop.

To create a Desktop shortcut

- In **Windows Explorer** or **My Computer**, select the file, folder or drive that you want to create a shortcut to - select any file in **My Documents**

- From the **File** menu, select **Create Shortcut**

A new shortcut file is created with the name **Shortcut to** *file name*. The arrow in the bottom-left corner identifies a shortcut file. Otherwise the icon is the same as the destination file, folder or drive.

- If necessary, **restore** the window so that the **Desktop** is visible behind the window then drag the shortcut file onto the Desktop

---

Review of Using the Computer

Review the topics covered during the module and identify areas for further practice and goals for the future

---

Review

(Check **objectives**) ☐
(Complete **consolidation** exercise) ☐
(Identify topics for **further** study) ☐
(**Answers** to practice questions) ☐

Check Objectives

Congratulations on completing the lessons for ECDL Module 2 "Using the Computer and Managing Files".

You have learned to:

♦ Use basic features of **MS Windows**.

♦ Create **text files** using the applications included with MS Windows.

♦ Understand the **structure** of drives and directories (folders) and to create **folders** and **subfolders**.

♦ **Print** files, select different printers and manage the print queue.

♦ Change the appearance of the **Desktop** and alter some system settings.

Make sure you have checked off each syllabus item and identified any areas you do not fully understand or remember.

Consolidation and Going Further

Tests for Module 2 can either be practice-based or question-based. Practical tests will give you a series of tasks to perform in Windows.

There are further test-style exercises for you to try on the CD in the folder **ECDL Tests\2 Using Computers**

Print the document **Using Computers Questions** and try to complete the test unaided.

Note   These questions are provided as a consolidation exercise. They do not make up an approved ECDL test. See page 689 for more information about the extra tests.

Going further

Windows contains many more complexities than are covered in this course. You can get further training as an **Advanced User** (to learn how to configure system and networks settings, install applications and so on). You could also go on to learn as a **Technical User** (to learn how to install the operating system, support others and troubleshoot problems).

Practice Answers

Q1. Write down the file path

C:\Documents and Settings\davidm\My Documents\Windows.doc

Word Processing

Creating a New Document

Recognise features of the screen and create a basic document

Lesson 14

Start the MS Word application ☐
(Identify the different **elements** of the Word screen) ☐
Customise the display of **toolbars** ☐
Change **page display** modes ☐
Create a **new** document and **save** ☐
Insert and delete **text** and **paragraphs** ☐
Get **help** from the **Office Assistant** ☐
Close a document ☐
Close Word ☐

What is a Word Processor?

Microsoft Word is a sophisticated **word-processing** application.

A basic word-processor is designed to create text **documents** such as letters, memos and reports. Most word processors also have features to let you **format** (enhance the appearance of text and paragraphs) and **proof** (check spelling and layout) documents. MS Word also has several **desktop publishing** (DTP) features, allowing you to incorporate tables, graphics and data from other applications in a document.

Word is the first application in a suite of products called **Microsoft Office**. The applications in Office have basically the same window layout and share many features. Once you have learned to use these features in one application, you will be able to master them in all the others.

Open Word

Word can be started by opening its application icon **W**, wherever it is found.

To start Word from the Start menu

- On the **Taskbar,** click once on the **Start** button

The **Start** menu is displayed.

- Click once on the **Programs** menu item

The **Programs** submenu is displayed.

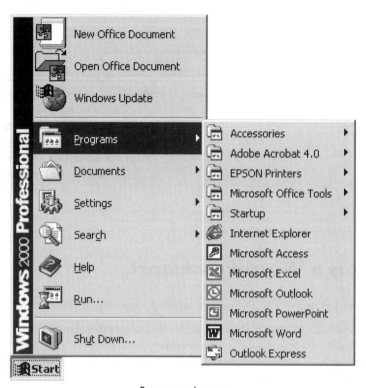

Programs submenu

- Click the **Microsoft Word** program item ▣ Microsoft Word

> **Tip** You may also be able to start Word from a **Desktop shortcut** or from the **Office 2000 Shortcut bar**. Look for the Word program icon ▣.

The Word Window

Word's **application window** may look more complex than the other
Windows programs you have seen so far, but it does contain basically the
same elements.

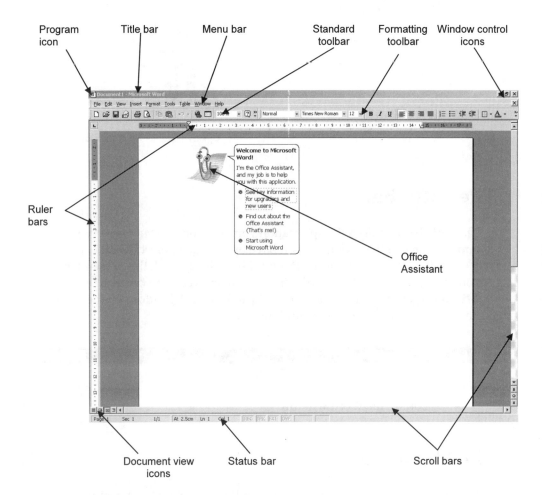

Program icon · Title bar · Menu bar · Standard toolbar · Formatting toolbar · Window control icons · Ruler bars · Office Assistant · Document view icons · Status bar · Scroll bars

The Office Assistant

Depending on how your computer has been setup, when you first start
Word the Office Assistant may appear, providing you with the **Tip of the
Day**. The Tip of the Day is a learning aid that contains useful suggestions
and shortcuts for using Word more effectively.

You will learn more about the Office Assistant later in this lesson.

To close the Tip of the Day

- Click **OK** (or click **Start Using Microsoft Word** if this is the first time you have started the application)

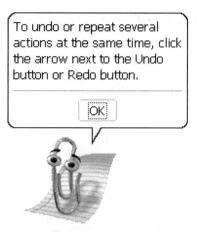

To undo or repeat several actions at the same time, click the arrow next to the Undo button or Redo button.

OK

Office Assistant - Tip of the Day

The Title Bar

The **Title** bar identifies the application you are running (Microsoft Word) and the name of the document you have open (Document 1). On the left-hand side of the Title bar is the **Program Icon**. If you click this, a menu of commands to control the Word window is displayed. You can also use the **Minimise**, **Maximise** / **Restore** and **Close** buttons on the right-hand side of the Title bar to control the window.

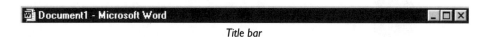

Document1 - Microsoft Word

Title bar

- Maximise the Word window

The Menu Bar

Each word on the **Menu** bar represents a different menu. Each menu contains the commands you use to activate features of Word. If a command is also found on a **toolbar** (see below) then the icon representing the command is displayed in the menu too. This makes recognising commands easier.

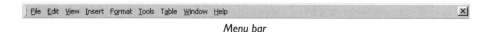

File Edit View Insert Format Tools Table Window Help

Menu bar

Word Toolbars

Toolbars contain icon button shortcuts to selecting a command from a menu. When you first start Word the **Standard** and **Formatting** toolbars are displayed. These toolbars contain commonly used commands. There are many other toolbars available in Word, used for tasks such as editing tables and completing a mail merge.

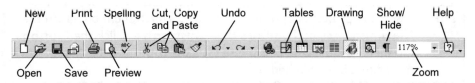

Standard toolbar

Formatting toolbar

To display/hide a toolbar

- From the **View** menu, select **Toolbars**

A list of available toolbars is displayed. The toolbars that are checked are currently displayed.

- Click an unchecked toolbar to display it - select the **Drawing** toolbar

- Display the **Toolbars** menu again and select **Drawing** once more - the toolbar is hidden

If the toolbar does not fit on the screen, you will see a chevron above the **More Buttons** icon - click the **More Buttons** chevron to display the rest of the toolbar.

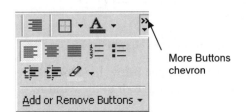

More Buttons chevron

- Click the **More Buttons** chevron on the **Formatting** toolbar

- Click away from the toolbar without selecting a command

Tip	If only part of a toolbar is visible, Word will display the buttons you select often on the visible part and hide the commands you do not use.

- Look for the [?] icon button at the end of the **Standard** toolbar - if you cannot see it, click the **More Buttons** chevron

- Point to the [?] icon with the mouse - a **ScreenTip** describing its function is displayed

ScreenTip

Tip   If ScreenTips do not appear you need to switch them on. From the **View** menu, select **Toolbars** then **Customize**. Click the **Options** tab then click the **Show ScreenTips on toolbars** checkbox. A tick means that it is switched on.

To move toolbars

You can move toolbars around the screen to make them easier to access. Toolbars can be attached to any window border (top, bottom, left or right) and "stacked" in rows (a **docked** toolbar). Alternatively, you can drag a toolbar into the middle of the screen (a **floating** toolbar).

Move Handle

- Point to the **Move Handle** on the **Formatting** toolbar

- With the mouse pointer in the move shape ✛, click-and-drag the handle to move the toolbar into the middle of the screen

Floating toolbar

- Click-and-drag on the borders of the toolbar to change its shape

- Click-and-drag the toolbar's **Title** bar up to just below the **Standard** toolbar - when the **Formatting** toolbar attaches itself to the window release the mouse button

- Try moving each toolbar around the top of the screen - you can drag the move handle left and right and move the toolbars over one another

- On completion leave the **Standard** toolbar above the **Formatting** toolbar

Scroll Bars

Scroll bars are used to move quickly around the document.

The **scroll button** on the scroll bar changes size in proportion to the overall size of the document.

You can scroll around the document by clicking the scroll arrows at either end of the scroll bar or by dragging the scroll button in the scroll bar.

The browse buttons allow you to move through a document in different ways. The default setting is by page.

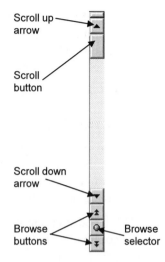

Scroll up arrow

Scroll button

Scroll down arrow

Browse buttons

Browse selector

Tip If your mouse has a **wheel** on it, you can use the wheel to scroll up and down a window.

The Status Bar

The **Status** bar displays relevant document information including page numbering, insertion point location, insert/overtype setting, spelling check and saving status.

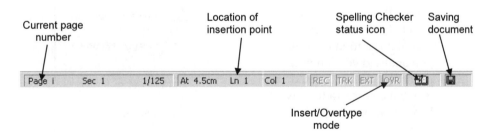

Current page number

Location of insertion point

Spelling Checker status icon

Saving document

Insert/Overtype mode

Menus and Dialogue Boxes

Commands are displayed on drop-down menus that appear below menu headings. When selecting a command from a menu you can use the mouse or the keyboard. Some commands open a dialogue box, which is used to specify further options.

Refer back to page 123 to see how to use menus and dialogue boxes.

Personalised menus

The Office 2000 programs, including Word, have "intelligent" menus that are automatically personalised for you, based on how often you use certain commands. When you first start Word, the most frequently used commands are displayed on the selected menu.

As you spend longer working in Word, the menus change to contain just the commands that you select most often.

To re-display a menu command

If you are looking for a specific command you do not use very often or have never used before, you need to adjust the menu so that it displays it.

- Click the **chevron** ☒ arrows at the bottom of the menu **OR** double-click the menu name (for example, **View**) to **extend** the menu

When one menu is extended, the other menus are also expanded, until you click on a command or perform another action. When a command is selected from an extended menu, it is added to your personalised version of that particular menu. If you do not use that command for a while, Word will stop displaying it.

An extended menu

To show all commands on a menu

As a new user to Word you may prefer to have every menu option available all of the time.

- From the **Tools** menu, select **Customize...**

The **Customize** dialogue box is displayed.

Dialogue boxes often have a series of **tabs** (or **pages**) to group related commands.

- Click the **Options** tab (or press O)

The **Options** tab in the **Customize** dialogue box is displayed.

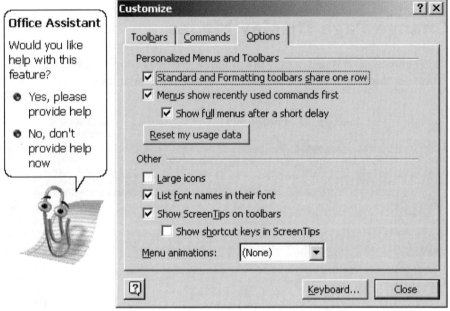

Customize dialogue box

- If the Office Assistant appears offering help, click **No**

- If you want to show full menus now, click the **Menus show recently used commands first** check box to clear the tick then click the **Close** button

Note Selecting or de-selecting the **Menus show recently used commands first** check box will affect every Office 2000 application on your PC.

Keyboard Shortcuts

As you become more proficient with Word it is often easier to use keys instead of the mouse to carry out a command. Most of the major commands have keyboard shortcuts (referred to as *SpeedKeys* in this book) that are displayed beside the command name on the menu. For example, to open a file the SpeedKey is `Ctrl`+`O`.

Sometimes there is more than one SpeedKey option. For example you can also open a file with `Ctrl`+`F12` (Control and Function Key 12). To see a full list of SpeedKeys, open the Office Assistant (see "Getting Assistance" below) and ask for help on "Keyboard shortcuts".

Change Page Display Modes

When you start Word, a new document is created automatically. The main area of the Word window is taken up by the document itself.

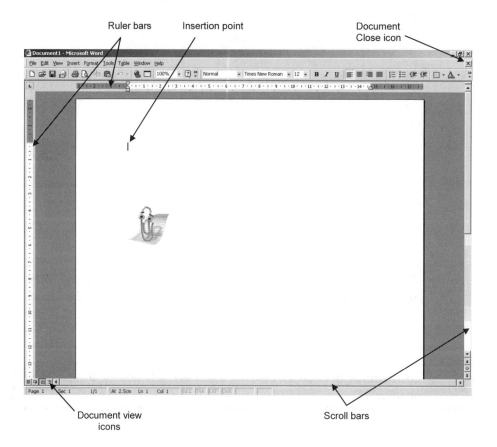

Ruler bars   Insertion point   Document
                                                     Close icon

Document view   Scroll bars
icons

The Insertion Point

The **insertion point** (or **typing cursor**) shows you where text will appear if you start pressing keys on the keyboard.

Hidden Text

As you work in Word, you may see strange characters and wavy lines appear on the screen. This is **hidden text** (that is, it does not appear when you print the document). Hidden text is used to format and proof your document. You will be learning about it in later lessons.

Views

As you work in Word, the document can be displayed in several different ways. The two basic views are **Normal** view and **Print Layout** view. You can switch between Normal view and Print Layout view whenever necessary.

- **Print Layout** view (shown above) displays the text as if it were on a piece of paper, including the **page margins**. This view is probably the easiest to work in.

- **Normal View** displays the text space as if it were a long strip of paper. Dotted lines indicate the end of a page. This view displays the text area only, not the page margins. It is best suited to entering large amounts of text.

To select a document view

- On the left-hand side of the horizontal scroll bar, click the **Normal View** button

Normal view   Outline view

Web Layout view   Print Layout view

View menu

- From the **View** menu, select **Print Layout** view

- Use the **View** menu to display the **Ruler** if it is not turned on

Create a New Document and Save

When entering text into a Word document the insertion point automatically returns to the left margin when you have typed beyond the right margin (this is known as **word-wrap**). Press $\boxed{\text{Enter}}$ to start a new **paragraph**.

> **Tip** When you start Word, a new document is created automatically. To create another new document, on the **Standard** toolbar, click **New** $\boxed{\text{D}}$ (*SpeedKey:* $\boxed{\text{Ctrl}}$+$\boxed{\text{N}}$).

To enter some text

- Type the text below - hold down the $\boxed{\text{Shift}}$ key to type capital letters

- Press $\boxed{\text{Enter}}$ in place of the ¶ symbol

The·Title·Bar¶
Shows·the·name·of·the·application·and·current·document·and·allows·control·of·the·window.¶
¶
The·Menu·Bar¶
Contains·all·the·commands·used·to·operate·the·application,·grouped·under·menu·headings.¶
¶
Toolbars¶
Contain·shortcut·buttons·to·frequently·used·commands.¶
¶
Scroll·Bars¶
Allow·you·to·move·around·a·large·document.¶
¶
View·Buttons¶
Present·different·ways·of·looking·at·a·document.¶
¶
The·Status·Bar¶
Displays·information·about·the·document.¶

To save a document

It is important to save your document as a **file**. You need to do this **regularly** (every 10 minutes) to prevent accidental loss of data. Word saves document files with a .DOC extension and the icon .

The first time you save a document you will need to give it a **file name** and select a folder in which to save it.

- On the **Standard** toolbar, click **Save** 🖫 **OR** from the **File** menu, select **Save** (*SpeedKey:* `Ctrl` + `S`)

The **Save As** dialogue box is displayed.

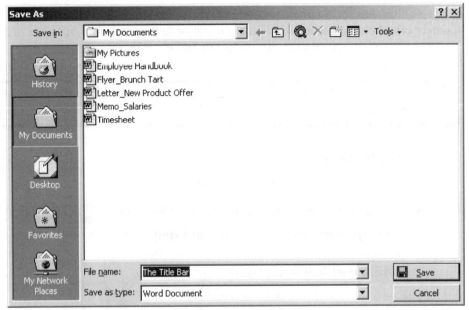

Save As dialogue box

- Open the folder you want to save the document in (for this exercise, save it in **My Documents**)

The default file name is taken from the first line of text in your document.

- Enter a new **File name:** Word Window

Note You do not need to add a .DOC extension to the file name because Word does this automatically. If you see .DOC displayed in the **File name:** box, you can safely overtype it.

- Click **Save**

The **Status** bar will briefly display a line of blue dots, followed by a pulsing floppy disk symbol while the save is in progress 🖫 . When the save is complete, the new file name is displayed on the **Title** bar.

Get Help with Word

Word contains an extensive series of Help topics explaining how the application works. The default way of accessing these help topics is to use the **Office Assistant**.

The Office Assistant remains on-screen while you work. At certain points, it may offer help on the feature you are using or display relevant tips. The Office Assistant will also display warning and error messages.

> **Note** If the Office Assistant is turned off, warning and error messages are displayed in a **dialogue box**.

To display the Office Assistant

The Office Assistant may be hidden. To display it:

- On the **Standard** toolbar, click **Microsoft Word Help** [?] **OR** from the **Help** menu, select **Microsoft Word Help** (*SpeedKey:* F1)

The **Office Assistant** is displayed.

The assistant usually appears as a paper clip, but your copy of Office may be setup to display a different character.

To move the Office Assistant

- The assistant should keep out of the way while you are working on a document, but you can also move it manually by clicking-and-dragging - try dragging the assistant around the screen

To hide the Office Assistant

- Right-click the **Office Assistant** and from the shortcut menu, select **Hide OR** from the **Help** menu, select **Hide the Office Assistant**

The **Office Assistant** is hidden.

To get help from the Office Assistant

- Display the **Office Assistant** again

The **Office Assistant** tries to guess what kind of help you might need and provides a list of relevant Help topics.

If the list of "guessed" **Help** topics does not include anything relevant, you can ask the assistant a question.

- Type "How do I spell check my document" into the text box

- Click [Search] - a new list of topics is displayed

Tip If the list of topics does not contain anything relevant to your query, try using different terms in your question.

- Click the topic **Ways to check spelling**

The **Microsoft Word Help** window is displayed alongside the Word window.

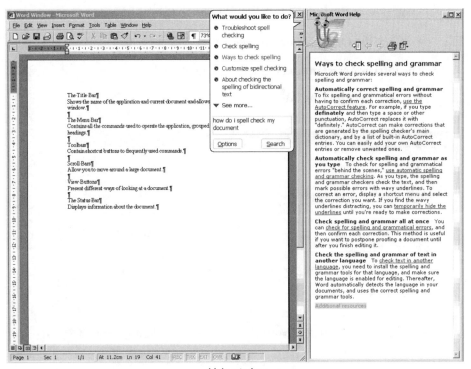

Help window

Help about the topic you have chosen is displayed.

- Read the help that is displayed

- Click **Print** 🖨 then **OK** to print a copy of the topic for future reference

- Where displayed, click the blue, underlined text to see related help topics

- Close the **Help** window by clicking the **Close** button ☒

To set different options for the Office Assistant

The assistant displays tips and help while you work. A light bulb is displayed when the **Office Assistant** has a tip. To see the tip, click the light bulb.

Office Assistant

You can change the type of tips that the assistant displays.

- Click the **Office Assistant** and select 　Options

The **Office Assistant** dialogue box is displayed.

- Click the **Options** tab

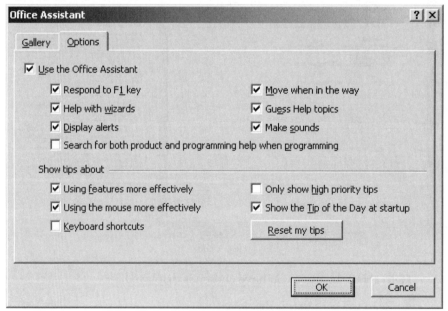

Office Assistant dialogue box

Select check boxes in the top panel to control the way the assistant behaves. Select options in the bottom panel to control what type of tips the assistant displays.

- For this course, turn off the office assistant by de-selecting **Use the Office Assistant**

> **Tip** If you use help without the Office Assistant, you can access topics using the **Contents**, **Index** and **Answer Wizard** (search) tabs. These work much like the **Windows** help system (see page 115).

- Click **OK**

> **Note** For the rest of the course, it is assumed that the office assistant will be turned off. Re-activate the assistant by selecting **Show the Office Assistant** from the **Help** menu.

To display ScreenTips for an area of the Word window

If you are uncertain about what an item is or does, you can display a ScreenTip description. ScreenTips are available for menu commands, toolbar buttons, dialogue boxes and other screen areas like scroll bars.

- From the **Help** menu, select **What's This?** (*SpeedKey:* `Shift`+`F1`)

The mouse pointer turns into an arrow with a question mark attached.

- Click on the item you require context sensitive help for - click the Ruler bar
- Read the tip then click the box to hide it

To display ScreenTips in a dialogue box

- Display the dialogue box for which you want help (From the **File** menu, select **Print...**)
- Click the **Question Mark** [?] on the top right-hand corner of the dialogue box

The mouse pointer turns into the **What's This** pointer.

- Click on the item you require context sensitive help for - click the **Name:** box

A **ScreenTip** is displayed with the appropriate help.

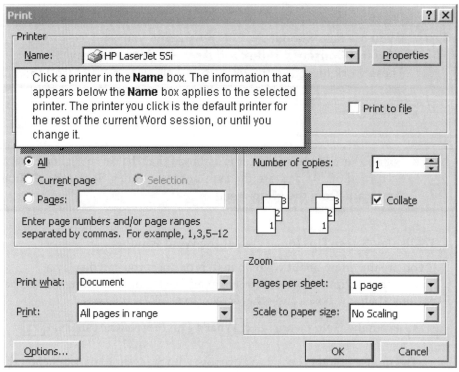

ScreenTip

- Press <kbd>Esc</kbd> to close the tip then click the **Cancel** button to exit the dialogue box

Practice

- *Add the following text about the Office Assistant at the end of the document*

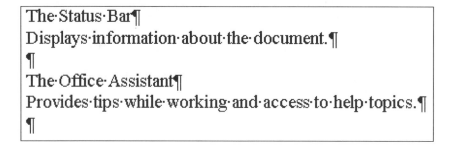

- *Do **not** save the document*

Close a Document

To close a document you simply close its window. Each document is contained in its own window **within** the Word application window.

To close a Word document

- On the **Menu** bar, click **Close** ☒ OR from the **File** menu, select **Close** (*SpeedKey:* Ctrl + F4)

If you have not saved the document or have made changes to it since it was last saved you are prompted to save the document now.

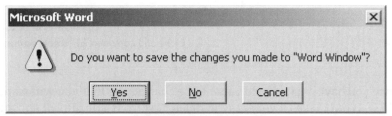

Save changes dialogue box

- Click **Yes** to save the document

Clicking **No** closes the document without saving. Clicking **Cancel** leaves the document on the screen unchanged.

Because there are no documents open, the main part of the screen is grey.

Close Word

You can exit from Word in several ways. If you have unsaved documents open when you exit Word you are prompted to save them as Word closes.

> **Tip** It is best to save or close all of your open documents before exiting Word, otherwise you may not be sure which document you are being asked to save.

To exit Word

- Double-click the **Word Program Icon** on the top-left of the Word window ⬜ OR click the **Close** button on the top-right of the **Word** window ☒ OR from the **File** menu, select **Exit** (*SpeedKey:* Alt + F4)

Editing a Document

Edit existing documents and use the Cut, Copy and Paste tools

Lesson 15

Open an existing document ☐
Use the **Zoom** tool ☐
Select text characters, paragraphs and documents ☐
Use the **Undo** command ☐
Insert **special characters** and **symbols** ☐
Move and **copy** text ☐
Save a document onto hard disk and floppy disk ☐
Open **several** documents ☐
Move and copy text **between documents** ☐

Once you have created a document, the chances are that you will want to edit it. Word makes it very easy to delete text from a document and add new text to it. It also provides an invaluable **undo** tool, allowing you to reverse changes.

As well as normal text characters that you can type from the keyboard, Word lets you insert special characters and symbols (such as the copyright and trademark signs).

There are also **Cut**, **Copy** and **Paste** tools, which allow you to move or copy text around a document or to reuse text in another document.

Open an Existing Document

You can open an existing document when you want to make changes or add information to it.

To open an existing document

- Start Word if necessary

- On the **Standard** toolbar, click **Open** 📂 OR from the **File** menu, select **Open** (*SpeedKey:* Ctrl + O)

The **Open** dialogue box is displayed. The layout of this dialogue box is very similar to **Save As**. It is used to browse drives and folders so that you can locate and open a document.

Your **My Documents** folder is usually displayed by default. If necessary, you can use the **Look in:** box to select a different disk drive or network folder.

Select a folder icon and click **Open** to browse a subfolder. Use **Up One Level** to move from a subfolder to its main folder. Click **Back** to go back into the folder you were in previously.

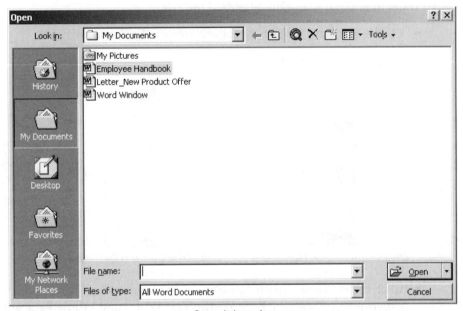

Open dialogue box

- Select **Letter_New Product Offer** and click **Open**

Tip	To access a document quickly, create a shortcut to it in the **Favorites** folder. In the **Open** dialogue box, select the document then click the **Tools** button and select **Add to Favorites**. Whenever you want to open the file, simply click the **Favorites** button in the left-hand panel and select the document to open.

Tip	You can also open any of the four most recently saved documents by selecting it from the list at the bottom of the **File** menu.

Note	If you open a document file icon in Windows Explorer, Word will start and open the document automatically.

Use the Zoom Tool

The **Zoom** tool allows you to enlarge what you are looking at or zoom out to see several pages on the screen at the same time.

You can change the size at which to view and work in your document from as little as 10% up to 500% of normal size.

To zoom in and out using the Standard toolbar

- On the **Standard** toolbar, click the arrow on the **Zoom** box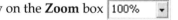

The **Zoom** menu is displayed.

 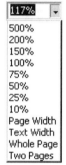

Zoom Control menu in Normal view   *Zoom Control menu in Print Layout view*

- Click the required size - practise zooming in and out of the document, experimenting with the **Page Width**, **Text Width** and **Whole Page** options

To zoom in and out using the menu

- From the <u>V</u>iew menu, select <u>Z</u>oom...

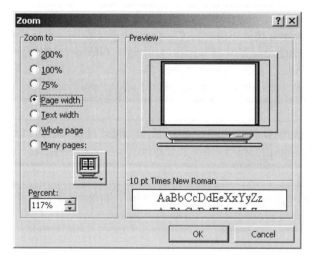

From the **Zoom to** panel select a scale to use, or in the **Percent:** box, enter the percentage required.

The effect of the selected scaling factor is displayed in the **Preview** panel. In **Print Layout** view the legibility of text at the selected scale is displayed beneath the **Preview** panel.

- Click the **Many Pages:** button

- Click-and-drag over the menu to select **2 x 2 Pages**

- Click **OK**

- Change the zoom setting back to **Page Width**

Zoom dialogue box - Many Pages menu

Work with Paragraphs

A **paragraph** may be a character, a word, a line or multiple lines. What defines text as a paragraph is the fact that it is ended with the `Enter` key.

> This is a paragraph containing one line.¶
>
> This is a paragraph containing several lines. This is a paragraph containing several lines. This is a paragraph containing several lines.¶

Tip   To force a new line to start without creating a new paragraph, press `Shift`+`Enter`.

It can be useful to see exactly where a paragraph ends. The **paragraph mark** (¶) represents the end of a paragraph. The paragraph mark is **hidden text**. It can be displayed on-screen but does not print out.

To display hidden text

- On the **Standard** toolbar, click the **Show/Hide** button ¶ (*SpeedKey:* `Ctrl`+`Shift`+`*`) - this button toggles on and off

You will see the following hidden text characters used in documents.

This Character	Represents
¶	End of a paragraph
▪	Space
→	Tab (see page 233)
°	Non-breaking space (see page 258)

Move the Insertion Point

The **insertion point** (sometimes referred to as the cursor) is a blinking vertical black line where new text is inserted. When you move the mouse pointer ⅍ into the typing area it changes to an **I-beam** shape Ⅰ, which is used to position the insertion point.

To move the insertion point with the mouse

- If necessary, use the **scroll bars** or the **Zoom** tool to display the last paragraph of text in the document

- Point the **I-beam** mouse pointer Ⅰ just below the last line of text

- Click the left mouse button

The insertion point is moved to the same position as the I-beam.

- Press Enter to create a new paragraph, then type the salutation, your name and a job title as shown below

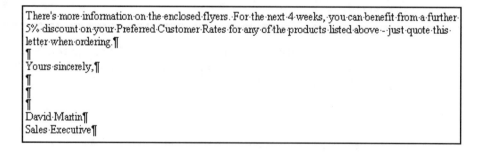

Note Scrolling does not move the insertion point.

To move the insertion point with the keyboard

Press	To Move
↑	Up one line
↓	Down one line
←	Left one character
→	Right one character
Home	To the beginning of the current line
End	To the end of the current line
Ctrl + Home	To the top of the document
Ctrl + End	To the bottom of the document
Ctrl + ←	To the beginning of the previous word
Ctrl + →	To the beginning of the next word
Ctrl + ↑	To the top of the current paragraph
Ctrl + ↓	To the beginning of the next paragraph
Page Up	Up one screen
Page Down	Down one screen

Practice

Use the keyboard to complete this exercise:

- *Move to the top of the document*

- *Move to the end of the second line "new addition"*

- *Move to the beginning of the second paragraph*

Note that the second "paragraph" does not contain any text.

- *Move the cursor before "Chilli Meals" in the third paragraph*

Use Click-and-Type

In **Print Layout** view, you may notice that the insertion point appears with lines next to it when you move it over blank areas of the page.

Many word processors only let you add text to existing text - if you want to type at the bottom of the page, you need to press $\boxed{\texttt{Enter}}$ to move down.

With Word, you can double-click anywhere on the page and start typing.

ECDL Using the Click-and-Type feature is not part of the ECDL syllabus. It has been included so that you understand why the cursor sometimes changes shape.

Note If you do not see the click-and-type cursors, this feature may be turned off. To activate it, from the **Tools** menu, select **Options**. Click the **Edit** tab and make sure the **Enable click and type** box is checked.

To use click-and-type

- If necessary, click the **Status** bar button 🖹 to switch to **Print Layout** view

- Click to position the insertion point in the words "Sales Executive" then point to the space below the line

The cursor may change to show you how the text you type will be **aligned** (You will learn more about aligning paragraphs on page 229).

This Cursor	Means
I≡	Text will be left aligned
I≡	Text will be centred on the page
≡I	Text will be right aligned

- With the pointer about two lines below "Sales Executive", double-click the left mouse button and type Encl.

- On the **Standard** toolbar, click **Save** 🖫 to save changes to the document

Select Text

Selecting text is one of the most important actions in Word. You need to select text before you do something with it - for example, copy, delete or format it.

Normal text appears like this, but selected text appears highlighted.

To select text with the mouse

To Select	Do This
Characters	Click-and-drag across the character(s).
A word	Double-click the word.
A whole line of text	Click in the **selection border** (the space to the left of the paragraph text).
A sentence	Press Ctrl and click within the sentence.
A paragraph	Double-click in the selection border or triple-click within the paragraph.
A block of text	Click-and-drag down and across OR click at the beginning of the text, then press Shift and click at the end.
The document	Triple-click in the selection border.

Note If you click-and-drag to the top or bottom of the screen, the selection will scroll down the document automatically. If the screen scrolls too quickly, use the keyboard to select text (see overleaf).

To use Automatic Word Selection

When you are selecting a block of text, **Automatic Word Selection** selects whole words even if you click-and-drag from the middle of a word. You can turn the option on or off to suit the way you work.

- From the **Tools** menu, select **Options...** then click the **Edit** tab

- In the **Text** panel, remove the tick from the **When selecting, automatically select whole word** box and click **OK**

- Keep the setting activated if you prefer (try completing the practice exercise below with it turned off and on)

To select text with the keyboard

Press	To Select
Shift + ➜ or Shift + ◄	A character or multiple characters
Shift + Ctrl + ➜ or ◄	A word
Shift + End	To end of line
Shift + Home	To beginning of line
Ctrl + Shift + Home	To top of document
Ctrl + Shift + End	To bottom of document
Ctrl + A	The whole document

Practice

Use the mouse and keyboard to select the following:

- *The first line of text*
- *The paragraph starting "As you know"*
- *"new additions"*
- *The whole document*
- *"Custom" (from "Preferred Customer Rates")*
- *All paragraphs except the first*

- *Move to the top of the document and add the following text (use the* Caps Lock *key to type the subject)*

```
Victoria·Dunn¶
General·Manager¶
Courtyard·Restaurant¶
Yorebridge·House¶
Bainbridge¶
Leyburn·DL8·3PB¶
¶
12·December·2000¶
¶
BENEFIT·FROM·EXTRA·DISCOUNTS¶
¶
Dear·Mrs·Dunn¶
¶
I'm·writing·to·thank·you·for·the·support·you've·given·Joe·Chilli's·over·the·last·six·years.·As·one·of·our·
```

- *Press* Caps Lock *to turn it off again*

To switch between Insert and Overtype mode

When editing a document, new text is usually **inserted** (existing text is moved to the right). The alternative is to type over the existing text by switching into **Overtype** mode.

Normally you are in Insert mode and **OVR** appears dim on the **Status** bar.

- Double-click the **OVR** box on the **Status** bar OVR
  (*SpeedKey:* Insert)

OVR now appears bright. You are in **Overtype** mode.

- Click at the beginning of the line "General Manager" and type Head
  Chef

Do not worry about the additional characters at the end of the line, we will get rid of those next.

- Double-click the **OVR** box on the **Status** bar OVR (*SpeedKey:* Insert)

OVR is dimmed again. You are back in **Insert** mode.

Tip It is easy to press the Insert key by mistake, so if your text starts disappearing when you type, check that you are not in Overtype mode.

Typing Replaces Selection

If you have selected text in your document, anything you type will replace it, even if you press Space Bar or Enter . Therefore, always make sure nothing is selected before you enter new text, unless you are replacing it intentionally.

Tip This option can be switched off by selecting **Options...** from the **Tools** menu and then selecting the **Edit** tab. Remove the tick from the **Typing replaces selection** box.

Delete Text

To delete individual characters

- Press the Delete key to remove the character to the **right** of the insertion point - delete the "anager" text from the end of the job title

- Press the Backspace key to remove the character to the **left** of the insertion point - delete the job title "Head Chef"

- Press Backspace again - the **paragraph mark** is deleted, removing the paragraph

To delete selected text

- Select the address text then press Delete or Backspace

Use the Undo Tool

Word allows you to **undo** previous actions.

To undo the last action

- On the **Standard** toolbar, click **Undo**  **OR** from the **Edit** menu, select **Undo** (*SpeedKey*: Ctrl + Z)

The address text is restored to the document.

To undo a previous action

The **Undo** button stores over **300** actions.

- Click the arrow on the **Undo** button to display a list of your previous edits

| Typing C |
| Typing |
| Typing d |
| Typing a |
| Typing e |
| Typing H |
| Undo 25 Actions |

Undo menu

- Scroll down the list until you find the point where you typed capital "H" then click that item

All of the edits back to that point are undone in one action.

Insert Symbols and Special Characters

There are many **symbols** available from the font styles installed on your computer.

To insert a symbol

- Click at the start of the "Tomato, Basil and Garlic Tart" line

- From the **Insert** menu, click **Symbol...** then click the **Symbols** tab if not already displayed

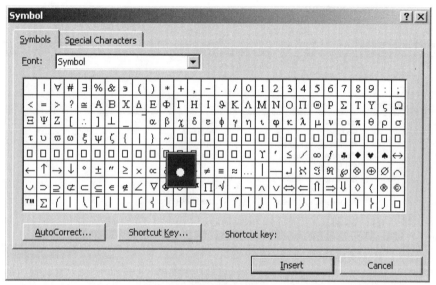

Symbol dialogue box

- Select the **Symbol** font from the **Font:** box

- To get a close-up view of a symbol, click it - select the black dot as shown above

- Click **Insert**

- You can select another symbol to insert if you wish, but for this exercise click **Close**

- Repeat the above steps to add the same symbol to each item on the list

Tip	If you are using an expanded font, such as **Arial** or **Times New Roman**, the **Subset** list appears. Use this list to choose from an extended list of language characters, including Greek and Russian (Cyrillic).

Note To insert the symbol for the **Euro** currency, press `Alt`+`Ctrl`+`4`
(UK keyboard layouts).

To insert a special character

You can easily insert special characters, such as © (copyright), ® (registered) and ™ (trademark), into your document.

- Click after the text "Chilli Meals" in the first main paragraph

- From the **Insert** menu, select **Symbol...** and select the **Special Characters** tab

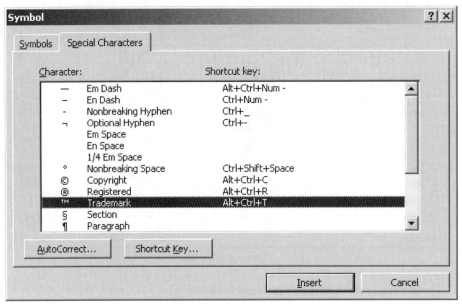

Symbol dialogue box

- Select the **Trademark** character then click **Insert**

- Click **Close**

- Click after the words "Chilli Meals" in the next block of text

- Press `Alt`+`Ctrl`+`T` - the ™ character is inserted again

- Save the changes you have made to this document by clicking **Save** 🖫 (*SpeedKey* `Ctrl`+`S`)

The Windows Clipboard

At times you will want to reorganise your document by moving or copying text to different locations. You can move and copy text using the **Clipboard**.

The Clipboard is a temporary storage area used by Windows to hold text (or graphics) while it is being moved or copied. The Clipboard can be used to transfer information within an application, or between applications. The information remains on the Clipboard until you replace it or until you exit from Windows.

The terms used for these actions are **Cut, Copy** and **Paste**.

◆ **Cut** removes the information from an application and places it on the Clipboard.

◆ **Copy** leaves the information in an application and places a copy of it on the Clipboard.

◆ **Paste** copies the information from the Clipboard and places it into an application.

Word also features an **Office Clipboard** that can be used to collect **multiple** items for pasting into MS Office 2000 applications.

Note The Office Clipboard may appear while you are completing this exercise. If so, hide it by clicking its **Close** button ⊠. You will learn to use the Office Clipboard on page 559.

Move Text (Cut and Paste)

Text (and graphics) can be moved within the same document, between documents or between files in different applications.

To move text using the Standard toolbar

- Select the "• Chicken and Garlic Pasta" paragraph

- Click the **Cut** button ✂ (*SpeedKey:* `Ctrl`+`X`)

The text is **removed** from the document and placed into the Clipboard. The previous contents of the Windows Clipboard are removed.

- Move the insertion point before "• Brunch Tart"

- Click the **Paste** button 📋 (*SpeedKey:* `Ctrl`+`V`)

The contents of the Clipboard are copied from the Clipboard to the destination. Note that because you selected the whole paragraph, the "Brunch Tart" text is moved down.

Note   You can paste the contents of the Clipboard again. The same data stays on the Clipboard until you select Cut or Copy or exit Windows.

Tip   As an alternative way to move text, after selecting the text, click the **right** mouse button and from the shortcut menu, select **Cut**, then right-click where you want to put the text and select **Paste**.

To move text using the keyboard

- Use `Shift` + `→` to select the text "• Tomato, Basil and Garlic Tart" exactly as shown below, that is, do not select the paragraph mark

> • Tomato, Basil and Garlic Tart
> • Chicken and Garlic Pasta
> • Brunch Tart
> • Ham and Onion Cream Tart

- Press `F2`

Move to where? is displayed in the Status bar.

- Move the **insertion point** before "• Brunch Tart" and press `Enter`

- This time, because you did not cut a whole paragraph, the text is pasted into the same paragraph - press `Enter` to move "• Brunch Tart" to a new line

---

Tip   There are several other ways to move text.

As an alternative way to move text using the menu, select the text to be moved then from the **Edit** menu, select **Cut**. Move the **insertion point** to the new position for the text and from the **Edit** menu, select **Paste**.

To move text using a mouse shortcut, select the text to be moved then point to the destination while holding down the `Ctrl` key and click the **right** mouse button.

Copy Text (Copy and Paste)

Text (and graphics) can be copied within the same document, between documents or between files in different applications.

To copy text using the Standard toolbar

- Select the list of the four products

- Click the **Copy** button ▣ (*SpeedKey:* `Ctrl`+`C`)

The text is copied from the document and placed into the Clipboard. The previous contents of the Windows Clipboard are removed.

- Use Click-and-Type to move the **insertion point** to the end of the document (below "Encl.")

- Click the **Paste** button ▣ (*SpeedKey:* `Ctrl`+`V`)

The contents of the Clipboard are copied from the Clipboard to the destination. You can paste the contents of the Clipboard again.

- Delete the bullet symbols "•" from each paragraph

To copy text using the menu

- Type the word `Flyer` at the end of the line that reads "Ham and Onion Cream Tart"

- Select the word "Flyer" then from the **E**dit menu, select **C**opy

- Position the **insertion point** at the end of the line above

- From the **E**dit menu, select **P**aste

- Position the **insertion point** at the end of the line above and click **Paste** ▣ - the same text is pasted again

- Finally repeat this at the end of the line that reads "Chicken and Garlic Pasta"

To copy text using a mouse shortcut

- Select the text "Flyer" again

- Hold down `Ctrl`+`Shift`

- Point to the end of the line with the word "Encl." on it and click the **right** mouse button - "Flyer" is pasted at the end of the line

Save a Document

When you use the basic **Save** command (**Save** 🖫 , **File** - **Save** or `Ctrl`+`S`), the existing file is updated.

You can use the **Save As** command to create a new file for the same document. You might do this to create a backup copy of the document. It is also useful to keep a copy of an existing document before making major changes to it.

You can change the file name and/or the file location.

> **Note** If you use the same file name but save to a different location, make sure you can identify which version to work on in the future. If you are backing up a file, it is a good idea to add something like "Backup 12Sep2000" to the end of the file name.

To save with a different name or in a different location

- Firstly, preserve the changes you have made to the document in the **existing** file, by clicking **Save** 🖫

- From the **File** menu, select **Save As....** (*SpeedKey* `F12`)

- Enter the new file name and/or select a new location by clicking the **Save in:** list box - add the current date to the end of the file name

- Click **Save**

> **Note** You are now working in the **new** file - not the old one.

To save to a floppy disk

In most circumstances, it is not a good idea to work on a file saved to a floppy disk, as Word will perform quite slowly and there is a greater chance of errors occurring. Use Windows Explorer to copy and move files between disks.

If you must use **Save As** to save to a floppy disk, use the following steps.

- Save any changes to the existing file if necessary

- From the **File** menu, select **Properties...** then click the **General** tab

- Look at the **Size** attribute

If the file is much more than 1400 KB it will not fit on a normal floppy disk. The current file will fit easily.

- Click **OK** to close the dialogue box

- Put a floppy disk in the drive then select **File**, **Save As**

- In the **Save in:** box, select **3½ Floppy (A:)**

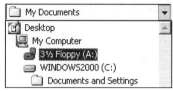

Save In list box

- Keep the same file name and click **Save**

- Wait until the disk activity stops and the LED goes out then close the document

- Remove the disk from the drive

- From the bottom of the **File** menu, select the original **Letter_New Product Offer** document

Open Several Documents

While using Word you can have several documents open at one time; you do not have to close one before opening another. The advantage of this is that you can quickly look up information in one document whilst working on another or you can transfer data between documents.

To open a second document ☺

o On the **Standard** toolbar, click **Open** 🖗 OR from the **File** menu select **Open...** (*SpeedKey:* Ctrl + O)

o Select the second document to open

To move between document windows

Each open document appears as a separate button on the **Windows Taskbar**.

- On the **Standard** toolbar, click **New** 🗋 to create a new document

There are now two documents open.

- On the **Windows Taskbar**, click the **Letter Document** icon (*SpeedKey:* Alt + Tab)

Multiple document windows displayed on the Taskbar

- From the **Window** menu, select **1 Document2** to switch to it (*SpeedKey:* $\boxed{\texttt{Ctrl}}$ + $\boxed{\texttt{F6}}$)

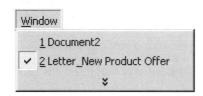

The name of the active window is displayed on the **Title** bar.

To view both documents on screen

- From the **Window** menu, select **Arrange All**

Both documents are displayed on the screen.

To copy and move text between documents

Text can be copied and moved between documents using the **Cut**, **Copy** and **Paste** buttons from the **Standard** toolbar. You can use the **Office Clipboard** to copy and paste multiple items. Also, if both documents are open the text can be dragged from one to the other.

Note   Drag-and-drop can be used to move or copy text and graphics within a document, between documents or between applications.

When both documents are visible select the document to work in by clicking on it with the mouse. The first click will activate the window but will not move the insertion point.

- Select the **Letter_New Product Offer** document

- Select the text from "Chilli Meals" in the second main block of text to the end of the list of new products

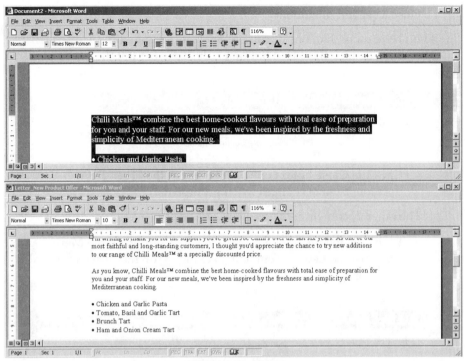

Drag-and-drop editing

- Hold down Ctrl to **copy** the selection then click-and-drag the text to the new document - release the mouse button *before* the Ctrl key

Note Holding down the Ctrl key *copies* the text. If you simply drag text it will be *moved*.

Tip If you cannot get both windows on-screen, drag the selection to the destination document's **Taskbar** icon. Hover the mouse over the icon for a few seconds. The destination document window will open and you can drop the selection into it as normal.

- Save the new document as **Flyer_Brunch Tart** in the **My Documents** folder

- Delete the bullet symbols "•" from each paragraph

To close a second document

If you have more than one document open at the same time, subsequent documents display the **Close** button on the **Title** bar not the **Menu** bar.

Multiple documents open

- Click the **Close** button on the **Title** bar of the **Flyer_Brunch Tart** document - save changes when prompted

The other document remains open.

- With one document open, click the **Close** button on the **Menu** bar to close just the **Letter** document (clicking ☒ on the **Title** bar will also exit Word)

One document only open

- If prompted to save any changes, click **Yes**

Tip   To exit Word in one step with several documents open, from the **File** menu, select **Exit**

- On the **Title** bar, click **Maximise** ☐

Formatting Text

Apply character and paragraph formatting to enhance documents

Apply a different font **style**, **size** and **colour** ☐
Apply bold, underline and italics **enhancements** ☐
(Apply several **formats** in one action) ☐
Align and **justify** paragraphs ☐
Change line and paragraph **spacing** ☐
Set **tabs** and **indents** ☐
Create **bulleted** and **numbered** lists ☐
Apply **borders** to paragraphs ☐
Use the **Format Painter** to copy formats ☐
(**Remove** character and paragraph formats) ☐

What is a Font?

Font is the term used (in Word) to describe the **typeface** of text (the shape of the characters). MS Office installs many varied fonts that can be applied to your text. Extra fonts may be installed by other software applications as well.

Cleverly mixing different typefaces and applying enhancements - varying size with bold, underline and italics - can improve the presentation of your document and create the right effect for the reader.

> **Note** Too many different typefaces and enhancements can have the opposite effect. Your document may become confusing and off-putting.

Fonts

There are three important kinds of typeface:

♦ **Serif** type has curly edges to help guide the eye, like the text in this paragraph. Serif type is suitable for large blocks of text. Examples include Times New Roman, Book Antiqua and Century Schoolbook.

♦ **Sans serif** type is plainer looking, like the text in the header at the top of this page. Sans serif type is suitable for smaller blocks of text, such as text in columns and headings and in some cases for documents intended to be read on-screen. Examples include Arial, Gill Sans and Tahoma.

♦ **Cursive** type is designed to look like handwriting. It should be used sparingly.

Use a typeface appropriate to the type of documents you are creating. Look at other books, letters and magazines to guide you.

The Formatting Toolbar

The **Formatting** toolbar gives you quick access to the basic font tools. You can use it to change the font style, size and colour and apply enhancements such as bold, italics and underline.

Formatting toolbar

If you apply formatting changes at the insertion point, text typed from there on will have the new formatting applied. If you have **selected** text, changes will only apply to the selection.

Practice

- *Add text to the **Flyer** document from the previous lesson as shown below - if you didn't complete the last lesson, open **Flyer_Brunch Tart (Fonts)***

Chilli Meals™ combine the best home-cooked flavours with total ease of preparation for you and your staff. For our new meals, we've been inspired by the freshness and simplicity of Mediterranean cooking.

Chicken and Garlic Pasta
Brunch Tart
Ham and Onion Cream Tart
Tomato, Basil and Garlic Tart

Brunch Tart

This new addition to our popular range of filo pastry tarts will satisfy customers with the heartiest appetites.

We only use the best ingredients for the Brunch Tart:

The finest Cumberland Sausage
The crispest Norfolk Bacon
Hand-picked mushrooms
Organically grown tomatoes
All surrounded by a delicious tangy sauce

Like each of our Chilli Meals™, the Brunch Tart is prepared by hand. We give our meals the care and attention that your customers deserve.

A special Three-for-Two Introductory Offer* is available to the first 100 customers to place an order in December 2000.

If you don't already have a Customer Account with us, to order simply phone 0800 540 540 to speak to a Sales Advisor, or buy online at our website www.joechillis.com

* Offer applies to two units per customer

Change the Font Style and Size

The **Font** list box on the **Formatting** toolbar contains a list of the font styles available on your PC.

Fonts that have the letters **TT** before them are called **True Type** fonts. True Type fonts are designed to match the screen display with what is printed. Fonts that are not True Type may look different when printed.

To change the font

- Select the whole document

- On the **Formatting** toolbar, click the arrow on the **Font** box

Drop-down type list

A list of typefaces available on your PC is displayed. The most recently used typeface appears at the top of the list and you can see what each style looks like.

- Select the **Book Antiqua** typeface

To change the font size

Fonts can be scaled in size using a measurement of **points**. 72 points (72 pt) will produce lines of text that are 1 inch (2.54 cm) in height. Typically 10-12 point fonts are used for body text.

- With the whole document still selected, on the **Formatting** toolbar, click the arrow on the **Size** box

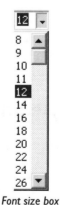

Font size box

- Select **12** to change the font size to 12 pt

Tip   Alternatively, type a font size into the box (any whole number between I and 1638) then press Enter.

Change the Font Colour

If you have a colour printer, you can use font colours to create attractive looking documents. Coloured text will print as shades of grey on a non-colour printer.

To change the font colour

- Select the character(s) you want to format - press Ctrl + A to select the whole document

- On the **Formatting** toolbar, click the arrow on the **Font Color** button

The **Font Color** menu is displayed.

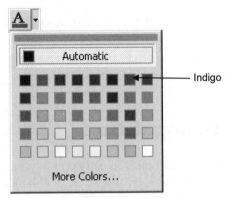

Font Color menu

- Point to each chip to see the name of the colour

- Select **Indigo** (top row, second from right)

Tip   Click **More Colors...** to select from a wider range of colours or mix a custom colour using specific values.

Font Enhancements

Basic font enhancements are easily applied using the toolbar or SpeedKeys.

Click	Or Press	To Apply
B	`Ctrl`+`B`	**Bold**
I	`Ctrl`+`I`	*Italics*
<u>U</u>	`Ctrl`+`U`	<u>Underline</u>

To apply enhancements

- Select the text "Chilli Meals" in the first paragraph

- Set the selected text to *italics*

- Select the text "www.joechillis.com" and <u>underline</u> it

The Font Dialogue Box

Using the **Font** dialogue box, you can apply several font enhancements at once. You can also access a greater range of enhancements, including ~~strikethrough~~, superscript, subscript, shadow, Outline, embossed and SMALL CAPS text. You can also preview effects before applying them.

ECDL Use of these additional enhancements is not required by the syllabus.

To apply several font enhancements at once

- At the top of the document, press `Enter` to insert a new paragraph

- Press `↑` to move back to the first paragraph

Note that the paragraph is formatted with italics. This is because the cursor was next to characters formatted with italics when you pressed `Enter`.

- From the **Format** menu, select **Font...** (*SpeedKey:* `Ctrl`+`D`)

The **Font** dialogue box is displayed.

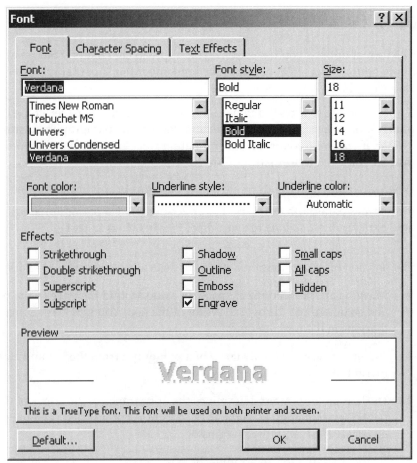

Font dialogue box

- Set the options shown above (the **Font color:** is **Gold**)

The **Preview** panel will display the selected options on either the font name or currently selected text.

- Click **OK**

Tip To keep the selected settings as standard for all new documents click the **Default...** button.

- Type New Ready Meals from Joe Chillis
- Save the document

Apply Alignment and Justification Options

The format options you have seen so far apply to **characters**. You can also apply options that affect **paragraphs**. Remember that a paragraph may be a character, a word, a line or multiple lines.

If you are going to format **one** paragraph, you do not *have* to select the entire paragraph, simply position the insertion point in the paragraph you want to format. If you want to format **several** paragraphs, click-and-drag through the text you want to format.

When you press ⌐Enter⌐ to create a new paragraph, any formats applied to the *previous* paragraph are carried over. If you delete a paragraph mark, the new paragraph retains the formatting of the *first* block of text.

The position of paragraphs on a page are determined by several factors:

♦ **Margins** are the amount of space set aside around the edge of the page and so determine the overall width of the text. You will learn about margins in the next lesson.

♦ **Indents** determine the distance of a paragraph from the left and right margins.

♦ **Horizontal alignment** determines the appearance of the edges of the paragraph: left aligned, right aligned, centred or justified (where both edges are flush with the margins).

♦ **Vertical alignment** determines the position of text on the page relative to the top and bottom margins (for example, the title page on the front cover of a report could be centred between the top and bottom margins and so appear in the middle of the page).

To display margin guides

As well as viewing the hidden text markers, when working with paragraphs, it is quite helpful to be able to see where the margins are on the page.

• Switch to **Print Layout** view if necessary then from the **Tools** menu, select **Options** and click the **View** tab

• Under **Print and Web Layout options**, make sure the **Text boundaries** box is checked then click **OK** - dotted margin guides will appear on the page (these do not print out)

To align text horizontally

Text can be aligned between the left and right margins in the following ways: left, right, centred or fully justified.

When text is left aligned, text aligns on the left margin with a ragged right margin.	When text is right aligned, text aligns on the right margin with a ragged left margin.	When text is centred it is evenly centred between the left and right margins with ragged left and right margins.	When text is fully justified it aligns on both the left and right margins (Extra spaces are automatically inserted to spread the words out, except on the last line of a paragraph).

Example of paragraph alignment

- Click in the heading you just created then click each toolbar button, leaving the paragraph **centred**

Click	Or Press	To Align
≣	Ctrl + L	Left
≣	Ctrl + E	Centre
≣	Ctrl + R	Right
≣	Ctrl + J	Justified

Change Line and Paragraph Spacing

When you change the **line spacing** of text, you increase the white space between individual lines in a paragraph.

This paragraph is single-spaced. This paragraph is single-spaced. This paragraph is single-spaced. This paragraph is single-spaced. This paragraph is single-spaced.	This paragraph is one-and-a-half-spaced. This paragraph is one-and-a-half-spaced. This paragraph is one-and-a-half-spaced.	This paragraph is double-spaced. This paragraph is double-spaced. This paragraph is double-spaced. This paragraph is double-spaced.

Example of paragraph line spacing

To change line spacing using the keyboard

- Select the paragraphs for which you want to change line spacing then press the appropriate SpeedKey

Press	To Apply
`Ctrl` + `1`	Single line spacing
`Ctrl` + `2`	Double line spacing
`Ctrl` + `5`	1.5 line spacing

- Test the different options on the title but leave the paragraph set to single line spacing

To alter the white space before and after a paragraph

You can also add space between **paragraphs**.

- With the insertion point blinking in the title, from the **Format** menu, select **Paragraph...**

- Enter a measurement in the **Before:** box to set the spacing to be included at the beginning of each paragraph - leave this set to **0 pt**

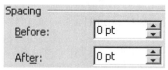

Paragraph dialogue box - paragraph spacing boxes

- In the **After:** box, use the spin controls or type to set the spacing to **24 pt** then click **OK**

Tip   Clicking on the up or down arrows changes the number by **6 points** each time, but you can type any whole number (between **0** and **1584**). **12pt** is equivalent to one line.

Practice

- *Format the "Brunch Tart" subheading using any options you think appropriate*

- *Remove blank paragraphs from the document, applying Space Before and Space After to paragraphs instead*

- *Save the document*

Indent Text

Indents are the positions where text begins and ends on a line relative to the page margins. Indenting is a way of offsetting a paragraph from the rest of the text, creating different indents for the first line or all lines in the selected paragraph(s).

Page margins are indicated at each end of the Ruler bar by dark shading. The white space in between is the normal typing space.

The indents for the selected paragraph are also indicated on the horizontal Ruler bar. The left indent symbols are two triangles and a rectangular box. The right indent symbol is a single triangle.

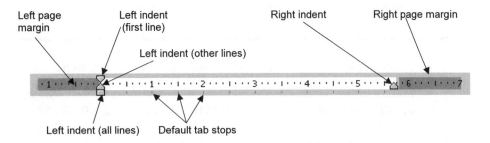

Horizontal Ruler bar

Tip   If you cannot see the horizontal ruler, from the **View** menu, select **Ruler**.

As well as setting text in from the margin, indents can extend **into** both the left and right margin areas. There are also two special types of indent. A **hanging** indent means that the first line of text begins to the left of the rest of the paragraph. A **first line** indent means that the first line begins to the right of the rest of the paragraph.

To change the measurement units

You can set the units used to measure indents, tabs, margins, paper size and so on, to centimetres, millimetres, inches, points or picas. The settings apply in all Word's dialogue boxes and on the rulers.

- From the **Tools** menu, select **Options** then click the **General** tab

- From the **Measurement units:** list box, select the unit to use (you will see units given in both centimetres and inches in this course)

- Click **OK**

To indent text using the Ruler bar

- Drag the indent markers to the required position

Drag	To Set
▽	The left indent - first-line only
△	The left indent - all other lines
□	The left indent - all lines
△	The right indent

> **Tip**   Selecting the indent markers can be quite difficult. If you click in the wrong place, you will probably create a **tab stop** (see 233). Delete the tab stop and try again.

- Select all the text from the "Brunch Tart" subheading to the end

- Practise using the markers until you are confident with them, leaving the **left** and **right** indents set in from the margin by 1 cm (½")

To indent text to tab stops ☺

Each document has a series of default **tab stops**, indicated as grey lines on the Ruler bar. You can indent text to these tab stops.

- o On the **Formatting** toolbar, click **Decrease Indent** ⊏ (*SpeedKey:* Ctrl + Shift + M), or **Increase Indent** ⊐ (*SpeedKey:* Ctrl + M)

The text is indented to the previous or next tab stop.

OR

- o Press the Tab key to create a first line indent to the first tab stop

- o Press Backspace remove the hanging indent or press twice to remove the indent completely

> **Note**   If the Tab or Backspace keys do not work as described above, select **Tools**, **Options**, **Edit** tab and check the **Tabs and backspace set left indent** box.

Practice

- *Indent the last line of text to the first tab stop*

Set Tabs

Tabs are used to align lists, indexes, and columns of numbers. Pressing the
Tab key inserts a hidden text tab character (→), which moves the insertion
point to the next **tab stop.** There are default tab stops every ½" (1.27 cm).
You can also set manual tab stops.

Tab types

Text can be aligned to the tab stop in different ways.

Bar	Left	Centre	Right	Decimal	Bar
	123	123	123	£123.00	
	48484	48484	48484	£48,484.25	
	Tom	Richard	Sam	-123	
	Letitia	Sue	Constance	(123)	

Decimal tabs line up numbers on the decimal point. Where whole negative
numbers are entered with parentheses, for example **(123)**, the closing bracket
will align on the decimal tab position.

Tab stops can be set, moved and deleted on the **Ruler** bar using the mouse.
Each of the five tab alignment styles can be selected by clicking on the **Tab
Alignment** button at the far left of the Ruler bar.

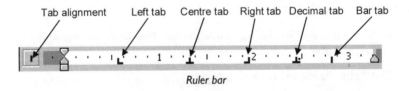

Tab alignment · Left tab · Centre tab · Right tab · Decimal tab · Bar tab

Ruler bar

Tip Tabs can be useful in some circumstances, but are quite difficult to
work with. If you want to create columns and rows of data in your
document consider using a table instead (see page 267).
If you are creating a tabbed list, remember to select **all** the
paragraphs to format before setting or altering the tab stops.

To set tabs ①

The following instructions are for reference. A practice exercise follows at
the end of the Tabs topic.

o   Select the paragraph(s) for which tabs are to be set

o   Click the **Tab Alignment** button at the far left of the **Ruler** bar until
the correct tab alignment button is displayed

Click To	To Set
L	A left tab
⊥	A centre tab
⅃	A right tab
⊥	A decimal tab
▮	A bar tab

- Click the **Ruler** bar at the required position for the tab

To delete a tab marker ①

o Select the paragraphs containing the tabs to be deleted then drag the tab marker up or down off the **Ruler** bar

To move a tab marker ①

o Select the paragraph(s) containing the tabs to move then drag the tab marker to the required position

To define tab settings ①

The **Tabs** dialogue box lets you set tab stops more accurately. You can also change the default tabs.

o Select the text to change tab stops for then from the **Format** menu, select **Tabs...**

The **Tabs** dialogue box is displayed.

o If necessary, remove existing tab stops with the **Clear** or **Clear All** buttons

o In the **Tab stop position:** box, enter the ruler position for the tab

o Choose an option button from the **Alignment** panel

o Click **Set**

Note Remember to click **Set** for each tab stop - just clicking **OK** will not apply the new setting.

o Define other tab stops if required

o To change the default tab stops, type the required setting in the **Default Tab stops:** box or select the new setting with the arrow keys

o Click **OK**

ECDL with MS Office 2000

Practice

- *Edit the list of products to create a tabbed list showing amounts and prices (as shown below)*

> → Chicken·and·Garlic·Pasta→ 12x330·gms→ £21.45¶
> → Brunch·Tart→8x → £13.80¶
> → Ham·and·Onion·Cream·Tart → 8x → £14.00¶
> → Tomato,·Basil·and·Garlic·Tart → 8x → £11.80¶

Note If pressing `Tab` at the start of the line sets an indent rather than inserting a tab stop, select **Tools**, **Options**, **Edit** tab and uncheck the **Tabs and backspace set left indent** box.

- *Alter the tab stops to use a bar, left, right and decimal tab stop respectively*

- *Use the tab stop positions shown below*

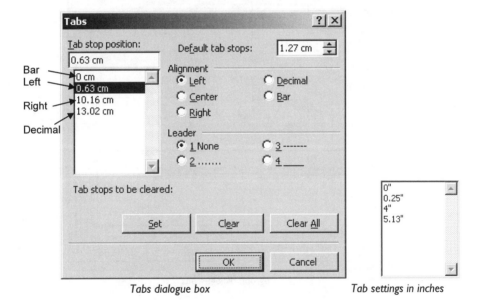

Tabs dialogue box   Tab settings in inches

The completed list should look like this:

→ Chicken·and·Garlic·Pasta	→	12x330·gms →	£21.45¶
→ Brunch·Tart	→	8x →	£13.80¶
→ Ham·and·Onion·Cream·Tart	→	8x →	£14.00¶
→ Tomato,·Basil·and·Garlic·Tart	→	8x →	£11.80¶

- *Save the document when you have finished*

The Paragraph Dialogue Box

The **Paragraph** dialogue box contains options to change all of the paragraph layout settings. You can use it to set several options at once, use more precise measurements or to set more advanced options for indents and spacing.

To change paragraph settings from the Paragraph dialogue box ①

This topic is included for reference - there is no exercise to complete.

   o From the **Format** menu, select **Paragraph...**

The **Paragraph** dialogue box is displayed.

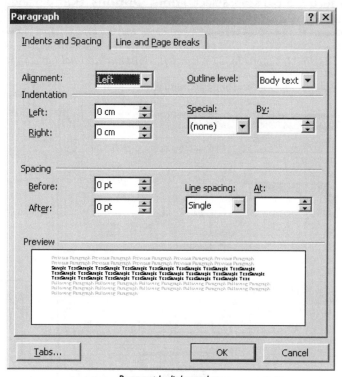

Paragraph dialogue box

   o Select the options to apply

The **Preview** panel will display either a text example or any highlighted text from the document with the selected options.

   o Click **OK**

Note Access **Tabs** by clicking the **Tabs** button in the **Paragraph** dialogue box.

Use Bulleted and Numbered Lists

A list of items is much more distinctive if each line starts with a bullet. You can select from a wide variety of characters to use as the bullet or you can use numbering.

To apply bullets and numbering from the Formatting toolbar

- Select the list of ingredients for the Brunch Tart
- Click the **Numbering** button ▤ then the **Bullets** button ▤

Tip Where sequential numbering is required but not all paragraphs are to be numbered, select all of the paragraphs starting from the one where numbering begins to the one where numbering ends. Apply numbering to all of the paragraphs, then switch it off on the paragraphs where it is not required by selecting the paragraph(s) and clicking the **Numbering** button.

To apply bullets or numbering from the menu

- With the list still selected, from the **Format** menu, select **Bullets and Numbering**

The **Bullets and Numbering** dialogue box is displayed.

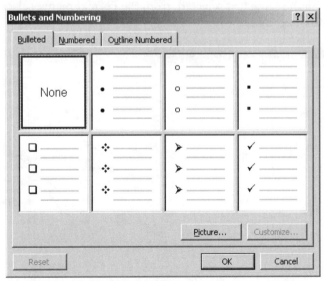

Bulleted dialogue box

- Select the **Bulleted** or **Numbered** tab and choose a style you think appropriate then click **OK**

Add Borders

Borders can be added to paragraphs, character selections and the page. You can apply lines to any or all sides of a paragraph or page, but characters can only have borders added all the way around.

To add borders using the Border toolbar

- Select the text from "This new addition" to "www.joechillis.com"

- Click the down arrow on the **Border** button - the **Borders** toolbar is displayed

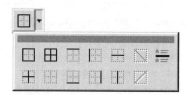

- Experiment with different buttons to change the position of the line or border (for example, top, bottom, left, right, or outline)

- On completion select the **No Border** button

To add borders using the menu

- With the same text selected, from the **Format** menu, select **Borders and Shading...**

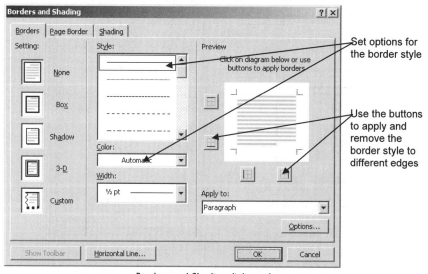

Borders and Shading dialogue box

- On the **Borders** tab, from the **Setting:** panel, select a border style (**Box**)
- From the **Style:** list, select a line style (**dotted**)
- From the **Color:** list box, select a border colour (**Gold**)
- From the **Width** list box, select a line thickness (**2 ¼ pt**)

Tip The **Apply to:** list box lets you select whether to apply the border around characters in the selection (**Text**) or around paragraphs.

Your chosen settings are displayed in the **Preview** panel.

- Click the **Preview** picture or the option buttons around it to customise the border - leave borders around the edges of the selection
- Click **OK**

Brunch Tart

This new addition to our popular range of filo pastry tarts will satisfy customers with the heartiest appetites.

We only use the best ingredients for the Brunch Tart:

- ✓ The finest Cumberland Sausage
- ✓ The crispest Norfolk Bacon
- ✓ Hand-picked mushrooms
- ✓ Organically grown tomatoes
- ✓ All surrounded by a delicious tangy sauce

Like each of our *Chilli Meals*™, the Brunch Tart is prepared by hand. We give our meals the care and attention that your customers deserve.

A special Three-for-Two Introductory Offer* is available to the first 100 customers to place an order in December 2000.

If you don't already have a Customer Account with us, to order simply phone 0800 540 540 to speak to a Sales Advisor, or buy online at our website www.joechillis.com

---

Note If your paragraphs have separate borders (for example if the bulleted paragraphs are in a separate box) you need to adjust the indents to make them the same as the rest of the text. Select the bulleted paragraphs and drag the **First Line Indent** into line with the other paragraphs.

Practice

You can apply a border to the edge of the page as well. If there are multiple pages in the document, the border will appear on every page.

- *Use the **Page Border** tab to create a border on the top and bottom edges of the page*

- *Use an appropriate **A̲rt:** border effect, such as the one shown below*

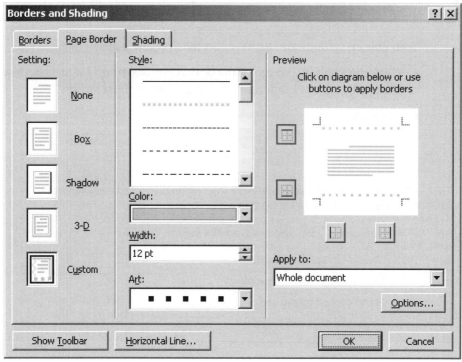

Applying a page border

- *Click **OK***
- *Save the document*

Use the Format Painter

The **Format Painter** is a tool that allows you to copy formats from existing text and apply it to other text in your document. This saves you having to remember which font, size, colour, line spacing and so on to use.

To copy enhancements

- Select the italic text "Chilli Meals" in the first paragraph

- On the **Formatting** toolbar, click **Format Painter** [icon] (*SpeedKey:* [Ctrl]+[Shift]+[C])

- Select the other occurrence of "Chilli Meals" (below the ingredients list) (*SpeedKey:* [Ctrl]+[Shift]+[V])

The text you select is formatted with the enhancements you copied - note that because you only selected some characters, the **paragraph** formatting is *not* copied.

> **Note** To copy enhancements to more than one piece of text, double-click the **Format Painter** button before copying the formats.
> After you have finished copying the enhancements click the **Format Painter** button again (*SpeedKey:* [Esc]) to switch it off.

- Save and close the document

Remove Formats

To remove all text enhancements ①

You can remove all character and paragraph formatting from text at one time. The text will revert to the default.

- o Select the text containing the enhancements to be removed

- o Press [Ctrl]+[Space Bar] to remove character formatting

- o Press [Ctrl]+[Q] to remove paragraph formatting

Setting Up a Document

Set the page layout, add headers and footers and proof the document

Lesson 17

Set the page **size** and **orientation** □
Set the page **margins** □
Insert **page breaks** and use **hyphenation** □
Apply **styles** to format a document □
Use the **Find and Replace** tool □
Insert and format **headers** and **footers** □
Insert document **fields** (page number, author, date...) □
Use the **Spelling and Grammar Checker** □

Modify Document Setup

When you start a new document, one of the first decisions you need to make is the **size** and **orientation** of the paper that it will be printed on.

Orientation is the direction of the paper when printing. Text is normally printed in **portrait** orientation with the short sides of the paper at the top and bottom. When the long sides are at the top and bottom the orientation is called **landscape**.

Portrait   Landscape

Depending on the printer attached to your computer you may be able to use different **sizes** of paper. Standard paper in the UK is A4 size.

You should setup the pages in your document to match the size and orientation of paper you are printing on, otherwise it may not print out correctly.

To change page orientation and paper size

- Open the document called **Employee Handbook**

- From the **File** menu, select **Page Setup**...

- Select the **Paper Size** tab

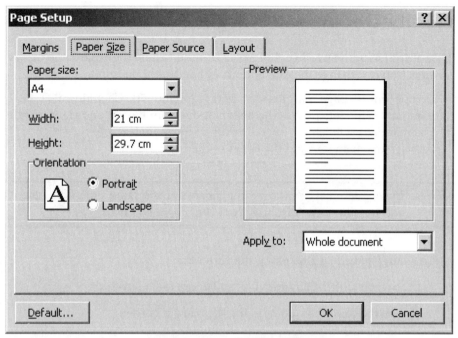

Page Setup - Paper Size dialogue box

You can use the **Paper size:** list box, to select a standard paper size, or enter custom page dimensions in the **Width:** and **Height:** boxes.

- Leave the paper size set to **A4**

- From the **Orientation** panel, select the **Portrait** option

The **Preview** panel displays the effect of the paper size and orientation settings.

- Click **OK**

Tip   To keep the selected settings as standard for all new documents click the **Default...** button.

Note   To use different units of measurement, from the **Tools** menu, select **Options** and click the **General** tab. Click the drop-down arrow on the **Measurement units:** list box and select a unit.

Modify Document Margins

In **Print Layout** view, the white space around text on the page is the margin area. You can change the top, bottom, left and right margins.

Do not confuse page margins with paragraph indents. Changing a paragraph's indents pushes the text in or out from the left and right margins. The margins establish the overall width of the main text and the space between the main text and the edges of the page.

> **Note** Moving the margins moves the indents at the same time. The indents will stay the same distance from the margins as before.

To change page margins using the Ruler bar

- Switch to **Print Layout** view and zoom to **Page Width**

- On the **Ruler** bar, point to the left margin border

> **Tip** This is the border between the grey and white sections on the **Ruler** bar.

The pointer will change to a double-headed arrow and a ScreenTip is displayed.

Setting the left margin

- Click-and-drag the margin to the left by about 1 cm (½")

> **Note** It is quite difficult to position the mouse over the margin border when the indent marker is in the same place. Point to the bottom of the top triangle and watch for the double-headed arrow.

> **Tip** To see margin guides in **Print Layout** view, from the **Tools** menu, select **Options**. On the **View** tab make sure the **Text Boundaries** box is checked. The margin appears as a dotted outline.

To change page margins from the menu

- From the **File** menu, select **Page Setup...** and click the **Margins** tab

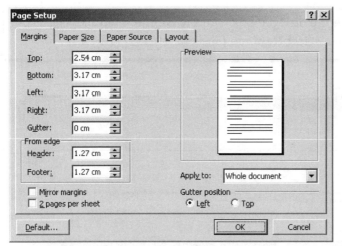

Page Setup - Margins dialogue box   *Measurements in inches*

- Set the **Top:**, **Bottom:**, **Left:** and **Right:** margins as shown above by clicking in the box and typing a value or by using the spin arrows to adjust the value

The **Preview** panel displays the effect of the new margin settings.

- Click **OK**

Use the Find and Replace Tool

The **Find and Replace** tool simplifies updating names or phrases or other text in a document.

To find a word or phrase

- From the **Edit** menu, select **Find** (*SpeedKey:* `Ctrl`+`F`) - the **Find and Replace** dialogue box is displayed.

- In the **Find what:** box, type `etc`

- Click the **Find Next** button - the word is highlighted in the document

---

Tip   Click the **Find Next** button again to find the next occurrence, or if the **Find and Replace** dialogue box is closed, use the **Browse** buttons (*SpeedKey:* `Shift`+`F4`).

To replace text

- In the **Find and Replace** dialogue box, click the **Replace** tab

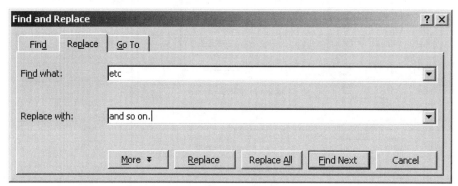

Find and Replace dialogue box

- Type the replacement text (and so on.) in the **Replace with:** box
- Select **Replace** to replace the selected word ("etc")

The word is replaced in the document and the next occurrence of the **Find what:** text is selected.

- Edit the **Replace with:** text to remove the period (.) then click **Replace**
- Repeat to replace the next "etc"
- When no more instances of the word are found, click **OK**
- In the **Find what:** box, type i.e. and in the **Replace with:** box type that is,
- Click **Replace All** to replace text throughout the document
- Click **OK** to remove the message box
- Close the **Find and Replace** dialogue box

Apply Existing Styles to a Document

A **style** is a collection of formats you can apply to text. A style can include attributes such as font type, size and enhancements, spacing, indents and borders. Styles enable you to format your documents quickly and consistently. Word contains a substantial number of different styles for creating headings, bulleted and numbered lists, indented text and so on.

There are two types of styles available for you to use: **paragraph** styles and **character** styles.

Paragraph styles can be applied to a minimum of one paragraph. They can store any of the formats in the **Paragraph, Tab** and **Border** dialogue boxes and can also contain character formatting.

Character styles can be applied to a minimum of one character. They can store any of the formats from the **Font** dialogue box.

To apply a paragraph style

- Select the paragraph "Attendance"

Note Do not select a group of characters in just one paragraph. If you do this, you will apply any character formats in the paragraph style to the selected text. You will not apply the paragraph style.

Drop-down list of available styles

- On the **Formatting** toolbar, click the arrow on the **Style** list box

A drop-down list is displayed, previewing the key formats associated with the styles available.

This Attribute	Represents
Style name indented	Whether text is indented negatively or positively from the left margin
Style name's appearance	The formatting of the style (Font sizes of less than 8pt and greater than 16pt are displayed as 8 or 16pt respectively)
Four horizontal lines	Left, right, centred or justified alignment
a (Underlined a)	A character style
¶ (Paragraph mark)	A paragraph style

- Select the **Heading 1** style

To apply styles using the menu

The **Style** list box only contains styles that you have already used. If you want to apply a new style, you must use the **Style** dialogue box.

- Select the title at the top of the page then from the **Format** menu, select **Style...**

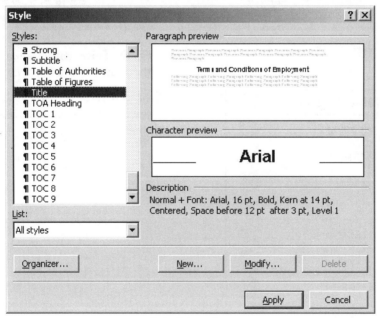

Style dialogue box

A list of styles is displayed. The letter **a** appears beside character styles.

- From the **List** list box, select **All styles** then from the **Styles:** list box, select **Title**

The formatting of the style is displayed in the preview panes.

- Click **Apply** - the style is applied to the selected text and is also added to the **Style** list box for future use

- *Continue to apply relevant styles to the document*

- *Use Heading 1 for text formatted in bold*

- *Use Heading 2 for text formatted with underlining*

- *Use Heading 3 for text formatted in italics*

- *Use indent, list and bullet list styles where appropriate*

- *Save the document regularly*

- *Return to the top of the first page in the document*

Add Headers and Footers to a Document

A **header** is space in the top margin. A **footer** is space in the bottom margin. Headers and footers are used to print the same information at the top and/or bottom of every page, such as titles and page numbers. You can put text and graphics in a header or footer.

To insert a header or footer

- From the **View** menu, select **Header and Footer**

Word switches to **Print Layout** view and displays the page header and the **Header and Footer** toolbar. A non-printing dashed line encloses the header and footer spaces. Text on the page is faded out.

Page header outline

- In the header, type `Joe Chillis Ltd. Employee Handbook`

Header and footer text is formatted using the same tools as any other text. Note that header text is formatted with **Header style**. You can also apply formatting to the text directly.

- Select the header text and change the font to **Arial 9 pt italic**, right-align the paragraph and apply a single-line top border

Insert Page Numbering

Automatic page numbers can be inserted in a header or footer. When pages are created or deleted in the document the numbering changes accordingly. The numbers can be formatted in a variety of styles (for example, Arabic or Roman).

To insert a page number

- To edit the footer, click **Switch Between Header and Footer** or simply scroll down to the footer area

- Change format options to **9 pt** and **centre** align then type `Page` (follow with a space)

> **Note** A ScreenTip will appear with the text "Page x of x". This is Word's AutoComplete tool. You can press `Enter` to accept the suggestion, but for this course simply ignore the tips.

- On the **Header and Footer** toolbar, click **Insert Page Number**

To format page numbers

At times you may want to use a different numbering format, such as Roman numerals or letters.

- On the **Header and Footer** toolbar, click **Format Page Number**

The **Page Number Format** dialogue box is displayed.

- From the **Number format:** list box, select the Roman numbering style (i, ii, iii)

- Click **OK**

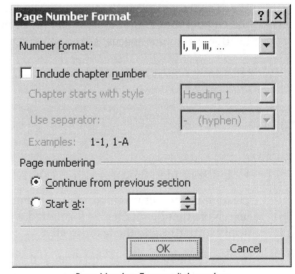

Page Number Format dialogue box

The Header and Footer toolbar

The toolbar buttons can be used to enter document information and control the way the headers and footers operate. Click the appropriate button for the action required.

Click	To
AutoText ▾	Insert AutoText. To insert the author's name, click the button then select **Author, Page #, Date**. You can delete the **Page #** and **Date** parts.
[⌗]	Insert the current page number at the insertion point. It is useful to type the word **Page** and leave a couple of spaces before inserting the number (for example, **Page 2**).
[⊞]	Insert the total number of pages in the document at the insertion point (for example, **Page 2 of 5**).
[⌗]	Display the **Page Number Format** dialogue box to set the page number formatting options.
[📅]	Insert the current date at the insertion point in the default format.
[🕐]	Insert the current time at the insertion point.
[▣]	**Show** or **Hide** the body text in the document. The body text normally appears faded while viewing headers and footers. This button hides it completely.
[▤]	Switch between the header and footer sections of the page.
Close	Close **Headers and Footers** view.

These buttons insert information as a **field**, which means that it is updated automatically.

- Make sure that the cursor is blinking after "Page i"

- Press Enter twice and change the formatting of the new paragraph to **left** align

- Type Prepared by *Your Name* on followed by a space

- On the **Header and Footer** toolbar, click **Insert Date** [📅]

- To return to the document click **<u>C</u>lose OR** double-click in the body text area

The **Header and Footer** toolbar is hidden and the document text is displayed.

Tip In Print Layout view a header/footer appears as dimmed text. You can edit it quickly by double-clicking.

Use the Spelling and Grammar Checker

Word's **Spelling and Grammar Checker** constantly tests your document to look for words and phrases that it does not recognise or thinks may be incorrect. This text is marked with a wavy line: a red line indicates a spelling error; a green line an error of grammar.

Not all words marked incorrect are errors. Word can only recognise words from its dictionary. Proper names and specialised words (jargon) that relate to your work can be added to a **Custom Dictionary** to prevent Word from marking them.

Word's Grammar Checker can be setup to test for Casual, Formal and Technical writing styles.

> **Note** Neither the Grammar checker or the Spell Checker are infallible (for example, they rarely pick up words that have been omitted). Also, they do not always make appropriate suggestions. You should always proofread your documents carefully before distributing them.

To use the automatic Spelling Checker

As you type, the **Spelling Checker** icon on the Status bar displays a pencil ⊞ . When errors are detected, the Spelling Checker icon displays a cross ⊞ and the errors are underlined with a wavy red line. This line is **hidden text** and does not print out. When no errors are detected the Spelling Checker icon displays a tick ⊞ .

- Position the insertion point somewhere in the first word marked incorrect ("Chillis")

- Double-click the **Spelling Checker** icon ⊞ **OR** right-click the misspelled word

The **Spelling Checker** shortcut menu is displayed.

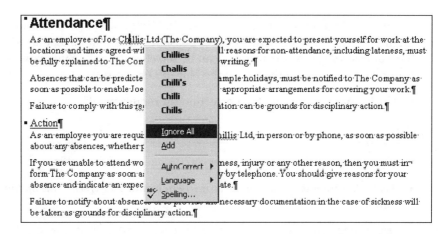

- You can select a correction from the top of the shortcut menu but in this case select **Ignore All** - the error markers are removed from both instances of "Chillis"

To use the Spelling Checker

You will often need to check the whole document or a section of text that has been added or amended. The **Spelling and Grammar** dialogue box works through selected text (or from the insertion point) and stops at each error.

- On the **Standard** toolbar, click **Spelling** ![ABC] OR from the **Tools** menu, select **Spelling and Grammar...** (*SpeedKey:* F7) OR right-click an incorrect word/phrase and from the shortcut menu, select **Spelling** or **Grammar** as appropriate

The **Spelling and Grammar** dialogue box is displayed.

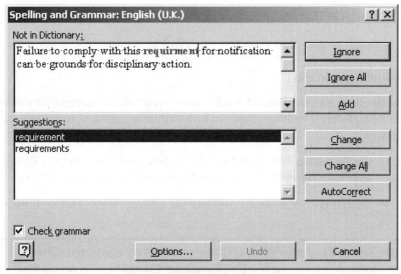

Spelling and Grammar dialogue box

The error is highlighted in red in the **Not in Dictionary:** box, and also highlighted in the document. A list of possible corrections is displayed in the **Suggestions:** box. Corrections can be selected from the **Suggestions:** list or made by editing the text in the **Not in Dictionary:** box.

- Click **Change** to accept the correction to "requirement"

Practice

- *Continue the spelling and grammar check to the end of the document*

- *For each word highlighted in the **Not in Dictionary:** box, select the option button to use*

Click	To
Change	Replace the misspelled word with the word you select from the **Suggestions** box, or with the correction you enter in the **Not in Dictionary:** box.
Change All	Change the first and all subsequent occurrences of the misspelled word with the word you select from the **Suggestions** box, or with the correction you enter in the **Not in Dictionary:** box.
Add	Add the word to the Custom dictionary.
Ignore	Leave the word unchanged, but stop at it the next time it is found.
Ignore All	Leave the word unchanged, and do not stop at it in any documents until you restart Word.
AutoCorrect	Add the misspelled word and its correction to the AutoCorrect list.
Options...	Set the writing style applied by the Grammar Checker.

Note that the spelling checker's suggestions are not always correct.

- *Save the document when you have finished*

To hide error markers

The Spelling and Grammar Checker can leave your document covered in red and green wavy lines. You can hide either type of line to tidy the screen display.

- On the **Status** bar, click the **right** mouse button on the **Spelling Checker** icon then select **Hide Spelling Errors** or **Hide Grammar Errors**

- To display errors again, reselect the option - leave both options on

Note To switch the Grammar Checker on or off check the **Check grammar** box in the **Spelling and Grammar** dialogue box.

Insert a Page Break into a Document

When text gets to the bottom of a page, Word inserts a **soft page break** to start a new page. In Print Layout view, each page is represented on-screen. In Normal view, soft page breaks are represented by a dotted line. They appear, disappear and move up or down the text depending entirely on the page setup and formatting options used.

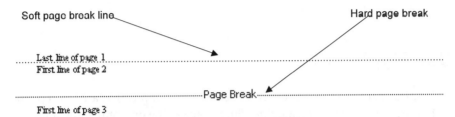

Example of soft and hard page breaks in Normal view

To *control* where a page ends you can insert a **hard page break**. Hard page breaks are identified by the words **Page Break** on the dotted line. Page break markers are always visible in **Normal** view, but are only visible in **Print Layout** view when the **Show/Hide** button is on ¶ .

To insert a hard page break

- Switch to **Normal** view and click after the first soft page break (this may appear somewhere around "Leave of Absence" depending on the styles you have applied)

- From the <u>I</u>nsert menu, select <u>B</u>reak then <u>P</u>age Break (*SpeedKey:* `Ctrl` + `Enter`) to replace the soft page break with a hard one

To delete an inserted (hard) page break

Only hard page breaks can be deleted. Soft page breaks created automatically by Word cannot be deleted.

- Select the page break marker

- Press `Delete` - the soft page break marker re-appears

- *Work through the remainder of the document inserting hard page breaks where appropriate*

- *You might find it easier to work in Print Layout view and to use Zoom to view one or more pages at the same time*

- *Try to keep body text on the same page as its heading*

- *Save the document*

Use Hyphenation

Hyphens are used to create even lines of text. Long words are often pushed to the next line, creating a lot of white space at the **end** of the line if the paragraph is **left aligned** or a lot of white space **within** the paragraph if it is **justified**.

Hyphens can be inserted to break words that do not fit the end of a line into two parts. Hyphenation needs to be used with care. If hyphens occur on every other line, your document will be very hard to read.

In Word, you can hyphenate text manually or automatically. You can also insert non-breaking hyphens (when you want to keep all parts of a word that is actually **spelled** with a hyphen on the same line).

To hyphenate a document

- Move to the start of the document then from the **Tools** menu, select **Language** and then **Hyphenation...**

The **Hyphenation** dialogue box is displayed.

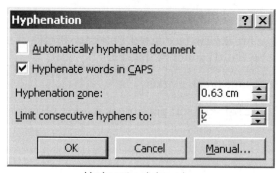

Hyphenation dialogue box

- In the **Hyphenation zone:** box, enter the amount of space (**.63 cm** or ½") to allow between the end of the last word in a line and the right margin

Tip   To reduce the number of hyphens, make the hyphenation zone
wider. To reduce the raggedness of the right margin, make the
hyphenation zone narrower.

- In the **Limit consecutive hyphens to:** box, enter **2** as the number of
  consecutive lines that can be hyphenated

- Click **Manual...**

It is quite likely that the **Hyphenation** feature has not been installed. If
so, a dialogue box is displayed.

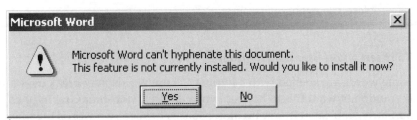

Installer message box

- You will need your **Office 2000 Setup Disk** to install the feature - seek
  assistance from your IT support person or refer to the appendix on
  page 687

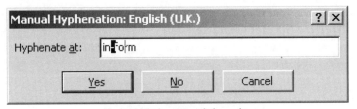

Manual Hyphenation dialogue box

If you want to insert a hyphen in the location Word proposes, click **Yes**.
To insert the hyphen in another part of the word, use the arrow keys to
move the insertion point to that location and then click **Yes**.

If you make a lot of changes to the document regularly, you can make
Word hyphenate it automatically.

- Click **Cancel** to abandon the manual hyphenation then select **Tools**,
  Language and **Hyphenation...** again

- Click the **<u>A</u>utomatically hyphenate document** check box then **OK**

Word will now add and remove hyphens using the options you set.

- Save and close the document

Note If you do not want to apply automatic hyphenation to a particular block of text, select the text, and from the **F<u>o</u>rmat** menu, select **<u>P</u>aragraph**. Click the **Line and <u>P</u>age Breaks** tab, and then select the **<u>D</u>on't Hyphenate** check box.
To remove automatic hyphenation, uncheck the **<u>A</u>utomatically hyphenate document** check box. To remove manual hyphens, delete the hyphen character (‐).

To insert a non-breaking hyphen ①

Some words are spelled with a hyphen. These words may break over a line. If you do not want this to happen, you can use a **non-breaking** hyphen. Similarly, you can use non-breaking spaces to keep two words together.

- o To insert a non-breaking hyphen, press `Ctrl`+`Shift`+`-`

- o To insert a non-breaking space, press `Ctrl`+`Shift`+`Space Bar`

OR

- o From the **<u>I</u>nsert** menu, select **<u>S</u>ymbol...** and select the space or hyphen from the **Special Characters** tab

Printing a Document

Preview and print a document

Preview a document on-screen ☐
Use basic print **options** ☐
Print a document ☐

Preview a Document

Print Preview is designed for checking the overall layout of a document before printing it. Like Print Layout view you can see one or more pages, zoom in or out and adjust margins. You can also edit text. Unlike Print Layout view you cannot show the non-printing characters such as paragraph, tab and space bar markers.

To preview a document

- Open the **Employee Handbook** document

- On the **Standard** toolbar, click the **Print Preview** button 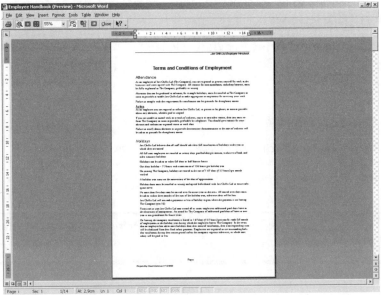 **OR** from the **File** menu, select **Print Preview** (*SpeedKey:* Ctrl + F2)

Print Preview

The **Print Preview** toolbar is displayed above the document.

Tip   To zoom in on the document, click on the area to view. Click again anywhere to zoom out.

Practice

- *Preview the document using the tools on the toolbar*

Click	To
 🖨	Print the document.
🔍	1. Click anywhere on the previewed page to magnify that section of it. Click again to turn off the magnification.
🔍	2. Click the magnification button to switch between magnifying the preview and editing the document.
 ▣	Preview a single page at a time.
 ▦	Preview multiple pages. Click the button and select the number of pages from the menu.
40% ▼	Zoom.
 ▥	Display or hide the Ruler bar.
 ▦	Shrink to fit. Reduces the font size of your text to squeeze it onto one less page.
Close	Close the **Print Preview** window.
 ▶?	Get Help.

- *View the document 2 pages at a time*
- *Use* 🔍 *to switch to edit mode and adjust page breaks if necessary*
- *Click* **Close** *to return to the document*

Tip   Press `Ctrl` + `F2` to switch between **Print Preview** and your document.

Use Basic Print Options

There are a variety of different options for printing a document, ranging from clicking a button to print a copy quickly to printing multiple copies of a range of pages.

The following steps are for reference. There is a practice exercise on printing at the end of the topic.

To print the whole document ☝

   o   On the **Standard** toolbar, click **Print** 🖨

The **whole** document is printed using the default printing options.

OR

   o   From the **File** menu, select **Print** (*SpeedKey:* `Ctrl` + `P`)

The **Print** dialogue box is displayed.

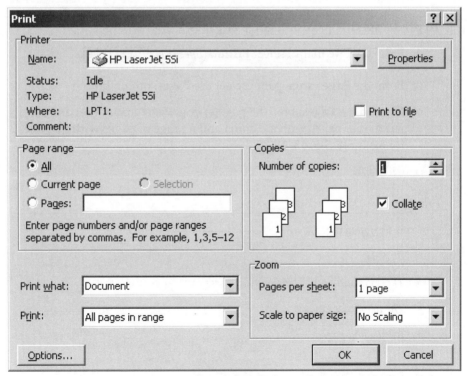

Print dialogue box

   o   From the **Page range** panel, select the **All** button

   o   Click **OK**

To print selected text ①

Rather than printing the whole document, you can print only a selected part of it. The selection may be just a few words, sentences or paragraphs, or may extend across several pages.

o   Select the text you want to print

o   From the **File** menu, select **Print...** (*SpeedKey:* `Ctrl`+`P`)

o   From the **Page range** panel, click the **Selection** option button

o   Click **OK**

To print the current page ①

o   Position the **insertion point** anywhere on the page to print then from the **File** menu, select **Print...** (*SpeedKey:* `Ctrl`+`P`)

o   From the **Page range** panel, select the **Current Page** option button

o   Click **OK**

To print a specific page or a range of pages ①

o   From the **File** menu, select **Print...** (*SpeedKey:* `Ctrl`+`P`)

o   From the **Page range** panel select the **Pages:** option button

o   Enter in the **Pages:** box, the page(s) you wish to print - separate individual pages with a comma and a range of pages with a hyphen, for example, **5-9, 13, 15-20**

o   Click **OK**

Practice

Print the following:

- *Page 12*

- *The "Training and Development" section*

- *The whole document*

- *All the odd pages*

- *Save and close the document*

- *Open the **Letter_New Product Offer** document and print a copy to refer to for the next lesson*

- *Close the document*

Cancel Printing

When you print, Word creates a temporary file on the hard disk called a **print** file. This collects all of the information to be printed then sends it to the printer. While the print file is being created you can cancel the print.

To show the progress of the print file a **Printing** icon is displayed on the Word Status bar in place of the Spelling Checker icon. A counter lists each page as it is sent to the print file.

ECDL This topic is not required for the syllabus, but it may save you from wasting a lot of paper.

To cancel printing from Word ⊕

o   Double-click the printer icon on the **Status** bar 🖨 6

The print is immediately cancelled.

OR

o   From the **File** menu, select **Print...** (*SpeedKey:* [Ctrl]+[P])

The **Background Printing** message box is displayed.

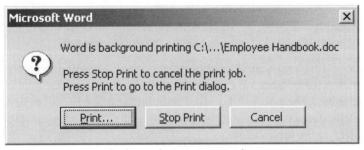

Background printing message box

o   Click **Stop Print**

Note You can also cancel printing from the Windows Print Queue, but if the print file you want to cancel is still being created and the **Printer** icon 🖨 6 is visible on the **Status** bar you should cancel it from Word or Word will continue to create a print file.

Templates

Use templates to create standard documents quickly

Choose an appropriate document **template** ☐
Work within a template ☐

Choose a Template to Create a Document

Word uses two types of file - **documents** and document **templates**. You have already created **document** files. These store a piece of work, such as a letter or a report.

You have also used a **document template**, though you may not have realised it. A template is a "pattern" for a document that you can use repeatedly. For example, you might base each letter you create on a **Letter** document template.

A template contains the default **Page Setup**, **styles** and other **formatting** to use in a document. It can also contain default text and graphics.

Every Word document is based on a document template. The template you will probably use most is called **Normal**. When you start Word, the new blank document created is based on the **Normal** template.

Word contains a number of additional templates to help you create documents. Templates are divided by document type under tabs in the **New** dialogue box. The range of tabs and templates available will depend on how your system is setup, but some of the commonly used types of document are explained in the table below.

Select	To
Letters & Faxes	Create letters and faxes in various styles
Memos	Create memos in various styles
Reports	Create a marketing or business report
Publications	Create a brochure, manual or thesis
Web Pages	Create pages for display on the world wide web with various different layouts
Other Documents	Create a resume (CV) or a calendar

> **Note** The templates available by default are developed for the US market and so might not fit your requirements very well. However, your company may have created its own templates for you to use.

To create a new document based on a template

- From the **File** menu, select **New...**

The **New** dialogue box is displayed.

- Click the tab containing the type of document you want to create (select **Letters & Faxes**)

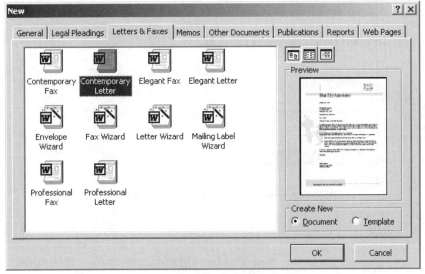

New document dialogue box

- Select the best template for the type and style of document you are creating (select the **Contemporary Letter**)

The document template style is displayed in the **Preview** panel.

> **Note** If no preview is displayed, the template is not fully installed. You will need your Office 2000 Setup Disk to use the template.

- Select the **Document** option button in the **Create New** panel
- Click **OK**

> **Tip** **Wizard** templates display a series of dialogue boxes to help you customise the document and add text.

Work Within a Template

There are a wide variety of templates, from simple memos to complex brochures and reports. Most of the Office templates work on the basis that you click to replace standard text with your own. Templates created for you at work may simply contain the basic layout and formatting of the document though.

To work in a template

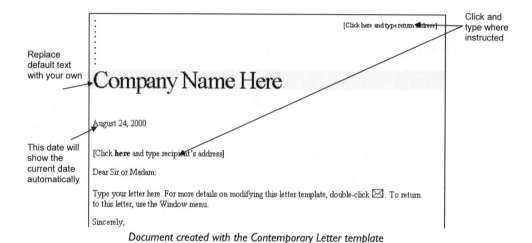

Document created with the Contemporary Letter template

Practice

- *Recreate the **Letter_New Product Offer** document using the template*

- *Use Copy and Paste to add text from the original document*

- *Make the return address* The Ranch, 42 Broadway, Maidenhead SL6 1LU

- *The slogan (at the bottom of the page) is "Fresh Food First"*

- *Apply any extra character or paragraph formatting you think appropriate*

- *Save the new letter as **Letter_New Product Offer (Formatted)***

- *Close any open documents*

> **Note** The letter template uses **text boxes** to hold some of the text. A text box is a drawing object, which you will learn about on page 279.

Tables

Create and format tables to improve the page layout

Create standard **tables** ☐
Change cell attributes ☐
Insert and delete **columns** and **rows** ☐
Add **borders** to a table ☐
Use the **AutoFormat** tool to apply table formatting ☐

Create a Table

A **table** consists of a series of **columns** and **rows** into which text and graphics can be entered. The intersection of a row and column is a **cell**. Tables are ideal for creating forms, lists or documents with a complex page layout.

To create a table using the toolbar

- Create a new document based on the **Blank Document** template

- Save the document as Timesheet

- Change the paper orientation to **Landscape** and adjust the view and zoom settings to **Page Width** in **Print Layout** view

- On the **Standard** toolbar, click **Insert Table** ⊞

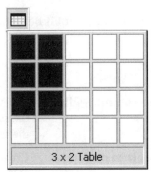

A menu is displayed allowing you to select the dimensions of the table.

- Drag over the menu to create a table 3 rows by 2 columns (as shown) then click the left mouse button

3 x 2 Table

Insert Table drop-down menu

Tip   If you make a mistake and create a table with too many or too few rows and columns, look at page 270 to find out how to modify it.

To create a table using the menu

- Press ⌈Enter⌋ below the first table to insert a paragraph then from the Table menu, select Insert then click Table...

The **Insert Table** dialogue box is displayed.

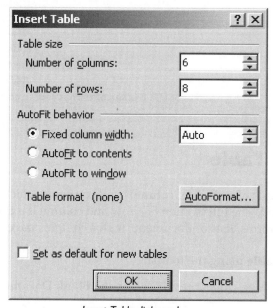

Insert Table dialogue box

- In the **Table size** panel, set the number of rows (8) and columns (6) that you want

- In the **AutoFit behavior** panel, select an option according to the table below

Select	To
Fixed column width	Create a table where the width of columns is fixed to the size you enter in the spin box. If you select Auto, the table will fill the space between document margins.
AutoFit to contents	Create a table where the columns will automatically resize to contain any text you type in them.
AutoFit to window	If you save your document as a web page, this option creates a table that will resize to fit in the web browser's window.

- Select **Fixed column width** and click **OK**

- Save the document

Select Parts of a Table

You can move around in a table by using the keyboard or by clicking on a cell with the mouse. With the mouse you can select whole columns, whole rows, blocks of cells, individual cells or text within a table.

To move the insertion point with the keyboard

Press	To
← → ↑ ↓	Move to the next column or row in blank cells, or move to the next character or line in text
Tab	Move right one cell, or add a new row when pressed in the bottom right cell
Shift + Tab	Move left one cell
Alt + Home	Move to the first cell in the same row
Alt + End	Move to the last cell in the row
Alt + Page Up	Move to the top cell in the column
Alt + Page Down	Move to the bottom cell in the column

To select in a table with the mouse

Mouse Pointer	Do This	To
I	Click over text, or to the right of the cell marker ¤ in a blank cell	Position the insertion point
I	Click-and-drag over the text only	Select text
⬈	Click in the left margin of the cell	Select a single cell
I ⬋	Click-and-drag over the cells	Select a group of cells
⬋	Click to the left of the first column or drag to select several columns	Select a whole row
↓	Click at the top of the column or drag to select several columns	Select a whole column

Practice

- Enter text in the table as shown below

Employee¤			¤			¤
NI·Number¤			¤			¤
Week·commencing¤			¤			¤

Day¤	Start·Time¤	Finish·Time¤	Hours·(Basic)¤	Hours·(Overtime)¤	Hours·(Break)¤	¤
Monday¤	¤	¤	¤	¤	¤	¤
Tuesday¤	¤	¤	¤	¤	¤	¤
Wednesday¤	¤	¤	¤	¤	¤	¤
Thursday¤	¤	¤	¤	¤	¤	¤
Friday¤	¤	¤	¤	¤	¤	¤
Saturday¤	¤	¤	¤	¤	¤	¤
Sunday¤	¤	¤	¤	¤	¤	¤

- Select the first column in the first table and format the text to **Arial 14 pt**

- Select the first row in the second table and format the text to **Arial 12 pt italic**

- Select the cells containing the days and make the text **bold**

Insert and Delete Columns and Rows

To insert and delete a column and/or row ①

o Select the same number of rows or columns as the number of rows or columns you want to insert

o On the **Tables and Borders** toolbar, click the down arrow on the **Insert Table** button ▦ ▾ then select an **Insert** command

OR

o From the **Ta̲ble** menu, select **I̲nsert** then select the appropriate command

OR

o Right-click the selected rows or columns and select an option

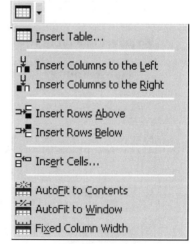

Table Insert menu

Practice

- Select both columns in the first table then from the **Ta̲ble** menu, select **I̲nsert** then **Columns to the R̲ight**

- Select the last row in the second table then choose **Ta̲ble, I̲nsert, Rows B̲elow**

To delete columns and rows

- Select the two columns you inserted in the first table

- From the **Table** menu, select **Delete** then **Columns OR** right-click the selection and select **Delete**

Change the Width of Columns and Rows

You can change the width/height of rows and columns in the table or change the way the contents fit in cells.

To change the width of columns

- Select the first column in the first table

- On the **Ruler** bar, point to the column grid box (level with the right-hand edge of the column)

- Hold down the Shift key then drag the box to the left, up to the edge of the word "commencing"

- Release the mouse button first followed by the Shift key

Note The Shift key keeps the table at the same overall size. If you did not hold down Shift, the right edge of the table would be dragged in as well.

Tip To make the columns in a table automatically fit the contents, from the **Table** menu, select **AutoFit** then **AutoFit to Contents**.

To change the height of rows

- Select the first row in the second table then click-and-drag the box down on the vertical ruler to make the row twice its current height

---

Note To change a column width or row height to a specific measurement, click in a cell then, from the **Table** menu, select **Table Properties** and click the **Row** or **Column** tab. Select the options you want.

To resize a table using the mouse

- In **Print Layout** view, point to the second table

A **Resize Table** handle is displayed on the bottom-right corner of the table.

- Move the cursor over the **Resize Table** handle

The cursor will change shape to show a double-headed arrow.

- Click-and-drag the table down and left to make the columns narrower and the rows taller by about 2 cm (½") each way

Note A dotted outline shows the table's new size.

- Save the document

Change the Alignment of a Table

You can use the normal Align commands to change the horizontal position of text relative to cell margins. You can also set the indents and spacing of text and paragraphs as normal.

In addition to this, you can apply horizontal **and** vertical alignments from the **Tables and Borders** toolbar. You can also change the **orientation** of text in a cell, so that it runs up or down instead of left to right.

To change the orientation of text in a cell

Cell alignment can be adjusted using the **Tables and Borders** toolbar.

- Display the **Tables and Borders** toolbar (right-click a toolbar and select **Tables and Borders** from the shortcut menu)

- Select the first row of the second table then on the **Tables and Borders** toolbar, click **Change Text Direction** until you get the direction shown below (click **2** times)

Day	Start Time	Finish Time	Hours (Basic)	Hours (Overti me)	Hours (Break)

Table text with vertical orientation

To change the vertical and horizontal alignment of text in a cell

Text in a table cell can be aligned between any edges of the cell using the **Alignment** button on the **Tables and Borders** toolbar.

If text is **oriented** vertically, the buttons adjust to show this.

- With the first row of the second table selected, on the **Tables and Borders** toolbar click the arrow on the **Align** button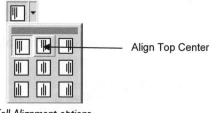

- Select **Align Top Center**

Align Top Center

Cell Alignment options

To change the alignment of a table relative to the margins

You can align the position of a table on the page just as you can a paragraph.

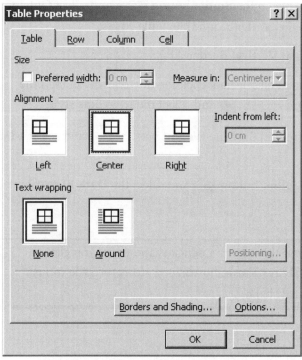

Table Properties dialogue box

- Click in the second table then from the **Table** menu, select **Table Properties**

- From the **Alignment** panel, select **Center** then click **OK**

The **Table Properties** dialogue box is also a convenient way to change table dimensions, borders and cell properties.

Apply Table Borders and Shading

When a table is created, Word includes a printing single-line border around each cell. You can apply and remove borders in a table in much the same way as with paragraph borders.

If you remove borders, gridlines on the screen will still identify the location of each cell, but do not print out.

You can apply borders and shading to a table using the **Format, Borders and Shading** command (see page 238) and also with the **Tables and Borders** toolbar.

To add borders and shading using the Tables and Borders toolbar

Tables and Borders toolbar

- Select both columns in the first table

- Click the down arrow on the **Border** button 🔲 ▾ and select **Outside Border** to remove the border around the table edges

- Remove the **Internal Vertical Border** ⊞

- Keeping the whole table selected, click the down arrow in the **Line Style** box [———————— ▾] and select the wavy line style

- Click the down arrow in the **Line Weight** box [1 ▾] and select a 1½ **pt** line

- Click the **Border Colour** button 🖌 and select the **Dark Blue** colour chip

---

Note If the mouse pointer changes to a pencil shape when you click buttons, click the **Draw Table** button 🖉 to return the mouse pointer to its normal shape.

- On the **Border** button, select the **Inside Horizontal Borders** button to apply the new line style

- Apply the same line to the **Bottom Border**

- Select the first column in the first table then click the down arrow in the **Shading Colour** box [icon] and select a shading colour of your own choice

---

Tip   You can also use the **Tables and Borders** toolbar to apply borders to paragraphs.

AutoFormat a Table

The **Table AutoFormat** tool creates a table with preset borders, shading and font effects. You can AutoFormat new and existing tables.

- Click in the second table then from the **Table** menu, select **Table AutoFormat...**

The **Table AutoFormat** dialogue box is displayed.

- From the **Formats:** list box, select a format to apply (select **Grid 8**)

- You can apply different options to the table by selecting or deselecting the check boxes (uncheck the **Font** and **AutoFit** boxes)

The results of the options you select are displayed in the **Preview** panel.

- Click **OK**

- Save and close the document

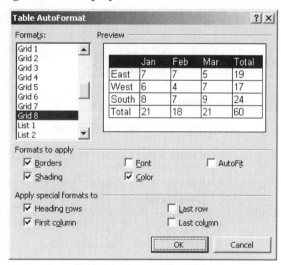

Table AutoFormat dialogue box

Tip   To format a new table quickly, click the **AutoFormat...** button in the **Insert Table** dialogue box.

Graphics

Improve a document by adding graphics and drawings

Lesson 21

Insert **clip art** in a document ☐
Import an **image file** into a document ☐
Add **AutoShapes** to a document ☐
Move and **resize** drawings and images ☐

Graphics are an important part of presenting a document effectively. Apart from using lines and shading, you can add a logo, use a graphic from an image library (clip art) or create a drawing.

Tip   Refer to the picture of the finished document on page 284 to help you complete this lesson.

Add an Image File to a Document

The **Microsoft Clip Gallery** contains a variety of pictures, sounds and photographs and video clips.

To insert clips

- Open the **Employee Handbook** document

- Create a page break before the "Attendance" heading

- Insert a new paragraph after the main heading "Terms and Conditions"

- With the insertion point in the new paragraph, from the **Insert** menu, select **Picture** then **Clip Art...**

The **Insert ClipArt** dialogue box is displayed. The Clip Gallery is divided into categories. You can browse for clips by clicking a category or enter search text to look for clips relating to a particular subject.

- In the **Search for clips:** box, type book and press `Enter`

The dialogue box displays any clips related to the search term.

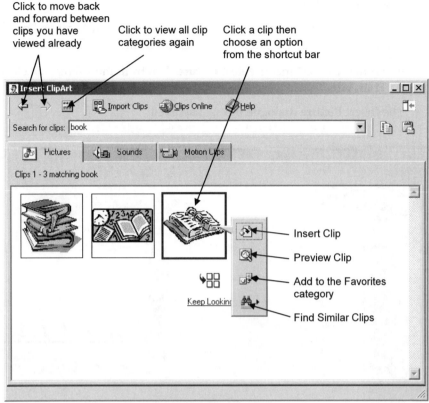

Click to move back
and forward between
clips you have
viewed already

Click to view all clip
categories again

Click a clip then
choose an option
from the shortcut bar

Insert ClipArt dialogue box

- Click the book clip shown above

- On the shortcut bar, click **Insert Clip** ⬚ - the clip is inserted into
  the document

- On the **Insert ClipArt Title** bar, click the **Close** button ✕

To insert other pictures

As well as clip art, you can use images that you might have scanned or taken with a digital camera or created in another application.

- From the **Insert** menu, select **Picture** then from the submenu, select **From File...**

The **Insert Picture** dialogue box is displayed.

Insert Picture dialogue box

- In the **Files of type:** box, select **All Pictures** - this option lets you view any type of picture file

- In the **Look in:** box, make sure that the **My Pictures** folder is selected

- Select the **chilli logo** picture file then click **Insert**

Tip	You can change the properties of some graphics using the Picture toolbar. See page 563 in the Presentation module for more details.

Tip	You can also import graphics by copying them from other files and pasting in Word.

Move and Resize Objects

Anything in your document that is not plain text is an **object**. Examples of objects include clip art, inserted pictures, worksheets and graphs, AutoShapes and lines.

Each **object** in a Word document has a **wrapping style**, which controls how it interacts with normal text paragraphs.

Inline with Text

When you paste or insert an image, it is shown **inline with text**. This means that it is located within a paragraph can be selected as though it were a text character.

Selected picture in Inline With Text mode

Float Over Text

You can make objects float over the text. You cannot select a float over text object with the keyboard, you have to use the mouse.

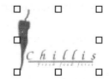

Selected picture in Float Over Text mode

There are many sub-types of float over text, which determine how the object affects the normal text paragraphs surrounding it.

Note   This course will explain the basics of changing the wrapping style only. The simplest way of using graphics is to keep them inline with text.

To change the wrapping style

- Click the chilli logo picture to select it then from the **Format** menu, select **Picture**

- Click the **Layout** tab

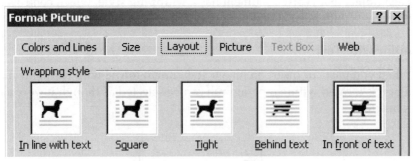

Format Picture dialogue box - Layout tab

- Select the wrapping style **In front of text** and click **OK**

To select a float over text object

- Click the object with the mouse - it appears with white resize handles

To move a float over text object

You can drag an object around the screen with the mouse or use the Cut, Copy and Paste tools.

- With the logo selected, on the **Standard** toolbar, click **Cut**

- View the document **header** and click **Paste** 📋

- Point to the selected logo

The mouse pointer shape changes to a four-headed arrow ⊕.

- Click-and-drag the logo to the left margin

| **Tip** | To move an object, **either** up/down **or** left/right, hold down the ⟨Shift⟩ key when you drag. |

To resize an object

- Point to the bottom-right handle on the selected logo

The mouse pointer changes shape to a double-headed arrow ↘.

- Click-and-drag the handle to make the logo fit into the header area

---

Tip   Hold down the ⌈Ctrl⌉ key to resize the object from the centre outwards.

Tip   If the object contains text (see below), click the shape's border to select it for moving or resizing.

To delete an object

- Select the logo then from the **Edit** menu, select **Clear** (*SpeedKey:* ⌈Delete⌉)

- Undo this action to restore the logo

- Return to **Print Layout** view then save the document

Add an AutoShape to a Document

The **Drawing** toolbar provides a palette of tools and features you can use to create your own drawings and diagrams.

This lesson shows you the basics of using the drawing tools. You can learn more drawing techniques in the Presentation lesson on page 544.

Tip   Objects added to the page directly from the Drawing toolbar cannot be made inline with text. To create a complex drawing, from the **Insert** menu, select **Object...** then from the **Object Type** list, select **Microsoft Word Picture**. This displays a blank page on which you can draw multiple shapes.

When you have finished, on the **Edit Picture** toolbar, click **Reset Picture Boundary** 📷 then click **Close Picture** to insert the picture into the document.

To draw lines, arrows, rectangles and ovals

- If necessary, display the **Drawing** toolbar by right-clicking any toolbar and selecting **Drawing** from the shortcut menu

The **Drawing** toolbar has several buttons for drawing simple shapes: **Line** \ , **Arrow** ↖ , **Rectangle** ☐ and **Oval** ○ .

- Click the **Oval** ○ tool then place the pointer over the top-left corner of the clip art book picture

The mouse pointer changes to a cross-hair shape ┼.

- Click-and-drag to the bottom-right corner of the book then release the mouse button to draw an oval around the picture

White handles are displayed at the ends of the object indicating the object is selected. The oval is currently in front of the text. Because the clip art is inline with text, the oval shape obscures it.

- Use the **Format AutoShape** dialogue box to change the wrapping style of the oval to **Behind Text**

> **Note** You may find it quite hard to select the shape. Point to its border and watch for the cursor changing shape.

Drawing tips

> **Tip** Click to draw an object at a default size - this will draw either a square or circle.

> **Tip** Hold down the Shift key while you draw to create a line at 15° intervals or to create a perfect square or circle

> **Tip** Hold down the Ctrl key to draw an object extending from its centre outwards

> **Tip** By default Word draws shapes in steps - hold down the Alt key to draw more precisely.

> **Tip** You can combine the effects of Shift, Ctrl and Alt.

To draw an AutoShape

The **AutoShapes** menu on the **Drawing** toolbar gives you access to a number of useful shapes, including lines, arrows, stars, banners, and shapes for creating flowcharts. After you draw an AutoShape you can add text to it.

- Cut the text in the title "Terms and Conditions" but leave the insertion point in that paragraph

- On the **Drawing** toolbar, click the **AutoShapes** button to display the **AutoShapes** menu

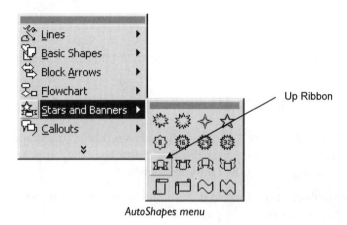

AutoShapes menu

- Select the **Stars and Banners** option then click the **Up Ribbon** tool

- Click-and-drag out the AutoShape across the top of the document

To add text to an AutoShape

Rectangles, circles, triangles, and other closed shapes drawn with the **AutoShapes** tool can have text attached to the shape.

- Right-click the ribbon and from the shortcut menu, select **Add Text**

- Paste the text "Terms and Conditions of Employment"

- If necessary, on the **Formatting** toolbar, click **Center** ≡ to align the text in the middle of the ribbon

Note When you type in a shape, Word treats the text as part of the shape. When you move the shape, the text moves with it.

Tip Use the **Text Box** button 🖹 on the **Drawing** toolbar to create a text box quickly.

To adjust AutoShapes

Many AutoShapes have adjustment handles you can use to adjust a unique aspect of the shape.

- Click-and-drag the yellow diamond handle(s) on the shape ▷

- Adjust the shape so that it looks like the picture below

- Use **Space Before** to put the text in the middle of the banner)

Change Object Properties

Word graphic objects (including clip art, WordArt, AutoShapes and drawing objects) have properties that define how they appear. Properties can be changed using the **Drawing** toolbar.

These tools are explained in more detail in the lesson on Drawing in the Presentation module (see page 552).

Practice

- *Select the banner*

- *On the **Drawing** toolbar, click the down arrow on the **Font Color** button* **A** ▾ *and select **Dark Blue***

- *Use the **Line Color** button* ▾ *to change the border to dark blue also*

- *Use the **Fill Color** button* ▾ *to change the colour of the banner to **Gold***

- *Click the **Shadow** button* ■ *and apply **Shadow Style 6***

- *Save and close the document*

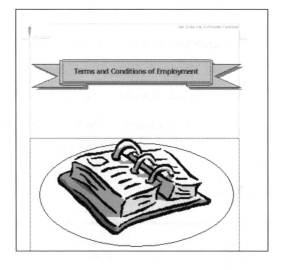

Working with Other Applications

Integrate Word with other Office applications by sharing data

Insert a **spreadsheet** or **chart** into a document ☐
(**Modify** an imported object) ☐
(**Append** text from another document) ☐

Import Data into a Document

MS Office applications use **Object Linking and Embedding** (OLE) to share data with each other and with other Windows software. OLE is a software **technology** that enables different applications to share data.

You can copy and paste text and edit it in Word as normal. You can also use **objects** (data such as pictures, spreadsheets, graphs and so on) in Word by copying them from the source application and pasting into Word (or by using drag-and-drop). Using objects like this is called **embedding**.

Note This lesson involves some use of the Excel spreadsheet application. If you cannot follow the instructions given for using Excel, complete the first few lessons in the Spreadsheets module (starting on page 307) before continuing with this lesson.

To import an Excel spreadsheet

In this exercise, you will import a list of customer addresses from an Excel worksheet into a Word document, which you will use later to complete a **mail merge**. As the worksheet contains quite wide columns, we need to create as much space as possible in the Word document.

- In Word, create a new document and save it as **MailMerge_Customers**

- Set the page orientation to **Landscape** and set the margins to **0** (zero) then click **OK**

When you try to exit the **Page Setup** dialogue box, a warning message is displayed.

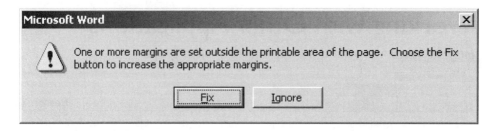

- Click **Fix** to set the margins to the minimum required by your printer

- Click **OK**

Tip   Another way of creating a document with a lot of space is to use a custom paper size, but you can only do this if you know you will not want to print the document.

- In **Windows Explorer** or **My Computer**, open the **Customers** Excel

  workbook file ![icon] - this starts Excel automatically

  Customers

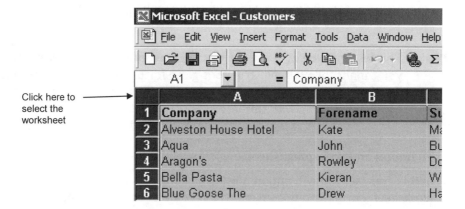

- Click the **Select All** button on the worksheet then on the **Standard** toolbar, click **Copy**

- Close Excel - a message box is displayed prompting you to keep the data you copied

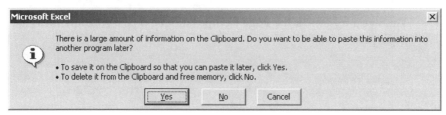

- Click **Yes** to keep the data on the Clipboard then switch back to the Word document and click **Paste**

The worksheet is pasted into Word as a standard table. The data can now be edited in Word like any other table.

- You do not need the **Telephone Number** field for the mail merge, so select that column and delete it

- Save and close the document

To import an Excel graph

The same procedure (Select, Copy, Paste) can be used to import data from most applications. The only thing that varies is the appearance of the data after pasting.

- Create a new document and save it as **Memo_Salary Chart**

- Enter text as shown below

- Use Windows Explorer to open the **Employees** Excel workbook

Employees

- Click anywhere on the **Salary Totals by Department** chart to select it, then copy it using the toolbar, menu or SpeedKey

- Close Excel without saving changes to the workbook

- Switch to the Word document and select **Paste**

This time the data has been pasted as an **embedded object**.

- Resize and position the chart on the page then save the Word document

Modify an Embedded Object

Embedded objects can very easily be modified from Word by double-clicking. The toolbars and menus will change to those of the source application, allowing you to edit the object using those commands. When you have finished, you simply click away from the object to return Word to normal. The object is saved as part of the Word document file.

To modify an embedded object

- In Word, double-click the chart

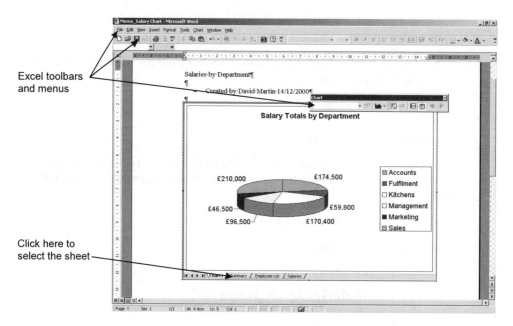

Excel's toolbars and menus replace those of Word. Note that the worksheet tabs are present at the bottom of the chart - when you copied the chart object you also selected all the data linked to it.

- Click the **Summary** worksheet tab, as shown in the picture above

- Click anywhere outside the object - Word's toolbars return and the object now displays the data from the worksheet rather than the chart

- Double-click the object again to open it

- Click-and-drag from cell **A1** down to cell **B7** as shown

- Click **Copy** 📋

- Click the **Chart1** tab to re-display it then click outside the worksheet

	A	B
1	Department	Total Salaries
2	Accounts	£174,500
3	Fulfilment	£59,800
4	Kitchens	£170,400
5	Management	£95,000
6	Marketing	£46,500
7	Sales	£210,000

- Save and close the document

Note Do not use the Cut or Copy command again - you are going to use the copied data in the next exercise.

Insert a File into a Document

As well as using copy and paste to import data, you can use the **Insert File** command to import data from a file into a document. You can use this method to import text from other Word documents, graphics, charts and worksheets.

To add text from one document to another by inserting a file

- Open the **Memo_Salaries** document and click at the end of the document

- From the **Insert** menu, select **File...**

The **Insert File** dialogue box is displayed.

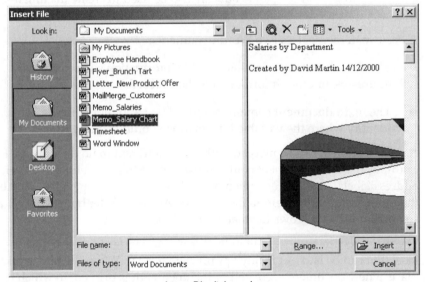

Insert File dialogue box

- Select the **Memo_Salary Chart** document and click **Insert**

The contents of the file (the text you typed plus the chart object) are inserted at the insertion point.

Even though you have performed several other actions, the data you copied is still on the Clipboard.

- Click in the document after the text "Here are the department totals you requested", create a new paragraph and select **Paste**

The worksheet you copied is pasted as a Word table.

- Resize the chart to fit on the same page

- Save and close the document

Mail Merge

Create a mail merge document to print letters and labels with different addresses

---

Objectives

Create a **mail merge** document ☐
Create and edit a mail merge **data document** ☐
Merge a data document with a mail merge document ☐

A **Mail Merge** is the process of combining information from two sources to make a new document. It is normally used to produce a form letter addressed to several recipients but can also be used to create documents such as a directory or catalogue.

A basic mail merge uses two Word documents:

♦ The **data document** contains variable information such as names, addresses, or other information (called **records**).

♦ The **main document** contains standard text and merge **fields**, which identify where the variable information should be placed.

A data document can be merged with many different main documents. For example, the data document could be used to address envelopes and print address labels. The data document is always in the form of a table, where the first row provides **field names** (Name, Address, Telephone Number and so on) and the other rows the mail merge **data**.

The main document is usually in the form of a standard letter or address label, but can be laid out in any appropriate format. When the merge takes place, a new document is created or the document is printed, in which the merge fields are replaced with the actual data (names, addresses and so on).

Create a Main Document

A main document contains the standard text and fields that position variable information.

To create a mail merge document

- Open the document **Letter_New Product Offer** document **OR** if you have not been completing all the lessons, use **Letter_New Product Offer (MailMerge)**

- From the **Tools** menu, select **Mail Merge...**

The **Mail Merge Helper** dialogue box is displayed.

- Click the **Create** button

The **Create** drop-down list is displayed.

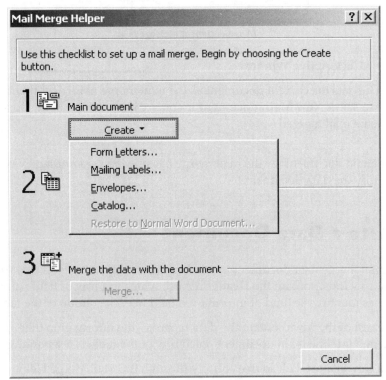

Main document menu

You can create the following documents:

Select	To
Form Letters...	Create a series of records separated by **section breaks** (a type of formatting to divide a document into discrete parts).
Mailing Labels...	Create a table with several records on each page, sized to the label type.
Envelopes	Create a series of envelope-sized pages.
Catalog...	Create the records sequentially (without section breaks).

- Select **Form Letters...** - the merge document message box is displayed

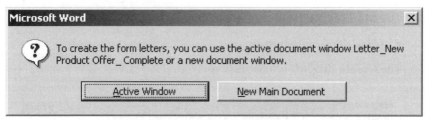

Merge document message box

- Click **Active Window**

This sets the current document as the mail merge main document. You can select **New Main document** if you are not working in the document to be mail merged.

The main document for the mail merge has now been identified. Next, identify the data document.

Create a Data Document

A mail merge data document must always be a table of at least two rows. The first row must contain the **Header** record, which is a row of field names. Field names identify the kind of information held in each column of the table.

The rest of the rows contain the data records - the information that is merged into the main document. Each row of the table is a separate record.

You can create a data source entirely through the Mail Merge Helper, but it is more common to use existing data. In this exercise, you will use the **MailMerge_Customers** document. If you did not create this document, go back to page 285 and complete the exercise or try using the Excel workbook **Customers** as the data source.

To create the data source

After identifying the main document you are returned to the Mail Merge Helper.

- Click **Get Data**

The **Get Data** drop-down list is displayed.

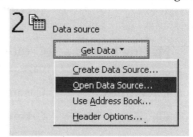

Data source menu

- Click **Open Data Source...** to open a browse style dialogue box

- Select the **MailMerge_Customers** document and click **Open**

Tip You can easily use a different data source, such as the original Excel spreadsheet, by selecting the correct application from the **Files of type:** box.

The **Edit** document message box is displayed.

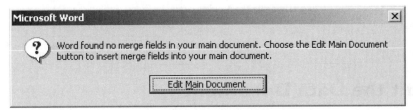

Edit document message box

Merge fields are placeholders put in the main document that will display the data from the data source when the document is merged.

Insert a Merge Field

To complete the main document

- Click **Edit Main Document** - an additional toolbar appears on-screen

- If you have typed in an address already, delete the text first then click at the top of the document

- On the **Mail Merge** toolbar, click **Insert Merge Field**

The field name list from the data document is displayed.

Data document field list

- Select the **Forename** field

The field is inserted inside chevrons, for example <<Forename>>. Merge fields can be inserted in any order, and the same field can be inserted any number of times.

- Press Space Bar then insert the **Surname** field

- Press Enter to create a new paragraph

- Add the **Contact_Title** field

- Repeat for each field name required in the document, including replacing "Mrs Dunn" with the **Salutation** and **Surname** fields after "Dear"

- Save the main document

«Forename» «Surname»
«Contact_Title»
«Company»
«Address_1»
«Address_2»
«Address_3» «Post_Code»

12 December 2000

BENEFIT FROM EXTRA DISCOUNTS

Dear «Salutation» «Surname»

Merge fields

Edit the Data Document

To view merged data from the main document

You will want to browse the actual data to check that it fits correctly in the space allowed.

- On the **Mail Merge** toolbar, click **View Merged Data** to see the actual data in place of the field names

Kate MacKenzie
General Manager
Alveston House Hotel
28 Corisbrook Road
Gloucester GL1 2TN

12 December 2000

BENEFIT FROM EXTRA DISCOUNTS

Dear Mrs MacKenzie

Viewing merged data from the main document

Note Where there is no data in a field, the space reserved for the data is closed up. If the field is the only entry in the paragraph, the whole paragraph is closed up. In the example above, the paragraph containing the **<<Address_2>>** field is gone, because there is no data to show.

- Use the record selector buttons on the **Mail Merge** toolbar to browse different records

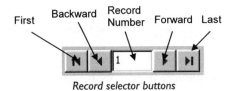

Record selector buttons

- Click in the **Record Number** box, type 5 and press `Enter`

Record number five is displayed.

To open the data form

A **Data Form** is easier to work with than a table, particularly if there are many fields. The field names are listed down the left side of the form, with the fields beside them. The fields scroll across if the data entered is longer than the box.

Alternatively, open the data document in the normal way and edit the table directly.

- On the **Mail Merge** toolbar, click **Edit Data Source**

  (*SpeedKey:* `Alt` + `Shift` + `E`)

The **Data Form** dialogue box is displayed.

Data form

To add and edit a record

- Change the **Company** name to `The Blue Goose`

- Click **Add New** to open a blank form for a new record

- Enter details about yourself and your company - press `Enter` or `Tab` to move forward between fields and `Shift`+`Tab` to move backward between fields

- When you press `Enter` on the last field a new, blank record is displayed

- Click **Delete** to remove the empty record

- Click **OK** - the main document is displayed

Create a Mail Merge Document

Mail merge documents can be printed directly to the printer or to a new document, which can be edited, saved and printed as normal.

To merge all records to a new document

It is a good idea to merge to a new document so that you can check it for mistakes.

- On the **Mail Merge** toolbar, click **Merge to New Document**
  (*SpeedKey:* `Alt`+`Shift`+`N`)

The new document is opened ready for editing, printing or saving.

To merge all records to the printer

Use this option only when you want to print every record in the data document and are sure the mail merge will print correctly.

- On the **Mail Merge** toolbar, click **Merge to Printer**
  (*SpeedKey:* `Alt`+`Shift`+`M`)

- Close any open documents, saving everything except the new merged documents

Practice

- *Use the Mail Merge Helper to create a document for printing mailing labels, using the same data source*

A dialogue box will be displayed for you to select the type of labels to use.

- *Create labels for the paper you use in your office, or select **L7163** from the Avery A4 types*

- *Save the labels main document as **MailMerge_Labels** and close it*

Exchanging a Document

Save a document in different file formats

Lesson 23

Save an existing document in a different **file format** ☐
Save a Word document as a **web page** ☐
(Create **hyperlinks** between documents) ☐

Save a Document in Another File Format

If you want to share a document with colleagues using a different word processing application to Word (or an earlier version of MS Word), you can use the **Save as type:** box to save a document in a different **file format**.

Note that not all Word features will convert exactly to other file formats.

To convert a Word document to a different file format

- Open the **Flyer_Brunch Tart** document **OR** if you have not completed all the lessons, open **Flyer_Brunch Tart (Complete)**

- From the **File** menu, select **Save As...**

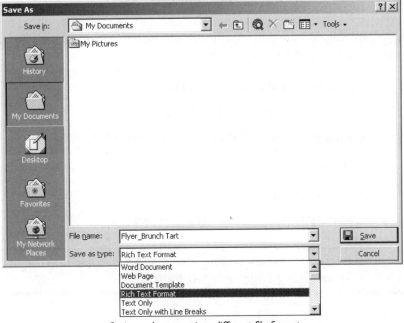

Saving a document in a different file format

- In the **Save as type** box, pick an appropriate file format for the target application version - for this exercise select **Rich Text Format**

Tip **Rich Text Format** is a "neutral" format that most word processors can open.

- Click **Save**

Note If you select **Document Template** from the **Save as type:** box, the document will be saved as a template in the Office Templates folder. You can use the template to create new documents, containing the same text and formatting as the original. You will see the document listed in the **New** dialogue box.

Save a Document as a Web Page

Word documents can be saved as web pages for publishing on the internet or an intranet in a single step. Word will warn you if you have included any features in your document that will not display correctly in a web browser.

Note An intranet is a company network setup to offer the same sort of services, such as web pages, as the internet.

If you are unsure how your document will look if saved as a web page, preview it first in **Web Page Preview**.

To preview a document in Web Page Preview

- From the **File** menu, select **Web Page Preview**

The document is opened in your web browser window.

- Close the web browser window to return to the document

To save a Word document as a web page

- From the **File** menu, select **Save as Web Page...**

Tip Make sure you have saved any changes to a document in the normal way before using **Save as Web Page.**

The **Save As** dialogue box is displayed.

The **Page Title** is displayed on the **Title** bar of the web browser when viewing the page. It also identifies the subject of the page to internet search engines. The default page title is taken from the first line of text in your document.

- To change the default page title, click **Change Title...**

The **Set Page Title** dialogue box is displayed.

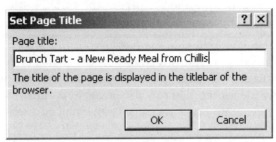

Set Page Title box

- In the **Page title:** box, type a new title for the web page as shown above then click **OK**

- Save the web page in **My Documents** leaving the file name the same

- Click **Save**

If you have used unusual formatting or page layout features, Word will try to convert them to a more standard feature.

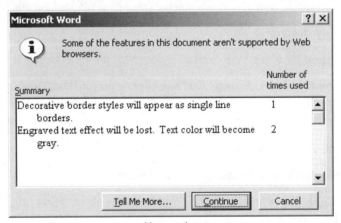

Message box

- If you do not want to accept the default changes, click **Cancel** and change the affected text manually but for this exercise click **Continue** to create the web page

Your document will be redisplayed in **Web Layout** view. Note that you can continue to edit it and make changes in MS Word, but the document you are working in is now an **HTML** file not a **DOC** file.

Create Hyperlinks

A hyperlink is a shortcut that will open another document or file. The file could be stored on a network server, an intranet or on the internet.

> **ECDL** Hyperlinks are not a specific part of the ECDL syllabus, but they are important if you want to create working web pages.

Hyperlinks can be created to any Microsoft Office file, HTML (HyperText Markup Language) web page or other file on any internal or external website or any file server. You can also create hyperlinks that will automatically generate a new message to an email address.

Hyperlinks can be created in documents using text or graphics. A text hyperlink (also called **hypertext**) is usually formatted as blue, underlined text.

Practice

To complete the hyperlinks exercise, first create some documents to link to. This and the following topic are optional.

- *Use the **Save As** command to create a copy of the flyer web page document called **Flyer_Ham&Onion Tart***

- *Edit the document to contain details about a delicious ham and onion tart*

- *Save changes*

- *Repeat the above steps to create a document for the Tomato Tart flyer*

- *Open the **Flyer_Brunch Tart** web page again (in Word) when you have finished*

To create a hyperlink to another file or web page

- Select the text "Ham and Onion Cream Tart"

- Right-click the selected text and from the shortcut menu, select **Hyperlink**

> **Tip** You can also create hyperlinks from graphics. Also the command can be selected on the **Standard** toolbar (**Insert Hyperlink** 🖫) or from the **Insert** menu, select **Hyperlink...** (*SpeedKey:* Ctrl + K).

The **Insert Hyperlink** dialogue box is displayed.

- From the **Link to:** panel, click **Existing File or Web Page**

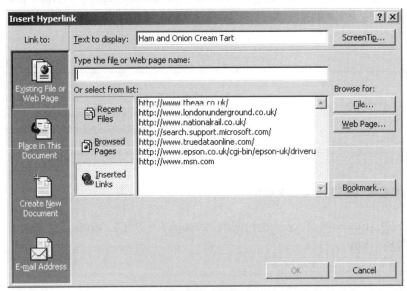

Insert Hyperlink dialogue box

There are several options for choosing the type and location of the file or web page, as shown in the table below.

Select	To
Recent Files, Browsed Pages or Inserted Links	Create a link to a file or web page you have opened recently.
File...	Browse for a file on your PC's hard drive or a network folder.
Web Page...	Find a web page on the internet or on an intranet. Clicking this button starts your web browser. Browse to the web page you want to link to then close the web browser.

- Use the **File...** button to select the **Flyer Ham&Onion Tart** web page

- Click **OK** to create the link

- Create links to the **Tomato Tart** document then open both other flyers and create hyperlinks between them

- Follow the hyperlinks to test them in the web browser

- Close any open windows

Review of Word Processing

Review the topics covered during the module and identify areas for further practice and goals for the future

---

Review

(Check **objectives**) ☐
(Complete **consolidation** exercise) ☐
(Identify topics for **further** study) ☐

Check Objectives

Congratulations on completing the lessons for ECDL Module 3 "Word Processing".

You have learned to:

♦   Recognise features of the **screen** and create a basic **document**.

♦   Use **application help** functions.

♦   **Edit** existing documents and use the **Cut, Copy** and **Paste** tools.

♦   Apply character and paragraph **formatting** to enhance documents.

♦   Set the **page layout**, add **headers** and **footers** and **proof** the document.

♦   **Preview** and **print** a document.

♦   Use **templates** to create standard documents quickly.

♦   Create and format **tables** to improve the page layout.

♦   Improve a document by adding **graphics** and **drawings**.

♦   Integrate Word with other Office applications by **sharing data**.

♦   Create a **mail merge** document to print letters and labels with different addresses.

♦   Save a document in different **file formats**.

Make sure you have checked off each syllabus item and identified any topics you do not fully understand or remember.

ECDL with MS Office 2000   © CWC (90) 2001

Consolidation and Going Further

Tests for Module 3 can either be practice-based or question-based. Practical tests will ask you to create, edit, format and print a series of documents in Word.

There are further test-style exercises for you to try on the CD in the folder **ECDL Tests\3 Word Processing**

Print the document **Word Processing Questions** and try to complete the test unaided, using the data files from the folder.

> **Note** These questions are provided as a consolidation exercise. They do not make up an approved ECDL test. See page 689 for more information about the extra tests.

Going further

There is plenty of opportunity for further training in Word. For example, there is much more to be learned about Word desktop-publishing-type tools to create more advanced page layouts with columns, sections, text boxes and graphics.

Other areas of study include collaborating on documents in a workgroup, tools for working with long, highly structured documents and using fields. You can also learn to use macros and VBA programming to automate tasks in Word.

Many of these topics can be studied under the **ECDL Advanced Syllabus**.

Refer to page 744 for more details about further courses in gtslearning's range of **Learn IT** training books.

Notes

_____

_____

_____

_____

_____

_____

_____

_____

_____

_____

_____

_____

_____

Spreadsheets

Getting Started with Excel

Identify parts of the Excel window and learn the layout of a spreadsheet

Lesson 24

Open MS Excel □
(Identify the different elements of the Excel **screen**) □
Create, open, save and close **workbooks** □
Select cells, rows and columns □
Exit **Excel** □

What is a Spreadsheet?

A spreadsheet is a tool for managing data and making calculations.

You can use a spreadsheet in a variety of ways: to store lists of data, to calculate and analyse financial or sales information, to create graphs from data, to create invoices or expense forms, to perform complex mathematical calculations, and so on.

An Excel spreadsheet (called a **worksheet**) is easy to revise and update and can be printed or published to the world wide web.

Open Excel

Excel can be opened in the same way as MS Word, using the program shortcut icon � wherever it appears.

To start Excel from the Start menu

- On the **Windows Taskbar,** click the **Start** button ▢Start and select the **Programs** menu

- Click the **Microsoft Excel** program item ▢ Microsoft Excel

The Excel Window

The layout of the Excel window is similar to that of Word. The menus and toolbars contain different items, there is a **Formula Bar** and the main part of the window displays the spreadsheet(s).

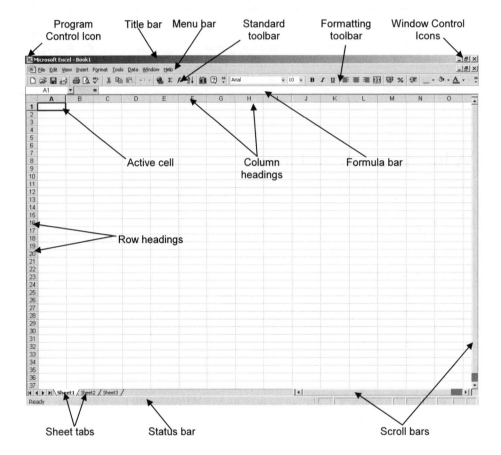

Excel Toolbars

When you first start Excel, the **Standard** and **Formatting** toolbars are displayed. These toolbars contain the most commonly used commands. There are many other toolbars available in Excel used for specialised tasks such as editing charts.

Working with toolbars is the same as for Microsoft Word. Refer back to page 185 for notes on changing the display of toolbars.

- Optionally, move the **Formatting** toolbar below the **Standard** toolbar so that you can see all the buttons

- Maximise the window

The Formula Bar and Name Box

The **Formula** bar displays the data being entered or edited. When entering or editing data, a green tick ✔ and a red cross ✘ appear on the Formula bar to confirm or cancel the entry. The ▪ button on the **Formula** bar is used to create mathematical functions.

The **Name** box displays various types of information depending on the current action. Usually it displays the grid reference or name of the active cell. When the ▪ button on the **Formula** bar is selected the **Name** box is used to select an arithmetic function and show the result of the calculation being entered.

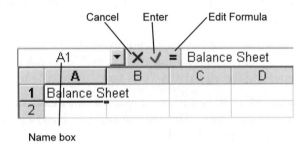

- Type Balance Sheet

As you type, the text appears in the active cell (A1) and in the **Formula** bar.

- Press Enter

The Status Bar

The **Status** bar displays information while you are working on a sheet. For example, a total is displayed on the Status bar whenever two or more numbers are selected on the sheet.

The **CAPS** and **NUM** boxes show whether Caps Lock and Num Lock respectively are on.

Status bar

The Active Cell and Column and Row Headers

The main part of the screen is taken up by the **worksheet**. This is where you enter data and formulae. It is divided into alphabetic columns and numbered rows. The point where a column and row intersect is called a **cell**. Cells are identified by their column and row reference. For example, the first cell in column **A** and row **1** is called cell **A1**.

The **active cell** is the location on the sheet where editing takes place. If the active cell is the only cell selected it has a black border around it, and is identified in the **Name** box by its grid reference or by a **Name** given to the location. If more than one cell is selected the whole selection is displayed with a blue tint, except for the **active cell**, which is displayed normally.

The **column** heading identifies each column across the sheet with letters of the alphabet. There are 256 columns, from **A** to **Z**, then **AA** to **AZ**, **BA** to **BZ** and so on, repeating the alphabet several times up to column **IV**.

The **row** heading identifies each row down the sheet with a number. There are 65,536 rows in each sheet. The column and row Headings appear raised and in bold to help locate selected cells.

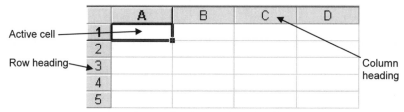

Active cell, column and row headings

Move Around the Sheet

The **active cell** is where text will appear if you start typing.

You can move around the sheet by moving the active cell with the keyboard or by clicking with the mouse. You can also view other parts of the sheet by using the scroll bars.

Note Scrolling does not move the active cell.

ECDL with MS Office 2000   © CWC (90) 2001

To move the active cell with the keyboard

Press	To Move
⬆ ⬇ ⬅ ➡	To the next cell in the direction of the arrow
Enter	To the next cell down (Confined to the selected range if several cells are highlighted)
Shift + Enter	To the next cell up (Confined to the selected range if several cells are highlighted)
Home	To column A on the current row
Ctrl + Home	To cell A1
Ctrl + End	To the last entry on the sheet
Page Up	Up one screen
Page Down	Down one screen
Alt + Page Up	Left one screen
Alt + Page Down or Tab	Right one screen
Ctrl + ⬆ ⬇ ⬅ ➡	To the end of a block of non-blank cells

Practice

- *Move to cell **AZ100***

- *Type* Last Entry *and press* Enter

- *Move to column **A***

- *Move to cell **A1***

- *Move to cell **D2***

- *Move to cell **D1***

- *Move to the "Last Entry" cell*

- *Move to cell **A1***

The Mouse Pointer

The mouse pointer takes on different shapes depending on where it is on the sheet. Each pointer shape relates to a specific type of action.

Pointer	Action
⇧	**Normal** sheet pointer. Used for selecting cells, columns, or rows for editing. Point to the middle of the cell, column or row to ensure correct selection.
	Fill pointer - appears when the pointer is positioned over the fill handle in the bottom-right corner of the selected cell(s) Used for copying the active cell contents to one or more adjacent cells.
	Move pointer - appears when the pointer is moved to any edge of the selected cell(s). Used to drag cell contents around the sheet. Can also be used make a single copy of the cell contents in a non-adjacent cell.
E ↔ F	**Sizing** pointer - appears when the pointer is over a divider on the column or row heading. Used for changing the width of columns or the height of rows.
C Formula Bar	**Editing** pointer - appears when the pointer is on the Formula bar or on a cell being edited. Used for entering and editing data on the sheet.

    ECDL with MS Office 2000   © CWC (90) 2001

Select Cells, Rows and Columns

Selecting cells (highlighting) is one of the most important actions in Excel. You need to select cells before you do something with them, for example enter data, copy, delete or apply enhancements. Selecting can be done with the mouse or the keyboard.

To select a single cell with the mouse

- Click on cell **A1**

The cell appears white with a black border around it.

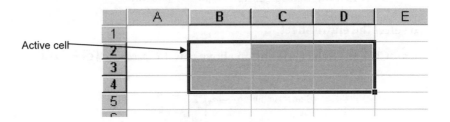

Active cell

To select a group of adjacent cells with the mouse

- Click on the first cell to be selected (**B2**) and holding the mouse button down, drag to the last cell to be selected (**D4**)

Active cell

Multiple cell selection

The active cell is the first cell selected. A black border appears around all of the selected cells and they are shaded blue.

To select a group of non-adjacent cells with the mouse

- Click-and-drag to select cells **A2:A4**

- Hold the $\boxed{\texttt{Ctrl}}$ key and select **D2:E2**, then **C3:C6** and finally **E4:E6**

	A	B	C	D	E	F
1						
2						
3						
4						
5						
6						
7						

Group of non- adjacent cells selected

The active cell is the first cell of the last group selected. A faint border appears around each group of cells.

To select whole columns or whole rows

- Point to the grey column header for column **B** and click once to select the column

- Click-and-drag across the row headings **1** to **5** to select adjacent rows

- Click on the column **B** heading, then hold the $\boxed{\texttt{Ctrl}}$ key and click on other headings to select non-adjacent columns

To select the entire sheet

- Click the **Select All** button above row 1 (*SpeedKey:* $\boxed{\texttt{Ctrl}}$+$\boxed{\texttt{A}}$)

Select All button

	A
1	

Every cell on the sheet is selected. The active cell is **A1**.

To clear the highlighted selection

- Click on any cell with the mouse **OR** press an arrow key on the keyboard

---

Tip   Excel remembers what is selected on the sheet when you close the file. It is good practice to clear the current selection before closing.

To select a group of adjacent cells with the keyboard

Selecting with the keyboard can save time if the selection is small, or if it extends beyond the edge of the screen. The keyboard can be used to extend or reduce a selection already highlighted using the mouse. You cannot use the keyboard to select whole columns or rows or groups of non-adjacent cells.

- Use the arrow keys (⬅, ➡, ⬆ and ⬇) to move to cell **A1**

- Hold the ⸢**Shift**⸣ key down and use the arrow keys to move to the last cell to be selected (**D4**)

- Press an arrow key to de-select the cells

The Sheet Tabs

An Excel spreadsheet file (called a **workbook**) is more than just a single sheet. It is a collection of sheets arranged like pages in a book.

Every new workbook contains three sheets, each of which can be used independently of the others or setup to share data. This allows spreadsheets that relate to a common activity to be grouped together in a single file, and all be opened, closed, and saved at the same time.

The Sheet tab at the bottom of the worksheet window identifies each sheet within the workbook. A sheet is selected by clicking on its tab. The **sheet scroll** buttons allow viewing of sheet tabs that extend beyond the tab space.

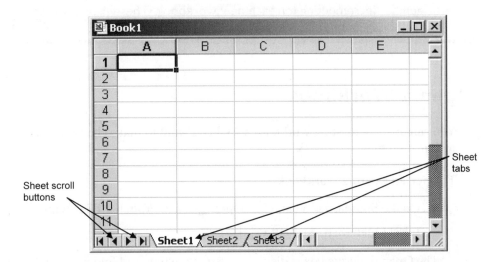

- Click each sheet tab in turn then return to **Sheet1**

Save and Close a Spreadsheet

It is important to save your work regularly to prevent accidental loss of data.

The **Save** and **Save As** commands in Excel work in exactly the same way as for Word. Excel files are saved as workbooks with an .XLS file extension and the icon ▣.

Refer back to the topics on saving and closing in Word (page 216 and 199) if you need to refresh your memory.

- Save the workbook as Moving Around then close it

Create a New Workbook

A new workbook is created automatically when you start Excel, but you can also create more workbooks after starting the application.

To create a new blank workbook

- On the **Standard** toolbar, click **New** ⬜ (*SpeedKey:* Ctrl+N)

A blank new workbook is opened.

Note Every time you start Excel the first workbook you create is named **Book1**. The second is named **Book2**, the third is **Book3**, with the number incrementing for each new workbook. These names are only temporary until you save or close the workbook window.

Open a Workbook

You can open an existing workbook when you want to make changes or add information to it.

To open an existing workbook

- On the **Standard** toolbar, click **Open** 📂 OR From the **File** menu, select **Open** (*SpeedKey:* Ctrl+O)

The **Open** dialogue box is displayed listing the files and folders available.

- Select **Moving Around** and click **Open**

> **Tip** You can also open any of the four most recently saved workbooks by selecting it from the list at the bottom of the **File** menu.

> **Tip** If you open a workbook icon from Windows Explorer, Excel will start automatically if it is not running already.

Get Help with Excel

The Help system in Excel works in the same way as for Word. Refer back to page 194 if you need reminding.

Close Excel

You can exit from Excel in several ways. If you have unsaved workbooks open when you exit, you are prompted to save them as Excel closes.

> **Tip** It is best to save or close any open workbooks before exiting Excel, otherwise you may not be sure which workbook you are being asked to save.

To exit Excel

- Double-click the **Excel Program Icon** at the top-left of the Excel window

OR

- Click once on the **Close** button at the top-right of the Excel window

OR

- From the **File** menu, select **Exit** (*SpeedKey:* Alt + F4)

Creating a Worksheet

Enter text and values in a sheet and use basic functions

Understand what **data types** a cell can contain ☐
Enter **numbers**, **dates** and **text** in a cell ☐
Use the **Undo** command ☐
Use the **AutoFill** tool to copy data ☐
Enter simple **formulae** in a cell ☐
Use **arithmetic** and **logical** operators in formulae ☐
Use the **SUM** and **AVERAGE** functions ☐
(Use other functions) ☐
Understand and use **relative**, **absolute** and **mixed** cell references ☐
Recognise standard **error messages** ☐
(Use **range names** in formulae and on the worksheet) ☐

Spreadsheet Data Types

A worksheet is built up by entering data into cells. There are four **data types** that can be entered in a cell: **Text**, **Values**, **Dates** and **Formulae**.

In most cases, Excel will identify the type of data you are trying to enter and **format** the cell appropriately. You can also apply your own formatting to a cell to make it look the way you want.

> **Tip** If you know the different types of data that can be used in spreadsheets, you can start the exercises on page 321.

Text

Text cells are often used as **labels** to identify the information entered in columns or rows, or you may want to store text data, such as names.

Text can include any letters, numbers and symbols on the keyboard. Up to 32,000 characters can be entered as text in a single cell. Text cells have a **value** of **0** (zero) if used in a calculation.

Entries containing a mix of letters and numbers are always treated as text. Typing an apostrophe (') at the beginning of the entry forces Excel to format the entry as text. For example, if you want to store a telephone number in a cell, it should be treated as text not a value, so you would type:

```
'01628 546000
```

Text will automatically align on the left of a column, but can be moved to the right or centre. If text is wider than the column it is entered into, it will overflow onto the adjacent cell if that cell is blank, otherwise the text will appear truncated. Changing the column width affects how much of the entry can be seen. (A formatting option allows text to word wrap onto multiple lines within the width of a column, with a corresponding increase in the height of the row).

Values

Values are usually **number** entries and used in **calculations** on the sheet. Numbers can be formatted to appear in different ways, for example with or without currency symbols or with as many decimal places as required.

Numbers that contain too many digits for the width of the column are displayed as hash symbols (####). The number displays correctly when the column is wide enough.

Numbers can be formatted to display in many different ways by using the formatting commands.

Value Type	Formats
Numbers	123
	123.00
	00123
	0.123
	1.23
Currency	£1,234.50
Percentage	17.5%
Fraction	3.825

All number formats are aligned to the right-hand side of the cell by default.

Note Leading and trailing zeros on numbers are ignored. If a currency symbol other than a £ sign is used when typing the entry, it is treated as text, not a number (You should **format** an entry to show the currency symbol rather than type it).

Dates

Dates (and **times**) are **values** that can be used in calculations to create new dates or calculate time intervals. Excel counts dates as the number of days from **January 1st 1900** and **stores** the date as a number. For example, 1st May 2000 is stored as **36647**. However the date is **formatted** to display in a more traditional manner.

Excel recognises dates separated with a slash (/) or a hyphen (-) or dates entered using the month name. Times should be separated by colons (:).

When you enter a date that Excel recognises, the cell will be formatted in one of the default styles, depending on what you typed. All date and time formats are aligned to the right-hand side of the cell.

You Type	Excel Displays
28/9	28-Sep
28/9/2000	28/9/2000
28 Sep	28-Sep
28 September 2000	28-Sept-00
28-9-2000	28/09/2000
9:00	09:00
9:00 a	9:00 AM
9:00 p	9:00 PM
21:00	21:00

> **Note** The default formatting used depends on the options set on the **Date** tab of Windows Regional Options, so you may see different results on your own PC.

Formulae

Formulae are instructions that perform calculations on the sheet. Formulae can be very simple or extremely complex and the **result** (the data that actually appears in the cell) may be text, a value or a date.

A formula begins with an equals sign (=) followed by one or more **values** and **functions** to calculate. The values can be entered directly into the formula, but it is more effective to enter the values into cells on the worksheet and **refer** to those cells in the formula.

Formulae can include arithmetic operators, specialised functions such as averaging or totalling, or be used to transfer data around the sheet.

Function	Description	Example
+	Add	=A1+A2
-	Subtract	=A1-A2
*	Multiply	=A1*A2
/	Divide	=A1/A2
^	Exponential	=A1^3
SUM	Total of values	=SUM(A1:A20)
AVERAGE	Average of values	=AVERAGE(A1:A20)
Cell reference	Transfer data	=A1

Enter and Edit Data

Most data entry is performed with the keyboard, although the mouse can be used to create formulae and for copying entries.

To enter data into a cell

As entries are typed they will appear in the active cell and on the **Formula** bar at the same time. The **Formula** bar displays exactly what is *stored* in the cell, which may be different from what is *displayed* in the cell, depending on the formatting options being used (see page 341).

- Start Excel if necessary

- **Save** a new workbook as `Sales Data`

- In cell **A1**, type `Sales`

- Click the green **Tick** button ✔ on the **Formula** bar to complete the entry and remain on the cell (**OR** press the `Enter` key, `Tab` key, or an arrow key to complete the entry and move to the next cell)

> **Tip** When entering text **AutoComplete** will automatically complete the entry if it recognises a similar pattern to a previous entry. If it is not correct continue typing the entry.

To cancel an entry ☺

o Click the red **Cross** button ✖ on the **Formula** bar or press `Esc` to cancel the entry before it is completed

To replace an entry

- Select cell **A1**

- Type the new entry - `First Quarter Sales`

- Click the green **Tick** button ✔ or press `Enter` to complete the entry

The existing entry is overtyped and replaced by the new one.

To edit an entry

- Double-click cell **A1** to edit directly in the cell (*SpeedKey*: `F2`) **OR** click on the **Formula** bar to edit the cell there

- Amend the text to `First and Second Quarter Sales`

- Click the green **Tick** button ✔ or press `Enter` to complete the entry

> **Tip** You can use all the normal text editing and selection techniques to modify cell entries. Refer back to page 204 of the Word module to see a list of keyboard and mouse commands.

To delete an entry

- Select cell **A1** and press `Delete`

Undo Incorrect Edits

Excel allows you to **undo** the last **16** actions (quite a lot less than Word). If you make an editing, formatting or other mistake it is often quicker to undo and start again rather than trying to correct the mistake.

To undo the last action

- On the **Standard** toolbar, click **Undo** ↶ ▾ OR From the **Edit** menu, select **Undo** (*SpeedKey:* Ctrl + Z)

The contents of cell **A1** are restored.

Tip As with Word, you can click the arrow on the **Undo** button to display a list of previous edits and select a point to go back to.

AutoFill

AutoFill copies the entry in the active cell into a range of adjacent cells. The fill can only be in a horizontal or vertical line along rows or columns, not diagonal.

AutoFill can be performed using the mouse or from the menu. **AutoFill** using the menu will **duplicate** the original entry exactly.

AutoFill using the mouse can produce **incrementing** lists, for example:

Selected Cell(s)		AutoFill Using the Mouse		
January		February	March	April
Monday		Tuesday	Wednesday	Thursday
21/5/2000		22/5/2000	23/5/2000	24/5/2000
Gate 1		Gate 2	Gate 3	Gate 4
5	10	15	20	25

To AutoFill using the mouse

- In **B2**, type `April`
- Point to fill handle of the selected cell(s)

The pointer changes to a crosshair ✛.

- Click-and-drag to cover the required range

As the pointer moves to each cell a **ScreenTip** displays the entry that will be copied into the cell.

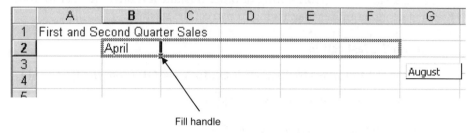

Fill handle

AutoFill ScreenTip

- Drag the range out to **G2** (September)

> **Tip** To increment numbers by 1, hold down $\boxed{\texttt{Ctrl}}$ while you drag. The cursor shows a plus sign $+$ and a ScreenTip displays the next value in the sequence as you move the mouse. To increment numbers by a different amount, enter two values in consecutive cells, then select both cells before AutoFilling. Each cell will increment by the difference between the second and first cells.
>
> Holding down $\boxed{\texttt{Ctrl}}$ **stops** a **date** from incrementing.

Practice

- *Complete the worksheet as shown below*

	A	B	C	D	E	F	G
1	First and Second Quarter Sales						
2		April	May	June	July	August	September
3	Ready Meals	61178	53305	57628	50855	63427	50189
4	Meat Produce	23689	24949	22240	23902	26771	20258
5	Vegetable Produce	16627	15708	18603	17355	17987	15129
6	Dairy Produce	24877	24109	27936	27859	30590	24781

- *Select column **A** then point to the right edge of the column button - the mouse pointer will change to this shape* ↔

- *Click-and-drag to make the column wider, as shown above*

- *Select columns **B** to **G** then click-and-drag on one border to make each column wider*

- *Save the worksheet*

What is a Formula?

Performing calculations is one of the main uses of spreadsheets. Excel allows you to build complex formulae using the arithmetic operators. You can also select from a long list of predefined functions for performing statistical analysis, financial and scientific calculations, tabular searches, and conditional actions.

What is a range?

You will remember that a cell is referred to by its column and row header, so the cell three rows down and four columns to the right is cell D3.

A range is a **block** of cells. A range is referred to by the cells in the top-left and bottom-right corners separated by a colon (:). So the range from the top corner of the worksheet, down to D3 is **A1:D3**.

Ranges are used extensively in performing calculations.

What is a formula?

Formulae are composed of a number of different elements that must be combined in a specific way to ensure the formula produces an accurate answer.

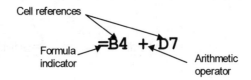

An example of a simple formula

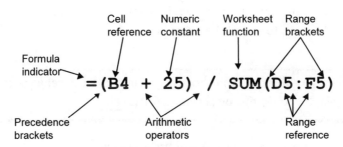

An example of a more complex formula

Use the AutoSum Tool

One of the most common features of a spreadsheet is column and row totals. Instead of using lots of + signs to add a group of cells, the **SUM** function can be used. SUM will add up and total a group of figures.

The SUM function requires a **range** to work with and can be entered manually on the **Formula** bar. For example, =SUM(A1:A20). AutoSum Σ is a toolbar shortcut for creating a SUM formula.

To use AutoSum for a single total

- Select the cell where the total is to be entered (select **B7**)

- On the **Standard** toolbar, click **AutoSum** Σ

The formula is displayed in the cell and on the **Formula** bar. A flashing border is displayed around the selected range.

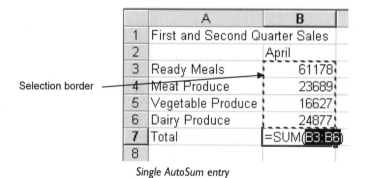

Single AutoSum entry

- If the wrong cells are selected, you can click-and-drag to select a different range, but for this exercise click the green **Tick** button ✓ or press ⌷Enter⌷ to accept the formula

---

Note Clicking anywhere on the sheet will change the cell references in the formula. If you do this by accident, press ⌷Esc⌷.

- Click-and-drag the fill handle of **B7** out to **G7**

Note that when the formula is copied across the columns, the cell references update to SUM the contents of the new column.

To sum multiple columns in one action

- Click in cell **H2** and enter the text `Total`

- Enter `Total` in cell **A7** as well

- Select the range **B3:G6**

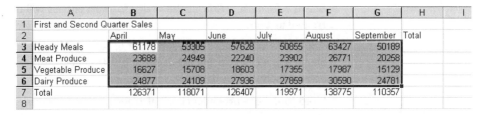

	A	B	C	D	E	F	G	H	I
1	First and Second Quarter Sales								
2		April	May	June	July	August	September	Total	
3	Ready Meals	61178	53305	57628	50855	63427	50189		
4	Meat Produce	23689	24949	22240	23902	26771	20258		
5	Vegetable Produce	16627	15708	18603	17355	17987	15129		
6	Dairy Produce	24877	24109	27936	27859	30590	24781		
7	Total	126371	118071	126407	119971	138775	110357		
8									

- On the **Standard** toolbar, click **AutoSum** Σ

Totals are created beneath each column of figures (in **B7:G7**). Note that the existing formulae were replaced without a warning.

To sum multiple columns and/or rows

- Delete the totals formula you just created (**B7:G7**)

- Select the range **B3:H7**

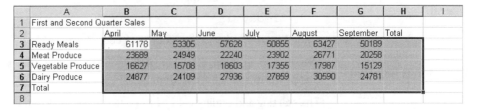

	A	B	C	D	E	F	G	H	I
1	First and Second Quarter Sales								
2		April	May	June	July	August	September	Total	
3	Ready Meals	61178	53305	57628	50855	63427	50189		
4	Meat Produce	23689	24949	22240	23902	26771	20258		
5	Vegetable Produce	16627	15708	18603	17355	17987	15129		
6	Dairy Produce	24877	24109	27936	27859	30590	24781		
7	Total								
8									

- On the **Standard** toolbar, click **AutoSum** Σ

Column totals are created in **B7:G7** and row totals in **H3:H6**.

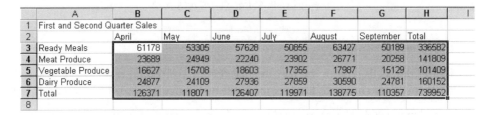

	A	B	C	D	E	F	G	H	I
1	First and Second Quarter Sales								
2		April	May	June	July	August	September	Total	
3	Ready Meals	61178	53305	57628	50855	63427	50189	336582	
4	Meat Produce	23689	24949	22240	23902	26771	20258	141809	
5	Vegetable Produce	16627	15708	18603	17355	17987	15129	101409	
6	Dairy Produce	24877	24109	27936	27859	30590	24781	160152	
7	Total	126371	118071	126407	119971	138775	110357	739952	
8									

- Save the workbook

Enter a Formula

Formulae contain the following elements:

Element	Description
=	Begins a formula. Without the = sign formula entries will be treated as text. The + or - signs may be used in place of = if the next element is a cell reference, but not if it is a function name. For example, +A1 / B1.
Brackets ( )	Used to denote precedence in calculating sections of the formula, and to enclose function ranges.
Cell reference	A location on the sheet containing a value to work with. Storing values in cells rather than in the formula makes a spreadsheet much easier to maintain.
Arithmetic operators	The arithmetic signs + - / * ^.
Constant	A number. This will remain the same until the value is changed in the formula. As mentioned above, this is not usually a good idea.
Literal " "	The text in quotes is displayed at the relevant point in the formula result. For example: `="Today is " & TEXT(TODAY(),"dddd")` ...will display "Today is Thursday" in a cell.
Worksheet functions	Words such as SUM, COUNT, AVERAGE and many others that perform specialised arithmetic.
Range reference	The starting and ending cells of a group of cells enclosed in brackets. Separated with a colon (:) if the cells are contiguous, for example SUM(A1:A20). Separated with a comma (,) if the cells are non-contiguous, for example SUM(A1,A5,A15,A20).

Calculating formula results

By default, cells containing formulae show an up-to-date result. If values on the worksheet are changed, the formula will be recalculated and the cell updated.

It is also possible to use manual recalculation. If so your cells will not always display the correct results.

- From the **Tools** menu, select **Options** and click the **Calculation** tab

- Make sure the **Automatic** option button is selected

A formula can be typed into a cell manually or built up using the **Formula** bar. Cell references can be added by selecting a range with the mouse or by typing in the reference.

To enter a formula using the Formula bar

- Click in cell **J2** and type the heading Average then press Enter

- With the active cell at **J3**, on the **Formula** bar, click the = button

The **Function** button is displayed in the **Name** box and the **Formula Palette** is displayed beneath it. As the formula is built up a running total is displayed in the **Formula Palette**.

- Type a left bracket (then click in cell **B3** - the cell reference is added to the formula

- Type + then click cell **C3**

- Complete the formula = (B3+C3+D3+E3+F3+G3) /6

Note the running total displayed on the **Formula Palette**.

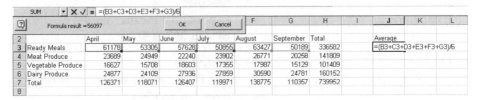

	April	May	June	July	August	September	Total		Average		
Ready Meals	61178	53305	57628	50855	63427	50189	336582		=(B3+C3+D3+E3+F3+G3)/6		
Meat Produce	23689	24949	22240	23902	26771	20258	141809				
Vegetable Produce	16627	15708	18603	17355	17987	15129	101409				
Dairy Produce	24877	24109	27936	27859	30590	24781	160152				
Total	126371	118071	126407	119971	138775	110357	739952				

- Click **OK** or the green **Tick** button ✓ or press Enter to accept the formula

This formula calculates the average value of values in cells B3, C3, D3, E3, F3 and G3.

- Change the value in **B3** to 2000 - the average value in **J3** is updated automatically

- Undo the change

Note You do not have to click the = button on the **Formula** bar to enter a formula; you can press the = key on the keyboard first, then create the formula as above or type it. However, the **Formula Palette** will not be displayed to show you a running total.

Note If you start a formula by mistake, press Esc to abandon changes to the cell.

> **Tip** If the **Formula Palette** covers the cells you are using, you can drag it out of the way.

Sequence of calculation

Formulae are calculated from left to right according to strict precedence. The precedence can be changed by enclosing sections of the formula in brackets (). These sections are calculated first and the result held as subtotals for further calculations.

Element	Sign	Order of Precedence
Brackets	( )	**First** The result is held as a subtotal for further calculations. Where brackets are enclosed within brackets, they are calculated from the inside set to the outside set.
Exponential	^	**Second** Exponential means "To the power of" (so 2^2 is 4).
Division Multiplication	/ *	**Third** Calculated in the sequence entered from left to right.
Addition Subtraction	+ -	**Fourth** Calculated in the sequence entered from left to right.
Functions	SUM()	These are calculated separately and included in the result depending on the adjacent arithmetic operators.

> **Tip** Try to work out the expected result before entering a formula, for example, by using simple numbers to verify the formula is calculating correctly. If the result is wrong either the formula has been typed incorrectly, or the sequence of calculation is not in the order required.

Edit a Formula

When you select a cell containing a formula all of the cells referenced by the formula are highlighted on the screen with coloured borders. The same colours highlight the cell references in the formula.

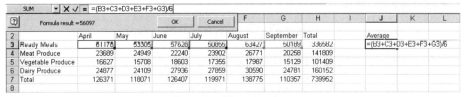

			April	May	June	July	August	September	Total			Average		
	SUM		▾ ✗ ✓ =	=(B3+C3+D3+E3+F3+G3)/6			F	G	H	I		J	K	L
?		Formula result =56097			OK		Cancel							
2			April	May	June	July	August	September	Total			Average		
3	Ready Meals		81178	53305	57628	50855	63427	50189	336582			=(B3+C3+D3+E3+F3+G3)/6		
4	Meat Produce		23689	24949	22240	23902	26771	20258	141809					
5	Vegetable Produce		16627	15708	18603	17355	17987	15129	101409					
6	Dairy Produce		24877	24109	27936	27859	30590	24781	160152					
7	Total		126371	118071	126407	119971	138775	110357	739952					
8														

Example of formula editing

To edit a formula ⑤

o   Double-click on the cell to edit the formula (*SpeedKey:* Select the cell then press F2)

o   Edit the cell references in the cell or on the **Formula** bar by typing

OR

o   Point to the edge of a cell reference and click-and-drag the border highlight to a different cell or range

OR

o   Point to the small box in the bottom-right corner of a highlighted cell(s) and click-and-drag to extend the cell range

Practice

- *Edit the formula in **J3** to read =* (H3+H4+H5+H6) /4
- *Write down the result* _____
- *Edit the formula to read* =H3+H4+H5+H6/4
- *Write down the new result* _____
- *Explain why the results are different*

_____

_____

_____

Use a Function

Excel contains a large number of functions to speed up the creation of formulae. For example, the **AVERAGE** function gets the same results as the formula we entered above, but it is much quicker to create.

To use a function

- Select **J3** and press `Delete` to remove the existing formula

- On the **Formula** bar, click the `=` button

- The **Function** button is displayed in the **Name** box with the SUM function selected - click the arrow on the button

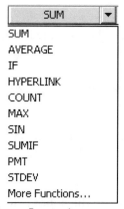

Function button

- Select the **AVERAGE** function

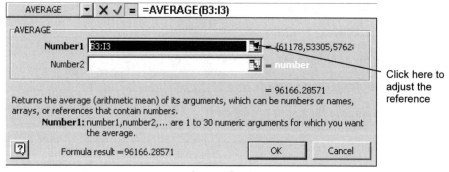

Average function

The **Formula Palette** displays a description of what input the function requires to work. Excel has chosen a range to use with the function, but it is not the correct one (you do not want to include the row total in the Average results).

- To edit the formula, you can click in the **Formula** bar to re-type the reference, but for this exercise, click ▦ at the end of the **Number1** box

The **Formula Palette** shrinks to let you select the correct range on the worksheet.

- Click-and-drag to select **B3:G3** then press `Enter`

- The **Formula** bar is redisplayed with the correct range - click **OK** or press `Enter` again to complete the formula

---

Tip If the **Formula Palette** covers the cells you are using drag it out of the way, or click the **Shrink** button ▦ to collapse it while you select the cells then the **Expand** button ▦ to enlarge it again afterwards.

Paste a Function

If you do not know which function to use, you can use **Paste Function** to browse a list of functions and find out what they do.

ECDL You only need to be able to use the **SUM** and **AVERAGE** functions for ECDL, but it is useful to know how to access others.

To use Paste Function

You do not need to complete this exercise to continue with the rest of the lesson. If you want to omit it, go forward to page 336.

- In **K2**, type the heading Best then in **K3** start a formula by clicking ▦

- Click the down arrow on the **Function** button and select **More Functions...** from the list

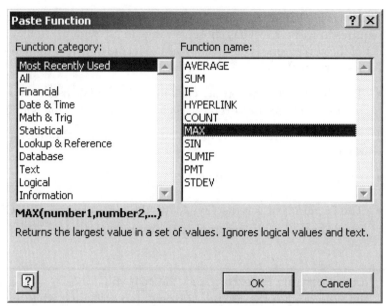

Paste Function dialogue box

The **Paste Function** dialogue box organises functions into categories. Select the relevant category or select **All** to see the complete list.

- Select the **MAX** function (from **Most Recently Used, All** or **Statistical**)

- Click **OK**

The **Formula Palette** is extended to display the selected function arguments.

- Select the range **B3:G3** and click **OK**

This function displays the **highest** value in the selected range.

- Copy the formula down to **K6**

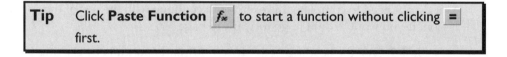

Tip   Click **Paste Function** f_x to start a function without clicking $=$ first.

Other useful functions

Category	Function	Use To
Math & Trig	SUM()	Total all numbers in range or in a list of values. Text has a value of 0 (zero).
Statistical	COUNT()	Count how many numbers there are in a range. Blank cells and text not included.
	AVERAGE ()	SUM values in a range and divide by COUNT of values in the range. Blank cells and text not included.
	MAX()	Find the largest value in range. Blank cells and text not included.
	MIN()	Find the smallest value in range. Blank cells and text not included.
Date & Time	DATE (yyyy,m,d)	Calculate with a date value. Enter the date in the format shown.
	NOW()	Find (and display) the current date and time.
	TODAY()	Find (and display) the current date.

Note When working with date formulae, you should always **type in** 4-digit year values and setup your system so that dates are displayed with 4 digits for the year to avoid any year 2000-type problems. If used correctly, Excel's functions will not cause any year 2000 errors.

Use Relative and Absolute Cell Addresses

Relative cell referencing occurs when a formula is copied and the cell references adjust to a new location on the sheet automatically. For example, if the formula **=SUM(A1:A5)** is copied to the next column on the right the formula would automatically adjust by one column to **=SUM(B1:B5)**.

To use relative cell referencing

- Click-and-drag the fill handle of **J3** to copy the formula down to **J6**

- Look at each new formula and note that the row references have changed each time

Absolute cell referencing means that a cell reference stays the same when you copy the formula. An absolute reference is created by putting a dollar sign (**$**) before the part of the cell reference to remain constant. For example:

◆ When copying across columns, **$A1** fixes the column reference, but the row reference will adjust.

◆ When copying down rows, **A$1** fixes the row reference, but the column reference will adjust.

◆ When copying in any direction, **$A$1** fixes both references and neither will adjust.

To create an absolute cell reference ①

o Enter the dollar signs manually into the formula where required

OR

o Click on the cell reference to remain fixed in the formula

o Press function key [F4] on the keyboard to insert dollar signs

o Keep pressing [F4] until the dollar signs are positioned as required

Practice

- *Select **J6** and on the **Standard** toolbar, click **Copy***

- *Select **B10** and on the **Standard** toolbar, click **Paste** - the cell displays an error message **#REF!***

When you copy the cell, Excel tries to update the references to the new location, but these would lie out with the left edge of the sheet, so an error is generated.

- *Edit **B10** to read* =AVERAGE($B$3:$G$6) *- to create an average for all types of products in all months*

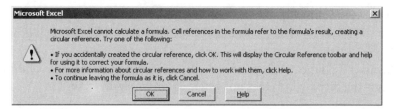

- *Try copying the cell to other cells - note that the value stays the same*

- *Delete the copied cells and add a label in **A10*** Cross Product Average

- *Save the workbook*

Circular References

Occasionally a formula that loops back on itself is created and cannot produce a valid result. This usually happens because you are trying to use a value from the cell in which the formula is stored. When this occurs, the following message box is displayed.

To resolve a circular reference

o   Click **Cancel** if the circular reference has been created intentionally

The formula is calculated as correctly as possible and flagged as **Circular** on the **Status** bar.

OR

o   Click **OK** if the circular reference is not intentional

Blue dots and linking arrows will appear in each cell within the loop. The **Circular Reference** toolbar is displayed and the **Help** window is opened with an explanation on how to use it.

Deleted References

It is possible to delete **columns** and **rows** from a worksheet. If cell(s) referenced by formulae on the worksheet are deleted in this way, an error message **#REF** is displayed in the cell containing the formula.

Reference error message

If you click in the cell, the missing references are displayed within the formula. For example, consider the formula **=C2+D2+E2**. If column D had been deleted from the worksheet, the formula would become **=C2+#REF!+E3**.

When the **contents** of the cell are deleted, as opposed to deleting the cell itself, the cell counts as blank. In a SUM or AVERAGE formula, this will not produce an error, as the cell will be counted as zero.

Error Messages

Apart from **#REF**, there are other common error messages that you will see displayed when a formula is invalid. All error messages are indicated by the hash symbol (#).

To recognise and resolve error messages ①

#####

This usually indicates that the cell contents are wider than the column. This affects the display but does not generally indicate an error.

- o Increase the size of the column to see the cell contents or use a smaller font

#NAME?

This error message indicates that text in a function is not recognised. This generally occurs because some element of the formula is misspelled.

- o Check the spelling of **function** names, **range** names and **cell references** in the formula

- o If using text in a formula, check that it is enclosed by quotes ("...")

#VALUE!

This means that one or more values used for a function or operator is the wrong type.

For example, the + operator expects the values to be added to be numbers or dates. If one or more of the values are text, the error message is displayed.

- o Check the references in the formula to make sure they point to the correct cells

- o If you need to perform a calculation on a range with a mixture of text and values, use a function such as SUM (which will ignore cells containing text)

#DIV/0!

This means that the formula is attempting to divide by zero, which cannot be resolved. This could be because a formula reference points to a blank cell or to a cell with the value zero.

- o Check the reference(s) to make sure that they do not point to blank cells or to zero values

Range Names

A **range name** is an alternative way of referring to one or more cells. Range names help to make formulae more comprehensible and are useful when it comes to sharing worksheet data with other applications. They can also be used to navigate a large worksheet quickly.

> **ECDL**   Range names are not part of the syllabus, but you should find them useful when creating worksheets.

To name a selection

- In the **Sales Data** workbook, select the range **A2:G6**

- Click in the **Name** box and type `Sales_Data` then press `Enter`

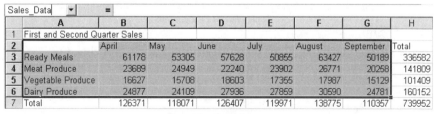

	A	B	C	D	E	F	G	H
1	First and Second Quarter Sales							
2		April	May	June	July	August	September	Total
3	Ready Meals	61178	53305	57628	50855	63427	50189	336582
4	Meat Produce	23689	24949	22240	23902	26771	20258	141809
5	Vegetable Produce	16627	15708	18603	17355	17987	15129	101409
6	Dairy Produce	24877	24109	27936	27859	30590	24781	160152
7	Total	126371	118071	126407	119971	138775	110357	739952

Example of a cell name

> **Note** Names must start with a letter or underscore (_), and can include numbers, full stops (.), or underscores, but no spaces or other punctuation.

- Name the range **B3:G6** Sales_Data_Without_Labels

To go to a location with the Name box

- Click the down arrow on the **Name** box and select **Sales_Data**

Name box

The named cells are selected on the sheet, exactly as they appeared when the name was created.

To use a name in a cell reference

To use a name instead of a reference, you can simply type it in the formula. If you select a named range, Excel will use the name automatically.

You can also convert an existing formula reference to a named reference.

- Select cell **B10** then from the **Insert** menu, select **Name** then **Apply...**

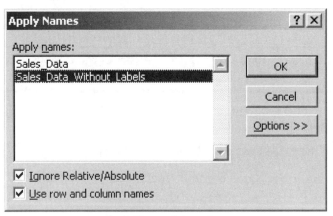

Apply Names dialogue box

- Select the name **Sales_Data_Without_Labels** and click **OK**

The range name is used in place of cell references in the formula.

- Save and close the workbook

Formatting a Worksheet

Apply format options to show values correctly and to improve the appearance of the worksheet

Format cells to display different **number, currency, percentage** and **date** formats ☐
Change the **font**, font **size**, font **colour** and apply **enhancements** ☐
Adjust **text orientation** and **cell alignment** ☐
Resize columns and rows ☐
Add **border effects** to a range ☐
(Add **shading** to a range) ☐
(Clear cell **contents** and/or **formats**) ☐
Insert **symbols** and **special characters** ☐

Apply Cell Value Formats

There are two types of formatting that you can apply to worksheet cells. As well as applying cosmetic formatting (font enhancements, borders, shading and so on) you can define the format of cell data. This is important for displaying numbers and dates clearly and unambiguously.

On a new sheet, numbers are entered with **General** formatting - aligned on the right, as they are typed, with a leading zero for fractions. The quickest way to apply basic value formatting is to use the **Formatting** toolbar.

To apply number formats from the toolbar ①

o   Select the cells to be formatted and click the format button required

Button	Value	Effect	Description
🖫	1234	£1,234.00	**Currency** - £ sign, 2 decimal places, commas between thousands, always right aligned.
%	.5	50%	**Percent style** - converts fraction to a percent. For example 1 = 100%, .175 = 17.5%.
🗎	1234	1,234.00	**Comma style** - as currency, without the £ sign.
.0 .00	1234	1234.000	**Increase Decimal** - each click displays an extra decimal place.
.00 .0	1234.567	1235	**Decrease Decimal** - each click hides a decimal place, rounding up or down each time.

Practice

- Open the **Sales Data** workbook OR if you did not complete the previous lesson, open **Sales Data (Formatting)**

- Select the range **B3:H7** and click 📋 to apply **Currency** formatting

- If you see ###### signs displayed in the cells, click-and-drag across the column headers then from the **Format** menu, select **Column** then **AutoFit Selection**

- In **A12**, type the heading Target then in **A13** enter % of Target

- Use AutoFill to enter 120000 from **B12:G12**

- In **B13**, enter the formula =B7/B12 then copy the formula across to **G13**

- Select the ranges **J3:J6**, **K3:K6** (if present), **B10**, **B12:G13** (use Ctrl +click-and-drag to select multiple ranges)

- Click , to apply **Comma** format

- Select the ranges **B3:H7**, **J3:J6**, **K3:K6** (if present), **B10**, **B12:G12** and click **Decrease Decimal** .00→.0 twice to remove all decimal places

- Select **B13:G13** and click % to apply **Percent** format then **Increase Decimal** →.00 twice to show 2 decimal places

- Save the workbook (as Sales Data)

	A	B	C	D	E	F	G	H	I	J	K
1	First and Second Quarter Sales										
2		April	May	June	July	August	September	Total		Average	Best
3	Ready Meals	£ 61,178	£ 53,305	£ 57,628	£ 50,855	£ 63,427	£ 50,189	£ 336,582		56,097	63,427
4	Meat Produce	£ 23,689	£ 24,949	£ 22,240	£ 23,902	£ 26,771	£ 20,258	£ 141,809		23,635	26,771
5	Vegetable Produce	£ 16,627	£ 15,708	£ 18,603	£ 17,355	£ 17,987	£ 15,129	£ 101,409		16,902	18,603
6	Dairy Produce	£ 24,877	£ 24,109	£ 27,936	£ 27,859	£ 30,590	£ 24,781	£ 160,152		26,692	30,590
7	Total	£ 126,371	£ 118,071	£ 126,407	£ 119,971	£ 138,775	£ 110,357	£ 739,952			
8											
9											
10	Cross Product Avera	30,831									
11											
12	Target	120,000	120,000	120,000	120,000	120,000	120,000				
13	% of Target	105.31%	98.39%	105.34%	99.98%	115.65%	91.96%				

To apply a cell value format

Other value formatting is applied from the **Format** menu. The **Format Cells** dialogue box gives you access to a wide variety of formats for currency, accounting, date, mathematical and scientific value formats.

- In cell **H1**, type the date (for example, 18/12/2000)

- With **H1** selected, from the **Format** menu, select **Cells...**
  (*SpeedKey:* Ctrl + 1)

The **Format Cells** dialogue box is displayed.

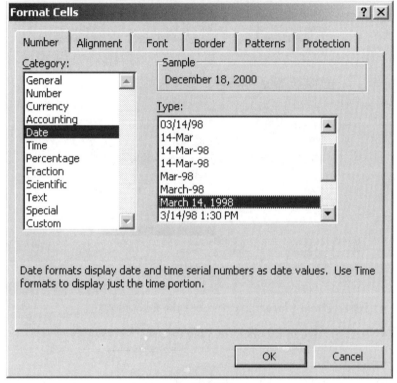

Format Cells

- On the **Number** tab, from the **Category:** list, select **Date**

- From the **Type:** box, select **March 14, 1998**

Note Always use a 4-digit year style when formatting dates.

The effect on the cell's actual contents is displayed in the **Sample** panel.

- Click **OK**

To apply different number formats

Numbers and currency values can be formatted to display a different number of decimal places and to show negative values with a minus sign or in red or both.

With currency, the default symbol and layout is the one specified for your PC in the Windows Regional Options. If you need to show that cell values are for a different currency, you can select the appropriate symbol from the drop-down list box.

- Select the range **B3:H7** then from the **Format** menu, select **Cells...** (*SpeedKey:* `Ctrl`+`1`)

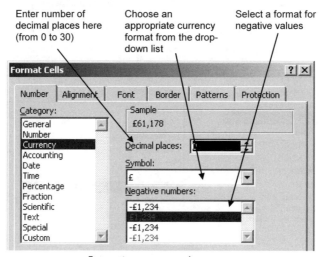

Enter number of decimal places here (from 0 to 30)

Choose an appropriate currency format from the drop-down list

Select a format for negative values

Formatting currency values

- Set **Decimal places:** to **0** and use the £ symbol

- Set negative numbers to display in red

- Click **OK**

The same options apply to the **Number** category, except that you can choose whether to use comma separators (1,000) or not (1000) and there are no currency symbols.

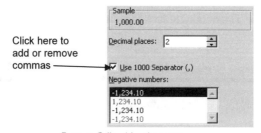

Click here to add or remove commas

Format Cells - Number options

Format Text

Text enhancements can be used to draw attention to important areas of the sheet. Enhancements include changing the font (typeface) and its size and colour; applying bold, italics and underlining, and applying shading to cells.

The **Formatting** toolbar contains shortcuts for frequently used formatting commands.

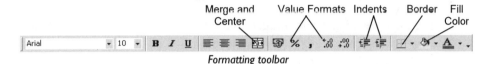

Formatting toolbar

The text and alignment formatting buttons work in the same way as for Word. Refer back to page 222 if you need to see explicit instructions.

Tip   You can apply formats to multiple cells at once. Also, use the **Font** tab on the **Format Cells** dialogue box to apply multiple formats in one go.

Note   Values formatted with the **Currency** or **Comma Style** formats override the alignment button options.

Practice

- *Select **A1** and apply **Bold** formatting and **12 pt** font size*
- *Select row **2** and apply **Italic** formatting*
- *Select **A3:A7** and apply **Italic** formatting*
- *Select row **7** and apply **Bold** formatting and font colour **Green***
- *Select rows **10-13** and apply font colour **Dark Blue***
- *Select row 1 and apply **Times New Roman** font*
- *Save the workbook*

To centre headings

Worksheet headings can be centred across several columns and/or rows by merging a group of cells into a single large cell. If any of the columns or rows are resized the heading is re-centred.

- Select the cells to centre across, including the cell containing the heading - select the range **A1:G1**

- On the **Formatting** toolbar, click **Merge and Center** ⊞

The highlighted cells are merged, with the heading aligned in the centre.

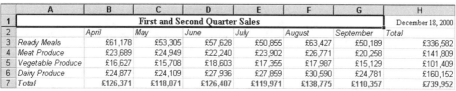

	A	B	C	D	E	F	G	H
1			First and Second Quarter Sales					December 18, 2000
2		April	May	June	July	August	September	Total
3	Ready Meals	£61,178	£53,305	£57,628	£50,855	£63,427	£50,189	£336,582
4	Meat Produce	£23,689	£24,949	£22,240	£23,902	£26,771	£20,258	£141,809
5	Vegetable Produce	£16,627	£15,708	£18,603	£17,355	£17,987	£15,129	£101,409
6	Dairy Produce	£24,877	£24,109	£27,936	£27,859	£30,590	£24,781	£160,152
7	Total	£126,371	£118,071	£126,407	£119,971	£138,775	£110,357	£739,952

Centred heading

Modify Column Width and Row Height

Text entries wider than the column will flow over the next column if it is blank. Rows will increase in height automatically to accommodate the font size. Columns and rows can be resized at any time and adjusted to a specific size, or sized automatically to fit the contents of the column or row.

To resize a column or row ①

- o Point to the divider to the right of the column header, or the bottom of the row header to be resized

The pointer changes to a double-headed arrow pointing in the direction of movement ↕ ↔ .

- o Click-and-drag to resize manually

OR

- o Double-click to resize the column or row to fit the largest entry automatically

---

Tip To resize several adjacent columns or rows at the same time, select all of the columns or rows, then click-and-drag any one of the selected dividers. All of the highlighted columns or rows are resized equally.

Practice

- *Select row **1** then click-and-drag to double the height of the row*

- *Make row **7** about 1½ times its height*

- *Click-and-drag to select columns **A:K***

- *Point to the divider between A and B then double-click to resize all the columns to fit their contents*

To align and orient cell contents

You can change the vertical alignment of text in a cell. As the height of a cell is normally the same height as the text, this effect will not be seen unless you change the row height.

You can also change the **orientation** of text to make it run up/down instead of left to right.

- Select row **1** then from the **Format** menu, select **Cells...** (*SpeedKey:* `Ctrl`+`1`) and click the **Alignment** tab

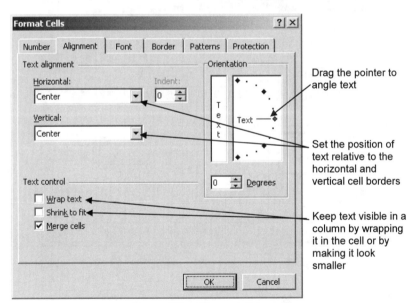

Format Cells - Alignment dialogue box

- From the **Vertical:** list box, select the required option (**Center**)

- Click **OK** then save the workbook

Insert Symbols and Special Characters

You can apply different types of currency symbols by using an appropriate cell format, but if you want to insert special characters (such as the trademark or copyright symbols) into a cell, you must use the Windows feature **Character Map**.

To use Character Map

- From the **Start** menu, select **Programs** then **Accessories**

- Select the **Character Map** menu item 🔳 Character Map

Tip If you cannot see **Character Map**, try looking in a subfolder (**System Tools** for example). If **Character Map** is not on the **Start** menu, ask your IT support person to install it.

The **Character Map** window is displayed.

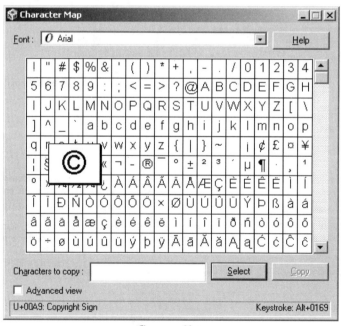

Character Map

- In the **Font:** box, select the font style containing the symbol(s) you want to use (select **Arial**)

- Click the symbol character you want (©) then click **Select**

The character is displayed in the **Characters to copy:** box.

- You can select another character if required, but for this exercise just click **Copy** then click **Close** ☒ to exit **Character Map**

- In Excel, select **I1**, click in the **Formula** bar or press F2 and from the **Edit** menu, select **Paste** (*SpeedKey:* Ctrl+V)

- The character is inserted in the cell - type Joe Chillis Ltd. after the © symbol to complete the entry

---

Note With some symbols, if the character is not formatted with the correct font, it will not look like the symbol you copied. In the **Formula** bar, select the character(s) using click-and-drag. Click the drop-down arrow on the **Font** box and select the same font as appeared in Character Map when you copied the character(s).

ä	™

™ *symbol formatted in Arial...*   *...and Symbol font*

Add Borders and Shading

The grey gridlines on the worksheet do not print out. Borders and shading can be used to define areas of the worksheet, such as line totals, more clearly, both on-screen and on paper.

Tip Applying borders may be easier with cell gridlines turned off. Use the **Tools**, **Options**, **View** tab to do this.

There is a practice exercise at the end of this topic.

To add borders from the toolbar ①

o Select the cell(s) to have borders added

o On the **Formatting** toolbar, click **Border** ▼ to apply the border style shown **OR** click the arrow on the **Border** button to select a border style from the menu

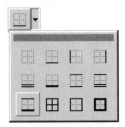

Border pull-down menu

To add borders from the menu ①

- o Select the cell(s) to have borders added

- o From the **Format** menu, select **Cells...** (*SpeedKey:* Ctrl + 1)

OR

- o Right-click and from the shortcut menu, select **Format Cells**

- o Select the **Border** tab

The **Border** tab of the **Format Cells** dialogue box is displayed.

- o From the **Line** panel, select a line **Style:** and **Color:** from the pull-down lists

- o From the **Presets** panel, select an outline style

OR

- o From the **Border** panel, click the buttons to add/remove borders from the edges and inside of the range

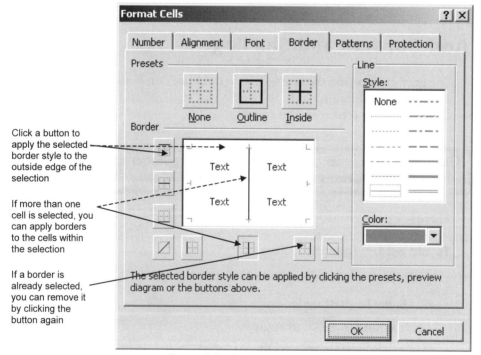

Click a button to apply the selected border style to the outside edge of the selection

If more than one cell is selected, you can apply borders to the cells within the selection

If a border is already selected, you can remove it by clicking the button again

Format Cells - Border dialogue box

To add shading from the toolbar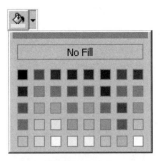

o   Select the cell(s) to have shading applied

o   On the **Formatting** toolbar, click **Fill Color** to apply the colour shown

OR

o   Click the arrow on the **Fill Color** button to select a fill colour from the colour palette

Fill Color palette

Practice

- *Select columns **A:K** then from the **Format** menu, select **Cells...** (SpeedKey:* `Ctrl` + `1`*) and click the **Border** tab*

- *Set the **Color:** to **Grey - 50%** then click the internal vertical border button*

- *Click **OK***

- *Select cells **H1:J1** and use the **Border** button to apply **No Borders***

- *Select column **K** then apply an external right border*

- *Select **A1:K1** and apply a thick external border and **Light Yellow** shading*

- *Select **A7:K7** and apply a **Top and Thick Bottom Border***

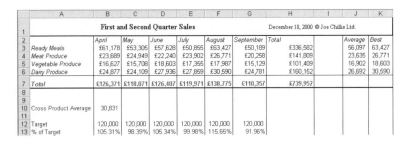

	A	B	C	D	E	F	G	H	I	J	K
1		First and Second Quarter Sales						December 18, 2000 © Joe Chillis Ltd.			
2		April	May	June	July	August	September	Total		Average	Best
3	Ready Meals	£61,178	£53,305	£57,628	£50,855	£63,427	£50,189	£336,582		56,097	63,427
4	Meat Produce	£23,689	£24,949	£22,240	£23,902	£26,771	£20,258	£141,809		23,635	26,771
5	Vegetable Produce	£16,627	£15,708	£18,603	£17,355	£17,987	£15,129	£101,409		16,902	18,603
6	Dairy Produce	£24,877	£24,109	£27,936	£27,859	£30,590	£24,781	£160,152		26,692	30,590
7	Total	£126,371	£118,071	£126,407	£119,971	£138,775	£110,357	£739,952			
8											
9											
10	Cross Product Average	30,831									
11											
12	Target	120,000	120,000	120,000	120,000	120,000	120,000				
13	% of Target	105.31%	98.39%	105.34%	99.98%	115.65%	91.96%				

- *Save and close the workbook*

Clear Cell Values and Formats

When you delete a value from a cell using the Delete key or by overtyping, the cell's formatting is not affected. If you want to remove the format, you can use the **Clear** command.

To clear a cell ⊕

o   Select the cell(s) to be cleared then from the **Edit** menu, select **Clear**

The **Clear** submenu is displayed.

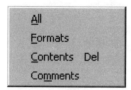

Clear submenu

From the submenu select:

o   **Contents** to clear only the data and leave the formatting (*SpeedKey:* Delete)

o   **Formats** to clear only the formatting and leave the data

o   **All** to clear both the data and formatting

Editing a Worksheet

Revise the worksheet and share data between workbooks

Lesson 27

Use the **Zoom** tool ☐
Move and **copy** cell contents ☐
Insert and **delete** rows and columns ☐
Use **multiple worksheets** ☐
Open **several** workbooks ☐
Use the **Find and Replace** tools ☐
(Create **lists** of data) ☐
Sort data alphabetically and by value ☐

Use the Zoom Tool

Like Word, Excel has a Zoom control that you can use to magnify or shrink the size of the worksheet on-screen.

To use the Zoom control

- Open the workbook **Customers** and select the range **A1:J50**

- On the **Standard** toolbar, click the drop-down arrow on the **Zoom** list box and select **Selection**

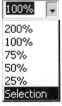

Zoom Control

Picking **Selection** causes the selected range to fill the screen. You can also zoom to a custom percentage.

- Click in the **Zoom** list box, type the level of magnification you want (**80%**) then press ⌈**Enter**⌋

- Click in cell **A1**

Cut, Copy and Paste

As with Word, the Cut, Copy and Paste tools are very flexible. You can click-and-drag to select then copy text within the **Formula** bar. You can move and copy cells or ranges of cells. You can paste text or data into a worksheet from other worksheets, workbooks or other types of file.

> **Note** A practice exercise demonstrating the next few topics can be found on page 359.

To move cells ①

o   Select the cells to be moved

o   On the **Standard** toolbar, click **Cut** ✄ OR from the **Edit** menu, select **Cut** (*SpeedKey:* [Ctrl]+[X])

The selected range is displayed with a flashing border. The action of moving and copying cells is rather different in Excel. Normally when you cut or copy, the data is placed on the Windows Clipboard and can be pasted back into the file at any time. In Excel you must choose Paste as the next command, or the Cut selection will disappear and you will need to re-select it.

> **Note** The data is on the Windows Clipboard however, and you **can** paste it into *other applications* normally.

o   Move the active cell to the new location

o   On the **Standard** toolbar, click **Paste** 📋 OR from the **Edit** menu, select **Paste** (*SpeedKey:* [Ctrl]+[V])

The cell is moved and the selection border disappears.

To copy cells ①

o   Select the cells to be copied

o   On the **Standard** toolbar, click **Copy** ▣ OR from the **Edit** menu, select **C**opy (*SpeedKey:* Ctrl + C)

The selected range is displayed with a flashing border. As with Cut, the cells must be pasted (in Excel) before selecting other commands.

o   Move the active cell to the new location for the cell contents

o   On the **Standard** toolbar, click **Paste** ▣ OR from the **Edit** menu, select **P**aste (*SpeedKey:* Ctrl + V)

Unlike Cut, the original cells remain selected and can be pasted multiple times.

o   Press Esc to cancel the original selection

Note   To move or copy entire rows and columns, click-and-drag across the row/column header then use Cut, Copy and Paste as normal.

Tip   You can use Cut, Copy and Paste to move and copy the some or all of the **contents** of cells as well. Simply click-and-drag across the text you want then Cut or Copy it as usual. When you paste, either select the cell to replace any existing contents or select the cell for editing to paste text at the insertion point.

Note   If you are editing the contents of the cell, do not try to select another cell to copy its data, as Excel will think you are creating a reference to the selected cell. If this happens, press Esc to abandon changes, copy the text you want from the cell, then go back to editing the original cell, pasting the text where required.

Insert and Delete Rows and Columns

Columns and rows can be inserted into an existing worksheet at any time. Rows, columns and cells can also be deleted. This is different from deleting the contents of cell(s) as any references to the deleted cells are also removed. Formulae that reference deleted cells will display an error message **#REF** (see page 338).

To insert columns and rows ①

o   Select the column(s) or row(s) where the new ones are to be inserted

o   With the pointer over the highlighted selection, click the **right** mouse button

o   From the shortcut menu, select **Insert** (*SpeedKey*: `Ctrl`+`+`) **OR** from the **I**nsert menu, select **C**olumns or **R**ows

> **Tip**   If you select multiple columns/rows, you will insert as many columns/rows as you selected.

To delete columns and rows ①

o   Select the column(s) or row(s) to delete

o   With the pointer over the highlighted selection click the **right** mouse button

o   From the shortcut menu, select **Delete** (*SpeedKey*: `Ctrl`+`-`) **OR** from the **E**dit menu, select **D**elete

> **Tip**   You can insert cut or copied cells by selecting the first option from the **I**nsert menu.

Move and Copy a Worksheet

A new workbook contains three worksheets named **Sheet1**, **Sheet2**, and **Sheet3**. You might use multiple worksheets to store related data (for example, expense claims for different people or sales data in different months of the year). Data can be moved, copied or transferred between sheets.

To copy a worksheet

- Point to the worksheet tab to copy

- Hold the Ctrl key then click-and-drag to the right

A small arrow pointing down appears above the sheet tabs.

Copying a worksheet

- Release the mouse to insert the duplicate sheet where the arrow is positioned

The new sheet has the same name as the original, with a number after it to identify it as a duplicate. For example, if the original sheet is named **Summary**, the duplicate is named **Summary (2)**.

To rename a worksheet

- Double-click on the sheet tab **OR** right-click and from the shortcut menu, select **Rename**

- Enter the name on the highlighted sheet tab and press Enter

To move a worksheet

- Click-and-drag to move the sheet

A small arrow pointing down appears above the sheet tabs.

- Release the mouse to move the sheet to where the arrow is positioned

To delete a worksheet

- Select the worksheet tab to delete

- Click the right mouse button and from the shortcut menu, select **Delete OR** from the **Edit** menu, select **Delete Sheet**

- A message box is displayed to confirm the deletion - click **OK**

Open Several Workbooks

Opening extra workbooks without closing the first one can save time when you are busy. The first workbook will sit in the background until you are ready to use it again. You can view and work on both workbooks at once, or switch between them with the keyboard, the mouse or from the menu.

To open a second workbook ①

o Open the first workbook

o On the **Standard** toolbar, click **Open** 🖾 and open the second workbook **OR** create a new workbook

To move between workbook windows ①

o On the **Windows Taskbar**, click the **Workbook** icon
   (*SpeedKey:* `Alt`+`Tab`)

Open workbooks on the Windows Taskbar

> **Tip**   If your workbooks do not appear on the Taskbar, from the **Tools** menu, select **Options**. Click the **View** tab and select **Windows in Taskbar**.

OR

o From the **Window** menu, click on the workbook name to switch to
   (*SpeedKey:* `Ctrl`+`F6`)

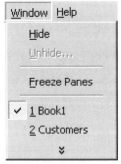

Open workbooks on the Window menu

The name of the active workbook is displayed on the **Title** bar.

To view both workbooks on screen ⑨

o   From the **Window** menu, select **Arrange...**

The **Arrange Windows** dialogue box is displayed.

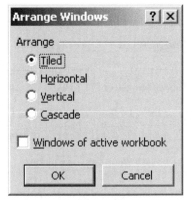

Arrange Windows dialogue box

o   From the **Arrange** panel select an arrangement method

o   Click **OK**

Tip   When more than one workbook is visible, select the workbook to work in by clicking on it with the mouse. The first click will activate the window but will not change the active cell. Alternatively, you can use `Ctrl` + `Tab` to switch between workbooks.

Practice

- *Do not save any changes to **Customers** during this exercise*

- *In the workbook **Customers**, right-click the **Customers** sheet tab and select **Move or Copy...***

- *Select (**move to end**) and check the **Create a copy** box*

- *Click **OK***

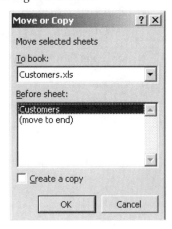

- Right-click the copied sheet and name it Customers Mail Merge

- Create a new workbook and save it as **MailMerge_Customers**

- From the **Window** menu, select **Arrange...** then choose the **Horizontal** option

- In **Customers**, select the range **A1:J50** on the **Customers Mail Merge** sheet

- Point to the edge of the selection, hold down the Ctrl key and drag the selection over cell **A1** in the **MailMerge_Customers** workbook

- Release the mouse button then the Ctrl key

- Close the **Customers** workbook without saving changes

- Maximise the workbook window

- In the new workbook, rename **Sheet1** to Customers Mail Merge

- Select columns **B** and **C** and on the **Standard** toolbar, click **Copy**

- Select cell **A1** on **Sheet2** then on the **Standard** toolbar, click **Paste**

- On the **Customers Mail Merge** sheet, select column **I** then click **Cut**

- Select column **C** on **Sheet2** then click **Paste**

- Rename **Sheet2** to Customers Telephone

- Make the column widths fit the cell contents

- Click in cell **A1**

- Switch back to the **Customers Mail Merge** sheet, select column **I** then from the **Edit** menu, select **Delete**

- Make the column widths fit the cell contents

- Click in cell **A1**

- Save the workbook

Setup a Data List

In addition to performing calculations, spreadsheets can also be used to work with long lists of data (a **database**). Two database terms that are useful to know are **Record**, and **Field**.

♦   A **record** is all of the data on a single row.

♦   A **field** is each separate column along the record.

Fields have column headings at the top to identify the type of data that should be entered in the field.

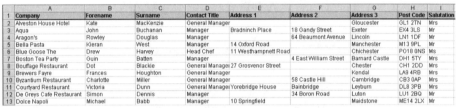

	A	B	C	D	E	F	G	H	I
1	Company	Forename	Surname	Contact Title	Address 1	Address 2	Address 3	Post Code	Salutation
2	Alveston House Hotel	Kate	MacKenzie	General Manager			Gloucester	GL1 2TN	Mrs
3	Aqua	John	Buchanan	Manager	Bradninch Place	18 Gandy Street	Exeter	EX4 3LS	Mr
4	Aragon's	Rowley	Douglas	Manager		64 Beaumont Avenue	Lincoln	LN1 1DF	Mr
5	Bella Pasta	Kieran	West	Manager	14 Oxford Road		Manchester	M13 9PL	Mr
6	Blue Goose The	Drew	Harvey	Head Chef	11 Westhampnett Road		Chichester	PO18 0NS	Ms
7	Boston Tea Party	Guin	Batten	Manager		4 East William Street	Barnard Castle	DH1 5TY	Mrs
8	Bouffage Restaurant	Dot	Blackie	General Manager	27 Grosvenor Street		Chester	CH1 2DD	Mrs
9	Brewers Fayre	Frances	Houghton	General Manager			Kendal	LA9 4RB	Mrs
10	Byzantium Restaurant	Charlotte	Miller	General Manager		58 Castle Hill	Cambridge	CB3 0AP	Mrs
11	Courtyard Restaurant	Victoria	Dunn	General Manager	Yorebridge House	Bainbridge	Leyburn	DL8 3PB	Mrs
12	De Greys Cafe Restaurant	Simon	Dennis	Manager		34 Boron Road	Luton	LU1 2BQ	Mr
13	Dolce Napoli	Michael	Babb	Manager	10 Springfield		Maidstone	ME14 2LX	Mr

Example database containing nine fields

Lists can be created and used with or without a heading row; Excel will recognise and use it if it is there, but formatting the heading row differently from the rest of the list helps to make it obvious to users. A blank row or column denotes the end of a list.

Sort a List

A list consists of column headings with rows of data beneath them. The end of a list is marked by a blank row or column.

Lists can be sorted by using the toolbar buttons or from the menu. Excel will find and sort any data adjacent to the active cell. Selecting the data manually will limit the sort area to the selection only.

To sort by a single column

•   Click cell **C1** then on the **Standard** toolbar, click **Sort Ascending** and **Sort Descending**

The entire list is sorted by the chosen column.

> **Note**   If you select a column and then sort, only the selection is sorted, leaving the remainder of data in the same place. In order to sort the whole list by a column, just click in any cell in that column.

To sort by more than one column

- Click anywhere in the list then from the **Data** menu, select **Sort...**

The **Sort** dialogue box is displayed.

Sort dialogue box

- In the **Sort By** list box, select **Salutation**

- In the **Then By** list box, select **Surname**

- Click the **Ascending** option button for each sort selected

- Make sure that the **Header row** option in the **My list has** panel is selected

This prevents the column labels from being included in the sort.

- Click **OK**

> **Tip** If more than three columns need to be sorted on, select and sort on the three *least* important columns first and click **OK**. Re-open the **Sort** dialogue box and sort by the three *most* important columns.

Use the Find and Replace Tool

Use **Find and Replace** to locate specific items of text or numbers on a worksheet that you either want to review or edit. You can also replace data.

To replace text or numbers on a worksheet

- Switch to the **Customers Telephone** worksheet

- Select the range of cells on the worksheet that you want to search **OR** to search the entire worksheet, click in any cell (click in any cell)

- From the **E̲dit** menu, select **F̲ind** (*SpeedKey:* Ctrl + F) **OR Re̲place** (*SpeedKey:* Ctrl + H) - select **Replace**

The **Replace** dialogue box is displayed.

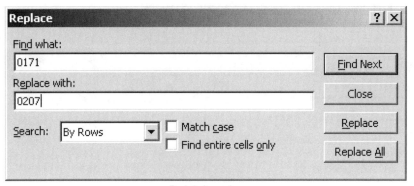

Find dialogue box

- In the **Fi̲nd what:** box, enter the text or numbers that you want to search for (type 0171)

- In the **Re̲place with:** box, enter the text or numbers that you want to replace it with (type 0207)

- In the **S̲earch:** box, select an option to either search by rows or by columns (select **Columns** in a large sheet for faster searching)

> **Note** With the **Find** command, there is an option to select **Values** or **Formulas** from the **L̲ook in:** box.

- If you want to distinguish between upper and lowercase characters in your search, select the **Match c̲ase** check box - leave this blank

- If you want to search for an exact or complete match, select the **Find entire cells o̲nly** check box - leave this blank too

- Click **Find Next**

- To replace the highlighted characters found, click **Replace**

- Click **Find Next** again and exit all dialogue boxes when no further matches are found

Note To replace all occurrences of the characters found, click **Replace All**

Tip To cancel a search, press Esc.

- Click in cell **A1**

- Close the workbook, saving any changes

ECDL with MS Office 2000 © CWC (90) 2001

Worksheet Page Layout and Printing

Setup the worksheet for printing

Setup the **page size, orientation** and **margins** ☐
Resize a worksheet to fit on one page ☐
Add a **header** and **footer** to a worksheet ☐
Use the **Spelling Checker** ☐
Preview a worksheet for printing ☐
Print a worksheet ☐
Print **part** of a worksheet ☐

Change the Page Setup

If you are designing a spreadsheet that will need to be printed often, for example an invoice or expenses form, you should determine the page setup (paper size, orientation and margins) before entering data.

To change the page setup

- Open the workbook **MailMerge_Customers OR** if you did not complete the previous lesson, open **MailMerge_Customers (Page Layout)**

- With the **Customers Mail Merge** worksheet selected, from the **File** menu, select **Page Setup...** and click the **Page** tab

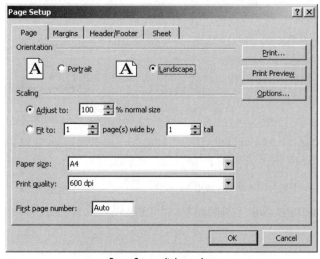

Page Setup dialogue box

From the **Paper size:** list box, you can select the type of paper on which to print (A4, Letter, B5...). From the **Orientation** panel, select **Portrait** (if the worksheet contains more rows than columns) or **Landscape** (if there are more columns than rows or if the columns are very wide).

- Select **Landscape** for this sheet

Modify Document Margins

To change the margins and print alignment

- From the **Page Setup** dialogue box, select the **Margins** tab

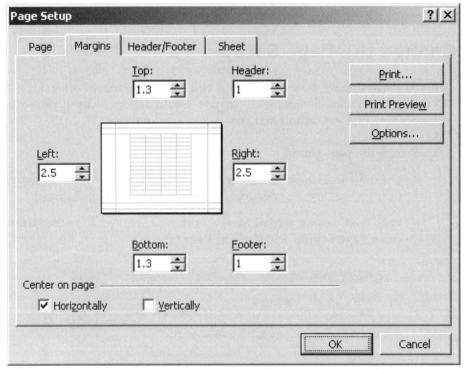

Page Setup - Margins dialogue box

- Enter the new margin dimensions (as shown above) in the boxes around the example page

- From the **Center on page** panel, click the **Horizontally** tick box

The example page displays the alignment and margin settings.

Change Print Scaling

The **Page Setup** dialogue box contains a feature to fit a worksheet onto an exact number of pages.

To print a worksheet on a specified number of pages

- From the **Page Setup** dialogue box, select the **Page** tab

From the **Scaling** panel, you can click the **Adjust to:** option button and enter a scaling factor in the **% normal size** spin box.

A number less than 100 can be used to shrink the print to any required size, a number greater than 100 can be used enlarge it to fill the page.

- For this exercise, click the **Fit to:** option button

- In the **page(s) wide by** and **tall** boxes, enter the maximum number of pages that the print must be limited to (enter **1** by **2**)

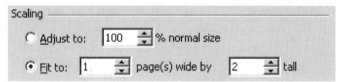

Page Setup - Scaling options

If the print is bigger than one page it will shrink equally in both directions until it fits the smallest dimension. If the print already fits on one page the **Fit to:** option has no effect.

Tip   Check the legibility of the resized sheet in Print Preview (see page 371).

Add a Header and Footer

As in Word, you can add a header and/or footer to display information on each page of the worksheet. You can add fields such as the page number, date, file name and so on.

To create page headers and footers

- From the **Page Setup** dialogue box, select the **Header/Footer** tab

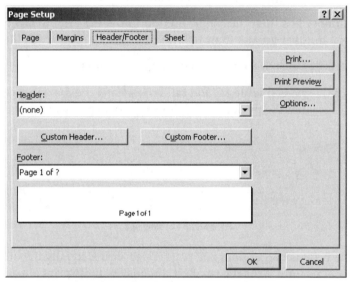

Page Setup - Header and Footer dialogue box

- Click the arrow on the **Footer:** box to select the **Page 1 or ?** footer
- Click the **Custom Header...** button to create a custom entry

The **Header** dialogue box is displayed.

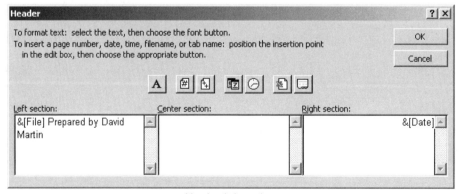

Header dialogue box

The three section panels will align any entries to that section of the page. The buttons can be used to insert information as a **field** (the page number, current date and so on).

Click	To
A	Change Font
[#]	Insert Page Number
[+]	Insert Total Number of Pages
[z]	Insert Current Date
⊘	Insert Current Time
[▦]	Insert File Name
[▭]	Insert Sheet Name

- In the **Left section:** box, click [▦] and type Prepared by *Your Name*

Automatic entries are enclosed in brackets and preceded by an ampersand on the screen, for example **&[Date]**.

- Click in the **Right section:** box and click [z]

- Click **OK**

The selected or custom entry is displayed in the preview panel.

- Click **OK** to exit **Page Setup**

Use the Spelling Checker

Excel uses the same **Spelling Checker** as Word, except that it does not check grammar. You can use it to check a selected range or an entire worksheet.

To use the Spelling Checker

- Select the cells to be spell checked or position the active cell where the spell check should begin (select **A1**)

- On the **Standard** toolbar, click **Spelling** OR from the **Tools** menu, select **Spelling...** (*SpeedKey:* F7)

Spelling dialogue box

- For each word identified as **Not in Dictionary**, select the option button to use

Click	To
Ignore	Leave the word unchanged.
Ignore All	Leave the word unchanged in all sheets until you restart Excel.
Change	Accept the spelling in the **Change to:** box. You can either replace the misspelled word with a selection from the **Suggestions:** box, or type your own correction in the **Change to:** box.
Change All	Change all occurrences of the misspelled word.
Add	Add the word to the custom dictionary.
Undo Last	Reverse the last change.

- Cancel the spell check

Use Print Preview

Print Preview lets you see how many pages your worksheet will take up, whether any data will not be printed because the columns are too narrow and whether the **Fit To** option has left the text illegible.

To use Print Preview

- On the **Standard** toolbar, click **Print Preview** OR from the **File** menu, select **Print Preview**

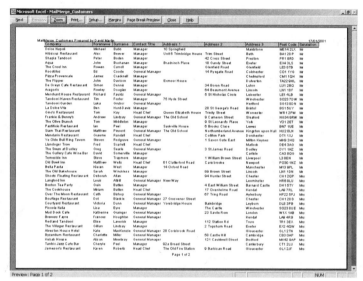

Print Preview

At the bottom of the screen the current page number and total number of pages in the print is displayed.

- On the **Preview** toolbar, click **Next** to advance to the next page then **Previous** to go back

On the preview screen the mouse pointer appears as a magnifying glass ⌕.

- To enlarge the preview move the pointer onto the page and click once, or on the **Preview** toolbar click the **Zoom** button

- Use the scroll bars to move around the page

- To view the whole page again click once anywhere on the page, or on the **Preview** toolbar click the **Zoom** button again

- Click **Setup...** and increase the top margin to **1.8**

- Click **OK** and check the results then click **Close** to exit preview mode

Print a Worksheet

To print the whole sheet

- On the **Standard** toolbar, click **Print** 🖨

All pages of the current worksheet are printed.

To print the sheet using options

- From the **File** menu, select **Print...** (*SpeedKey:* `Ctrl`+`P`) **OR** on the **Print Preview** toolbar, click the **Print...** button

The **Print** dialogue box is displayed.

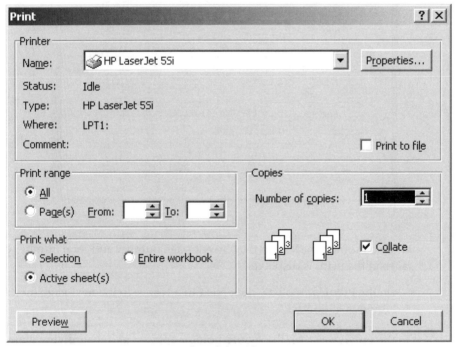

Print dialogue box

The default print settings are to print a single copy of every page from the current worksheet. From the **Print range** panel select **Page(s)** and enter the first and last pages to print in the **From:** and **To:** boxes. From the **Print what** panel click **Selection** to print only the highlighted range on the sheet, or **Entire workbook** to print every worksheet in the file.

From the **Copies** panel enter the **Number of copies:** to be printed and click the **Collate** tick box to set the copy sorting sequence

- For this exercise, just click **Cancel**

Print Part of a Worksheet

To restrict the print range

- From the **File** menu, select **Page Set<u>u</u>p...** then select the **Sheet** tab (This cannot be performed from the **Print Preview** screen)

- Click the worksheet selection icon 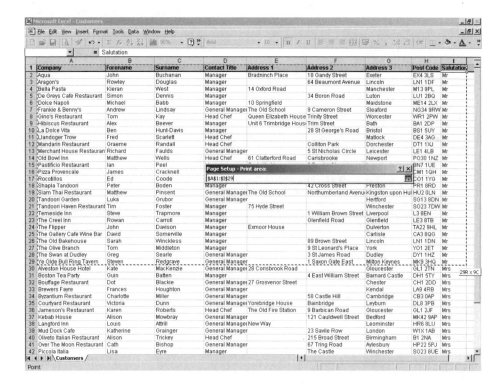 in the **Print <u>a</u>rea:** box

- Click-and-drag to select the range on the sheet (select **A1:I29**)

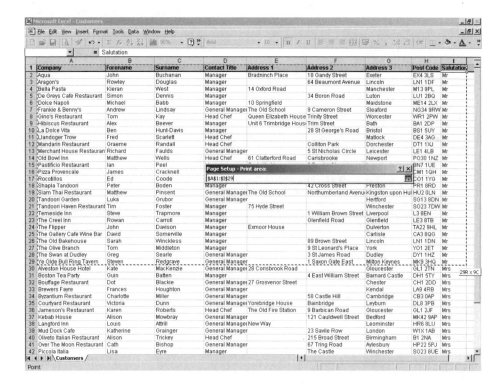

- Click **OK**

Tip You can create a print range quickly by selecting the range in the worksheet then from the **File** menu, select **Prin<u>t</u> Area** and then **<u>S</u>et Print Area**.

- On the **Standard** toolbar, click **Print** 🖨 - only the first 29 rows print out

- Save and close the workbook

Spreadsheets Consolidation Exercise

Get further practice in creating and formatting a worksheet

Lesson 29

(Create an **invoice** worksheet) ☐
(**Format** the worksheet for filling in online) ☐
(**Format** the worksheet for filling in by hand) ☐
(**Setup** the invoice for printing) ☐

Practice

- *Re-create the invoice shown below, making full use of copy and paste and the formatting tools*

- *Save the workbook as **Invoice***

- *Try to complete the exercise on your own, but use the notes if you get stuck or open **Invoice (ExchangingData)** to see a completed example*

	A	B	C	D	E	F	G	H	I
1			Joe Chillis Ltd. The Ranch 42 Broadway Maidenhead SL6 1LU				VAT Registration: 567 8232 46		
2			www.joechillis.com						
3		Invoice Address							
4		Name						*Invoice Number*	000001
5		Address						*Date*	12/19/2000
6		City		County		Post Code			
7		Telephone		Email					
8		Delivery Address							
9		Name							
10		Address							
11		City		County		Post Code			
12		Telephone		Email					
13		Qty	Product Description					Unit Price	Total
14									B14*C14
36									
37		Payment Details						Net Amount	SUM(I14:I36)
38		Cash/Cheque						VAT Amount	I37*0.175
39		Account #						Invoice TOTAL	SUM(I37:I38)
40		Credit Card							
41		CC# Expiry Date							
42									

Notes

- *Enter all the text before trying to create the border effects and row heights/column widths (also note that the product lines take up rows 14-35 - these have been hidden in the graphic)*

- *Use appropriate value formats for the price, total and date fields*

- *Type = before the formulae shown*

- *Use Format, Cells, Alignment to adjust the position of text in a cell - also use this dialogue box to indent B41 and B42*

- *Create line breaks in C1 by pressing* **Alt** *+* **Enter**

- *C2 will be formatted as a hyperlink automatically*

Practice

- *Copy the completed invoice to a new sheet, then add shading as shown below*

- *Use your own colour scheme or refer to the one in* **Invoice (ExchangingData)**

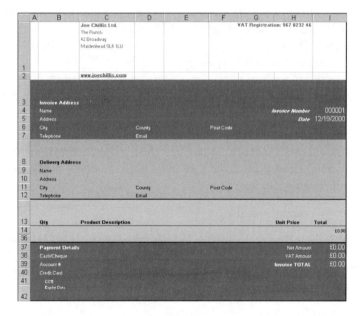

- *Create another copy of the original invoice on the third worksheet and set it up for printing on a black-and-white printer*

- *Make sure the invoice prints on one page only*

- *Add the word "Invoice" as a header in large type (36 pt, Bold)*

- *Refer to* **Invoice (ExchangingData)** *if you want to follow an example*

Charts

Display data graphically using a range of graphs and charts

Lesson 30

Create different types of **chart** from worksheet data ☐
Modify a chart (format, title, legend and scale) ☐
Change the chart **type** ☐
Move and **delete** charts ☐

Produce Different Types of Charts

Charts are an effective way of conveying complex numeric data, making the data easier to understand. Charts can demonstrate trends, highs and lows, or comparisons. They are linked to the underlying worksheet data, so amending the values on the worksheet will adjust the chart automatically.

There are a variety of chart formats (or **types**), such as **Line**, **Bar**, and **Pie** charts, which can all be presented in **2-D** or **3-D** layout. Combination charts compare related sets of figures such as staff levels and production output by means of bars *and* lines. Chart elements can be customised for colour, font, size, scale and in various other ways. Bars on a chart can be displayed in a variety of shapes including blocks, columns, cones, and pyramids.

Chart type

One of the main decisions to make is to choose the chart type. There are fourteen main chart types to choose from in Excel. Some of the most commonly used types are:

◆   **Bar** - to compare values.

◆   **Column** or **line** - to compare values (often over a period of time).

◆   **Area** - to compare values over time and show how the total value breaks down.

◆   **Pie** - to show how a total breaks down.

Each main chart type also has several subtypes or variations, such as adding a 3-D effect.

Plotting a chart

Data for a chart generally needs to be laid out in a table with column and row headings, but you do not have to select all the data. For example, the following selection could be made to compare how profits changed over time for different items. The **Totals** are not required.

	A	B	C	D	E
1			Profit		
2		Jan	Feb	Mar	Totals
3	Item 1	250	50	250	550
4	Item 2	150	150	150	450
5	Item 3	50	150	50	250
6	Item 4	1000	2000	1000	4000
7	Totals	1450	2350	1450	5250

Data selection for a column or line chart

Bar, column and line charts are made up of the **data series** (the values that are plotted), the **value** axis (displaying the range of values in the data series) and the **category** axis (displaying the range of items providing the values).

In this example, the **series legend** comes from the **column** headings (**Jan, Feb, Mar**), the **categories** are **Items 1-4** and the values to plot range from **50** to **2000**.

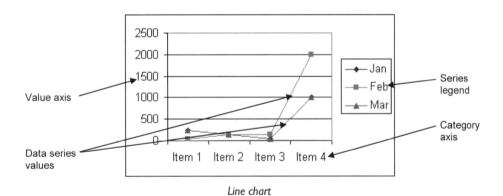

Line chart

Alternatively, you could select separate areas of the table to show how much of the total profit each item comprises.

	A	B	C	D	E
1			Profit		
2		Jan	Feb	Mar	Totals
3	Item 1	250	50	250	550
4	Item 2	150	150	150	450
5	Item 3	50	150	50	250
6	Item 4	1000	2000	1000	4000
7	Totals	1450	2350	1450	5250

Data selection for a pie chart

An appropriate chart to display this data would be the **pie** chart, which is designed to show how elements of one data series make up a total.

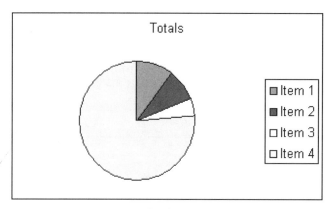

Pie chart

You could also use a bar chart to compare the totals with one another.

To create a chart

There are four steps to creating a chart. At each step you can go back and change previous selections.

- Open the **Sales Data** workbook **OR** if you have not been following each lesson, open the workbook **Sales Data (Charts)**

- Select the range from which to create the chart - select **A2:G6**

- On the **Standard** toolbar, click **Chart Wizard** ![icon] **OR** from the **Insert** menu, select **Chart...**

The **Chart Wizard Step 1** dialogue box is displayed.

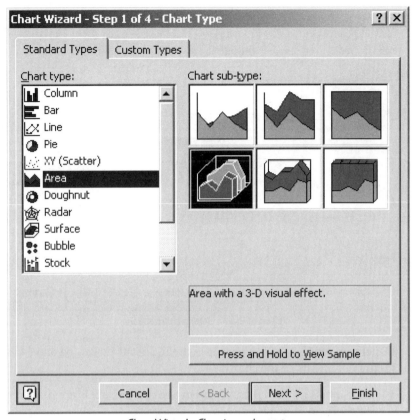

Chart Wizard - Choosing a chart type

- From the **Chart type:** list, select **Area**

- From the **Chart sub-type:** list, choose an appropriate 2-D or 3-D style (select the chart shown above)

- Click the **Press and hold to view sample** button to see how the selected data will appear as a chart

- Click **Next >**

Tip   If you are unsure which type of chart to use, lookup the topic "Examples of Chart Types" in the online help.

The **Chart Wizard Step 2** dialogue box is displayed. This dialogue box lets you adjust the range you selected and change plot options for the chart. See page 388 for further details on this step.

- Leave the options as they are and click **Next >**

The **Chart Wizard Step 3** dialogue box is displayed.

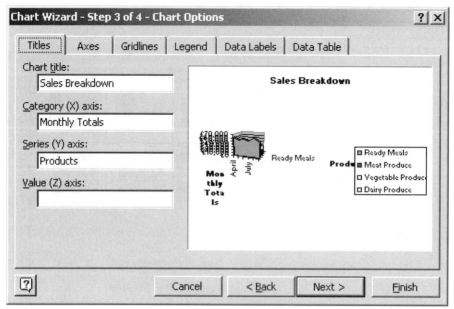

Chart Wizard - Setting chart options

Depending on the chart type selected various labels can be entered to identify elements of the chart.

- Enter labels in the boxes as shown above - the labels are displayed in the chart preview panel

- Click the **Legend** tab

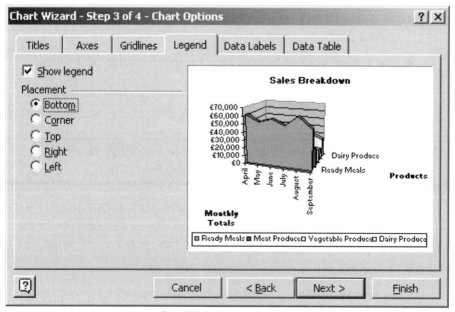

Chart Wizard - Legend options

- Select the **Bottom** option under **Placement** then click **Next >**

The **Chart Wizard Step 4** dialogue box is displayed.

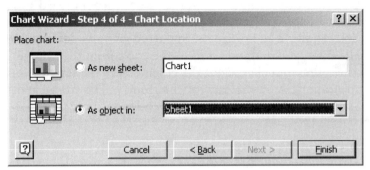

Chart Wizard - Locating the chart

The chart can be created in two ways. **As new sheet** creates a separate sheet that contains only the chart and is printed out separately to the worksheet containing the data. **As object in** creates a chart on the worksheet selected in the box. The chart can be resized and moved around the worksheet, and is printed out as part of the worksheet.

- Select **As object in: Sheet1**

- Click **Finish** - the chart is created floating over the worksheet

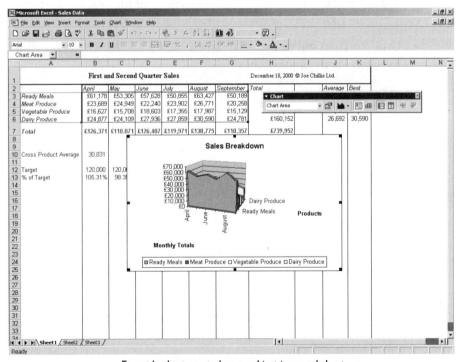

Example chart created as an object in a worksheet

> **Tip** If you have created a graph in another application and want to import it onto a worksheet, select the graph and from the **Edit** menu, select **Copy**. Switch to the Excel worksheet and from the **Edit** menu, select **Paste**. The graph is placed onto the worksheet as an **object**. You can move and resize the imported graph as described below. However, you must edit it using the tools from the original application (double-clicking the graph object will start the original application). Also, the data for the graph will be stored in datasheet attached to the graph, not in the Excel worksheet.

Move, Resize and Delete a Chart

To position, resize or delete a worksheet chart

- Click once on the chart to select it

Black selection handles appear around the edge of the chart.

- Use the arrow pointer to click-and-drag the chart around the sheet - move it below the worksheet data

Click-and-drag the sizing handles to enlarge or reduce the chart: the chart elements are redrawn automatically to fit the chart box

- Drag the chart out so that most labels are displayed, but do not make the chart larger than will fit on-screen

- Press ⌑Delete⌑ to delete the chart

- Click **Undo** to restore it

- Save the workbook

Print a Chart

Printing a chart is the same as printing a worksheet. If the chart is on a worksheet it is printed as part of the sheet. It can be sized and moved as required.

If the chart is on a chart sheet it can be printed separately, or printed along with a worksheet by selecting both sheet tabs before printing.

Modify a Chart

To edit chart elements

- Click once on the chart to display the **Chart** toolbar

Tip   If the **Chart** toolbar is not displayed when you select the chart, right-click any toolbar and from the shortcut menu, select **Chart**.

The **Chart** toolbar lets you select and edit elements of the chart quickly.

Click	To
Chart Area ▼ *Chart Objects*	Select an element of the chart to format.
🛠️ *Format Chart Objects*	Display a dialogue box to format the selected chart object.
📊 ▼ *Chart Type*	Select a different chart type.
📇 *Legend*	Show or hide the chart legend.
⊞ *Data Table*	Show or hide a table of the chart data below the chart.
🗐 *By Row*	Read the data across rows - use row headings as the data series and column headings as the categories.
🗒 *By Column*	Read the data down columns - use column headings as the data series and row headings as the categories.
✍ *Angle Text Downward*	Slope the selected text down.
✍ *Angle Text Upward*	Slope the selected text up.

To format chart elements

- Select the **Series "Ready Meals"** element (by clicking on it or by selecting it from the **Chart** toolbar)

- On the **Chart** toolbar, click **Format Chart Objects** 📝 OR from the **Format** menu, select **Selected Data Series...** (*SpeedKey:* [Ctrl]+[1])

The **Format** dialogue box is displayed. The **Format** dialogue box will have different tabs depending on which element is selected. You can usually change things like the border or background colours, line colours and styles, font formatting and so on.

- Click the **Series Order** tab

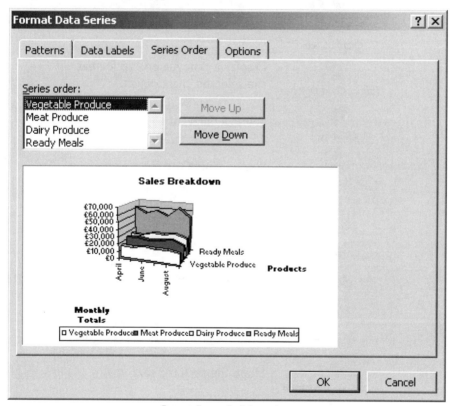

Format (Legend) dialogue box

- Use the **Move Up** and **Move Down** buttons to change the series order as shown above

- Click **OK**

To change the scale of the value axis

In some circumstances the scale of the value axis determined by Excel may not be appropriate. For example, if a chart contains many low values and one very high value, you may want to cut off the high value in order to show the spread of low values in more detail.

- Select the **Value Axis** then on the **Chart** toolbar, click **Format Chart Objects**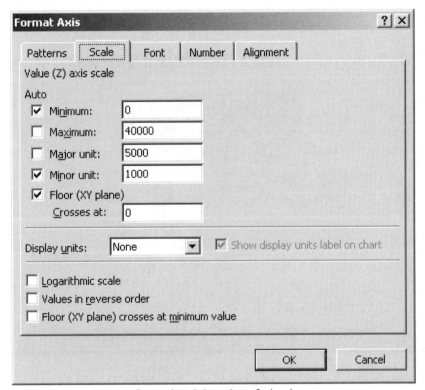

- Click the **Scale** tab

The **Minimum:** and **Maximum:** boxes allow you to enter the lowest and highest values you want to be displayed on the chart. Optionally, you can change the values of the units (which affects how gridlines are displayed).

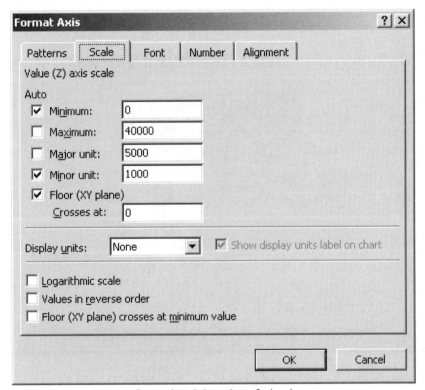

Format Axis dialogue box - Scale tab

- Set the values shown above and click **OK**

The higher values in the **Ready Meals** data series are removed and the changes in the other series are emphasised.

Practice

Use the **Format** *dialogue box and* **Formatting** *toolbar to make the following changes:*

- *Set the **Font Size** of each **axis** to 8 pt*

- *Set the **Font Color** of all text to **Dark Red***

- *Make all titles **Times New Roman** and **Underline***

- *Make the chart title 24 pt*

- *Make the **Legend** font size 10 pt*

- *Change the **Fill Color** of the **data series** to different shades of **orange***

- *Change the **Fill Color** of the **walls** and **floor** to **white***

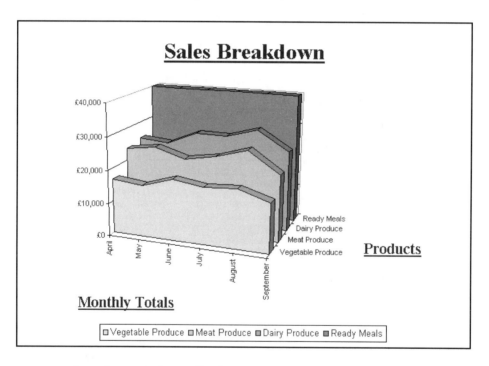

- *Save changes to the workbook*

Change the Chart Type

Excel contains a large library of chart types that can be chosen from the **Chart Wizard** when the chart is being created. The chart type can also be changed after the chart has been created.

To change the chart type

- Select the existing chart then on the **Standard** toolbar, click **Copy**

- Switch to **Sheet2** and click **Paste**

- Select the original chart on **Sheet1** then click the arrow on the **Chart Type** button

Chart type menu

- Select the **3-D Pie Chart**

The chart is immediately updated to the chart type selected.

Changing the chart type might mean that the new chart does not show the same data as before. In this example, because the chart is now a pie chart, only the first data series is displayed.

You can change the source data for a chart, but in some cases it will be better to delete the chart and start again.

Tip   Alternatively, you can re-display step 1 of the Chart Wizard to completely revise the chart type. To do this, from the **Chart** menu, select **Chart Type...**

To change the source data for a chart

The values displayed in the chart are updated whenever the data in the worksheet is changed. However, you can also change the ranges used for chart data, add and remove data series, plot by row or column and so on.

- With the new pie chart selected, from the **Chart** menu, select **Source Data...** - the dialogue box is the same as **Step 2** of the **Chart Wizard**

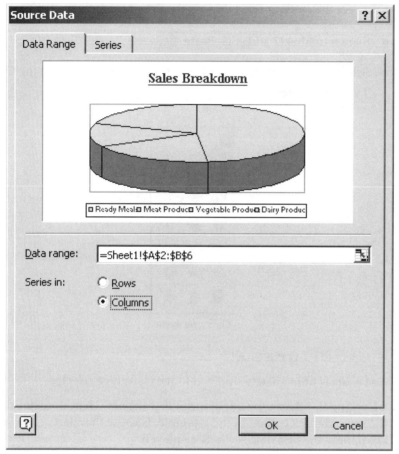

Chart Wizard - plotting data

- Click 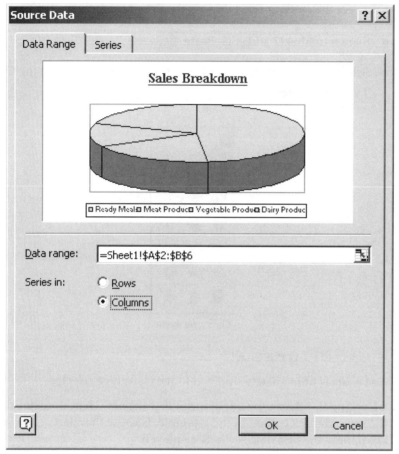 to select the range **A2:B6** and select the **Columns** option button
- Click **OK** - the chart preview panel changes to show the effect of your selection

---

Tip   Click the **Series** tab to make adjustments to the data you are plotting. You can add and remove data series and change the cells used to provide labels and names.

Practice

The **Chart Options** *dialogue box repeats step 3 of the wizard, allowing you to adjust the title, legend, labels and so on.*

- *Change the* **Fill Color** *of the data series to different shades of orange*

- *From the* **Chart** *menu, select* **Chart Options** *and click the* **Data Labels** *tab*

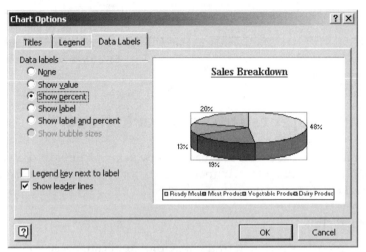

Chart Options dialogue box

- *Set labels to* **Show percent** *and change the chart title to* Sales Breakdown (April)

- *Save the workbook and close it if you do not want to complete the next exercise*

Practice

To get further practice in creating charts, try completing the following in the **Sales Data** *workbook (add each chart as a new sheet). These exercises are more advanced than would be expected in an ECDL test, so do not worry if you cannot complete them. Finished examples can be found in the* **Sales Data (Finished Charts)** *workbook.*

- *Create a chart to show the difference between the average values for each type of product (Tip: You can use* Ctrl *+click-and-drag to select two separate ranges for the chart source data)*

- *Create a chart to compare sales of* **Meat** *and* **Vegetable Products** *between* **April** *and* **September**

- *Create a combination chart showing* **Average** *and* **Best** *values together (use the Custom Types tab to create a combination chart, such as Line-Column)*

- *Add appropriate titles and formatting to each chart then save and close the workbook*

Exchanging Worksheet Data

Add data objects to a worksheet and save workbooks for use in different applications

---

Lesson 31

Import **objects** onto a worksheet □
Move and **resize** imported objects □
Save a workbook and/or worksheet under a different **file format** □
Save a worksheet as a **web page** □

Import Objects into a Worksheet

You may want to enhance a spreadsheet by using pictures or drawings. For example, you could add a company logo to an invoice or draw arrows to connect charts with data on the worksheet.

To insert clips

The **Clip Gallery** is shared by all MS Office applications, so you have already seen how to use it in the Word lesson (page 276).

- If you completed the **Consolidation Exercise**, open your **Invoice** workbook OR open the **Invoice (ExchangingData)** workbook

- Select the sheet where shading has been applied

- From the **Insert** menu, select **Picture** then **Clip Art...**

- Browse for a suitable clip - in the **Search for clips** box, type Handshakes and press Enter or try searching for Money

- Choose a clip and click **Insert Clip** on the shortcut bar

- Close the **ClipArt Gallery** dialogue box

To insert other pictures

The invoice also needs a logo to give it a corporate identity.

- From the **Insert** menu, select **Picture** then **From File...**

- Select the **chilli logo** picture and click **Insert**

Move and Resize Objects on a Worksheet

Pictures, clip art, drawings, charts and so on are all referred to as **objects**. You can move them around the worksheet, resize and delete them in the same way.

Objects "float over" the worksheet. They are not part of any cell and so can only be selected with the mouse.

To select an object

To edit any object you must first select the object you wish to change. When an object is selected, white handles appear around the edge of the object (except for charts, which have black handles).

A selected object

To move, resize and delete an object

- Select the chilli logo and then click-and-drag to move it to the left of the Chilli address

Tip To maintain the horizontal or vertical alignment of the object, hold down the `Shift` key when you drag.

Click-and-drag a centre handle to make the object taller or wider OR click-and-drag a corner handle to make the object larger or smaller.

- Drag the bottom right-hand corner to make the picture fit beside the address without obscuring it

Tip Hold down the `Ctrl` key to resize the object from the centre outwards.

- Select the clip art then from the **Edit** menu, select **Clear** then **All** (*SpeedKey:* `Delete`)

- If you liked your clip art, click **Undo** then resize and move it to a suitable location on the invoice

Practice

You can also use the drawing tools in Excel.

- *Create some AutoShape rectangles to mark off the address and payment details areas - see the **Invoice (Complete)** sheet in **Invoice (ExchangingData)** for an example*

- *Save the workbook*

Save a Workbook in a Different File Format

Excel includes file converters that enable you to open spreadsheets from other applications (such as Lotus 123 and Corel QuattroPro) or from text files (.CSV and .TXT) and to save your workbooks in the file format of other applications.

To open a spreadsheet from another application ⊕

There are no example files for this topic, but if you have spreadsheets in a different file format try opening one now.

o On the **Standard** toolbar, click **Open** 📂

o In the **Files of type** drop-down list box, select **All Files**

o Locate and open the file

If the file format is recognised, the spreadsheet will open as normal in Excel. You can make changes and then save it back in the original file format or in MS Excel format.

If the file format is not recognised, an error message is displayed.

Open File error messages

You can try running the MS Office 2000 setup program to install the correct file converters or open the spreadsheet in the original application and save it in a different format.

To save an Excel spreadsheet in a different file format

If you want to share worksheet data with colleagues using a different application to Excel (or an earlier version of MS Excel), you can use the **Save as type** box to save a workbook in a different **file format**. The table below describes some of the different formats you can choose.

Select	To
Excel 5.0/95 Workbook/ Excel 4.0 Workbook	Save the workbook so that it can be opened and edited in a previous version of Excel or in an older version of another spreadsheet application (for example, Lotus 123 or Corel QuattroPro).
Excel 4.0, 3.0, 2.1 Worksheet	Save the active worksheet only for use in an earlier version of Excel.
Template	Save the workbook in the Office Templates folder. You can then use the workbook as the basis of new workbooks, by selecting it from the New dialogue box.
Text/CSV	Save the active worksheet only in a text format. This option is used to save lists of data in a format that can be opened by most spreadsheet or database applications. The end of each cell is marked by a special character - either a tab (TXT) or a comma (CSV). There are also different formats for Apple MAC and MS-DOS computers.
QPW, WK*, DBF...	Save the workbook in the file format of another application.

> **Note** Applications such as Lotus 123 and Corel QuattroPro have **file converters** that let you open an Excel workbook in its original format. Not all Excel features will convert exactly to other file formats though.

> **Note** Take care when opening or converting spreadsheets containing dates that use 2-digit year formats. Different applications can use different methods to interpret the date intended. It is safest to convert all dates to a 4-digit year format in the original application before opening it in Excel.

As an example, you will save the **Invoice** you created as a template file. Firstly, you will move just the completed worksheet to a new workbook.

- Right-click the sheet tab containing the completed invoice and select **Move or Copy...**

- In **To book:** select **(new book)** and check the **Create a copy** box then click **OK**

- In the new workbook, from the **File** menu, select **Save As...**

The **Save As** dialogue box is displayed.

- From the **Save as type:** list box, select **Template**

Move or Copy dialogue box

Your Office **Templates** folder is automatically selected as the default location.

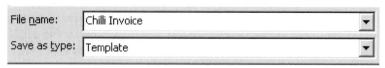

Save As dialogue box

- Enter the file name `Chilli Invoice` then click **Save**

- Close all open workbooks without saving

- From the **File** menu, select **New...**

- Select the **Chilli Invoice** icon and click **OK**

A new workbook is created with the same cell contents, formatting and graphics as the original.

- Close the new workbook without saving

To use text files

Plain text files are a useful way to transfer data, because almost any type of application (word processor, spreadsheet, database or presentation) can open text files.

Text files are usually used to store data **lists**, where each **field** is **separated** by a special character, such as a comma or tab. Such files are called **comma-delimited** (or **tab-delimited**).

However, you can also use text from another file within a cell. For example, you might have the text of a legal disclaimer or invoice terms stored in a Word document. You can copy and paste this text into a worksheet cell.

- Open the **Customers** workbook then save it as a tab delimited text file

- Excel will warn you that some formatting and features may not convert to the new format - click **Yes** to continue

- Open the **Customers.TXT** file using MS Word - in the **Open** dialogue box, make sure that the **Files of type:** box is set to **Text Files**

The file will look quite chaotic, but if you were to adjust the tab stops to fit each paragraph to a single line, you would see that the same columns and rows have been preserved.

- Press Ctrl+A to select all the text then **Copy** it

- Close Word then switch to Excel and create a new workbook

- Click in cell **A1** and select **Paste**

The text is inserted into the sheet. Excel recognises that the data is a list and so puts each field into its own cell.

- Close any open workbooks without saving

Tip If you paste text that is not in a delimited list format, it is put into just one cell.

Save a Worksheet as a Web Page

As with Word documents, you can save an Excel worksheet or workbook in **HTML** format for publishing on the world wide web or to a company intranet.

The advantage of saving data as HTML is that other users will not need a spreadsheet application to view it.

Before you can publish your worksheet as a web page the file should be saved as a normal Excel file. If at a later date you decide to change the information displayed, you will have access to the original file.

You can publish a worksheet as a **static** web page or as an **interactive** web page. In a static web page, the spreadsheet data can simply be viewed in a web browser. In an **interactive** web page, users can work with the data, if they are using the web browser **Internet Explorer 4.01** (or later).

To save a worksheet as a web page

- Open the **Sales Data** workbook OR (if you have not been following each lesson) use **Sales Data (Finished Charts)**

- From the **File** menu, select **Save as Web Page...**

The **Save As** dialogue box is displayed - if you save from here you will create a series of web pages for each worksheet.

- For this exercise, click the **Publish...** button

The **Publish as a Web Page** dialogue box is displayed.

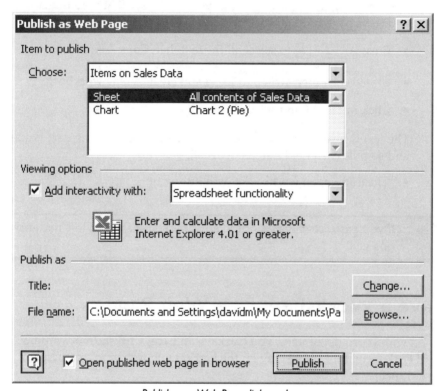

Publish as a Web Page dialogue box

You can create an **interactive** web page that lets users (with Internet Explorer 4.01 or later) work with the data on the sheet. However, you can only publish one object at a time.

- In the **Choose** box, ensure that **All contents of Sales Data** is selected

- To make the sheet interactive, from the **Viewing options** panel, select the **Add interactivity with:** check box and from the drop-down list, select **Spreadsheet functionality**

- To add a title to the web page, click the **Change...** button and enter the title Chilli Sales Data

- In the **File name:** box, click the **Browse...** button and save the page in **My Documents** as SalesData

- Click **OK**

- To view the published web page using your browser after you have published it, select the **Open published Web page in browser** check box

- Click **Publish**

The sheet is opened in your web browser.

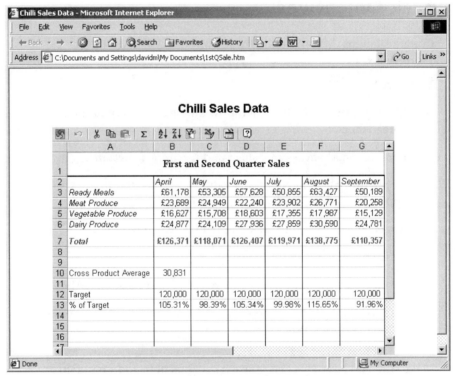

Viewing a spreadsheet published on a web page

- Experiment with the toolbar to work with the data then close your web browser

- Save and close the workbook

Review of Spreadsheets

Review the topics covered during the module and identify areas for further practice and goals for the future

---

Review

(Check **objectives**) ☐
(Complete **consolidation** exercise) ☐
(Identify topics for **further** study) ☐

Check Objectives

Congratulations on completing the lessons for ECDL Module 4 "Spreadsheets".

You have learned to:

♦ Identify parts of the Excel **window** and learn the **layout** of a **spreadsheet**.

♦ Enter **text** and **values** in a sheet and use basic **functions**.

♦ Apply **format** options to show values correctly and to improve the appearance of the worksheet.

♦ **Revise** the worksheet and **share data** between workbooks.

♦ **Setup** the worksheet for **printing**.

♦ Display data graphically using a range of **graphs** and **charts**.

♦ Add data **objects** to a worksheet and save workbooks for use in different **applications**.

Make sure you have checked off each syllabus item and identified any topics you do not fully understand or remember.

ECDL with MS Office 2000 © CWC (90) 2001

Consolidation and Going Further

Tests for Module 4 can either be practice-based or question-based. Practical tests will ask you to create, edit, format and print a series of worksheets in Excel.

There are further test-style exercises for you to try on the CD in the folder **ECDL Tests\4 Spreadsheets**

Print the document **Spreadsheets Questions** and try to complete the test unaided, using the data files from the folder.

> **Note** These questions are provided as a consolidation exercise. They do not make up an approved ECDL test. See page **689** for more information about the extra tests.

Going further

There is plenty of opportunity for further training in Excel. For example, there are a huge number of more complex functions and formulae to learn about and tools to change the layout and appearance of a worksheet.

Other areas of study include collaborating on workbooks in a workgroup, tools for analysing and consolidating data, such as PivotTables and importing data from other applications, such as an Access database. You can also learn to use macros and VBA programming to automate tasks.

Many of these topics can be studied under the **ECDL Advanced Syllabus**.

Refer to page 744 for more details about further courses in gtslearning's range of Learn the series training books.

Notes

Database

Using a Database

Open a database to add and edit records

Lesson 32

Understand the **functions** and **components** of a database ☐
Open and **logon** to a database ☐
Navigate through a database **table** ☐
Enter and **edit** data in a table ☐
Add and delete **records** ☐
Find a record ☐
Add and edit data using a **form** ☐
Close the database and Access ☐

What is a Database?

A database is a collection of information that has been organised so that the information easy to access and display in different ways. Databases are used everywhere: at work, in the home, in schools and leisure facilities.

Real world database examples are as obvious as a telephone directory, an encyclopaedia, or even a library.

Computerising a Database

The advantage of any database is that information is easy to find (we all know how to look up a friend's telephone number in the telephone directory). If the database is computerised, then information retrieval is faster and more accurate still.

More importantly, it is possible to manipulate the information in the database in different ways. A paper database can only be viewed in one way - the way it was printed. In a computer database, information can be re-sorted and filtered to display different views of the data. For example, with a computer telephone directory, you could easily create a list of the telephone numbers of people in your street.

The main disadvantage of a computerised database is that designing and creating an efficient database takes time. Also, a database has to be maintained carefully, to ensure that it is used properly and that the data stored is accurate.

Database Terms

The following terms are used to speak about databases.

Database

A **database** is a collection of **objects** used for storing and managing information. In Access, a database is stored on disk in an **.MDB** file. The MDB file saves the database objects and the data they contain.

Object

An **object** (in Access) means a database component, such as a **table**, **query**, **form** or **report**.

Table

A **table** is the place in the database where data is stored. A table consists of **fields**, which define what information is kept for each **record**. A **record** represents one entry in the database. For example, a table storing a simple telephone directory for a business might have three fields to store data for *Name*, *Desk* and *Telephone Number*. Each employee in the company would have a record in the table.

At its simplest, data in a table is shown as a **datasheet**. A datasheet looks like a spreadsheet. Each column in the datasheet represents a field. Each row in the datasheet is a record.

Forms

Datasheets show all of the records in a table at once. **Forms** are a more user-friendly way of presenting data. A form usually displays data in the table one record at a time, with fields arranged neatly on-screen.

Queries

Queries are a tool for selecting and sorting data to make it easier to work with. For many database operations, you may not want to see all records at the same time, or to analyse data, you may wish to see how many records fit certain criteria.

Queries can be used to update and modify data as well as to look at it. You can also use **expressions** in queries to perform calculations on data.

Reports

Tables, queries and forms can be printed as seen on the screen, but **reports** allow data to be presented in a more structured format. Reports based on queries print only the selected fields and records that the query produces. Reports can also include calculations and summaries of the data printed.

Open Access

Access can be opened using the program shortcut icon  wherever it appears.

To start Access from the Start menu

- Click the **Start** button **Start** then from the **Programs** menu, select the **Microsoft Access** program item Microsoft Access

Unlike Word and Excel, Access displays a **Startup** dialogue box, which provides several options for the creation of a new database, or the opening of an existing database.

Select	To
Blank Access database	Create a new database from scratch.
Access database wizards, pages, and projects	Create a database with help from Access.
Open an existing file	Open an existing database. Recently used files are listed in the scroll box.

- For this exercise, click **Cancel** to pass through the dialogue box without selecting an option

The Access application window is displayed.

Access Startup dialogue box

> **Tip**   If an existing database is not on the list, select **More Files...** to browse for it.

Open an Existing Database

Like other Office 2000 applications, there are several ways of opening an Access database.

To open a database ⓘ

o From the **Startup** dialogue box, select **Open an existing file** then double-click **More Files... OR**

o Use the **Open** toolbar button 📂 on the **Standard** toolbar **OR**

o Use the **File, Open** command (*SpeedKey:* Ctrl + O) **OR**

o Select a recently used database from the bottom of the **File** menu

Unlike other Office 2000 programs, you cannot open multiple files in one Access window. If you use the Open command from within Access, the current database will be closed before opening the new one. To open more than one database at a time, you must start another version of Access.

o Select a recently used file from the **Start, Documents** menu (Access will start automatically) **OR**

o Open a database file icon 📄 from **My Computer** (Access will start automatically)

Logon to a Database

Many databases are password protected, to prevent unauthorised users from viewing or editing records.

To logon to a password protected database

• On the **Standard** toolbar, click **Open** 📂 - the **Open** dialogue box is displayed

• Select the **Products_Database** icon and click **Open**

Because this database is protected, a **Password Required** dialogue box is displayed.

• Type the password ecdl and click **OK**

The database is opened.

Password Required dialogue box

> **Tip** If the database does not open, you probably did not type the password in lower case - in Access passwords are case sensitive. Make sure the Caps Lock key is not activated, and try re-entering the password.

The Access Window

The Access window contains most of the elements you might expect from an Office 2000 application.

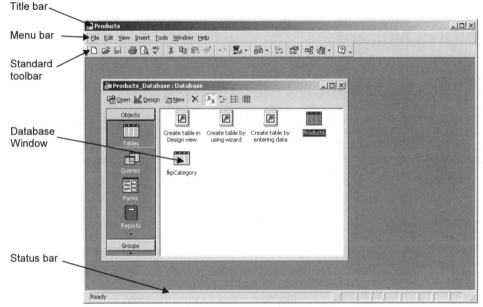

Access Opening Screen

The Access Standard Toolbar

Unlike other Office applications, the buttons on the Standard toolbar change depending on where you are in the application. Otherwise the toolbar is controlled in the same way.

Standard toolbar (with Database Window active)

The Database Window

Access allows only one database to be open at any one time. All of the contents of the database are displayed in the Database window.

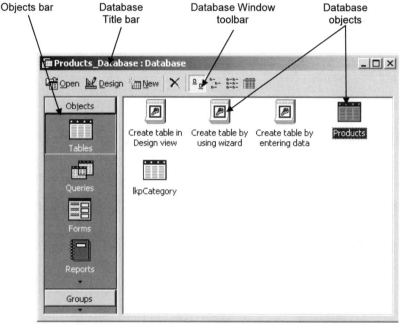

Database Window

The Database window has its own **Title** bar and its own toolbar. The **Objects** bar, on the left-hand side of the window lets you browse different types of database **objects**. The right-hand **object list pane** lists all of the available objects of the selected type, plus some additional icons for creating new objects.

In this course you will be looking at the following four object types: **table**, **form**, **report** and **query**. You will be creating and manipulating some of these objects later in the course.

- Click each icon on the **Objects Bar**

As you do so, the **object list** pane is updated with the list of currently available objects. Even in a blank database, there will be objects in some of the windows - usually wizards and other such useful objects. In some cases, there are two or three ways of creating each object.

The Database Window Toolbar

The **Database Window** toolbar allows you to perform various operations on the currently selected object, or to create a new object of the type currently selected in the **Object** bar.

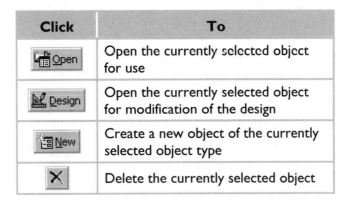

Click	To
Open	Open the currently selected object for use
Design	Open the currently selected object for modification of the design
New	Create a new object of the currently selected object type
X	Delete the currently selected object

Other buttons on the database window allow you to change the display.

The Status Bar

The **Status** bar displays information while you are working in a database. The left-hand part of the bar may display help text related to the field you are entering data in. **CAPS** and **NUM** show whether Caps Lock and Num Lock respectively are switched on.

Status bar

Get Help with Access

The Help system in Access works in the same way as for Word. Refer back to page 194 if you need reminding.

Open a Table

When you open a table, you see it in **Datasheet** view. Datasheet view looks like a **spreadsheet**. However, unlike a spreadsheet, you can **only** enter data into the fields defined, and any data you enter **must** be part of a record.

The table is a series of rows, which represent records, and columns, which represent fields.

To examine a table in datasheet view

- From the **Database** window, in the **Objects** bar, click **Tables**

The right-hand pane displays any table objects available in the database. Database tables are represented by the table icon ▦. The Access icon objects ▧ represent different ways to create new tables.

- Select the **Products** table

- On the **Database Window** toolbar, click **Open** Open

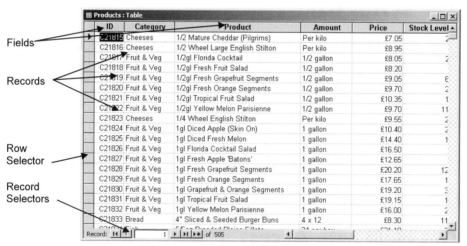

A table named Products in datasheet view

The table is opened in datasheet view. Note that the table opens in its own window and that an icon for the window appears on the **Windows Taskbar**.

Enter Data in a Table

When you are displaying a table in datasheet view, you can add a record to the end of the existing records. If you scroll to the bottom of the data, you will see that the last (empty) row is marked by an asterisk ⟦*⟧ in the row selector column.

This asterisk denotes that if you enter data into any of the columns in this row, Access will treat this as a new record to be added to the table, and will change the record selector button to display an **Editing** icon ⟦/⟧.

To add a record in datasheet view ①

Read through these steps then practise adding records on page 412.

o On the **Standard** toolbar, click **New Record** ⟦▶*⟧ **OR** type data into the row marked with an asterisk ⟦*⟧ **OR** from the **Insert** menu, select **Ne̲w Record**

Use the following key combinations to move between the fields in the record:

Press	To Go To
⟦Tab⟧ or ⟦➡⟧ or ⟦Enter⟧	Next field
⟦Shift⟧+⟦Tab⟧ or ⟦⬅⟧	Previous field
⟦Home⟧	First field
⟦End⟧	Last field

OR

o Use the mouse to select a field in which to enter data

Save Changes to Records

Once you have entered data into one or more fields, saving the changes is a simple case of moving off the record that you are currently editing. There is no need to select a **Save** command to save changes made to data.

To save changes to records ①

o Press ⟦Page Up⟧ , ⟦Page Down⟧ , ⟦⬆⟧ , ⟦⬇⟧ **OR** ⟦Shift⟧+⟦Enter⟧ **OR**

o Press ⟦➡⟧ from the last field **OR** press ⟦⬅⟧ from the first field **OR**

o Close the table

Practice

- On the **Standard** toolbar, click **New Record** ▶*

The first column in the table is an **AutoNumber** *field. Access updates this automatically when you add a record.*

- *Press* Tab *to move to the next field*

- *Add the records shown below to the table*

- *There is no need to type the £ sign in the* **Price** *field - this is added automatically*

- *Press* Tab *from the* **Discontinued** *field to start the next record without entering any data in the field*

Category	Product	Amount	Price	Stock Level	Reorder Level
Quiche	Spicy Prawn Quiche	12"	£9.70	25	25
Fruit & Veg	1/2gl Yellow Melon Parisienne	1/2 gallon	£4.35	11	15
Fillings	Chicken Tikka Mayonnaise	6x l litre jars	£9.15	95	0
Salads	Mexican Bean Salad	2kl	£9.65	67	25

Use the Undo Tool

You can use the **Undo** button on the **Standard** toolbar to reverse your last action. **You must use Undo before making any other change** - in Access there is only one "level" of undo.

While you are on a record, you can undo the last change you made to an individual field. When you move off a record, you can undo **all** the changes you made to it, **but only if you have not started editing another record**.

To undo changes to a record

- On the **Standard** toolbar, click **Undo** ↺ OR from the **Edit** menu, select **Undo** (*SpeedKey:* Ctrl+Z or Esc)

The last action you made was to add the **Mexican Bean Salad** record. Access warns you that this will be deleted.

- Click **No** to cancel undo and keep the record

Navigate Through a Table

The **active selection** is the location on the datasheet where editing takes place, for example text being entered or deleted. You can either select a single field for editing, or select an area for cut and paste operations. However the two are exclusive – you can have an active selection or an area selected but not both.

There are three main ways to select cells, rows (records) and columns:

♦   Using the **Record Selector** buttons.

♦   Using the **mouse**.

♦   Using the **keyboard**.

To use the Record Selector buttons

At the bottom of the datasheet, there are button controls used to navigate between records.

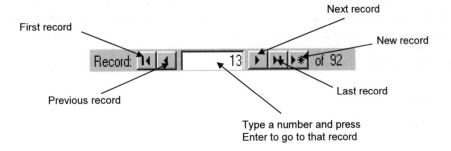

Practice

- *Write down the Product Names of the following records (Use the best navigation button to move to each record)*

316

_____

315

_____

First

_____

Last

_____

To select records using the mouse

As an alternative to using the Record Selector buttons, you can select records using the mouse simply by clicking in them.

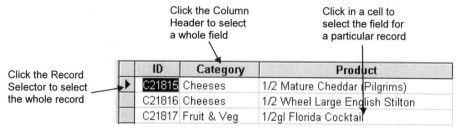

Selecting rows and columns with the mouse

Depending on the size of the **Datasheet** window, **scroll bars** may appear to the right and at the bottom of the table window.

Tip   Scrolling does not move the active selection. To edit after scrolling, click the mouse to select the field that you wish to edit.

Note Click-and-drag to select multiple records.

SpeedKeys

The following keystrokes are also useful for navigating around the datasheet:

Press	To
`Tab` or `→`	Select the next field in the record
`Shift` + `Tab` or `←`	Select the previous field in the record
`↓`	Select the same field in the next record
`↑`	Select the same field in the previous record
`Shift` + `←`, `→`, `↑`, `↓`	Select two or more fields in the datasheet
`Ctrl` + `Home`	Move to the first field of the first record
`Ctrl` + `End`	Move to the last field of the last record

Press	To
Page Up	Scroll the screen up one page
Page Down	Scroll the screen down one page
Ctrl + A	Select all records in the table
Ctrl + Space Bar	Select the entire column of the current active cell
Shift + Space Bar	Select the entire row of the current active cell

Practice

Use navigation keys to select:

- *The **Category** column*
- *Record #3 (all fields)*
- *The **Reorder Level** field of the last two records*

Find a Record

In a large database, it is difficult to locate a record simply by scrolling down the screen. The **Find** tool lets you search for records based on the data in a given field.

To find a record

- Select the **Product** column
- On the **Standard** toolbar, click **Find** 🔍 OR from the **Edit** menu, select **Find...** (*SpeedKey:* Ctrl + F)

The **Find and Replace** dialogue box is displayed.

- In the **Find What:** box, type the text you want to search for - type quiche

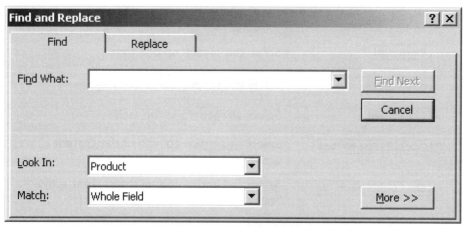

Find and Replace dialogue box

Note By default, the **Look In:** field shows the currently selected column. You have the choice of either using this default value or the entire table. Selecting the latter option may take a long time with a large table. If you have more than one column selected, the only option is to search the entire table.

The **Match:** field allows you to choose three matching options for the field on which you are searching.

Select **Whole Field** (default) to find records only where the whole of the field exactly matches the contents of the **Find What:** box. Select **Start of Field** to find records where the field **begins** with the contents of the **Find What:** box (This is slightly less restrictive than the **Whole Field** option). Select **Any Part of Field** to find records where the contents of the **Find What:** box occur in some part of the field.

- Select the **Any Part of Field** option and click **Find Next**

Record number **53** (Broccoli and Mushroom Quiche) is selected on the datasheet.

- Click **Find Next** - the next quiche (record 54) is located

- Click **Cancel** to close the **Find** dialogue box

Sort Data

The ability to sort data provides one of the most obvious examples of the flexibility of databases - imagine having a telephone directory in which you can view the information sorted by the first line of the address, or surname, initials, postcode, dialling code, telephone number...

When sorting information, you have the option to sort the information either:

♦ **Ascending (A to Z or 1 to 10).**

♦ **Descending (Z to A or 10 to 1).**

It should be noted that these sorts are not case sensitive. For example, words beginning with "a" and "A" will be mixed together in the sort.

To sort data by a single field

- Select the **Category** column

- On the **Standard** toolbar, click **Sort Ascending** to sort in ascending order

- On the **Standard** toolbar, click **Sort Descending** to sort in descending order

To sort data by more than one field

If you select more than one field in datasheet view, Access will sort by the fields in the order in which they are displayed in the view. Data will be sorted by the first selected column, then any duplicate values from that sort will be sub-sorted by the values in the second column, and so on.

- Select the **Category** and **Product** columns then click **Sort Ascending** - the data is sorted by category then by product name

---

Tip   To change the order of columns, click the column header and drag it left or right.

Modify Data in a Table

You will often want to make changes to a record after it has been added.

To select and edit fields ①

When you select a field with the keyboard, the entire field contents are selected.

- o If you begin typing into the field at this point, the existing contents will be overwritten

- o To edit the existing contents of a field, select the field then press F2

Practice

- • *Find the group of records where the Product Name field starts "1/2 gl" and "1 gl"*

- • *Edit each record to show just the product's name*

Tip Remember that you can use **Undo** to reverse the last edit you made to a field so long as you have not moved off the record. Once you move off the record, you can only undo **all** changes you made to it.

Also, you can only undo the last action you made.

Delete Data in a Table

To delete records in datasheet view

- • Sort the datasheet in descending order by the **Discontinued** column

- • Click-and-drag down the row selector column (the grey column to the left of the record) over the **discontinued** record(s)

- • On the **Standard** toolbar, click **Delete Record** ✖ OR from the **Edit** menu, select **Delete** (*SpeedKey:* Delete) OR right-click the row selector button and from the shortcut menu, select **Delete Record**

A warning box is displayed, telling you that the record(s) are about to be deleted permanently.

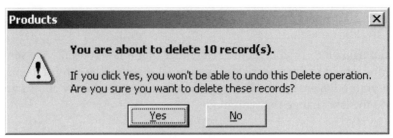

Delete Record(s) warning message

**Warning   You cannot undo this action. Once you click Yes, the
data cannot be recovered.**

- Click **Yes** to confirm the deletion

Close a Table

To close a table

- From the left-hand side of the datasheet's **Title** bar, click the
Document Control icon ▦ and select **Close**

OR

- Click the **Close** ✕ button on the right-hand side of the **Title** bar

OR

- From the **File** menu, select **Close** (*SpeedKey:* Ctrl + F4)

A message box prompts you to save changes to the layout of the table
(the changes you made to the sort order of the columns).

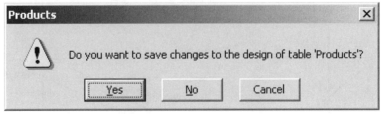

Close table warning message

- Select **Yes** to save changes

Enter Data Using a Form

When using a form you should remember that it is essentially the same as editing a field in datasheet view. You must therefore be careful to ensure that your edits are correct before moving on, as Access only allows you to undo the last change that you made.

To open a form

- In the **Database** window, select the **Forms** object

- Select the **Product Entry** form and click **Open** Open
  Product Entry

To navigate between records in form view

In **form** view, only a single record is displayed at any one time.

The controls at the bottom of the form allow you to navigate through the records, and to add new records, in the same way as in datasheet view.

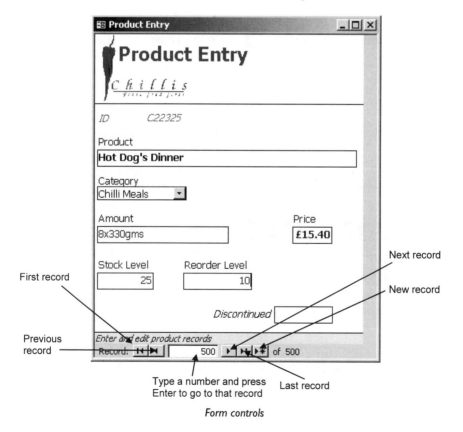

Form controls

- Enter a new record, using the details shown above

To use Find, Filter and Sort in forms

You can think of a form as a "special case" of datasheet view. You can apply filters (see page 463) and sorts to the data (except you click in a field rather than select a column) and use the Find dialogue box to locate records.

Note By default the toolbar is not displayed on forms in data entry view. You can show the toolbar using **View**, **Toolbars** and selecting **Form View**.

- Repeat some of the previous **Find** and **Sort** exercises using the form instead of datasheet view
- Close the form

Close the Database

Access can only display one database at a time. If you use the **Open** command to open a different database, the current one will be closed.

Note If you open another database directly from Windows Explorer (by opening the file icon), another **instance** of Access will start, so you will have **two** program windows open and two sets of database objects.

You can exit from Access in the same way as other Office 2000 products.

To close the database

- On the **Database Window** title bar, click the **Close** button ✖

To exit Access

- Double-click the **Access Program Icon** at the top-left of the Access window 🗗

OR

- Click the **Close** button at the top-right of the Access window ✖

OR

- From the **File** menu, select **Exit** (*SpeedKey:* [Alt] + [F4])

Designing and Creating Tables

Design and create a database

Lesson 33

Design and **plan** a database ☐
Create a new database file ☐
Create a **table** with **fields** and **properties** ☐
Define a **primary key** ☐
Setup an **index** ☐
Switch between **views** ☐
(**Import** data) ☐

Design and Plan a Database

Before creating a database, it is very important to plan it carefully. You need to know what information the database will store and analyse how the information stored will be used.

There are four steps in producing and using a database:

♦ Define the tables in which to store the data.

♦ Add data to the database - usually using a form.

♦ Extract information from the database - using a filter or query.

♦ Report - present the information in the database effectively.

At each stage of database design, when designing tables, forms, queries and reports, you should ask yourself the following questions:

♦ How can I ensure that data is entered quickly and without errors?

♦ How can I ensure that information is quick and easy to find?

Designing Database Tables

In a simple database, all data is stored in one **table**. A table consists of fields and records, stored in columns and rows. Each table can be defined with up to 255 fields.

Many Access databases use more than one table to store data. For example, in a database of customer orders, details about the customers, products and orders could all be stored in different tables. Storing data in several tables makes the database more flexible and easier to maintain.

This type of database is called a **relational** database, because relationships are created between certain fields in the different tables in order to tie the database together. For this course you do not need to understand how relational databases work, but you should be aware of what they are.

Designing a complex database can be a lot like developing a new piece of software. Requirements for the database need to be analysed and the new system needs to be tested. Refer back to the page 48 to remind yourself about the design process.

Here are a few basic hints and tips about designing database tables.

o Work out the design carefully and test it before starting to use the database. Think about what information you need to store in order to identify what **fields** to use for records. Study any existing examples, or similar databases, and get feedback from the people who will use the database.

o Choose a **name** for each field. Use names that make it obvious what data the field is storing without being too lengthy.

Some useful conventions to follow when naming fields are to capitalise words and use an underscore or hyphen instead of spaces between words. For example, a field containing a customer's address might be **Customer_Address** or **CustomerAddress**.

o Choose the **data type** for each field - see page 426

o Test the design with some "worst case" examples

o Decide if fields are missing or if any are not required

Adding Data to the Database

Once the database structure is in place, you need to enter your data. This is often referred to as **populating** the database. There are basically two ways of doing this:

♦ Manually enter data by **typing** it into a **form** or **datasheet**.

♦ **Import** existing data from another file.

Data entry is made more reliable and efficient by designing data entry forms.

Extracting Information From the Database

Once a database has been populated with some data, you will want to put it to work supplying you with information.

Data is extracted using **filters** and **queries**. A filter works something like the Find tool. It is basically a question asked of the data, such as "How many records with the word "Germany" in the Country field are there?" However, instead of **selecting** the records that match the **criteria**, a filter **hides** any records that do not match. You can apply a filter to any view of data, including datasheets and forms.

A **query** is a sophisticated tool for selecting and displaying records in different ways. In a query, you can specify which fields to display, the sort order of records and multiple selection criteria. You can also use queries to perform calculations and summaries.

Reporting Data

When you have extracted information from the database, you will often want to send it to someone. You can quite easily print what you can see on-screen, but for a professional-looking record you will need to create a **report**.

A report is used for data output in much the same way a form is used for data input. You can select what information to show (often using a **query** to select certain records), perform calculations on the data and present the data attractively by making good use of fonts and graphics.

Practice

- *Open the **Products_Database** and examine some of the completed objects (in the Database Window select the object icon then click* *on the toolbar)*

- *Close the database and exit Access*

Create a New Database

Unlike other Office 2000 applications, you must **save** the database as a file before you can start working.

To create a new database

- Start Access

- From the **Startup** dialogue box, select **Blank Access database**

- Click **OK**

The **File New Database** dialogue box is displayed.

- Select the **My Documents** folder to store the database in

- In the **File name:** box, type Employees_Database

- Click **Create**

The database file is saved and the **Access Application** and the **Database** windows are displayed.

Note Do not save a database to a floppy disk from Access. Not only will the application run very slowly, it is very likely that you will quickly run out of space.
If your database will fit on a floppy disk, you can make a backup copy of it by using Windows Explorer to copy the file (as described on page 153).
Most databases will need to be backed up to a disk with greater capacity, such as a Zip disk, CD-R(W) or tape cartridge.

Create a Table with Fields and Attributes

There are three ways to create a new table. These are listed in the table objects pane of the database window:

- **Create the table in design view** - this is the most widely used method and the one that you will learn in this course.

- **Create the table by using a Wizard** - this allows you to select from a predefined set of table designs.

- **Create the table by entering data** - if you are unsure about the data types that you should use to create the table, you can select this option. You will be presented with a new table in datasheet view.

Data Types

Before you start defining the fields for your table, you must understand **data types**. Data types determine the type of data allowed in a field. There are ten data types, as described below:

Data Type	Description
Text	Use this data type to enter text or a combination of text and numbers. You can enter up to 255 characters.
	You cannot perform calculations on numbers stored in a text field. For example, if you want to store a telephone number then use a Text field. If you want to store the number of items in stock, use a Number field.
Memo	Use this data type for lengthy text such as notes. Memo fields can hold up to 64,000 characters.
Number	Use this data type to enter numbers to be included in calculations, such as quantities or values.
Date/Time	Use this data type to enter dates and times.
Currency	Use this data type for currency values and any other values requiring up to four decimal places.
AutoNumber	The next number is automatically generated when a new record is added. This field is useful for creating a unique record ID.
Yes/No	Use this data type for fields that can only use one of two values. For example, whether a product is discontinued is either true or false, so a Yes/No field would be a good choice.
OLE Object	Use this for objects from other applications, such as a spreadsheet created in Excel or a picture file.
Hyperlink	Use this to store links to other files, documents or web pages in a field.
Lookup Wizard	This is not a data type in itself, but is used to choose a value from another table or to select a value from a list.

Tip   You may recognise some of these data types from the Spreadsheets module.

ECDL with MS Office 2000   © CWC (90) 2001

To create a table in design view

- From the **Database Window**, select **Create table in Design view**

Create table in
Design view

- On the **Database Window** toolbar, click **Open**

A new blank table is displayed in design view.

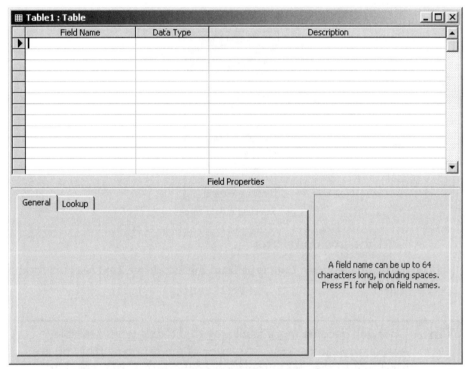

A blank table in design view

Each row in the top half of the **Table** window represents a **field**. The bottom half is split into two sections: the right-hand pane displays a short description of whatever is selected, while the left-hand side allows you to set additional **properties** (or **attributes**) for the field selected above.

To add a field to a table

A field is defined by giving it a **Name** and a **Data Type**. You should also enter a **Description**, though this is not required.

When you have defined the field, you can set additional **field properties** that control how data is entered and how it appears.

- In the first row, type `LastName` into the **Field Name** column

- Click in the **Data Type** field for the same row (*SpeedKey:* `Tab`)

The data type **Text** is selected by default. Since the data types are selected from a limited choice, the options are selected from a drop-down list in this field.

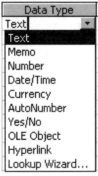

Selecting a data type

- Click the drop-down arrow

- Select the required data type from the list - leave **Text** selected for this field

---

Tip   Once you become more familiar with the data types available in Access, you can type the first letter of the data type that you are using, and Access will automatically choose that data type. For instance, you can type **Y** to define the fields as a **Yes/No** data type.

- Add a **Description** `Enter employee's surname`

Though they are not required, you are encouraged to add these comments, especially where the meaning of the field is not clear. The description is displayed in the **Status** bar when the cursor is in that field, so it can assist users during data entry. Also, it may help you and others to understand the decisions that you made when creating the table.

Practice

- *Add the fields shown below*

Field Name	Data Type	Description
► LastName	Text	Enter employee's surname
FirstName	Text	Enter employee's first name(s)
NI_Number	Text	Enter National Insurance number
BirthDate	Date/Time	Enter birth date
JobTitle	Text	Select from list
Department	Text	Select from list
Salary	Currency	Annual salary
StartDate	Date/Time	Employment start date
FinishDate	Date/Time	Employment finished…
SocialClub	Yes/No	In Social Club (yes/no)?

Employees : Table

Define a Primary Key

A **Primary Key** field uniquely identifies each record in a table. Most tables should have one field set as a primary key field.

The point of a primary key is to avoid creating identical records in the same table. Identical records (where **every** field contains the **same** data as another record) cause problems with many of Access's functions, particularly if you create a **relational** database, with several linked tables.

Duplicate values are not allowed in primary key fields. For example, you could not have two customer records with the customer ID **001**. For this reason, the primary key is often an AutoNumber field.

To set the Primary Key

- Select the **NI_Number** field to use as a primary key

- On the **Standard** toolbar, click **Primary Key** 🔑 OR from the **Edit** menu, select **Primary Key**

The row is marked with a small symbol 🔑 in the selector button, on the left-hand side of the field list.

> **Note** If you do not choose a primary key when first creating the table, Access will prompt you to let it create one. If you click **Yes**, Access will choose an appropriate field to use as a primary key or create a new AutoNumber field if it cannot identify a suitable field.

Save a Table

Once you have created your table, you should save it. In fact, Access will not let you close the table (or the database) or open it to add records without asking you if you want to save the design.

To save the table design

- On the **Standard** toolbar, click **Save** 🖫 **OR** from the **File** menu, select **Save** (*SpeedKey:* [Ctrl]+[S])

If the table has not been saved before, the **Save As** dialogue box is displayed.

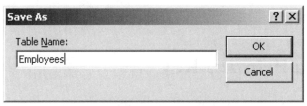

Table Save As dialogue box

- Enter Employees as the name of the table and click **OK**

Tip   When you are making changes to the design of a table, remember to save regularly.

Change Viewing Modes

It is useful to be able to switch between design and datasheet views, in order to check the results of any modification that you have made to the design.

To switch between design and datasheet views

- On the **Standard** toolbar, click **View** 🖩 ▾

The table is displayed in datasheet view, and the button changes to 🖉 ▾, which allows you to switch back to design view.

- Click 🖉 ▾ to return to design view

Tip   To open a table in design view from the **Database** window, select the table object then on the **Database Window** toolbar, click **Design** 🖉 Design .

Work with Windows

You will find that as you work with Access it is necessary to switch between windows regularly. There are several ways to do this.

To switch between windows

- If the table window is maximised, on the **Menu** bar, click the **Restore** icon 🗗

- Click the **Database window** to select it

- Click-and-drag the window's **Title** bar to move it around the screen

- Click-and-drag the window's borders to resize it

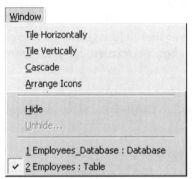

Window menu

- From the bottom of the **Window** menu, select **2 Employees: Table** (*SpeedKey:* Ctrl + F6)

- Select a **Tile** option to arrange all the windows on-screen together

- From the **Windows Taskbar**, click the icon for the **Employees_Database** (the **Database window**) (*SpeedKey:* Alt + Tab)

Access database objects in the Windows Taskbar

Note If each object does not have a Taskbar icon, from the **Tools** menu, select **Options**. Click the **View** tab and make sure the **Windows in Taskbar** check box is ticked.

Tip The shortcut key to switch to the **Database** window from any other window is F11 .

- Select the **Employees: Table** window again

What are Field Properties?

When creating a database, it is important to structure it in such a way as to allow as little human error as possible when keying in data. Common errors are numbers that are too large or too small, dates that are too early or too late or coded values that are not entered consistently. Errors like these make searching for data difficult and reports inaccurate.

Making effective use of field properties can solve many of these problems. Field properties define how data will be entered, stored and displayed. For example, the **Indexed** property can be set to prevent a user typing a duplicate value into a field (entering the same Customer name twice for example) or the **Required** property can be set to make sure the user enters some data in the field.

The properties you set in the field's table definition are carried through to forms and queries. Therefore, it is preferable to set the field's properties when designing the table in the first place. Whenever that field is used in a form, the field's properties will also apply to data entry performed using the form.

To examine field properties

To examine the properties of a field, you need to display the table in design view.

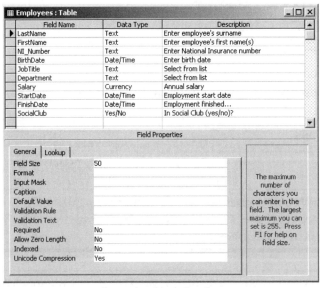

A sample table design view

Each data type has a number of appropriate properties that are displayed in the bottom left of the design view window. Some important properties are discussed below, with appropriate references to the different data types.

The Field Size Property

You can set the field size of **text** and **number** type fields. The field size property determines how much data the field can store. In the case of text this is the number of characters; in the case of numbers it is the range of values.

Larger fields take up more space and can slow the database down. However, these considerations only become really important in quite large databases and if you make the field too small, a lot of time could be lost changing the database design, so it best to over-estimate the space required in a field.

Text field size

Text fields can be up to 255 characters long. If you want a larger field in which to store text information, you should use the **Memo** data type, which allows for storage of up to around 64000 characters.

- Select the **NI_Number** field in the top half of the window

- In the **Field Size** box, enter 9

- Click **Save** 🖫

> **Tip** It is a good idea to save after each change, especially if a table already contains some data. See page 439 for a fuller discussion of how to modify existing fields.

Number field size

Several number field sizes are available. The most useful are summarised in the following table:

Field Size	Use	Decimals
Byte	Store values between 0 and 255	None
Integer	Store values between -32,768 to 32,767	None
Long Integer (Default)	Store values between -2,147,483,648 to 2,147,483,647	None
Single	Store larger numbers or decimal values	7
Double	Store even larger numbers or decimal values	15

It should be obvious that the greater the range of numbers that you allow in a field, the more space Access will use to store this information.

> **Note** The Byte, Integer and Long Integer sizes **cannot store decimal values**. If you need to store values with up to four decimal places only, use the **Currency** data type in preference to **Single** or **Double** number fields.
>
> The number of decimal places stored and displayed is set by the **Decimal Places** property. *Confusingly*, you can **set** the number of decimal places for bytes, integers and long integers! Be warned that during data entry **any data typed after a decimal point will be lost** if the field is one of these three sizes. For example, if you type **4.67** Access will store (and display) **5**.

- Select the **Salary** field and change the **Decimal Places** property to **0** (zero)
- Click **Save**

The Format and Input Mask Properties

The **Format** property allows you to specify the format of data as it is **displayed** (for example, you could specify that any text entered is displayed in upper case).

Input Mask allows you to specify the format of data **entry**, **storage** and **display**. For example, when National Insurance numbers are entered, an input mask will ensure that each NI number ends with a letter and is stored with spaces between the numbers).

The **Format** property is easier to apply but does not validate the information typed into the field. In this course, you will concentrate on using the Format property.

Text formats

The following formatting symbols can be used for the Text data type:

Symbol	Description
@	Must have a text character in this position
&	Optionally have a character in this position
<	All characters will be lower-case
>	All characters will be upper-case
space	Display a space between characters
"ABC"	Display the characters inside the quotes ("...")

The table below demonstrates the use of the text format property:

Format	You Type	Access Displays
>	Hello	HELLO
(@@@@)@@@@-@@@@	0123456789	(01)2345-6789
!(@@@@)@@@@-@@@@	0123456789	(0123)4567-89
<!"O/N 55"@@@@	BB8F	O/N 55bb8f

- Re-select the **NI_Number** field then click in the **Format** property box

- Type >@@ @@ @@ @@ @ (including spaces) then save

Number formats

The easiest way to apply a number format is to select from the list of predefined formats:

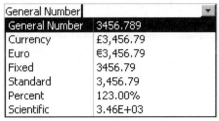

Predefined formats for the Number data type

Note Again, be warned that Access allows you to set a decimal format for the field even though this data may not be stored (if the field size is byte, integer or long integer).

Date/Time formats

The easiest way to apply a format is to select from the drop-down list. Use a 4-digit year style to make date data unambiguous.

Predefined formats for the Date/Time data type

If you want to use a custom format, use the following characters:

Symbol	Description
d	Display 1-2 characters for the Day (1,2,3...11,12,13)
dd	Display 2 characters for the Day (01,02,03...11,12,13)
m or mm	Display Month as a number
mmm	Display Month as a three letter code (Jan, Feb, Mar...)
mmmm	Display full Month name
yyyy	Display year with 4-digits
/ -	Display separator character (you can also use spaces)

Note Number and date formats are mostly derived from the Windows Regional Options (see page 166). If you want to experiment with your own formats, lookup "Format Property" in the online help for further examples of format codes.

- Select the **BirthDate** field from the top half of the window

- Click in the **Format** property field, then select the **Short Date** format

Note Your **Short Date** format should be set to use four digits for the year (**19/06/1994**). If it is not, change your **Windows Regional Options** to use this format.

- Use the same format for the **StartDate** and **FinishDate** fields too

Yes/No formats

This field can display one of two values in one of the formats shown below.

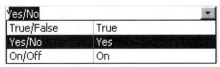

Predefined formats for the Yes/No data type

The Caption Property

The **Caption** property allows you to supply a plain English label to the field that you are defining. Labels are useful because they are not bound by Access limits on the names that you give to the field. The caption will appear at the top of columns in the table's datasheet view, and as a label for the field when it is displayed on reports and forms.

Adding an appropriate caption for each field speeds up the process of creating forms and reports later. This property applies to all fields.

- Add a caption to each field as shown below

Field	Caption	Field	Caption
LastName	Surname	Department	Department
FirstName	Forename(s)	Salary	Salary
NI_Number	NI Number	StartDate	Start Date
BirthDate	DOB	FinishDate	Finish Date
JobTitle	Job Title	SocialClub	Social Club Member?

- Save the changes on completion

The Default Value Property

When you add a new record to the table, Access will populate each field (where appropriate) with the specified default value. Default values are useful if the field contains information that is regularly filled in with the same data, since whoever is entering the record will be able to accept or update the default value.

- For the **Salary** field **delete** the **Default Value** of 0 that Access has used

The Required Property

Some of the fields in your database will contain mandatory information. If you set the **Required** property to **Yes**, Access will repeatedly display a dialogue box prompting the user to fill in the required field - until they do so or exit!

- Make the **LastName** and **NI_Number** fields required and save changes to the table

The Allow Zero Length Property

Specifically for Text and Memo fields, setting this property to **False** prevents someone bypassing the Required property by entering an empty string (a pair of quotes) into a field.

Setup an Index

To understand indexes, consider how you use the index at the back of this book. An index is a list of topics in alphabetical order. Alongside each topic is a list of page references where the topic is discussed. This makes it very easy to open the book to the page(s) on the topic you want - much easier than leafing through each page looking to see if the topic is discussed there.

In a similar way, indexes allow Access to locate information in a table quickly, assuming that the indexes are appropriate for the search being conducted.

You should consider indexing the following fields:

♦   Any field that you might want to use **regularly** to **search** the table.

♦   Any field by which you might want to **sort** the data **regularly**.

The key word for these points is **regularly**. Do not index **too many** fields in your database, because each index increases the amount of time required to update and modify records - imagine updating a book with 30 indexes!

When you choose to index a field, you have the option of whether or not to allow **duplicate values** in that column. In most cases you will want to **allow** duplicate values. For example, consider a **Country** field in a contact database. Obviously you want to be able to add different customers from the same country, so you would set the Country field to **Indexed (Duplicates OK)**.

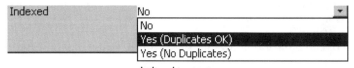

Indexed property

The primary key field in a table is always set to **Indexed (No Duplicates)** since duplicate values are not allowed in a primary key field.

- Set the **Indexed** property for the **LastName**, **JobTitle** and **Department** fields to **Yes (Duplicates OK)**

- Save changes to the table then close it

- The next topic is optional, so if you do not want to complete it, close the database

Import Data

It is often the case that there is already some data that can be used for the database. It may be in a different type of file, such as an Excel spreadsheet, or in a slightly different format (for example, with different field names or data types).

Rather than retype the data, it can be **imported** into the database.

ECDL This topic is not required for the ECDL syllabus. The exercise has been included so that you can work on your own data file throughout the course. This is only a very basic introduction to importing data.

To import data from an Excel worksheet

- From the **File** menu, select **Get External Data** then **Import...**

The **Import** dialogue box (similar to a standard **Open** dialogue box) is displayed.

- In the **Files of type:** box, select **Microsoft Excel** - the Excel workbooks in the **My Documents** folder are now displayed

- Select the **Employees** workbook and click the **Import** button

The **Import Spreadsheet Wizard** is started.

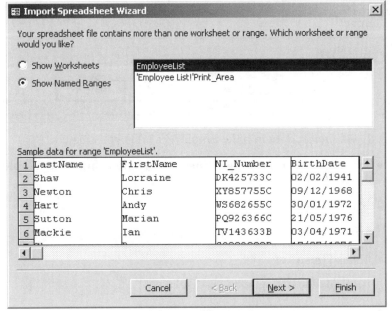

Import Spreadsheet Wizard

- Click the **Show Named Ranges** option and select **Employee List** from the box

The sample data shows the contents of the **Employee List** range. Remember that you learned to name worksheet ranges on page 339.

- Click **Next >**

- Leave the **First Row Contains Column Headings** check box selected and click **Next >**

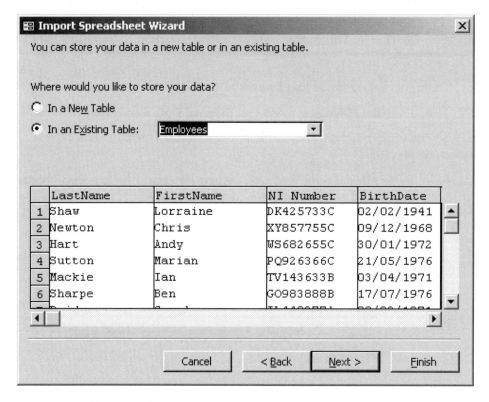

We will import data into the Employees table you created.

- Select the **In an Existing Table:** option button and select **Employees** from the drop-down list

- Click **Next >**

The final screen simply confirms the choices you have made.

- Click **Finish**

A confirmation dialogue box is displayed.

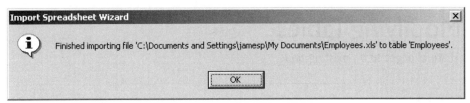

Import successful dialogue box

- Click **OK**

- Open the **Employees** table in datasheet view to browse the records

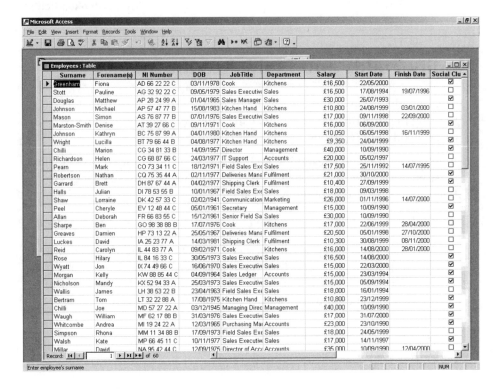

- Close all windows

Modifying Tables

Make changes to an existing table

Lesson 34

Modify **field properties** ☐
(**Delete** a table) ☐
Modify **table layout attributes** ☐
(Create a **lookup field**) ☐

Modify Fields and Field Attributes

You can add, remove and rename fields from a table at any time. As well as revising the structure of fields, you can change the data type and any associated field properties.

If you take care when designing your tables, you should not need to make these changes later on. However, when you do need to make changes to fields, be aware of the following:

♦ Deleting a field obviously deletes any data stored in that field as well.

♦ You will need to repeat any changes made to the field in the table in any existing forms, reports or queries using the field also. For example, if you delete a field in a table, Access will not delete the field control from a form based on the table, you must do so yourself.

Practice

For this topic, we will create a copy of the Employees table to practise on.

- *Open the **Employees_Database** OR if you did not complete the Import exercise in the previous lesson, open **Employees_Database (ModifyTables)***

- *Select the **Employees** table icon then from the **File** menu, select Save **As...***

- *In the Save Table '**Employees' To:** box, type* temp

- *Click **OK** - a copy of the table is added to the Database window*

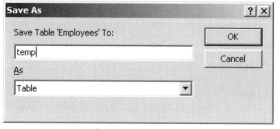

Save As dialogue box

ECDL with MS Office 2000 © CWC (90) 2001

To modify the layout of a table

- From the **Database** window, in the **Objects** bar, click **Tables**

- Select the **temp** table

- On the **Database Window** toolbar, click **Design**

The table is opened in design view.

> **Note** Remember, you must save changes to the design of a table by selecting the **Save** command. If you are making changes to multiple fields, it is a good idea to select **Save** after changing each field.

To insert a field

- Click the row selector (the grey box to the left of the field name) for the **Salary** field

- Right-click the row then from the shortcut menu, select **Insert Rows** (*SpeedKey:* `Insert`)

A new row is inserted **above** the **Salary** field.

- Enter the field name `AppraisalDate` and set the data type to **Date/Time**

To delete a field

- Select the **AppraisalDate** field

- Right-click the field and select **Delete Rows** (*SpeedKey:* `Delete`)

> **Note** When you delete a field, any data that you might have added to that field is also deleted.

To change the field name

- Click into the **Field Name** column for the **LastName** field

- Overtype the existing name with `Surname`

- On the **Standard** toolbar, click **Save** ![save icon]

To change the data type

- Click into the **Data Type** column for the **NI_Number** field

- Select the **Number** type from the drop-down list

- On the **Standard** toolbar, click **Save** 🖫

Access tries to convert any existing data to the new data type. The text data already stored in this field cannot be converted into numbers, so a warning is displayed when you try to save the table.

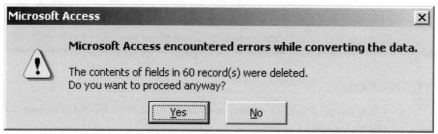

Microsoft Access ✕

⚠ Microsoft Access encountered errors while converting the data.

The contents of fields in 60 record(s) were deleted.
Do you want to proceed anyway?

[Yes]   [No]

Invalid data type warning message

- Click **No** to cancel the save then **OK** to the message box - note that the data type remains set to **Number**

> **Warning** **If you click Yes this operation deletes any existing data. You cannot recover the data and the operation cannot be undone.**

- Change the data type back to **Text**

To change the field size

- Click into the **Surname** field

- In the **Properties** panel, select the **Field Size** attribute and change it to 20

- On the **Standard** toolbar, click **Save** 🖫

Because you have selected a smaller field size than before, Access warns you that existing data in the field may be lost.

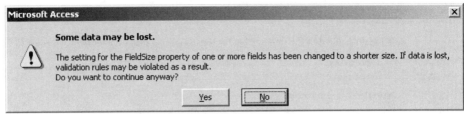

Field size warning message

- Click **Yes** - any data that does not fit will be cut from the field

Warning This action cannot be undone - the data cannot be recovered.

If you click <u>N</u>o the table will not be saved, but the **Field Size** attribute will remain set to **20**.

To change other field properties

When there is data in the table, changes to some fields may not be allowed or the change may be allowed but the data will not conform to the rules you have set.

As an example, we will make the **FinishDate** field a **Required** field. Because many of the existing records do not contain data in this field, Access will warn that the data does not comply with the new rule.

- Select the **FinishDate** field then in the **Properties** panel, change the **Required** property to **Yes**

- On the **Standard** toolbar, click **Save** ▣

Access prompts you to test existing data to see if it conforms to the new field property rules.

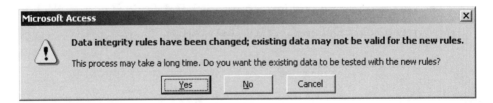

- Click <u>Y</u>es to check the data

Access comes across invalid data (that is, employees with no **FinishDate**) so it displays another message:

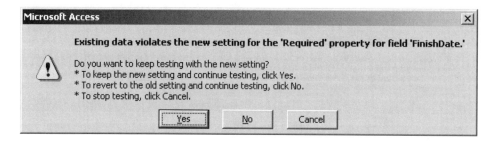

- Click **No** to abandon the changes you made - this time the field property is changed back to the original setting (**No**)

Note Access does not tell you **which** records are invalid, but you can open the table and sort the records to display blank fields.

Note Some changes cannot be made at all without changing the existing data first. For example, you cannot set the **Indexed (No duplicates)** property on a field if existing data contains duplicates!

- From the **File** menu, select **Close** to close the **temp** table

Delete a Table

You can delete any database object you no longer require from the **Database** window. Obviously, deleting a table also deletes any data stored in it.

To delete a table

- In the **Database** window, select the **temp** table icon

- On the **Database Window** toolbar, click **Delete** OR from the **Edit** menu, select **Delete** (*SpeedKey:* `Delete`)

- Click **Yes** in the warning box displayed

Note You can **undo** deleting a table, but only as your next action.

Modify Table Layout Attributes

Often, a column will not be wide enough to display all the data in the field. On the other hand, you may want to make certain columns narrower, in order to fit more fields on-screen. You can also change the order in which fields are displayed, hide columns and change the font used.

To change the width of columns

- Open the **Employees** table in datasheet view

- Point the mouse to the border between the **Surname** and **Forename(s)** columns

> **Tip**   Remember that the column headings used are those set in the **Caption** property, not the **Field Name**.

The mouse pointer changes to show a bar with arrows pointing left and right.

- Click-and-drag to the right to make the column about twice as wide

Click-and-drag the border to resize columns and rows

Surname	Forename(s)	NI Number	DOB	Job Title
Greenham	Fiona	AD 66 22 22 C	03/11/1978	Cook
Stott	Pauline	AG 32 92 22 C	09/05/1979	Sales Executive
Douglas	Matthew	AP 28 24 99 A	01/04/1965	Sales Manager
Johnson	Michael	AP 57 47 77 B	15/08/1983	Kitchen Hand

- Click the **Job Title** column field name to select the column

- From the **Format** menu, select **Column Width...**

The **Column Width** dialogue box is displayed.

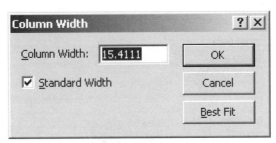

Column Width dialogue box

- In the **Column Width:** box, enter the number of characters to display (type 25) **OR** click the **Best Fit** button to display as much of the existing data as possible

- Click **OK**

To move columns

- Click the **Job Title** column field name to select the column

- Click-and-drag the column field name to the right of the **Department** column

A black line indicates where the field will be dropped.

- When the field is in the correct position, release the mouse button

To hide a column

Hiding a column does not delete the column permanently. It simply hides it from view. This is useful if you want to fit more columns on-screen or on the page (if you print the datasheet).

- Click-and-drag to select the **Salary**, **Start Date** and **Finish Date** columns

- From the **Format** menu, select **Hide Columns**

To unhide a column

- From the **Format** menu, select **Unhide Columns**...

The **Unhide Columns** dialogue box is displayed.

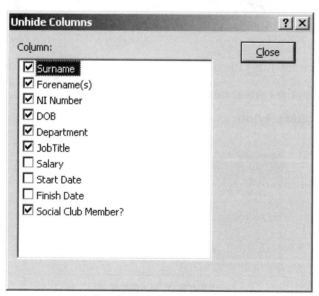

Unhide Columns dialogue box

- Click the unchecked boxes to display the columns again (You can also hide a column from here by **unchecking** a box)

- Click **Close**

To change the font of the datasheet

By default, the font used for the datasheet is Arial, which is an easy to read font found on all Windows PCs. However, you can use a different font on the datasheet or change the font size. You cannot change the appearance of individual columns however.

- From the **Format** menu, select **Font...**

The **Font** dialogue box is displayed.

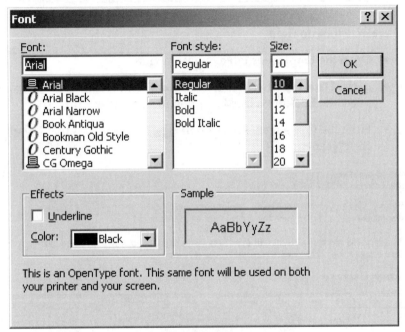

Font dialogue box

- Select the **Verdana** font and click **OK**

To save formatting changes to the datasheet

Any changes made to the way the datasheet is **displayed** (as opposed to editing records) need to be saved.

- On the **Standard** toolbar, click **Save** 🖫 **OR** from the **File** menu, select **Save** (*SpeedKey:* `Ctrl`+`S`)

- The next exercise is optional - if you do not want to complete it now, close the table and exit Access

Lookup Fields

Lookup fields help to standardise the entry of data by providing the user with a list of items to choose from. The items can be stored as a list in the field or in another table in the database.

ECDL Lookup fields are not required for the ECDL syllabus, but they are a very important part of efficient database design.

To create a lookup field

- Open the **Employees** table in design view

- In the **Data Type** field for **Department** click on the down arrow and select the **Lookup Wizard...** option to start the wizard

- From the first screen, select **I will type in the values that I want** and click **Next >**

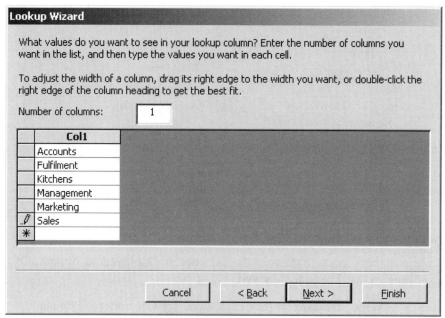

Lookup Wizard

- Enter the items that users will be able to select from the **Department** field, as shown above (use Tab to move to the next field)

- Click **Next >**

- In the last screen, enter the **label** as Department and click **Finish**

- When the table design is re-displayed, click the **Lookup** tab at the bottom of the window

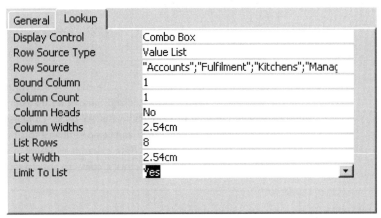

Lookup properties

You can see the list of items you entered stored in the **Row Source** property.

- Set the **Limit To List** property to **Yes** - this forces users to use values from the list only

- Save the table then open it in datasheet view to see the effect on the **Department** field

Practice

- *Create a new table and add a **Text** field* JobTitle

- *Save the table as* lkpJobTitle *and click **No** to have no primary key*

- *Add the records shown on the right to the table*

- *Close the **lkpJobTitle** table and open the **Employees** table in design view*

- *Start the **Lookup Wizard** for the **JobTitle** field*

- *In the next three screens of the wizard, select the option to lookup values, choose the **lkpJobTitle** table and add the **JobTitle** field by clicking the arrow*

- *On the fourth screen, adjust the width of the column so that all data is visible then **Finish***

Table to provide lookup values

- *A message box will be displayed prompting you to save the table - click **Yes***

- *Close the database*

Queries

Create queries to sort, analyse and filter records

What is a Query?

A query is created by specifying fields to display from a **data source** (a table or another query). Typically a query also specifies what data to look for in one or more fields (**criteria**). When you run a query, Access creates a **recordset**, essentially a table containing the data matching the criteria you specified. However, unlike a real table, a recordset is not saved as part of the database. Access creates a new recordset each time the query is run.

With a query you can:

♦   Extract records according to criteria you specify.

♦   Choose the fields you want to view in the result.

♦   Sort the records in a specific order.

♦   Calculate fields and summarise data.

Create a Simple Query

In the query pane of the **Database** window, two query objects are shown by default.

♦   **Create Query in Design view** allows you to build a query from scratch.

♦   **Create Query by using wizard** helps you to select the information in which you are interested.

It is quite easy to build a query in design view, but the second option is useful if you have never created one before.

To create a query using the Query Wizard

- If you completed the Lookup exercises in the last lesson, you can continue to use your **Employees_Database** file, otherwise open the **Employees_Database (Queries)** file

- In the **Database** window, click the **Queries** object

- Select **Create query by using wizard**

- On the **Database Window** toolbar, click **Open** Open

The **Simple Query Wizard** starts.

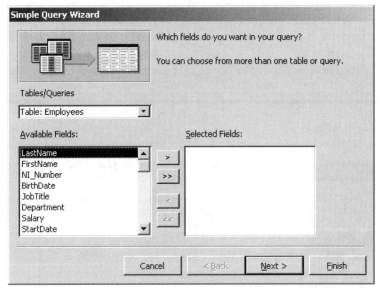

Query Wizard fields selection dialogue box

- In the **Tables/Queries** list box, select **Table: Employees** as the source of data

The four video controls allow you to perform the following operations:

Click	To
>	Move the **highlighted** field into the **Selected Fields** list box.
>>	Move **all** fields into the **Selected Fields** list box.
<	Move a selected field into the **Available Fields** list box.
<<	Move **all** fields into the **Available Fields** list box.

- Use the controls to add the fields shown below to the query

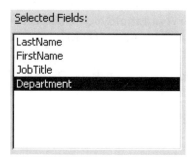

Selected Fields:

LastName
FirstName
JobTitle
Department

Note You must select any fields that you want to **display** in the query results, fields that you want to set **criteria** for or fields you want to **sort** by. You must select at least one field to continue with the wizard.
The choices you make here can be modified later in query design view.

- Click **Next >**

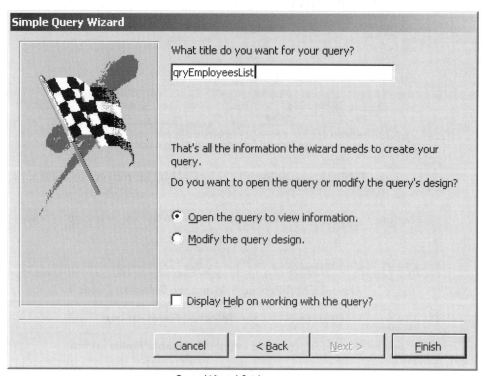

Query Wizard finish screen

The final screen of the wizard allows you to give an appropriate name to the query. This will appear in the **Title** bar of the query and identifies it in the Database Window.

- Type the title `qryEmployeesList`

You are also given the chance to either open the query in datasheet view to see the query results or modify the design. It is probably best at this point to examine the information that you have selected, to ensure that the results are what you expected.

- Select <u>**O**pen the query</u> and click <u>**F**inish</u>

The query recordset is displayed in a new window.

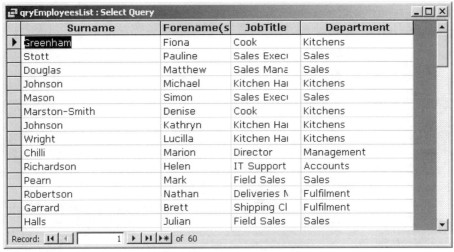

Surname	Forename(s)	JobTitle	Department
Greenham	Fiona	Cook	Kitchens
Stott	Pauline	Sales Exec	Sales
Douglas	Matthew	Sales Mana	Sales
Johnson	Michael	Kitchen Ha	Kitchens
Mason	Simon	Sales Exec	Sales
Marston-Smith	Denise	Cook	Kitchens
Johnson	Kathryn	Kitchen Ha	Kitchens
Wright	Lucilla	Kitchen Ha	Kitchens
Chilli	Marion	Director	Management
Richardson	Helen	IT Support	Accounts
Pearn	Mark	Field Sales	Sales
Robertson	Nathan	Deliveries N	Fulfilment
Garrard	Brett	Shipping Cl	Fulfilment
Halls	Julian	Field Sales	Sales

Results of the query in datasheet view

The information is presented in a datasheet, just like table datasheet view.

Warning The recordset represents the actual data from the source table. If you change data or delete records in the recordset, the data in the table is changed also.

Add and Remove Fields from a Query

The **Simple Query Wizard** lets you select records and fields but not much else. To create more sophisticated queries, for example where the query selects records matching certain criteria, you need to modify the query in design view.

To modify a query

- On the **Standard** toolbar, click **View** 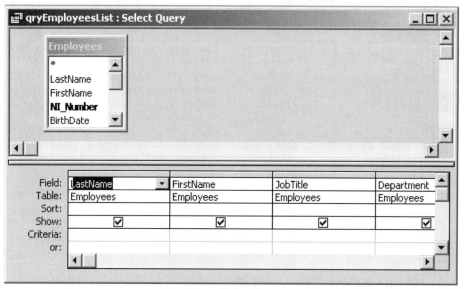 OR from the **View** menu, select **Design View**

The query is displayed in design view

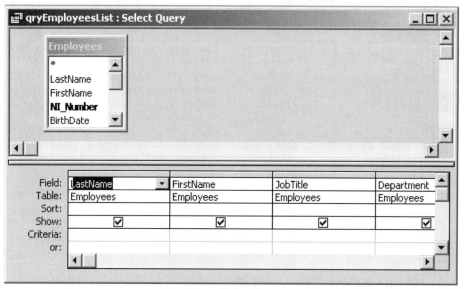

Query design view

The query design window is split into two halves. The top half displays the table(s) selected for the query.

Below that, the **query grid** shows which fields from the table(s) are included in the query. The top two rows of the grid show the name of the field and the table source. The other rows are used to set further options for the query.

To select a field

- Position your mouse over the field selector, located at the top of each field

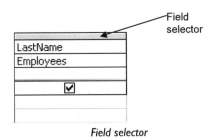

Field selector

When your mouse is in the correct position, the pointer will change to a down arrow (↓).

- Click to select the field

A selected field in the query design window

To remove a field from the query

- Select the **LastName** field then from the **E̲dit** menu, select **D̲elete** (*SpeedKey:* `Delete`)

Warning   You cannot undo the deletion of a field.

To change the position of a field

- Select the **Department** field and drag it to the left of the **JobTitle** field
- Put the fields back the way they were

Adding a field to the query

There are three ways to add fields to a query:

To add a field to the query by double-clicking

- In the table box in the top half of the window, double-click the **LastName** field

- This will add the field to the end of the grid - drag it to the beginning

To add a field to the query using drag-and-drop

- Scroll down to the **SocialClub** field in the table box in the top half of the design window

- If necessary, make the query window larger so that you can see a blank column at the end

- Drag the field and drop it onto the first blank column

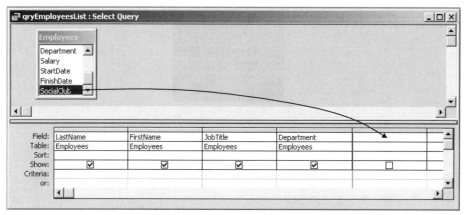

Adding a field to a query using drag-and-drop

Tip If you drop a new field onto an existing field, the existing field will move to the right.

Note You can find out the third method of adding fields on page 461.

- On the **Standard** toolbar, click **Save** and then **Run** to see the query results again

Note You can also use the **View** button to see query results.

To hide the display of query fields

The fourth row of the field list (**Show:**) in the query grid allows you to choose whether a field is displayed in the query output. You might want to **sort by** a field or set **criteria** for it without displaying it.

- On the **Standard** toolbar, click **View** 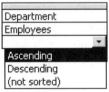 to return to design view

- Click the **Show:** check box for the **FirstName** field then run the query to observe the effect

- To display the field again, switch back to design view and ensure that the **Show:** check box is checked

> **Tip**   If you have modified an existing query and want to keep both the original query and the modified version, you can use **File, Save As** to save the modifications under a different name.

Sort the Query Results

The **Sort:** row of the table allows you to sort the query results by one or more fields.

To sort query data

- In the query grid, select the **Sort:** row for the **Department** field

- Select the drop-down control to display the available options

```
Department
Employees
                    ▼
Ascending
Descending
(not sorted)
```

Field sort options

The final option of **(not sorted)** is to allow you to reset a field to which you previously applied a sort.

- Select **Ascending** then run the query to check the results

> **Tip**   If you decide to sort by more than one field, the query will be sorted by the field order from left to right. Move the fields in the design grid to get the sort that you want.

Create a Query with Multiple Criteria

One of the most important functions of a query is to limit the number of rows that are displayed.

A query is what its name suggests: a question asked of the data. The "question" is defined by entering **criteria** for one or more fields in the query. If a record matches the criteria, it will be included in the query results.

Criteria are basically text or values with **operators** to determine how the criteria are to be matched. Text should be entered in quotes (" ") and dates between hash signs (# #).

The table below shows a few examples of operators and criteria.

Operator	Comment	Example
=	Equals	= "Johnson"
>, <	Greater Than, Less Than	>15, >#23-Jun-99#
>=	Greater Than or Equal To	>= "Gilmore"
<=	Less Than or Equal To	<= 10
<expr1> AND <expr2>	Both expressions in the selected field must be true	>5 AND <25
<expr1> OR <expr2>	Either expression in the selected field must be true	="Smith" OR ="Jones"
NOT <expr>	The inverse of the expression (usually used with AND, OR)	="John" AND NOT ="Johnson"
NULL or NOT NULL	Include (or exclude) 'empty' fields - into which data has not yet been added	Is Null Is Not Null
IN (<expr1>, <expr2>, ...)	Include values that match one of the items in the list	IN ("UK", "US", "JP") IN (1, 4, 8, 16)
BETWEEN <expr1> AND <expr2>	Include values between <expr1> and <expr2>, inclusive	BETWEEN #1-MAR-00# AND #31-MAR-00#

You can see a full list of criteria by asking the Office Assistant "I need help specifying criteria".

To create criteria for a field

- In design view, in the **Criteria:** line for the **SocialClub** field, type `True`

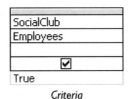

Criteria

- Run the query again - only records where the SocialClub box is ticked (that is, the field contents are True) are displayed

- Click the **Close** button ⊠ on the query window and click **Yes** to save changes

To filter by multiple expressions

You can add criteria for several fields on the **Criteria:** row - all of the criteria will have to be true for a record to be displayed in the query result.

You can add criteria to one or more of the **Or:** rows below the **Criteria:** row to create multiple sets of alternative criteria for the same field.

For this exercise we will create a new query in design view.

- In the **Database** window, select the **Create a query in Design view** icon and click **Open** 🔲 <u>O</u>pen

A blank query grid is opened with the **Show Table** dialogue box in front of it.

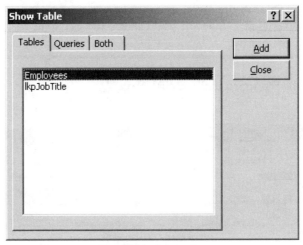

Show Table dialogue box

The **Show Table** dialogue box lets you select the source of data for the query. You can display it at any time in design view by clicking **Show Table**  on the **Standard** toolbar.

- Select the **Employees** table then click **Add**

A table box is added to the top half of the query grid.

- Click **Close**

Another way to add a field to the grid is by selecting it from an empty box in the **Field:** row

- Click in the **Field:** row in the first column then click the drop-down arrow

Selecting a field

- Select the **JobTitle** field

- Add the **Salary** field in the next column

Tip The first entry **Employees.*** is shorthand for "All fields from the Employees table". Using this means that the query will always display **all** the fields in the table, even when fields are added or deleted from the table itself. However, you cannot add **criteria** to this "field" or use it to sort by.

- On the **Standard** toolbar, click **Save**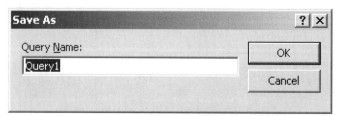

Save As dialogue box

- Type `qrySalaries` and click **OK**

This query will display a list of salaries paid to employees. We want to filter the results so that they do not show the salaries of Kitchen Hands or Shipping Clerks or salaries of over £25,000.

- See if you can work out what the criteria will be

_____

_____

_____

_____

- Enter the criteria and sort options as shown below

Field:	JobTitle		Salary
Table:	Employees		Employees
Sort:	Descending		
Show:		☑	☑
Criteria:	Not "kitchen hand" And Not "shipping clerk"		<=25000
or:			

- Run the query to check that the results are correct then save and close it

Add and Remove a Filter

Filters allow you to limit the number of records that are visible in a datasheet to a manageable sub-set of the records. You can apply filters to tables in datasheet view and to query recordsets.

To use Filter by Selection

The simplest way of filtering the display of records in a table is use **Filter by Selection**. This displays only records that have the same value in a field.

- Open the **qryEmployeesList** query in datasheet view

- In the **JobTitle** field, look for a record with **Kitchen Hand** in it then select that cell

- On the **Standard** toolbar, click **Filter by Selection**  OR from the **Records** menu, select **Filter** then select **Filter by Selection**

The datasheet is refreshed to display only records that pass the selected filter criteria.

You may further limit the records that are displayed by adding to the **Filter by Selection**.

If you select another field from this filter-limited list, and select **Filter by Selection** once more, the records displayed will be those that match both criteria. It follows that you can add successive filters by example, until the requirements match the criteria that you require.

To re-display all records

Once you have set a filter, the **Apply Filter** button ⛛ lets you toggle between the filter results and displaying all records.

- On the **Standard** toolbar, click **Apply Filter** ⛛ to toggle between filtered records and all records

Create an Advanced Filter

While **Filter by Selection** allows you to filter on exact values, it is often necessary to filter the information in your datasheet by a range of values. Access provides an option to **Filter by Form**. Filter by Form uses a blank record into which you can type an example of the data to filter by.

The filter criteria can be as complex as those defined for queries. Refer back to page 460 for a list of the main operators you can use.

Note that if you fill in more than one column with a filter expression, then the expressions must **all** be true for the record to be displayed (sometimes known as "AND-ing").

Access also allows you to "OR" several fields together, using the **OR** tab at the bottom of the filter window.

When you select the **OR** tab, another blank record is displayed at the top of the window, and you can fill in additional criteria for your filter.

To apply a Filter by Form

- On the **Standard** toolbar, click **Filter by Form** ▒ OR from the **Records** menu, select **Filter** then **Filter by Form**

The table window is redisplayed in **Filter by Form** mode.

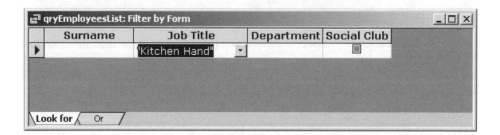

Tip   As the name implies, you can also use Filter by Form with data entry forms!

Filter by Form resembles an empty datasheet record, into which you can add your criteria.

- If you want to edit existing filter criteria, select the appropriate field and press F2 - for this exercise leave the field set to "Kitchen Hand"

- To add **OR** criteria for multiple fields, select the **OR** tab at the bottom-left corner of the window

- Select `Shipping Clerk` from the **Job Title** field drop down list

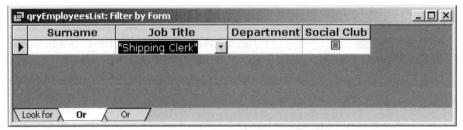

Using the Or tab to add criteria to the Filter by Form

Note that another tab has been added - you can go on adding multiple criteria if you wish

- To display filtered records, on the **Standard** toolbar, click **Apply Filter**

Only records where the employee is a Kitchen Hand or Shipping Clerk are displayed.

- Close the query window and save changes when prompted

Tip	When you sort or filter data, you are changing the structure of the datasheet. When you close the table, Access prompts you to save changes.

Create a Calculated Field

Queries become more powerful (and more interesting), when you consider that you are not limited to simply returning a sub-set of rows and/or columns from a table.

ECDL The last two topics in this lesson are not directly required by the ECDL syllabus. However, learning about calculated fields and summaries in queries will help you to understand how to group data in reports, which is covered on page 496.

As an example, it is possible to create a field in a query that is a value **calculated** from the data in one or more table fields. Here are some examples of calculated fields:

This Expression	Displays
[UnitPrice] * [Quantity]	The results of the multiplication of these two fields
[OrderDate] + 28	The value of the OrderDate field plus four weeks (28 days)
[FirstName] + [MiddleInitial] + [LastName]	The full name from three fields that contain name information
[TotalScore] / [NoOfQuestions]	The average score per question

Tip There are many other functions that you can include in expressions. Try looking up "What is an expression" in the online help to see further examples.

Calculated fields are a powerful feature of queries. If you can calculate data such as the order value from existing fields (unit price and quantity ordered), you remove the possibility of the data entry operator keying in the wrong amount. There is also less data to enter and one less field required in the database table.

To add a calculated field to a query

Using a calculated field in the query is simply a matter of typing the **expression** into the **Field:** box for a particular column.

For this exercise we will make a copy of the **qrySalaries** query and use it to calculate some seasonal bonus payments.

- From the **Database** window, select the **qrySalaries** query

- From the **File** menu, select **Save As...**

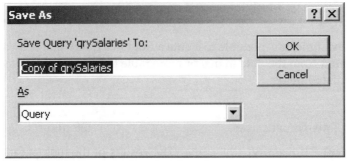

Save As dialogue box

- Type qryBonus in the **Save to** box and leave the **As** box as **Query**

- Click **OK**

- Select the **qryBonus** query icon and click **Design** Design to open it in design view

Firstly we will add a field to display each employee's full name.

- Select the first field then from the **Insert** menu, select **Columns**

A blank column is added to the front of the grid.

A calculated field is made by typing a name for the field followed by a colon (for example, **Line Total:**) then the expression itself.

- Click in the **Field:** row and type

        Name:[FirstName]&" "&[LastName] Enter

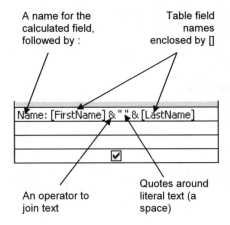

A name for the calculated field, followed by :

Table field names enclosed by []

An operator to join text

Quotes around literal text (a space)

Example calculated field

> **Note** When adding expressions, get into the habit of typing square brackets around the field name(s). This is **required** if you have used spaces in the field names when creating a table, but it is a good idea to use brackets around all field names.

- In the column to the right of **Salary**, in the **Field:** row, type
  `Bonus: [Salary]*0.005`

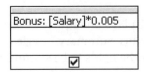

- Do you know what the results of this field will show?

- Save and run the query

The query calculates a festive bonus of ½ percentage point of the employee's salary. Note that the calculated field is not correctly formatted - it should display values as currency.

- Switch back to design view and select the **Bonus** field

- On the **Standard** toolbar, click **Properties** to display the **Properties** dialogue box

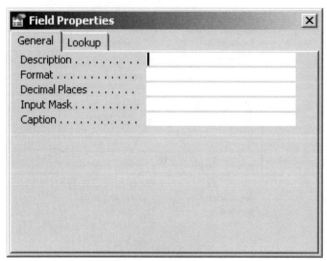

Properties dialogue box

- Click in the **Format** box and select **Currency** from the drop-down list

- Close the **Properties** dialogue box

- Save and run the query to check the results

Create a Summary Query

A simple select query displays one row for every record selected by the query. You can also produce **summary queries**, which display one row for every change in data for the fields to be summarised.

Two types of field are required for a summary query:

Group By field(s)

The field(s) by which you are grouping the data. For example, say you want a query to show the number of customers located in different countries. The **Group By** field in the query would be **Country**. The query results would display one line for each country.

If no grouping fields are included, you will get one summarised value based on all records selected by the query.

Aggregate fields

These are the fields that provide the values to calculate. Following the example above, the aggregate field would be **CustomerName**. Using the COUNT **function**, the query would group the data by country, then count how many records with a non-blank CustomerName appeared in each group.

You can also use a **calculated** field as an aggregate field. For example, having created a calculated field to show **OrderValue**, you could create a summary query to show the total value of orders from different customers. The group by field would be **CustomerName**, the aggregate field would be **OrderValue** and the **SUM** function would be used to add up the total of orders for each customer.

Aggregate Functions

Various functions are available for summarising data. You should recognise most of these from the Spreadsheets module.

Function	Description
SUM	Total of the values in a field
AVG	Average of the values in a field
MIN	Lowest value in a field
MAX	Highest value in a field
COUNT	Number of values in a field, not counting Null (blank) values

These functions will only work with **Number, Date/Time, Currency** and **AutoNumber** data types, with the exception of **Count**, which will work with *most* data types.

To create a summary query

We will adapt the **Bonus** query to show the total value of bonuses for each grade of employee.

- Switch back to design view

- To display summary criteria, on the **Standard** toolbar, click **Totals** Σ

An additional **Total:** row is added to the query grid.

By default, each field is set to **Group By**. We want a query that will group the results by **JobTitle** and display a total of bonuses for each record with the same JobTitle.

- Click in the **Total:** box for the **Bonus** field and select **Sum** from the drop-down list

- To prevent the results being grouped by Name and Salary, select the **Where** expression (which hides them from the query results)

- Sort the results by **Bonus** in **ascending** order

- Save changes - the query grid should look like this

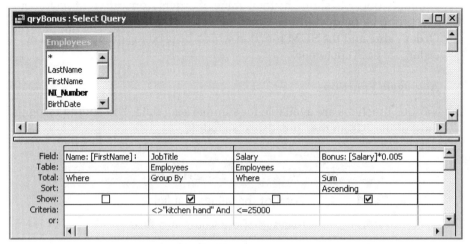

Summary query

- When you run the query you should get the following results

Job Title	Bonus
PO Clerk	£62.50
Secretary	£75.00
Sales Ledger	£75.00
Sous Chef	£80.00
Marketing Assistar	£82.50
Credit Controller	£95.00
Personal Assistant	£97.50
Purchasing Manage	£115.00
OP Clerk	£120.00
Fulfilment Manager	£190.00
Deliveries Manager	£207.50
Field Sales Executi	£357.50
IT Support	£382.50
Cook	£795.00
Sales Executive	£810.00

Record: 1 of 15

- Close the query and exit the database

Forms

Create and customise data entry forms

(Understand the differences between a **form** and a **datasheet**) ☐
Use the **Form Wizard** to create a simple form ☐
(Understand the different **sections** of forms) ☐
Change the **size** and **colour** of a form ☐
Add **controls** to a form/report using the **Toolbox** ☐
Change the **layout** of form controls ☐
Change the **properties** or **formatting** of controls ☐
Import an **image** onto a form and use **graphics** controls ☐
(Change a form's **tab order**) ☐

What is a Form?

Data entry using a datasheet is fairly straightforward. There are however several disadvantages in using datasheet view to enter records:

♦ It is often difficult to navigate across a record in datasheet view - especially if the set of fields is wider than the screen width.

♦ Although you can see information from several different records at once, it is often impossible to see all of the information from a single record.

♦ The display of information in datasheet view can become wearing on your eyes if you work in it for too long - it is difficult to keep your place on-screen.

♦ Datasheets do not present an ordered, professional view of your data.

♦ It is more difficult to use controls (such as check boxes and drop-down lists) on a datasheet to make data entry easier and more reliable.

♦ Large columns, such as those associated with memo and large text fields, are difficult to display and edit.

Many of these disadvantages are overcome by using a **form** for data entry and display.

A form displays database records **one at a time**. Most fields are displayed as a text box with a label next to it. Forms can be created with different layouts and can use graphics and effects as enhancements.

Create a Simple Form

The **Form Wizard** is usually the best way to create a basic form.

To design a form using the Form Wizard

- If you have completed all the exercises in each lesson, you can continue to use the **Employees_Database** file, otherwise open **Employees_Database (Forms)**

- In the **Database** window, select the **Forms** object

- Select **Create form by using wizard** and click **Open**

The **Form Wizard** is started.

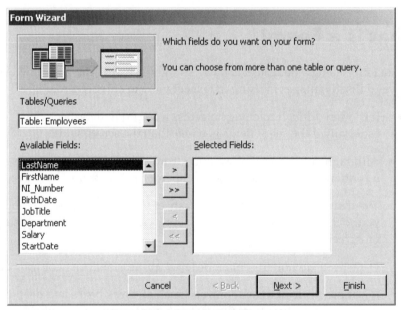

Form Wizard field selection dialogue box

The first screen lets you choose the **data source** for the form. This can be a **table** or a **query**. You can choose one or more fields from the data source to display on the form.

- Select the data source as **Table: Employees**, click [>>] to select all the fields and click **Next >**

Tip   Return to any of the previous **Wizard** forms by clicking **< Back**.

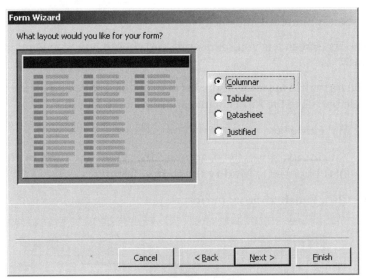

From Wizard - Layout screen

The form **layout** determines how the fields appear on the form. **Columnar** is suitable for most forms. It displays fields in one column down the page. The **Tabular** and **Datasheet** options both produce results similar to table **datasheet** view. **Justified** displays the fields in lines, without making any one line too wide to fit on-screen.

- Select the **Columnar** format then click **Next >**

This screen lets you select from a range of **styles** to give your form a professional appearance. If you want to customise the form yourself, it is best to select **Standard**.

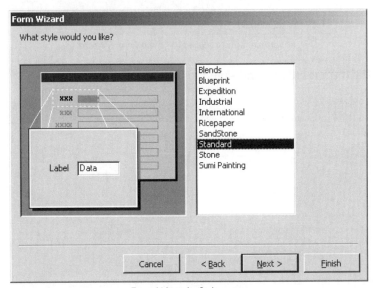

From Wizard - Style screen

- Select **Standard** and click **Next >**

The last screen lets you set the title and choose how you want to open the form.

The form **title** appears on the list of available forms and on the form's Title bar. Give the form a name appropriate to its use.

- In the **title** box, enter Employees Update

- You are also given the chance to either **Open the form to view** (select this option) or to **Modify the form's design**

- Click **Finish** to create the form

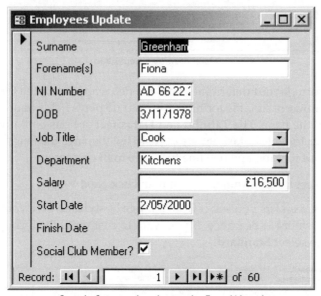

Sample form produced using the Form Wizard

The form is created and saved to the database file.

The Form Design Worksurface

Most forms will need at least some modification (for example, to make the data controls fit their contents). Often you will want to change a form quite radically to give it some individuality.

Forms are customised in design view using the following tools:

◆ The **worksurface** is the area on which you layout the form/report. The worksurface is divided into different **sections**.

◆ **Controls** display data and graphics. The **Toolbox** and **Field List** let you add controls.

◆ The **Properties** dialogue box lets you change the formatting of form/report **sections** and **controls**. You can also adjust some properties directly by using the **Formatting** toolbar.

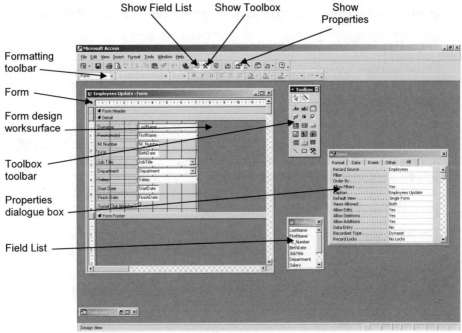

Form design view

In data entry form view, the toolbar is not usually displayed.

• To open the **Employees Update** form in design view, from the **View** menu, select **Design View**

- If they are not displayed, click the buttons on the **Standard** toolbar to display the **Field List** 📧 , **Toolbox** 🛠 and the **Properties** dialogue box 🖼

- If there is no ruler on the form, from the **View** menu, select **Ruler**

Tip You may want to maximise 🗖 the form window while customising a form.

Form Sections

Detail section

Each form must contain a detail section, which will contain fields from the currently selected record in the table or query that underpins the form.

Form Header/Form Footer sections

These sections are optional but if selected, the form header and/or footer will **always** be visible at the top and bottom of the form, no matter how large the detail section is.

This allows you to ensure that if the form is larger than the screen on which it is displayed, certain information will always be visible. This is especially appropriate when you have chosen to create a form that displays information in a tabular format.

Page Header/Page Footer sections

The main use for forms is for data entry and editing. However, it is also possible to print a form, which is where the **page header/footer** comes in.

The **page header** and **page footer** sections are never displayed as part of the form when it is on-screen, but are used when the form is printed. This is necessary because the **form header** and **form footer** sections only appear once when printed.

◆ The **form header** section is printed before the first form on the printout

◆ The **form footer** section is printed after the last form on the printout

In contrast to this, the **page header** and **page footer** sections will be printed at the top and bottom of the printed page, so making a multiple page printout much more readable.

> **Note** If you are not planning to print your forms, you can ignore the **page header** and **page footer** sections.

To show/hide the header and footer sections ✇

o The header and footers are not always displayed by default - to display them, from the **View** menu, select **Form Header/Footer** or **Page Header/Footer**

o The menu option is a toggle - to hide the sections again, simply select the menu option again.

> **Warning** If you hide a section, any controls in that section will be deleted.

Resize a Form Section

You can resize the height of form sections to make more or less space. You can also change the width of the whole form.

To change the height of a form section or the width of the form

- Point the mouse to the top of the Detail header - you will see the mouse pointer change to a resize pointer ✛

- Click-and-drag the border down about 2.5 cm (1")

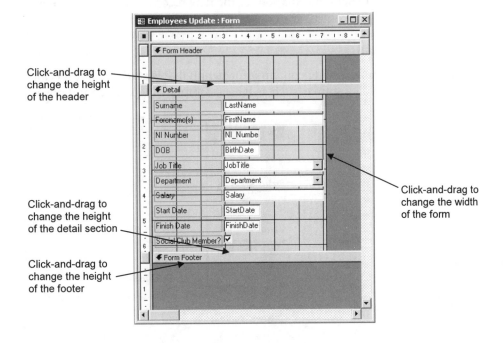

- Make the footer about 1 cm (½") high

- Click-and-drag the right-hand border to make plenty of space

- On the **Standard** toolbar, click **Save**

Note Access will only let you reduce the size of a section to the edge of the lowest/right-most control in the section. If you want to make the section smaller, you will have to re-position controls until this is possible.

Form Controls

Controls are the means by which you present data and other information on a form. Every object on a form is a control of one type or another. Controls are added from the **Toolbox** toolbar and from the **Field List**.

There are two basic types of control:

Bound controls

Bound controls display dynamic information on a form. When you use the Form Wizard to create a form, it automatically creates bound controls for each field you add to the form.

The control is bound to a field of the currently selected record in the underlying data source. As the record changes, so the bound control is updated with the field information for the new record. When the user enters or edits data in the control, the data source is updated.

Unbound controls

Unbound controls tend to contain information that is **static** with respect to the underlying data source, such as labels, company logos, lines and boxes.

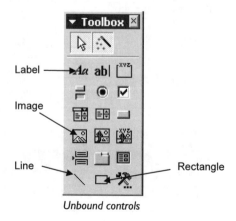

Unbound controls

To add controls to a form

The **Toolbox** toolbar is the main method by which you can add controls to the form.

- On the **Toolbox** toolbar, click the **Label** control

The button remains selected. When you move the mouse over the form, the pointer changes to a crosshair, along with a graphical representation of the tool (a letter A for the label control).

- In the **form header**, click-and-drag out the label control

- When you release the mouse button, the control is created - type the label Employee Update and press `Enter`

- Add another label to the footer with the text Enter and edit Employee records

> **Tip** The completed layout is shown on page 485 if you want to see where to place the controls. Do not worry about drawing them exactly, you can move and resize the controls after adding them to the form.

To add data-bound controls to the form

It is also possible to add controls directly from the underlying tables or queries using drag-and-drop. When you open a form in design view for the first time, Access also displays the **Field List** dialogue box.

- Click-and-drag the **LastName** field into the space you created on the right-hand side of the form

Access creates a control based on the **Display Control** property of the underlying table or query field (in this case a **text box**). Note that a label is also added containing the text from the **Caption** table field property.

Field list dialogue box

> **Tip** If you are designing a form from scratch, a good way to lay out data-bound controls is to select multiple fields in the Field List dialogue box using `Shift` and `Ctrl`. You can then drag them onto the form, where the resulting controls will be laid out in a column.

Change the Arrangement of Controls

To move and re-size controls

Controls are selected by clicking or by pressing `Tab` and `Shift`+`Tab` to move to the next and previous control respectively.

A selected control has handles around its borders, with an "extra-large" handle at the top left. If the control has a label, it will also display a large handle when the control is selected.

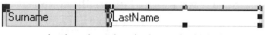

A selected text box (with attached label)

- Point to different parts of the control border to observe the different mouse pointers described below

Pointer	Point To	Operation
✋	Control border	Move *both* field and label
✋	Large handle	Move *either* field or label
↕	Top/bottom middle handle	Size the field horizontally
↔	Left/right middle handle	Size the field vertically
↘	Other corner handle	Size the field both horizontally and vertically

Mouse pointers and associated operations

- Practise resizing and moving the text box and label, both together and independently

- To re-size the label associated with a control, click the label

Tip You can **move** selected controls on a pixel-by-pixel basis using the keyboard arrow controls ⬆ ⬇ ⬅ and ➡ while pressing `Ctrl`.

Tip You can **re-size** the selected control(s) using the keyboard arrows when you are holding down the `Shift` key.

To delete a control

- Select the **LastName** text box control and press ⌷Delete⌷ - both the text box *and* the label are deleted

- Save the form

To resize multiple controls ①

The next few topics discuss different ways to work with multiple controls. There is a practical example at the end (on page 485).

If you want to re-size multiple controls so that they have the same dimensions, Access provides menu options to accomplish this quickly and easily.

Tip   To select multiple controls, drag an outline on the form. Any controls that the outline box touches will be selected. Alternatively, ⌷Shift⌷+click selects or deselects multiple controls.

---

o   Select the controls then from the **Format** menu, select **Size**

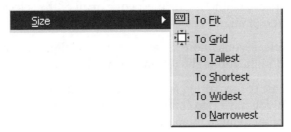

Format, Size command

The **To Fit** option sizes the controls so that expected data will be displayed in them.

To Grid "snaps" the object borders to an invisible grid, making it easier to line up controls.

The last four options should be self-explanatory.

To align controls ①

It can be fiddly and time consuming to align and space controls evenly by hand. Access provides several tools to help.

   o Select the controls that you wish to align

Tip   You can select a whole row or column of controls by dragging inside the rulers. If you are dragging inside the horizontal ruler at the top of the form, controls in **all** sections will be selected.

---

   o From the **Format** menu, select **Align**

Format, Align command

The first four options allow you to align the selected controls to one of the four sides of the control. The basic rule of alignment is that the controls are aligned to the furthest edge of all of the selected controls in the direction of alignment.

For example, if you choose several controls to align top, the controls will be aligned to the top of the top-most control.

Another rule of formatting is that controls aligned using Align will not overlap. If you have two controls which overlap in the direction in which you are trying to align them, then the controls will be aligned "as near as possible" without overlapping.

To space controls ①

With multiple controls, another layout requirement is to be able to set equal spacing between groups of three or more controls. Access provides horizontal and vertical spacing tools in order to help.

   o From the **Format** menu, select either **Vertical Spacing** or **Horizontal Spacing**

Format, Space command

The three options allow you to either make the spacing between objects the same or increase/decrease the spacing between them.

> **Note** If two or more controls are aligned in the direction that you are spacing them, they will be treated as a single unit. For example if, out of a group of controls two are aligned to top, then they will be treated as a single control for the purpose of spacing.

Practice

- *Adjust the size and position of the form controls to match the graphic*
- *Use the Size, Align and Spacing commands*
- *Switch between design and form view to check whether controls are displaying correctly*

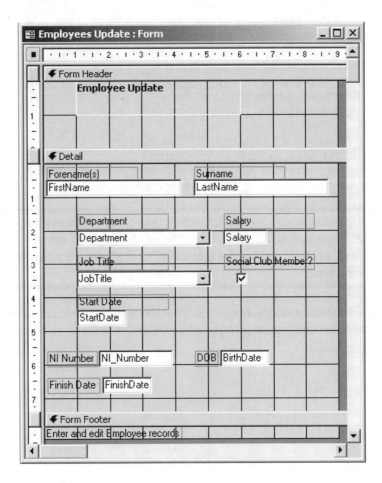

- *Save the form regularly*

What are Control Properties?

Control properties determine how controls and sections appear and behave.

Some properties are generic (applicable to all controls), some are applicable to several types of control and some are particular to individual controls. Also, the form itself and each section in the form have their own properties.

To display control properties

All of the currently selected object's properties are displayed in the **Properties** dialogue box.

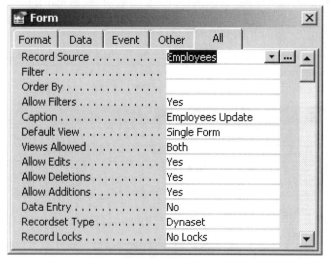

Properties dialogue box

Note If you select a form section rather than a control, the **Properties** dialogue box will display properties of the selected section. To display properties for the form, click in the grey area outside the form itself.

The **Properties** dialogue box has five tabs. The first four organise properties into logical groups, while the fifth tab displays all properties.

When you select a property, the following controls can be displayed at the end of the property text box. Where appropriate, both controls can be displayed for a property.

Click	To
...	Display a dialogue box from which appropriate values can be selected
▾	Display a list of appropriate values - you can either select from the values or type in your own

- Select the **Form** properties by clicking the dark grey worksurface background in the **Form** window

- Select the **Format** tab and set the **Record Selectors** property to **No**

This hides the grey bar on the left of the form, which would interfere the colour scheme we are going to setup.

> **Tip** Remember that you can double-click a Yes/No property to switch values.

The Formatting Toolbar

When you work in design mode, a **Formatting** toolbar is displayed below the **Standard** toolbar. This lets you set control properties, such as font type, size and colour and text alignment quickly. Any changes you make with the Formatting toolbar are automatically updated to the **Properties** dialogue box.

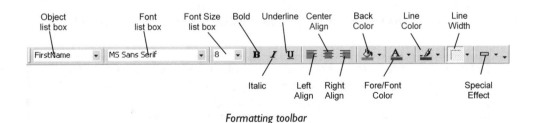

Formatting toolbar

Choosing fonts to use on a form

Different **font typefaces** are available for you to use on forms. Note that some fonts are not suitable for use on forms, as they are hard to read on-screen. Most forms use a **sans serif** font, such as **MS Sans Serif**, **Verdana** or **Tahoma**. Sans serif fonts are quite plain (they do not have curly ends) which make them easier to read on-screen.

Note that not all fonts are available on all systems. If a font you choose for the form is not available, the default system font will be used instead, which may spoil the layout of your form and make it difficult to read.

As well as changing the typeface of text, you can change its size. Most forms will use font sizes of between 8-12 points.

To change the font size and style

- Click-and-drag in the vertical ruler bar to select all the controls on the form

- Click the drop-down arrow in the **Font** box and select **Tahoma**

- Leave the size set to **8 pt**

Note When you select controls individually, note that formatting changes will only be applied to one part of a text box control. For example, if you select the label, the text in the label will change, but the text in the text box will be unaffected. If you want to change both parts of the control, or format several controls at once, Shift -click each one so that they are all selected.

Tip Alternatively, you can set the **Font Name** and **Font Size** properties on the **Format** tab of the **Properties** dialogue box.

To change the font colour of a control using the Property dialogue box

Note If your monitor is set to use 256 colours, you will see a different colour palette to the one described here. Work out your own colour scheme, based on those available to you.

- Shift +click to **deselect** the **SocialClub** check box control (but not its label)

Note The **Properties** dialogue box will not display a property unless it is available for all selected controls. The buttons on the **Formatting** toolbar are not so scrupulous.

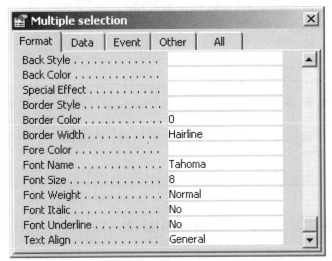

Format properties for a text box control

- Display the **Format** tab on the **Properties** dialogue box and scroll down to the middle of the tab, where most of the display properties are found

- Click in the **Fore Color** box then click the **Build** button ▪▪▪

The **Color** dialogue box is displayed.

- Select the **dark blue** colour chip and click **OK**

- Press Enter or click out of the box to apply the change

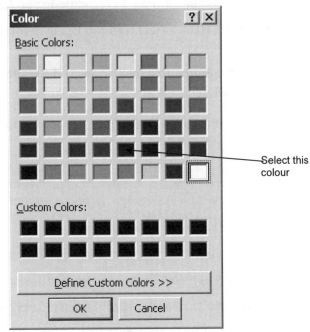

Select this colour

Color dialogue box

To change the border style of a control using the Formatting toolbar

- `Shift`+click to **deselect** all the **labels**, leaving the **controls** selected

- On the **Formatting** toolbar, click the drop-down arrow on the **Line/Border Color** button and select the **dark blue** chip

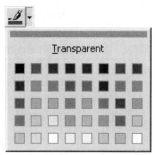

Line/Border Color

Line/Border Width

Special Effect

- Leave the width and special effect set to **Hairline** and **Flat**

- In the **Properties** box, change the **Back Style** property to **Transparent**

- Save the form

To change the form background colour

Each section of the form can have a different background colour.

- Click a blank area of the form header (without selecting a specific control)

- On the **Formatting** toolbar, select the **white** chip from the **Fill/Back Color** button

- Make the **Detail** section **pale yellow** and the footer the brighter yellow above it

Practice

- *Make the label in the header 18 pt and **bright red** and **bold***

- *Resize the label to fit the text if necessary*

- *Make the label in the footer **italic** and **dark red***

- *Make the **FinishDate** text and label **italic** and **blue** (3 down, 3 from right)*

- *Make the **LastName** and **JobTitle** text boxes (not the labels) **bold***

- *Save the form*

Import an Image onto a Form

Several unbound controls can be used to improve the design of forms.

To add a logo

You can use an **Image** control to add graphics to a form. You can use image types such as GIF, JPEG and BMP.

- On the **Toolbox** toolbar, click **Image**
- Click-and-drag a box to fill the left-hand quarter of the header

---

Tip   Do not attempt to match the size of the image control to the logo that you are adding to the form - you will be able to re-size the control later. Just ensure that the dragged area is large enough to manipulate once the control is created.

The **Insert Picture** dialogue box is displayed.

Selecting a graphic file for an image control

- Open the **My Pictures** folder, select the **chilli logo** image file and click **OK**

If the graphic that you have inserted does not fit the image control, you can automatically re-size the control to fit the graphic by double-clicking any of the (small) sizing handles to auto-fit the control. However, we need to keep the image quite small.

- In the **Properties** dialogue box, change the **Size Mode** property (on the **Format** tab) to **Zoom**

Clip (the default) displays the object at actual size, cropping any parts of the image that will not fit. **Stretch** sizes the object to fill the control. This setting may distort the proportions of the object. **Zoom** displays the entire object, resizing it as necessary without distorting the proportions of the object.

- From the **Format** menu, select **Send to Back** to stop the graphic from obscuring the label

To add line and rectangle controls

You can add line and rectangle controls to enhance the appearance of your form. Unfortunately, these controls also follow a rule that a control cannot span across a section boundary. If you want to draw a box around your form, you can build it from individual line controls.

- On the **Toolbox** toolbar, select **Rectangle** ▢ and draw a box around the indented controls

> **Tip** To create a horizontal or vertical line, hold down `Shift` *before you* drag to create the control.

- Change the fill and line colour of the rectangle to **pale green** and use **Format, Send to Back** to put it behind the controls

Change the Tab Order

The controls are no longer in their original sequence, so anyone using the `Tab` key to navigate between controls would get very confused when using the form.

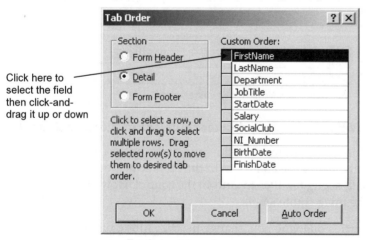

Click here to select the field then click-and-drag it up or down

To change the tab order

- From the **View** menu, select **Ta<u>b</u> Order...**

- Click-and-drag the fields into the order shown

- Click **OK**

Tab Order dialogue box

Practice

- *Put the finishing touches to your form, so that it resembles the one below*

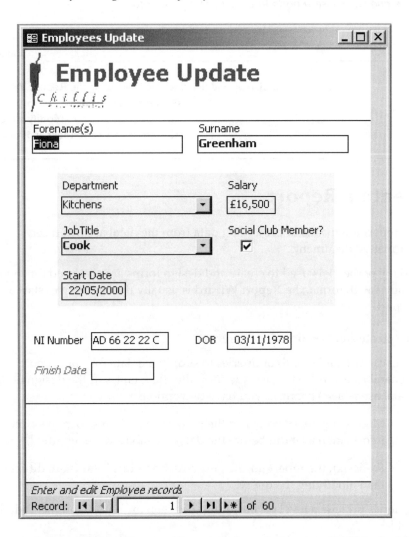

- *Use the form to add yourself as an employee (a **Personnel Officer** in the **Management** department)*

- *Personnel Officer is not on the list of Job Titles, but this field should not be limited to the list, so you can type it in*

- *Make up your salary*

- *Save and close the form*

- *Exit the database*

Reports

Create and customise reports to present and print data

Create a report to **display** and **print** selected data using the **Report Wizard** ☐
Group and **summarise** data in a report ☐
Modify a report ☐
Customise report **headers** and **footers** ☐

Create a Report

A report is a means of presenting data from the database in a nicely formatted document.

Many of the tools used to create and design forms are also used for reports, and as with forms, the **Report Wizard** is usually the best way to start a report.

To create a data source for the report

You can use tables and/or queries to supply the data for your report. As a general rule, it is best to use queries rather than tables. If the design of the database table(s) changes, you have two options:

♦ Modify the query on which the report is based, to return the same information as it did before the database tables were modified.

♦ Re-design the report for the new structure - this is far more difficult than modifying the query.

Queries provide a level of "buffering" between the report and the underlying table.

We will make some changes to the **qryBonus** query to use it as a data source.

Practice

- *If you have completed all the exercises in each lesson, you can continue to use the Employees_Database file, otherwise open Employees_Database (Reports)*

- *If you are using your own file, open the qryBonus query in design view*

- *Adjust the query grid to match the one below (remove the **Total:** line by clicking the button* Σ *again)*

Field:	LastName	FirstName	JobTitle	Salary	Bonus: [Salary]*0.005
Table:	Employees	Employees	Employees	Employees	
Sort:					Ascending
Show:	☑	☑	☑	☑	☑
Criteria:			<>"kitchen hand" And	<=25000	

- *Save and close the query*

To create a report using the Report Wizard

- In the **Database** window, select the **Reports** object

- Select **Create report by using wizard** then on the **Database Window** toolbar, click **Preview** ⊡ Preview

The **Report Wizard** starts.

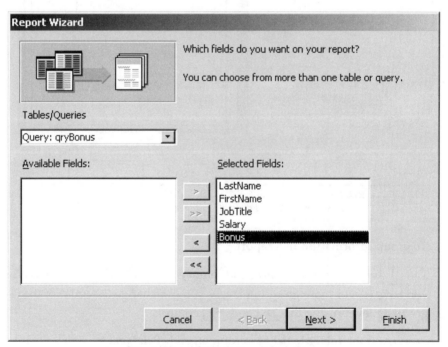

Report Wizard field selection dialogue boxes

- From the **Tables/Queries** list box, select **Query: qryBonus**

- Select all the fields from **Query: qryBonus** and click **Next >**

The next dialogue box is concerned with the grouping of information in the report. This allows you to group detailed information on the report, based on the values in one (or more) fields. Grouping is similar to the use of **Summary** queries (see page 470).

For grouping to be successful, you must choose a suitable field (or fields). For example, Country and City are good fields on which to group data, since there should (hopefully) be several Customers per country and/or city. Conversely, Address would not be appropriate, unless several of your customers happen to live at the same address!

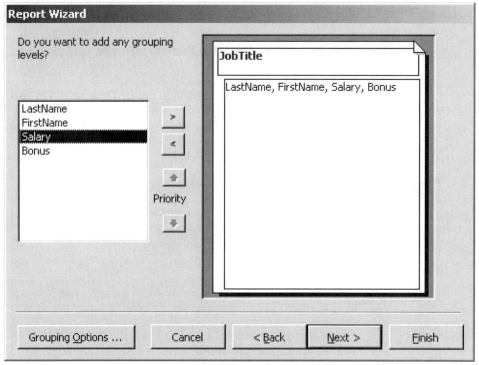

Report Wizard grouping selection dialogue box

To group information in a report

The `>` and `<` controls add and remove fields as grouping levels. When you have two or more grouping levels, you can change the order of the grouping levels using the `↑` and `↓` controls.

- Add the **JobTitle** field to group on and click **Next >**

Tip   You don't have to select any grouping levels.

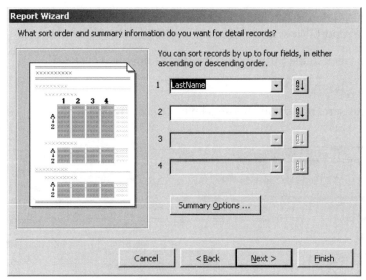

Report Wizard sort order selection dialogue box

The **Report Wizard** lets you apply up to four levels of sort to the records in the report. You cannot sort by any fields chosen for grouping (these are sorted in descending order automatically).

To apply a sort order to the report

- Select the **LastName** field to sort on and select **Ascending** order
- Click the **Summary Options...** button

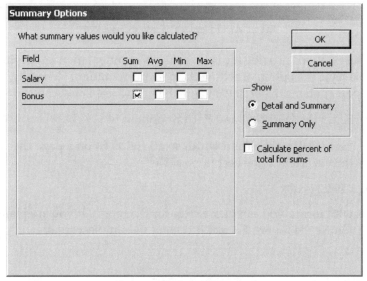

Summary Options dialogue box

This dialogue box lets you choose which function to use for subtotals on the report. We want to calculate the total value of bonuses.

- Click in the **Sum** box on the **Bonus** line then click **OK**

- Click **Next >**

This screen lets you choose a layout for the report.

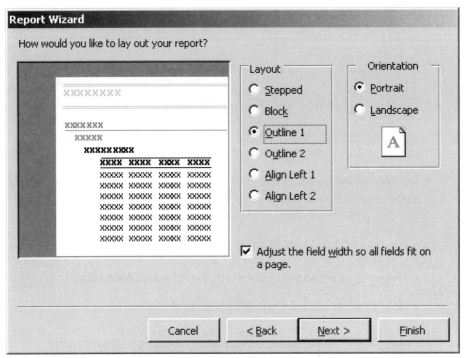

Report Wizard layout selection dialogue box

These options provide for various levels of indentation and styling. You also have the option of setting the paper **orientation**. Generally, if a report contains many fields you will need to use **Landscape** orientation.

- Select the **Outline 1** and **Portrait** options

- Leave **Adjust the field width so all fields fit on a page** checked to let the wizard find the best fit possible

- Click **Next >**

As with forms, you can pick a style for the report. If you are planning to customise the report, **Formal** produces the simplest results.

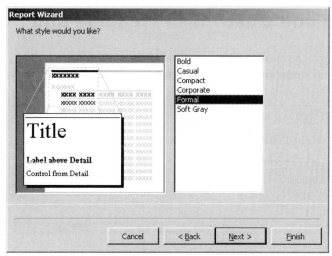

Report Wizard style selection dialogue box

- Select **Formal** and click **Next >**

The final dialogue box lets you give an appropriate name to the report.

- Enter the title `Bonus Payments Summary`

- Select **Preview the report** then click **Finish**

After some processing the report is displayed in **Print Preview**.

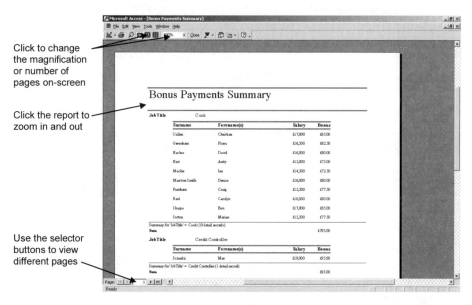

- Browse through the report then on the toolbar click **Close**

The report is opened in design view. The wizard has automatically named and saved the report for you.

Create and Customise Headers and Footers

Like a form, a report consists of several sections. However, the use of sections in a report is considerably more complex than it is on forms.

Report sections

The display of each section on a report is triggered by a different **event** during the processing of records. When designing reports, it is important to note that the sections are not always printed at a particular **position** on the page, rather they are printed as a result of **events** that occur during the processing of the report. If you understand **when** the report sections are printed rather than **where**, you will find that the design of report sections becomes far easier.

The height of each section determines how much vertical space it will take up on the printed page.

- Switch between design and preview mode while reading about each section so that you can relate the information to the actual report

Detail section

Each report contains a mandatory detail section, which will be printed once for each record supplied by the table or query that underpins the report. In our report the detail section contains records for each employee, sorted by **LastName**.

Report Header Section

This section is printed at the beginning of the report, **before** the first **Page Header** section is printed. This makes the report header suitable for a report **front page.** In our report this contains the title "Bonus Payments Summary".

Report Footer Section

The report footer section is printed at the end of the report, just **before** the last **Page Footer** section. This section tends to be used for grand totals (which appear in our report) and footnote information.

Page Header and Page Footer sections

These sections will always be visible at the top and bottom of each page of the report. Our report has a footer (showing the date and page number), but no page header.

Group Header and Group Footer sections

When you create groups within your report, Access provides a Group Header and Group Footer section for **each level of grouping** that you define. The sections are nested, as shown.

Group Header 1
> **Group Header 2**
> *Detail*
>
> **Group Footer 2**
>
> **Group Header 2**
> *Detail*
>
> **Group Footer 2**

Group Footer 1

Group Header 2
> **Group Header 2**
> *Detail*
>
> **Group Footer 2**

Group Footer 2

To show/hide the header and footer sections

If you are designing the report yourself, you may need to turn the display of some sections on and off.

o From the **View** menu, select **Report Header/Footer** or **Page Header/Footer**

Note If you hide a section, Access will delete any controls on that section.

Modify a Report

The layout of reports generated by the wizard is often quite clumsy and confusing.

However, it is quite easy to improve it with a few simple changes.

To work with controls on reports ①

o Use the same tools to move, resize, add and format controls on reports as for forms (see page on page 482)

Tip As you work through these steps, keep checking the report in preview mode and remember to save regularly.

Practice

We will modify the report to look like the one below:

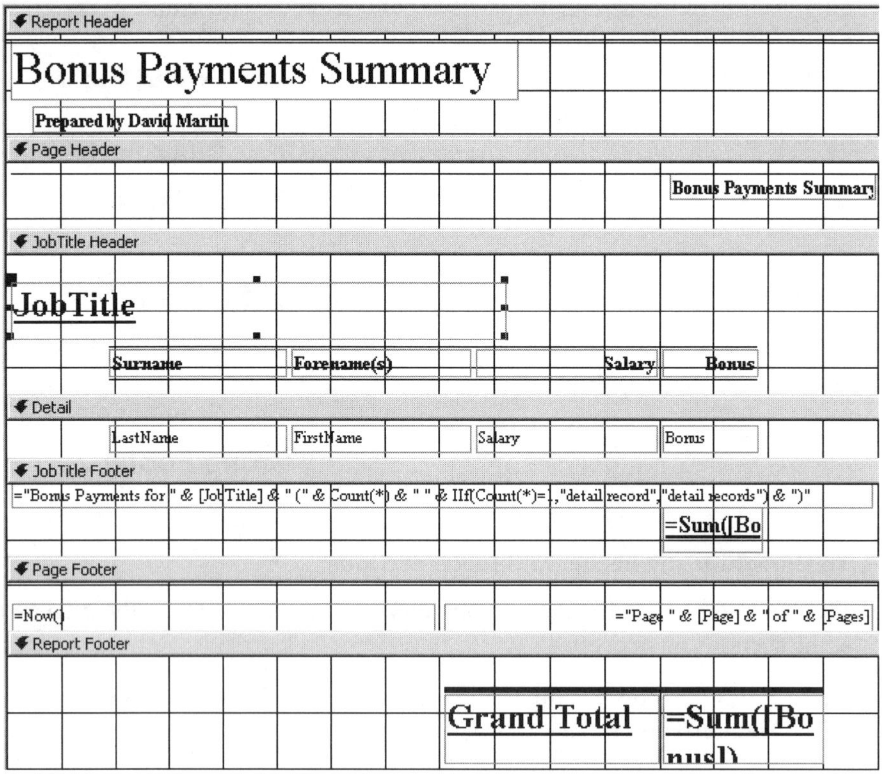

- *Click the drop-down arrow on the **Object** button on the **Formatting** toolbar*

Object button

- *Select **Line 22***

This selects the Line22 object on the report - it is much easier to use the list box than it is to click the line itself.

- *Press* `Delete` *to remove the line*

- *Delete **Line 24** as well*

This removes the double lines around the detail labels.

- *Drag down the bottom border of the **JobTitle** header section and move the controls in it to leave about ½" (1 cm) space at the top - this gap helps to make each group more distinctive*

- *Delete the **JobTitle** label, format the text box as **18 pt, bold** and **underline** then resize it and move it where the label was*

- *Replace the text "Summary" in the group footer control with* Total Bonus Payments *and delete the text & "'Job Title' = " & " "*

- *Shorten the line (Line 26) at the top of the footer so that it underlines the Bonus field only*

- *Delete the **Sum** label and make the total **12 pt, bold** and **underline***

- *Add a text label to the report header with the text* Prepared by Your Name

- *Make space in the page header to add a label showing the report title in 8 pt text with a line above*

- *Select the **Report Properties** and change the **Page Header** property (on the **Format** tab) to **Not with Rpt Hdr***

- *Finally, make the Grand Total stand out by using **18 pt, bold** and **underlining**, bring the label closer to the total, add a short 3pt line above it and make more space in the report footer*

Tip If you find that you get blank pages in your report, change the **Width** of lines **18, 19, 20, 21, 27** and **28** to **15 cm**. Drag the border of the report up to the edge of the controls.

Group and Summarise Data

The Report Wizard can setup sorting and grouping in a report. You can also set or modify these options in design view.

To set or modify Sorting and Grouping

- On the **Standard** toolbar, click **Sorting and Grouping** [⟨≣ **OR** from the **V**iew menu, select **S**orting and Grouping...

The **Sorting and Grouping** dialogue box is displayed.

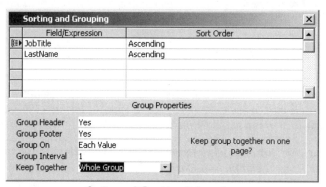

Sorting and Grouping dialogue box

To apply or modify grouping levels, from the **Field/Expression** box, select the field on which to apply sort or grouping options. **Sort Order** allows you to change the order between **Ascending (A...Z)** and **Descending (Z...A)**. To group a field, click into it in the top panel then in the bottom panel set **Group Header** and/or **Footer** to **Yes**.

- For our exercise, the only change to make is to set the **Keep Together** option (for **JobTitle**) to **Whole Group** - this forces a page break when the detail lines cannot all be included under their group header

Print a Report

To print the report

- Switch to preview mode to check that everything is in place then from the **F**ile menu, select **Print...**

As with other Office programs, you can select a range of pages to print and the number of copies.

- Click **OK** to print the report

- Close the report, saving any changes, and close the database

Review of Database

Review the topics covered during the module and identify areas for further practice and goals for the future

---

Review

(Check **objectives**) ☐
(Complete **consolidation** exercise) ☐
(Identify topics for **further** study) ☐

Check Objectives

Congratulations on completing the lessons for ECDL Module 5 "Database".

You have learned to:

♦   Open a database to add and edit **records**.

♦   **Design** and **create** a database.

♦   Make **changes** to an existing table.

♦   Create **queries** to sort, analyse and filter records.

♦   Create and customise data entry **forms**.

♦   Create and customise **reports** to present and print data.

Make sure you have checked off each syllabus item and identified any topics you do not fully understand or remember.

Consolidation and Going Further

Tests for Module 5 can either be practice-based or question-based. Practical tests will ask you to add and edit records and to create a database with table, query, form and report objects.

There are further test-style exercises for you to try on the CD in the folder **ECDL Tests\5 Database**

Print the document **Database Questions** and try to complete the test unaided, using the data files from the folder.

Note These questions are provided as a consolidation exercise. They do not make up an approved ECDL test. See page 689 for more information about the extra tests.

Going further

Access is a particularly powerful and complex application, and training in it can be taken to quite a high level. From a basic point of view, there are tools for importing and exporting data that have only been covered briefly in this course. There are also further field properties, which can be used to test and validate data.

The next big step is to learn about **relational** database design. This design stores data in multiple tables for greater efficiency and reliability.

Another area of study is database **management** (setting passwords and security options and supporting multiple users). You can also learn to use macros and VBA to create database **applications**, with customised forms and functionality.

Many of these topics can be studied under the **ECDL Advanced Syllabus**.

Refer to page 744 for more details about further courses in gtslearning's range of **Learn** training books.

Presentation

Getting Started with PowerPoint

Open a presentation and recognise elements of the screen

Lesson 38

Start PowerPoint and recognise elements of the screen ☐
Open a presentation, make some **changes** and **save** ☐
Move and **resize** text boxes ☐
Close a presentation and **exit** PowerPoint ☐

What is a Presentation?

A PowerPoint presentation is a set of **slides** designed to illustrate the main topics that the speaker is talking about. Presentation slides can be used to add impact to a business or marketing meeting, to a product launch, to staff inductions and training programs, and so on.

PowerPoint uses editing, formatting and drawing tools similar to those in Word. You can create slides consisting of text, graphics, charts and tables. Animation effects can be applied to the transitions between slides and to objects on each slide. You can also use PowerPoint to prepare notes pages and handouts to accompany a presentation.

With presentations, it is very important that all the slides look consistent. PowerPoint is setup to help you create slides with a similar look and feel without really thinking about it, leaving you to concentrate on the content of the show.

Open PowerPoint

By now you should be quite familiar with the way Office applications work. Open PowerPoint using its shortcut icon ⬚.

To start PowerPoint from the Start menu

- Click the **Start** button and display the **Programs** menu then click the **Microsoft PowerPoint** program item ⬚ Microsoft PowerPoint

The **PowerPoint** dialogue box is displayed. It enables you either to create a presentation (in one of three different ways), or to open an existing presentation.

PowerPoint dialogue box

Click	To
Auto**C**ontent Wizard	Get help with the content and design features of your presentation.
Design **T**emplate	Get help with the design features of your presentation, but not the content.
Blank presentation	Determine your own content and design features by starting with an unstyled, blank presentation.
Open an existing presentation	Open and edit a presentation you have already created.

- Select **O**pen an existing presentation

Open a Presentation

To open an existing presentation

If the name of the presentation is displayed in the lower section of the dialogue box, select the presentation you want to open (recently used presentations are listed here) then click **OK**.

- For this exercise, select **More Files...** then click **OK**

The **Open** dialogue box is displayed.

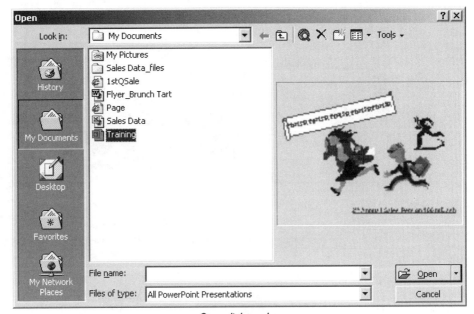

Open dialogue box

- Select the **Training** presentation file and click **Open**

To open a presentation when PowerPoint is already running ①

- o   On the **Standard** toolbar, click **Open** 📂

OR

- o   From the **File** menu, select **Open** (*SpeedKey:* Ctrl + O)

OR

- Select a recently used presentation from the bottom of the **File** menu

The PowerPoint Window

The PowerPoint window has the familiar MS Office layout.

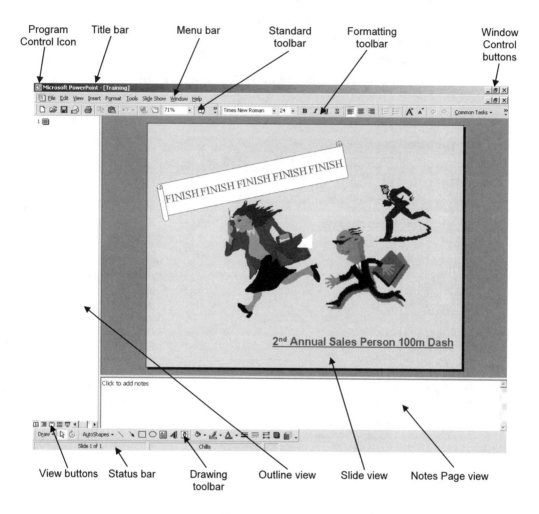

Program Control Icon | Title bar | Menu bar | Standard toolbar | Formatting toolbar | Window Control buttons

View buttons | Status bar | Drawing toolbar | Outline view | Slide view | Notes Page view

The PowerPoint Toolbars

When you first start PowerPoint, the **Standard**, **Formatting** and **Drawing** toolbars are displayed. These toolbars contain commonly used functions. There are ten other toolbars available for specialised tasks, such as working with animation. Refer back to page 185 for tips on working with toolbars.

- Optionally, move the **Formatting** toolbar below the **Standard** toolbar
- Maximise the window

The Scroll Bars

The vertical scroll bar allows you to move from slide to slide in your presentation.

To scroll around a presentation ⊕

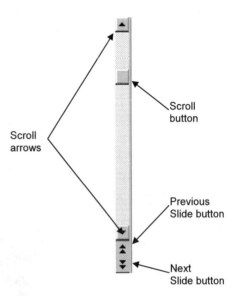

o   Click the scroll arrows either to scroll around the current slide, or to scroll to the next slide, depending on the current zoom setting

o   Click the **Next Slide** button to move to the next slide

o   Click the **Previous Slide** button to move to the previous slide

Scroll button

Scroll arrows

Previous Slide button

Next Slide button

o   Drag the **scroll button** up or down to move quickly to any slide in the presentation

The Status Bar

The **Status** bar displays information about the presentation, including the current slide number, the total number of slides in the presentation and the name of the design template you have used to create the presentation.

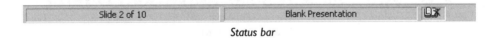

Slide 2 of 10   Blank Presentation

Status bar

Get Help with PowerPoint

The Help system in PowerPoint works in the same way as for Word. Refer back to page 194 if you need reminding.

Select Objects

A presentation slide is made up of a number of **objects**. Examples of objects are text boxes, graphics, drawings, pictures, tables, organisation charts and graphs.

Unlike Word and Excel, you can only enter data onto a slide by creating an object. For example, you cannot type text directly onto the slide; you must enter it into a text box object.

Every object can be selected, moved, copied and resized in the same way.

To select an object

To edit any object you must first select it.

- Click the picture of the salesman in the blue suit

When an object is selected, white "handles" appear around the edge of the object.

A selected clip art object

If an object contains text, it appears with white handles and a grey border.

- Click on some text in the "2nd Annual..." box

A selected text object

The text box is selected for editing. Notice the insertion point blinking where you clicked.

- Click-and-drag across "100" and type 1500

- Point to the border of the text box and click - the border changes to show a dotted line

2nd Annual Sales Person 1500m Dash

The text object is now selected for **moving** and **resizing**.

To select multiple objects

- With the text box still selected, hold down `Shift` and click the blue salesman again

Both objects are selected.

- Keep the `Shift` key pressed and click another salesperson then the "Finish" banner

All four objects are selected.

- Still holding down `Shift`, click one of the selected salesperson pictures

The object is de-selected, leaving the other three objects selected.

- Click a blank area of the slide or press `Esc`

All the objects are de-selected.

- If necessary, click the **Select Objects** button [cursor] on the **Drawing** toolbar so that it appears "pushed-in" [cursor]

- Click-and-drag a bounding box completely around all the objects except for the bottom text box

- From the **Edit** menu, click **Select All** (*SpeedKey:* `Ctrl`+`A`) - all objects are selected

- Press `Esc`

All the objects are de-selected.

Move, Resize and Delete Objects

After selecting an object, you can move and resize it using the mouse.

To move an object to a new position on the same slide

- Select a salesperson then point to the selected object

The mouse pointer shape changes to a four-headed arrow.

- Click-and-drag the salesperson towards the finish banner
- Select the "2nd Annual" box *for moving*
- Point to the grey border then click-and-drag the box to the left

---

Note To move the object **either** up and down **or** left and right, hold down the ⌷Shift⌷ key when you drag.

To resize an object

- Select the salesperson you moved
- Point to the right-hand corner handle on the graphic

The mouse pointer changes shape to a double-headed arrow.

- Click-and-drag to make the picture smaller

Tip Hold down the ⌷Ctrl⌷ key when you drag the handle to resize the object from the centre outwards.

To delete an object

- Select a salesperson
- From the **Edit** menu, select **Cle_ar** (*SpeedKey:* ⌷Delete⌷)

Use the Undo Tool

As with other Office programs, PowerPoint allows you to **undo** actions.

To undo the last action

- On the **Standard** toolbar, click **Undo** 🔄 ▾ OR from the **E**dit menu, select **U**ndo (*SpeedKey:* Ctrl + Z) - the picture is restored

To undo a previous action

By default, the **Undo** button stores the last 20 actions.

- Click the arrow on the **Undo** button to display a list of your previous edits and select back to **Typing**

Tip To increase the number of undos available, from the **T**ools menu, select **O**ptions. Click the **Edit** tab and pick a number from the **M**aximum number of undos: box.

Practice

- *Continue to move and resize the objects on the slide, making use of the Undo tool as well*

- *Use the different resize handles to discover their effect on the object's proportions and experiment with the* Shift *and* Ctrl *keys*

- *Notice the different effects when you resize objects containing text - you will learn about this later*

Save and Close a Presentation

All the different ways to save and close files and the application are the same in PowerPoint as in Word (refer back to page 216 if you need reminding).

To save and close a presentation

- Click **Save** 💾 to save changes to the current presentation

- Click the **Close** icon ✕ on the **Menu** bar to close the file

- If you are not continuing with the next lesson, click the **Close** icon ✕ on the **Title** bar to exit PowerPoint

---

Creating a Presentation

Create a basic presentation and work with views

Lesson 39

Create a **new** presentation ☐
Create a new **slide** and select an **AutoLayout** ☐
Add and delete **text** from a slide ☐
Switch between different **views** ☐
Use the **Zoom** tool ☐
Add **clip art** to a slide ☐
Change the **slide layout** ☐
Open **several** presentations ☐
Move and **copy** text and objects between slides and presentations ☐

A typical presentation starts with a title slide, showing the topic of the presentation and the name of the speaker.

Slides in the main part of the presentation generally follow the format of having a title, explaining the purpose of the slide, with 3-7 bullet points illustrating the key points of the topic. It is important not to put too much text on your slides. If a slide is too crowded and confusing, it is likely that your audience will not bother looking at it at all!

Graphics, pictures and charts are used to provide information and to add interest.

Create a New Presentation

You can create a new presentation when you first start PowerPoint, or you can create one from within the application.

To create a new presentation on starting PowerPoint

- If you have just started PowerPoint, from the **PowerPoint** dialogue box, select **Design Template** then click **OK**

OR

- If PowerPoint is already running, from the **File** menu, select **New**

The **New Presentation** dialogue box is displayed.

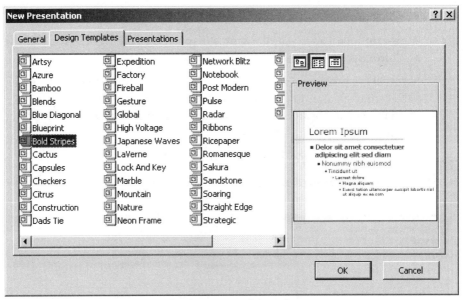

New Presentation dialogue box

Design Templates help you to create a nicely formatted presentation very quickly.

- Click the **Design Templates** tab if necessary then select the **Bold Stripes** icon - a preview of the slide design is displayed on the right

- Click **OK**

The **New Slide** dialogue box is displayed.

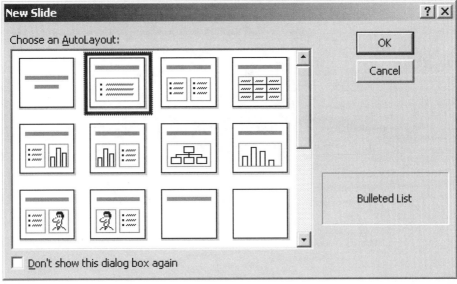

New Slide dialogue box

- Click on each **AutoLayout** in turn

A description of each AutoLayout is displayed to the right of the **Choose an AutoLayout:** list box.

Normally, a presentation would start with a **Title Slide** to introduce the subject and speaker to the audience. A Title Slide can also be displayed on the screen as the audience arrive for their presentation.

For this exercise we will practise editing techniques with some **Bulleted List** slides and add the **Title Slide** in a later lesson.

- Select the **Bulleted List** layout and click **OK**

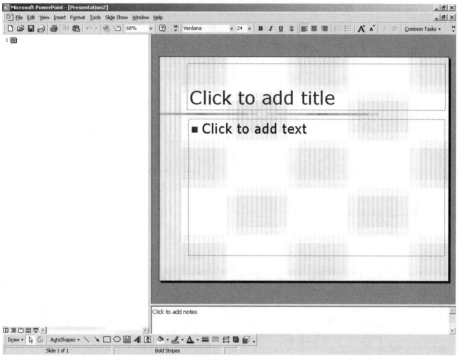

Slide placeholders

Most new slides contain **text placeholders** (the boxes with dotted outlines) for you to add text to the slide.

Add Text to a Slide

In any slide presentation, text is usually the most important component. Virtually every slide will contain text of some kind, even if it is just a title.

To enter text into a title placeholder

- Click into the text placeholder "Click to add title" to select it

When a text object is selected for editing, the border appears as a hashed line. The sample text disappears, and the insertion point is displayed in the placeholder, indicating that you can enter text.

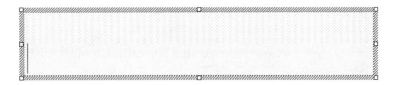

- Type Today's Program

Tip   Only press Enter when you want to begin a new paragraph.

PowerPoint automatically wraps text to the next line when you type to the edge of the placeholder.
On a slide, most paragraphs will only consist of one line.

- Click outside the text placeholder to deselect it

Tip   The F2 key toggles between selecting a text box for editing the text and selecting it for moving or resizing it.

To enter text into a bulleted list

Most text on a slide is presented as a bulleted list. Remember that slides are there to *support* what the speaker says, not to tell the whole story. The points on a slide must be short, easy to understand and develop the theme of the speaker's argument.

When you work with bullets you can choose from five indentation levels.

- Click into the bullet placeholder and type About Chillis

- Press Enter to start a new bullet at the same indentation level

- Type Departments and press Enter

- On the **Formatting** toolbar, click **Demote** ➡ (*SpeedKey:* `Tab`)

- Type Kitchens then press `Enter`

■ About Chillis
■ Departments
■ Kitchens

- Add these bullet points at the same indentation level Sales, Fulfilment, Management/Accounts

- Start a new paragraph then on the **Formatting** toolbar, click **Promote** ⬅ (*SpeedKey:* `Shift` + `Tab`)

- Type Training and Development

Tip	To start a new line **without** a bullet point, press `Shift` + `Enter`.

- Complete the slide as shown below then save the presentation as Recruitment

Note	When the text gets to the bottom of the slide, it is automatically made smaller so that it all fits.

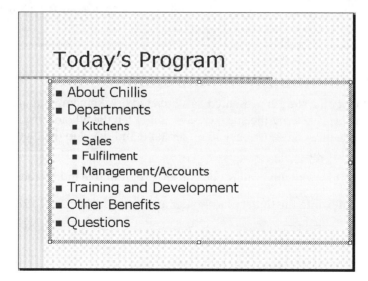

Create a New Slide

Every slide is based on an **AutoLayout**. Using the default AutoLayouts maintains a degree of consistency between slides, as each object appears in a predictable place.

AutoLayouts contain **placeholders** for the common types of object you will use on your slides: titles, bullet lists, pictures, charts and tables. If you want to create a custom layout, you can choose a title only or a blank AutoLayout. However, you should use these sparingly, so as not to complicate the presentation design too much.

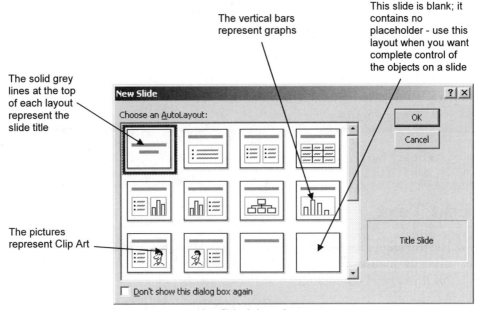

New Slide dialogue box

To create a new slide

- On the **Standard** toolbar, click **New Slide** [icon] OR from the **Insert** menu, select **New Slide...** (*SpeedKey:* `Ctrl`+`M`)

The **New Slide** dialogue box is displayed.

- Select the **Bulleted List** AutoLayout and click **OK**

The new slide appears, with placeholders indicating where to add text and other objects.

Tip   A new slide is always inserted **after** the currently selected slide.

- Add the following text to the slide

About Chillis

- Fresh Food First
- Growing Since 1994
- UK-wide Customer Base
- Sell Pre-cooked "Ready Meals" and Catering Products

> **Note** If you insert a new slide by mistake, from the **Edit** menu, select **Delete Slide**.

- Save the presentation

Edit Text

The techniques for selecting, editing and deleting text within a placeholder using the mouse or keyboard are the same as in Word (refer back to page 204 if you need reminding).

PowerPoint also uses **typing replace selection** and the **Automatic Word Selection** feature.

To use Automatic Word Selection

As with Word, when you are selecting a block of text, **Automatic Word Selection** selects whole words even if you click-and-drag from the middle of a word. You can turn the option on or off to suit the way you work.

- From the **Tools** menu, select **Options...** then click the **Edit** tab

- In the **Text** panel, remove the cross from the **When selecting, automatically select whole word** box and click **OK**

- Keep the setting activated if you prefer

Use the Zoom Tool

To zoom in and out ⊕

- o   As with Word and Excel, you can use the dialogue box (**View**, **Zoom...**) or the **Zoom** box on the **Standard** toolbar to zoom in and out

Change Display Modes

PowerPoint has six views, each of which gives you a different way of looking at your presentation.

Use This View	To
Normal	Simultaneously display Slide, Outline, and Notes Page views in their own adjustable panes. The advantage of this view is that it lets you work on all areas of your presentation from one screen.
Slide	Display just the slide. The advantage of this view is that there is more room on-screen for the slide, which can be useful for moving and editing objects.
Outline	Organise and develop the presentation text.
Notes Page	Create speaker notes for the presenter or as information for the audience.
Slide Sorter	Display the slides in miniature in order to arrange and order slides and preview animation settings.
Slide Show	Display each slide in full screen. This is the view in which you run the presentation slide show.

To change the view

- •   Switch to each view using the **View** buttons, located at the bottom left of the PowerPoint window
- •   Press Esc to exit **Slide Show** view
- •   From the **View** menu, select **Normal**

Normal View

The main working view is **Normal** view. The PowerPoint window is split into three panes so that you can work in **Outline** view, **Slide** view and **Notes Page** view simultaneously.

- Drag the **pane borders** to see more or less of each pane

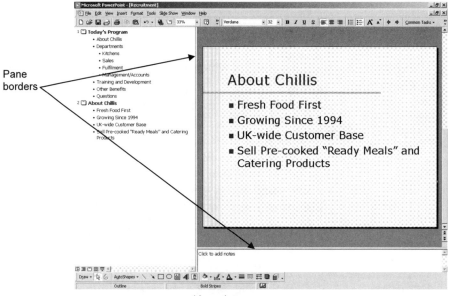

Normal view

Slide View

Slide view can be used to complete the format and content of each slide.

Outline View

Outline view is used to plan the presentation text. In Outline view slide titles are aligned at the left margin and other text indented. You can enter text at the appropriate outline level, move slides around, promote and demote headings and bullets, and so on.

A slide miniature is displayed in the top right-hand corner of the screen, allowing you to check the layout of any text entered on the slide. From Outline view you can also add any speaker notes to the **Notes Page** pane on the right-hand side of the screen.

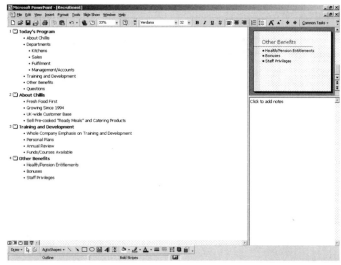

Outline view

- Use the view button to switch to Outline view then from the **View** menu, select **Toolbars** then **Outlining**

Use the **Outlining** toolbar to expand and collapse the outline or to promote and demote headings.

Click to promote and demote text | Click to move text/slides up and down | Click to expand or collapse text | Click to expand or collapse the whole presentation

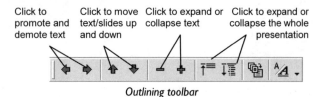

Outlining toolbar

Practice

- *Add the slides and text shown in the screenshot by typing into the Outline pane and using the Promote and Demote buttons to adjust the heading level*

- *Hide the Outlining toolbar again*

- *Save the presentation*

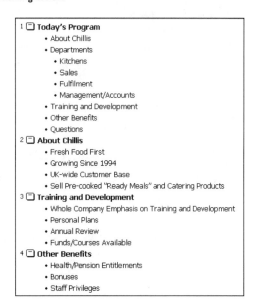

Slide Sorter View

Slide Sorter view gives you an overall perspective on your presentation by displaying a miniature version of each slide on a single screen. This view is used to reorganise slides and to apply transition and animation effects. You will learn more about working in this view on page 578.

Notes Page View

Notes Page view can be used to create speaker's notes or audience handouts, containing a reduced version of the slide at the top of the page with space at the bottom of the page for the notes.

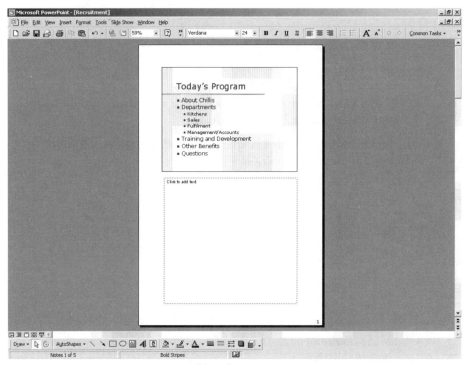

Notes Page view

To add notes to a slide

- From the **View** menu, select **Notes Page**

- Use the scroll bar to move to slide 1

- Zoom in so that you can see the text clearly

- Click the **Click to add notes** placeholder then type Welcome and introductions

You can use all the normal text editing, formatting and proofing tools that you use for slides to create notes pages.

Add Clip Art to a Slide

The **Microsoft Clip Gallery** contains a variety of pictures, sounds and photographs and video clips. It works in the same way as for Word and Excel (see page 276).

To insert clips

- Switch to **Normal** view

- Create a new slide at the end of the presentation based on the **Clip Art & Text** AutoLayout

- Add the title Questions to the slide

In PowerPoint, there are **three** ways to load the Clip Gallery.

- Double-click the **Clip Art Gallery** placeholder on the **AutoLayout**

OR

- You can also use the **Insert Clip Art** button on the **Drawing** toolbar **OR** from the **Insert** menu, select **Picture** then from the cascading menu, select **Clip Art...**

- In the **Clip Gallery**, search for question

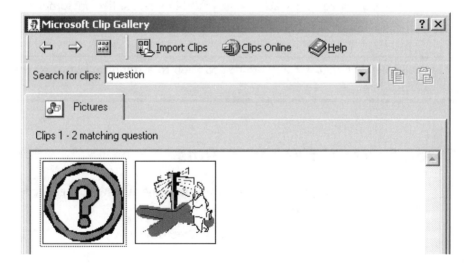

- Click the question mark clip then select the **Insert Clip** button on the shortcut bar

The Clip Art Gallery closes automatically when the clip is inserted. You can now work with the clip art object just as you can any PowerPoint object.

Modify Slide Layout

To change a slide's AutoLayout

If, while completing your slide, you decide that you have chosen the wrong slide layout, you do not need to it and start again.

- From the **Format** menu, select **Slide Layout...**

- Select the **Text & Clip Art** AutoLayout

- Click **Apply**

The slide is reformatted to the new layout, with the clip art moving to the right-hand side.

> **Note** You do not need to delete "unused" placeholders. If you do not add text or graphics to a placeholder, it will not be displayed or printed as part of a slide show.

- Save the presentation

To change the layout of objects on the slide ①

o   You can move, resize and delete placeholders just like any other object (see page 516)

> **Tip** Remember that it is a good idea to keep to a standard layout where possible.

Open Several Presentations

You can open up to 9 presentations at the same time and switch between them using the Window menu or Taskbar.

- Open the presentation **Department Overviews**

Move and Copy Objects

You should be quite confident using the Cut, Copy and Paste tools by now.

In PowerPoint, you can move or copy text within a placeholder and between placeholders. You can move and copy objects on a slide and between slides.

You can also move and copy data to another presentation or into another type of file, such as a document or worksheet.

To move a text object

- In the **Department Overviews** presentation, select both text placeholders on the first slide

- On the **Standard** toolbar, click **Cut** ✂ (*SpeedKey:* [Ctrl]+[X])

- From the **Window** menu, select **2 Recruitment**

- In the **Recruitment** presentation, select slide 2 then from the **Insert** menu, select **New Slide...** and choose the **Blank Slide** AutoLayout

- On the **Standard** toolbar, click **Paste** 📋 (*SpeedKey:* [Ctrl]+[V])

Notice that the formatting of the text boxes is not copied - the appearance of the text is changed to fit the rest of the presentation.

To copy text and graphics objects

- Switch back to the **Department Overviews** presentation and select the text and graphic objects on slide 3

> **Note** You will not be able to select or copy the pictures of chillies - these are part of the **Slide Master**, which you will learn about in the next lesson.

- On the **Standard** toolbar, click **Copy** 📋 (*SpeedKey:* [Ctrl]+[C])

- Switch to the **Recruitment** presentation and create a new blank slide

- On the **Standard** toolbar, click **Paste** 📋 (*SpeedKey:* [Ctrl]+[V])

- Close both presentations *without* saving

Formatting a Presentation

Use the formatting tools to customise slides and presentations

Lesson 40

Use a **master slide** to format the presentation □
(Modify a slide's **colour scheme**) □
Change font **style**, **size**, **colour** and **enhancements** □
Change the **case** of selected text □
Align text horizontally and vertically □
Change line and paragraph **spacing** □
Change the **bullet style** □
Create **numbered** lists □

Use a Master Slide

As well as keeping the layout of slides consistent, it is also important to keep the formatting of text on each slide similar.

Every presentation has a **Slide Master**, which sets the defaults for text formatting in the placeholders.

Example Slide Master

The Slide Master contains placeholders for the title, bullet text and for footers. You can also add objects to the master slide to have them appear on every slide.

When you want to make a change to the presentation that will affect all the slides, make the changes on the Slide Master, rather than changing each individual slide. PowerPoint will then automatically update the existing slides in the presentation. For example, if you change the colour of the title text to red on the Slide Master, this will change the titles on most slides in the presentation to red.

If you want to display your company logo in the same position on every slide in the presentation, insert the logo onto the Slide Master, then it will appear on most slides in your presentation automatically.

If you want the same piece of text to appear on every slide, use a text box to add text to the Slide Master. Do not add text to the placeholders on the Slide Master as these are only for setting formatting characteristics for the presentation.

The Title Master

The only type of slide **not** affected by the Slide Master is a **Title Slide**.

Title Slide AutoLayout

Title Slides are used as the opening slide in the presentation, or to introduce new topics or presenters in long presentations. They often have a different look to the rest of the presentation. For example, you may want your company logo in the bottom right-hand corner of every slide in the main body of the presentation, but on the Title Side have it enlarged and centred above the title. For this reason, the defaults for Title Slides are set on the Title Master.

> **Note** Presentations based on the **Blank Presentation** template do **not** have a Title Master Slide. Only presentations based on Design Templates have both Slide and Title Master slides.

Because any text formatting changes that you make to the Slide Master will be reflected on the Title Master, you should make changes to the **Slide Master** first.

To view a Master slide

- Open the **Recruitment** presentation **OR** if you did not complete the previous lesson, open **Recruitment (Formatting)**

- From the **View** menu, select **Master**

- Select **Slide Master**

Change the Colour Scheme

When you use colour on slides, bear in mind that there should be a strong contrast between text and background. Light text on a dark background is easier to read in a dark room, and vice versa, so consider where the presentation will be given. Also remember that people's reactions to colours can vary quite widely, so try to get feedback from your colleagues on what works and what does not.

PowerPoint uses a **colour scheme** to maintain consistency between slides. A colour scheme is a set of eight colours used as defaults for text, slide backgrounds and objects such as AutoShapes and charts. Each presentation design has a colour scheme, and there are several default schemes for you to choose from in blank presentations too.

As with other things in presentation design, use colours from the scheme consistently and be sparing with "stand-out" colour effects.

ECDL Modifying the colour scheme is not part of the ECDL syllabus. It has been included here as it is used throughout PowerPoint to ensure consistent formatting on your slides.

To change the colour scheme

You can give each slide a different colour scheme, but to ensure consistency throughout your presentation, you should create a default scheme for the Slide Master.

- From the **Format** menu, select **Slide Color Scheme...** then in the dialogue box click the **Custom** tab

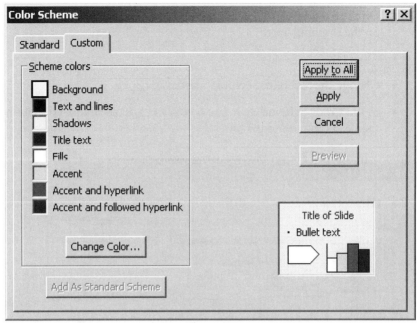

Color Scheme dialogue box

The **Scheme colors** panel displays the eight colours used for elements such as the slide background, title and bullet text, AutoShape fills and so on.

- Click the **Background** colour chip then click **Change Color...**

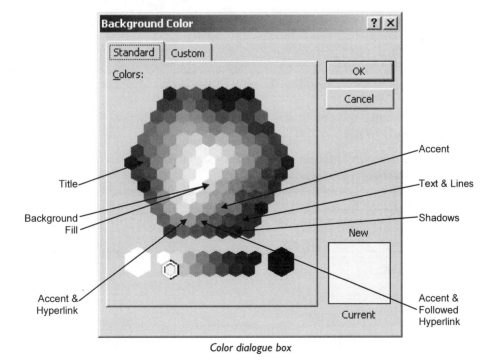

Color dialogue box

- On the **Standard** tab, click the chip labelled **Background** in the picture on the previous page

- Click **OK**

- Change the rest of the colours as shown above

- In the **Color Scheme** dialogue box, click **Add as Standard Scheme** then click the **Standard** tab

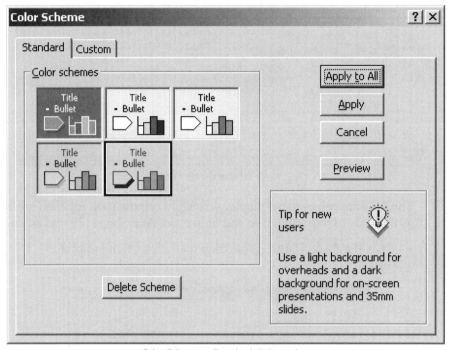

Color Scheme – Standard dialogue box

- Select the customised scheme from the **Color schemes** panel and click **Apply to All**

The background graphic used in the design template does not look good with the new colour scheme.

- Click an empty part of the slide to select the object (selection handles should appear around the edges of the slide) and press `Delete`

- To return to the slides in the presentation, click **Close** on the **Master** toolbar

- Save the presentation

Change Font Type and Enhancements

Formatting text on a presentation slide is much the same as formatting text in a Word document or Excel worksheet.

However, with presentation slides you will want to achieve different results to a printed document.

Use a font style that is easily legible and a font size that can be read from the back of the room in which you will be delivering your presentation. Use font enhancements sparingly to draw attention to important words and phrases.

PowerPoint makes it very easy to apply font styles and enhancements quickly. It is worth taking some time to consider the impact your slide formats will have on your audience however. Too many styles and enhancements and garish or illegible use of colour will only make your slides confusing and difficult to follow.

To change the font ①

o Bearing the above points in mind, the actual tools for changing the font are the same as for Word

o You can either select a block of characters or paragraphs to apply formatting to or select one or more placeholders (to apply formatting to all the text)

Practice

- *Open the* **Font Practice** *presentation*

- *Select the title placeholder and use the* **Formatting** *toolbar to make the font* **Arial**

- *Click the* **Increase Font Size** *button* **A** *twice to make the font larger*

- *Use the* **Font Color** *button to change the colour*

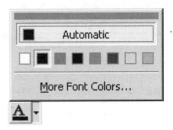

- *Use the toolbar buttons to apply the appropriate enhancement to the words* **italic**, *bold and* **underline**

- *Select the line **Change case** then from the **Format** menu, select **Change Case**...*

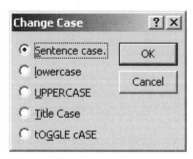

- *Select the **Title Case** option and click **OK***

- *Select the word **Shadow** then click the **Shadow** button* *on the* **Formatting** *toolbar*

- *Use the **Font** dialogue box to apply Superscript and Subscript effects to the text "subscript" and "superscript"*

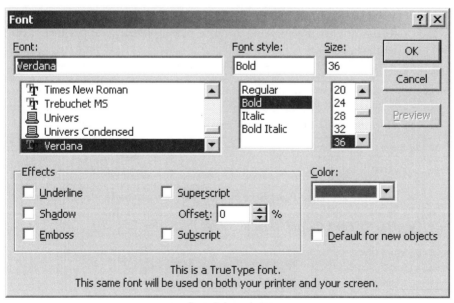

Font dialogue box

- *Use the **Font Colour** button on the **Drawing** toolbar to make the "Apply font colours" line **Dark Blue***

- *Save and close the **Font Practice** presentation*

Align Text

Text can be aligned to the right, left, centre, top or bottom of a text object.

To align text

- In the **Recruitment** presentation, from the **View** menu, select **Master** then select **Slide Master**

- Select the title text placeholder

- On the **Formatting** toolbar, click **Centre**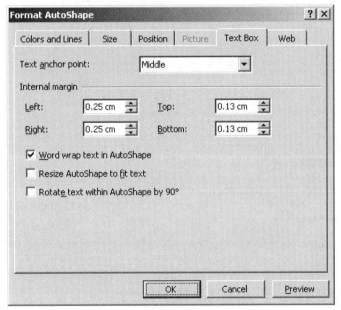

To align text between the top and bottom of a text box

- Select the title text placeholder

- From the **Format** menu, select **Placeholder...** then from the dialogue box select the **Text Box** tab

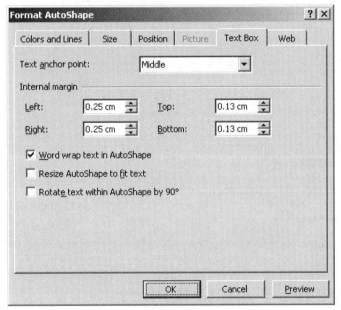

Format AutoShape dialogue box

- Click on the drop-down arrow to the right of the **text anchor point**: box and select **Middle**

- De-select the **Resize AutoShape to fit text** option and click **OK**

- Drag the bottom handle of the placeholder up to make the box about ¾ of its current size

- Drag the top border of the bullet placeholder by the same amount

Adjust Line and Paragraph Spacing

The space between lines and paragraphs is measured in multiples of line height.

To change paragraph and line spacing

- Click in the first level of bulleted master text "Click to edit master text styles"

- From the **Format** menu, select **Line Spacing...**

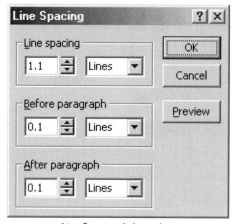

Line Spacing dialogue box

- In the **Line spacing** panel, use the arrows to set the amount of spacing to **1.1 Lines**

- In the **After paragraph** panel, select **0.1 Lines**

- Click **OK**

- Adjust the **After paragraph** spacing of the second level to **0.1 Lines**

Change the Type of Bullets

You can change the shape, colour and size of the bullets you use in bulleted lists. Bullet size is given as a percentage of the text size. A bullet size of 75%, for example, means the font size used for the bullet is 75% of the text font size.

To change the shape of bullets

- Click in the first bulleted level of text on the Slide Master

- From the **Format** menu, select **Bullets and Numbering...**

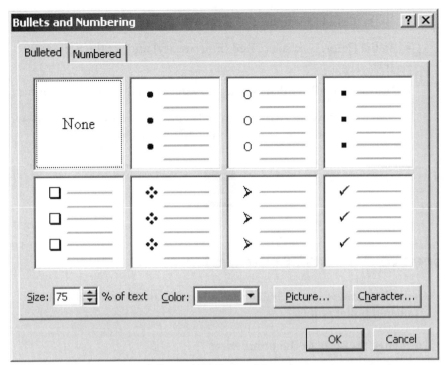

Bullets and Numbering dialogue box

- To change the bullet character, select from the displayed characters
  OR to choose a different bullet, click the **C<u>h</u>aracter...** button (select
  this option)

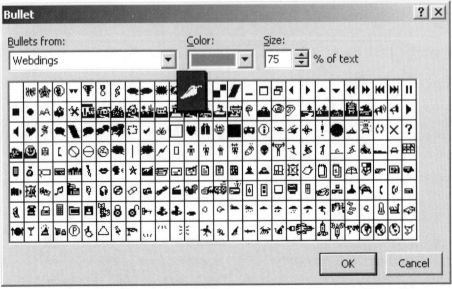

Bullet dialogue box

- In the **Bullets from:** list box, select **Webdings**

- In the **Color:** box, select **Red** (if necessary) and set the **Size:** to **90** % of text

- Select the **Chilli** bullet character as shown in the screenshot and click **OK**

- Use the following character from **Webdings** (on the fifth row down) for the second level of text, using a **Size:** of **70** %

Create a Numbered List

As an alternative to using bullet symbols, you can use automatically numbered bullet points.

To change the style of the numbering

- Select the third text level then from the **Format** menu, select **Bullets and Numbering...**

- Select the **Numbered** tab

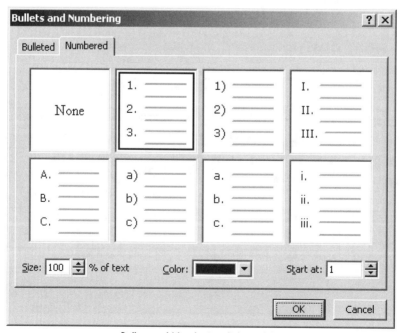

Bullets and Numbering dialogue box

- Select the Arabic numbering style as shown above

- Click **OK** to apply your number format

- Change the colour of the master text line to match their bullets

- On the **Master** toolbar, click **C̲lose**

The slides in the presentation are updated to show the new formatting.

Note Any formatting carried out on individual slides overrides the formatting applied on the Slide Master. To reapply Slide Master formatting, go to the individually formatted slide and from the **F̲ormat** menu, select **Slide L̲ayout....** From the **Slide Layout** dialogue box, select the appropriate layout and click **Re̲apply**. The formatting of the Slide Master is reapplied to the slide.

- Save the presentation

Note As with Word, the **Format Painter**  lets you copy formatting between bits of text. You can also select a text placeholder to copy and paste formatting to all the text.

Practice

- *Add a **Title Slide** to the start of the presentation*

- *Add the text "Working for Chillis" to the title placeholder and your name as the subheading*

- *Open the Title Master and remove the background graphics*

- *Close the Title Master and save the presentation*

- *Close the presentation file*

Drawing Tools

Add and format lines and shapes

Lesson 41

Draw different types of **line** on a slide ☐
Draw different **shapes** on a slide ☐
Move, resize, rotate and **align** shapes ☐
Change the **formatting** of a shape - line, fill, colour and shadow ☐
(**Group** shapes) ☐

The **Drawing** toolbar provides a palette of tools and features you can use to create your own drawings and diagrams.

The **Drawing** toolbar is divided into three sections:

♦ **General drawing controls** - use these tools to select and rotate objects and to determine their position and orientation.

♦ **Object drawing tools** - use these tools to create objects.

♦ **Object formatting tools** - use these tools to change the appearance of objects you create.

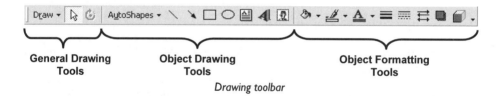

General Drawing
Tools

Object Drawing
Tools

Object Formatting
Tools

Drawing toolbar

• If the drawing toolbar is not displayed, from the **View** menu, select **Toolbars** then click **Drawing**

> **Tip** The drawing tools work in the same way in Word and Excel, so you can apply the techniques you learn here to create drawings in documents and worksheets.

Add Different Types of Line to a Slide

To draw lines and arrows

- Create a new, blank presentation and add a blank slide to it

- Save the presentation as **Drawing Practice**

- Click the **Line** button $\diagdown$ then point to where you want to start the line

The mouse pointer changes to a cross-hair shape.

- Click-and-drag the mouse pointer to draw the line across the top of the slide

- Release the mouse button to finish the line

The line is drawn. White handles are displayed at the ends of the object indicating the object is selected.

- Use the **Arrow** button $\nwarrow$ to add an arrow underneath the line - point to the middle of the slide and hold down the Ctrl key as you draw

---

Note The Ctrl key causes shapes to be drawn from the centre outwards.

To draw curves and freeform lines

As well as straight lines and basic shapes, you can use PowerPoint tools to create irregular shapes, freehand lines and curves.

- On the **Drawing** toolbar, click the **AutoShapes** button then from the **AutoShapes** menu, select **Lines**

A submenu of line drawing tools is displayed.

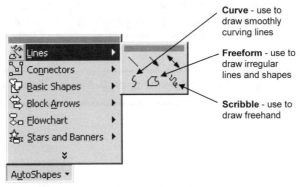

Line drawing tools

- Use the following tools to draw shapes on the left-hand side of the slide

- To draw freehand, as though the mouse were a pen, click the **Scribble** tool ✎

- Click-and-drag on the slide to draw the line, releasing the mouse button to finish

- To draw a smooth, curving line, click the **Curve** tool ∫

- Click on the slide to start the line, move the mouse then click again to add a bend in the line

- Add further curves if you wish, then **double-click** to end the line

The **Freeform** tool ⌐ combines the actions of the **Line** ＼ and **Scribble** ✎ tools. Use it to draw an object that has both curved and straight segments.

- From the **Lines** palette, click the **Freeform** tool ⌐

- Click the mouse to start the line then...

EITHER

- Click to add straight lines to the shape

OR

- Click-and-drag to add freehand segments

- Double-click to complete the shape

Tip   Using any of the above tools, if you **close** a shape by ending the line at the same point it starts, the shape will be filled with the default **fill** colour. You will learn how to change the fill colour below.

Note To deselect a tool without using it, click the tool again or press `Esc`.

Add Shapes to a Slide

To draw rectangles and ovals

- Click on the **Rectangle** button

- Point to where you want to start the shape

The mouse pointer changes to a cross-hair.

- Click-and-drag to draw the shape and release the mouse button to finish

The rectangle is drawn. White handles are displayed at the corners of the object indicating that it is selected.

- Use the **Oval** tool ◯ and hold down the `Shift` key to create a circle below the rectangle

---

Tip   Hold down `Shift` to constrain a shape. With the Oval tool, the `Shift` key produces circles; it also limits lines to 15° angles and draws rectangles as squares.

To draw an AutoShape

The **AutoShapes** menu on the **Drawing** toolbar gives you access to a number of useful shapes, including lines, arrows, stars, banners, and shapes for creating flowcharts. After you draw an AutoShape you can add text to it.

- Create a new blank slide

- Click the **AutoShapes** button on the **Drawing** toolbar to display the AutoShapes menu

Different types of AutoShape are organised in submenus.

- Select the **Stars and Banners** option and click the **Horizontal Scroll** tool

- Point to where you want the shape to start

- Click-and-drag the mouse pointer to draw the object then release the mouse button where you want the object to end

OR

- Click once to create an object at the default size

To adjust AutoShapes

Many AutoShapes have adjustment handles you can use to adjust a unique aspect of the object. The adjustment handles are yellow diamond shapes and they are only visible when an object is selected.

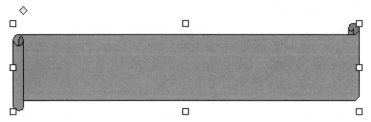

- Click-and-drag the diamond to the right to emphasise the scrolls on the banner

To add text to an AutoShape

Rectangles, ovals, triangles, and other **closed** shapes drawn with the AutoShapes tool can have text attached to the shape.

- With the banner shape selected, type your name

- If necessary, on the **Formatting** toolbar, click **Center** ≣ to centre align the text in the shape

Note When you type in a shape, PowerPoint treats the text as part of the shape. When you move the shape, the text moves with it.

Tip To make text word wrap to an AutoShape, select the shape and from the **Format** menu, select **AutoShape....** Click the **Text Box** tab and click the **Word wrap in AutoShape** to put a check in it. The same tab lets you set the internal margins of the shape and alter the text anchor point.

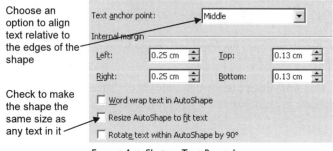

Format AutoShape - Text Box tab

Move, Resize and Rotate an Object

You already know how to move, resize and delete objects using the selection handles. However, there are several more tools for working with objects.

To resize objects using the Format AutoShape dialogue box

The **Format** dialogue box lets you set precise measurements for the size and position of an object.

- Right-click the banner object then from the shortcut menu, select **Format Auto̲Shape**

The **Format** dialogue box is displayed.

- Select the **Size** tab

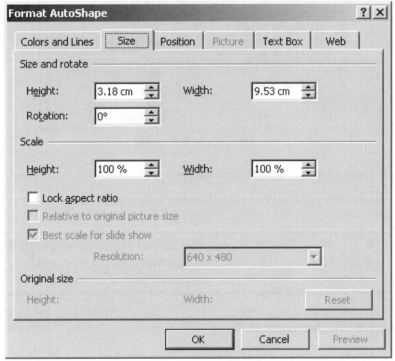

Format AutoShape dialogue box

- In the **Scale** panel, adjust the **Height:** and **Width:** spin boxes to make the object 75% of its current size

---

Note Check the **Lock a̲spect ratio** box (before making any adjustment) to keep the proportion between the height and width the same.

To align objects relative to one another

Aligning objects by eye can be quite tricky and time-consuming. It is easier to use the **Align** and **Distribute** tools.

- On the first slide, select three objects by ⟨Shift⟩-clicking them

- On the **Drawing** toolbar, click **Draw** then from the **Draw** menu, select **Align or Distribute**

A submenu of options is displayed.

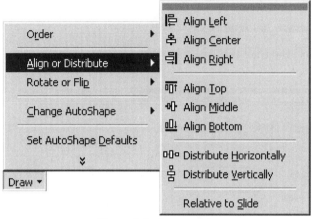

Align and distribute options

- Select an align option from the list

The objects are aligned along the edge you selected.

Tip	If you select more than two objects, you can choose to **distribute** them. This means that the space between each object will be equalised.

To align objects relative to the slide ⑩

o From the **Align and Distribute** menu, select **Relative to Slide**

The **Relative to Slide** option is checked. Any align options you choose will now apply in relation to the slide, until you uncheck the **Relative to Slide** option again by clicking it.

To rotate objects using the mouse

Most types of object created in PowerPoint can be rotated and/or flipped. Some other types of object can also be manipulated.

- Select an object to rotate

- On the **Drawing** toolbar, click **Free Rotate** 🗘

The **Free Rotate** icon is displayed as the mouse pointer and green rotation handles are displayed on the object.

- Click on one of the object's rotation handles and drag in the direction you want to rotate the object

To rotate objects using the menu

- Select the object you want to rotate

- On the **Drawing** toolbar, click **Draw**

- Select **Rotate or Flip** and select from one of the following options

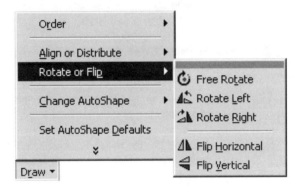

Rotate or Flip options

Change the Attributes of an Object

PowerPoint objects, including text boxes, graphics, clip art and charts have properties that define how the objects appear on a slide.

Click	To
Fill Color	Change the fill colour of the selected object (objects can be filled with colours, shades, patterns and bitmap pictures).
Line Color	Change the colour of the border around an object.
Font Color	Change the colour of the font in the object.
Line Style	Change the style of the border around an object.
Dash Style	Change the style of the border around the object to a dash style.
Arrow Style	Add and change the style of the arrows on a line.
Shadow	Add and change the style of the shadow of an object.
3-D	Add and change the style of a 3-D effect applied to an object.

To change fill, line and font colours

- Select the banner object on slide 2

- On the **Drawing** toolbar, use the following buttons to change the fill, line and font colours, using the eight colours from the scheme

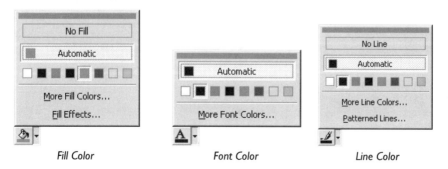

Fill Color   Font Color   Line Color

> **Tip**   To change a colour back to its default (following the colour scheme) click **Automatic**.

To change the fill effects of an object

- With the banner still selected, on the **Drawing** toolbar, click the down arrow on the **Fill Color** button 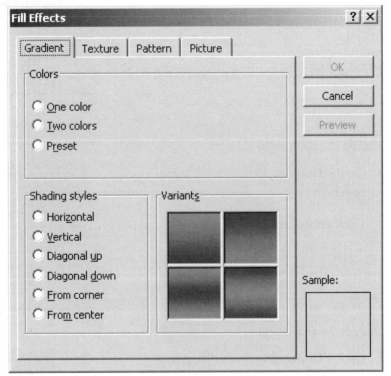 and select **Fill Effects...**

The **Fill Effects** dialogue box is displayed.

Fill Effects dialogue box

- Experiment with different options from the four tabs
- Click **OK** to apply

To change the line style

- Select the straight line on the first slide to experiment with the following options

- On the **Drawing** toolbar, click **Line Style** ≣

- Click the option you want

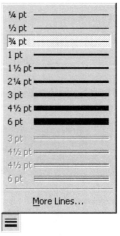

Line Style options

To change the dash style

- On the **Drawing** toolbar, click **Dash Style** ⋮⋮⋮

- Click the option you want

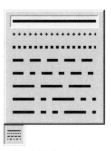

Dash Style options

To change the arrow style

- On the **Drawing** toolbar, click **Arrow Style** ⇄

- Click the option you want

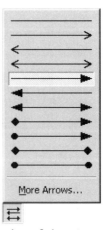

Arrow Style options

> **Tip**   All the previous options can be set using the **Colors and Lines** tab in the **Format AutoShape** dialogue box.

To add a shadow

You can add a shadow to any object you create, and you can change the size, direction, and colour of shadows.

- On the second slide, select the banner object then on the **Drawing** toolbar, click **Shadow**

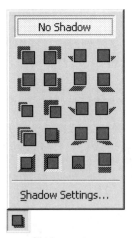

Shadow options

- Click the option you want

> **Tip**   To change the colour or offset of a shadow, click the **Shadow** tool, click **Shadow Settings...**, and then click the options you want on the **Shadow Settings** toolbar.

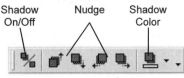

Shadow Settings toolbar

- Save and close the presentation

Group Objects

Grouping objects enables you to treat multiple objects as a single object.

ECDL This topic is not required for the ECDL syllabus.

For example, suppose you used the drawing tools to draw a window. Without grouping the objects that comprise the window moving or resizing the window is impossible. Grouping objects combines them so you can work with them as a single object.

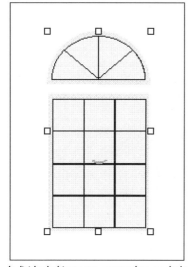

Individual objects are grouped as a whole

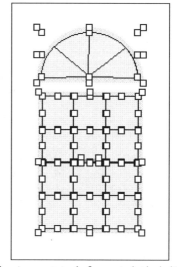

A drawing comprised of many individual objects

To group objects ⑨

o   Select the objects you want to group then on the **Drawing** toolbar, click **Draw** Draw ▾ and select **Group**

Tip   To ungroup the objects, click **Draw** then **Ungroup**. To regroup the most recently ungrouped objects, select one of the objects from that group and from the **Draw** menu, select **Regroup**.

Practice

- *Create a new slide and use the drawing tools to draw something, such as a plan of your room*

- *Use the Group tool where necessary, for example to combine objects that represent a desk and chair*

- *Save and close the presentation*

Tip	You can group two or more groups. For example, if you were drawing a person, you could group the objects making up the head then group them with another group representing the body.

Practice

- *To get further practice in using the drawing tools, add a new blank slide to the end of the **Recruitment** presentation*

- *Draw the map shown below - use the Notes overleaf to help*

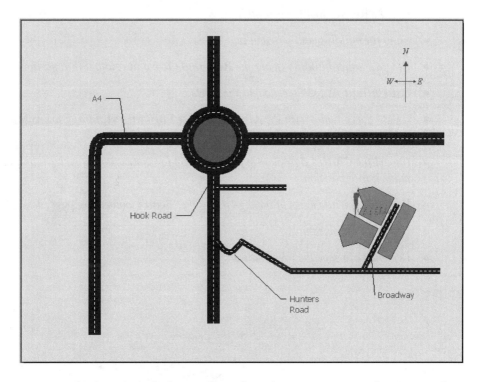

- *This exercise is fairly complex - if you do not want to complete it, copy the object from the **Visitor Map** presentation*

- *Save and close any open presentations when you have finished*

Notes

- _Draw the roads (ignoring the roundabout for now) using the line tools then use **Format AutoShape** to adjust the line thickness (20 pt and 10 pt)_

- _Group the roads as one object_

- _Copy the grouped roads object and paste it back over the drawing_

- _Use **Format AutoShape** to change the line to a white dashed line 1 pt thick_

- _Move the dashed line over the roads_

- _Draw a circle for the roundabout_

- _Make two copies for the road lines and green middle_

- _Adjust the size, format and positioning then group the three circles to make the roundabout and move it into position_

- _Group all the objects created so far_

- _Use the **Line** tool to create the first building shape (close the shape so that you can add shading), resize it and format as shown_

- _Use the **Rotate** tool to position it_

- _Copy the building and position it_

- _Create another building using the **Rectangle** tool and rotate it into position_

- _Use **Callout** AutoShapes to add the labels_

- _Create the compass with the **Arrow** tool (use **Format AutoShape** to create a double-headed arrow) and text boxes_

- _Import the **Chilli Logo** picture (see page 562 for instructions), resize it and move it into position_

- _Remove the white areas of the logo using the Picture toolbar (see page 563)_

- _Group all the objects_

- _Remember to save the presentation_

Pictures and Charts

Import data objects and create charts

Import **images** from other files onto a slide ☐
(Use the **Office Clipboard**) ☐
Move and **resize** imported objects ☐
Copy an imported object onto a **master slide** ☐
Create and edit different kinds of **chart** ☐
Create and edit an **organisation chart** ☐

One of the strengths of using Windows programs is that it is easy to share data between different types of file. The applications in MS Office are particularly well **integrated**.

This lesson will show you some of the ways to share data in different files in a PowerPoint presentation. Note though, that you can apply these techniques to any of the Office programs.

Practice

You will complete the first part of this lesson using a new presentation file.

- *Create a new presentation, using a design template of your choice*

- *Add a title slide* 1st Quarter Sales *and enter your name and the date as the subheading*

- *Save the presentation as* Sales Report

Import Other Objects

With presentations, the ability to share data is particularly important, because the source data for a presentation is often available in other documents. You can use the cut, copy and paste tools to add text, tables, charts, worksheets and graphics to a slide.

As well as using the normal Windows Clipboard to copy and paste objects, in Office 2000 the **Office Clipboard** can be used to copy or cut and paste **multiple** items, from more than one application.

For example, you can copy some text entered in a Microsoft Word document, switch to Excel and copy some spreadsheet data, switch to PowerPoint and copy a graphic, and so on, then paste the collection of items back into Word.

To display the Office Clipboard

The contents of the Office Clipboard are displayed on the **Clipboard** toolbar. This toolbar is displayed automatically when you use Cut or Copy twice in succession, though you can also display it manually.

- From the **View** menu, select **Toolbars** then from the submenu select the **Clipboard** toolbar

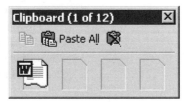

Office Clipboard

The Office Clipboard may already contain some data. File icons in the boxes represent data. The type of icon indicates the type of data.

- On the **Clipboard** toolbar, click **Clear Clipboard** 🖾 to remove any existing data

To use the Office Clipboard to import charts and text

- Use Windows Explorer to open the Word document **Flyer_Brunch Tart (Complete)** and the Excel workbook **Sales Data (Finished Charts)**

- In the workbook, click the chart on the first worksheet to select it then from the **Edit** menu, select **Copy**

An icon appears on the Clipboard toolbar.

- Select the range **A2:G6** and click **Copy** 🖹

Another icon appears on the Clipboard.

- Close Excel and switch to the Word document

- Copy the first block of text and the list of products

- Close Word and switch back to the **Sales Report** presentation

---

Note The Office Clipboard holds up to twelve items. When it is full you must clear it 🖾 to copy any more items. The items that have been collected will remain on the Office Clipboard until all open Office applications are closed.

- Point to each icon on the Clipboard in turn - a ScreenTip indicates what has been copied

Chilli Meals™ combine the best home-cooked ...

Office Clipboard

If the item has no text to display, or if it is a drawing object or a picture, the message "Item *x*" or "Picture *x*" will be displayed. This indicates the order in which the item was copied.

- Create a new **Title Only** slide with the title Sales Breakdown

- Click in the slide then click the first icon on the Clipboard - the chart is pasted onto the slide

- Resize the chart if necessary then create another **Title Only** slide called Sales Figures

- Paste the second icon - the table of data

The data is pasted as an object

- Select the object to adjust the font size and resize it so that it fits on the slide

- Create a **Bullet List** slide with the title Current Marketing

- Paste the third selection (the text from Word) into the bullet placeholder

- Edit the text and adjust the heading levels as shown below

> **Tip** To paste all the copied items, on the **Clipboard** toolbar, click **Paste All** 🖼️ Paste All .

- Hide the **Clipboard** toolbar then save and close the presentation

To insert a picture from a file

The **Insert Picture** command lets you add any picture file to a slide.

- Open the **Recruitment** presentation **OR** if you have not been following each lesson, open **Recruitment (Charts)**

- Select the title slide then from the **Insert** menu, select **Picture** then from the submenu, select **From File...**

- Locate the **chilli logo** file in **My Documents** then click **Insert**

Pictures can be moved, resized and deleted like any other object. You can also add border effects to them and crop parts of the image.

- Position the graphic in the bottom-left hand corner of the slide

To copy a graphic onto a slide

- Open the **Chillis Presentation Design** file and copy the chilli graphic under the slide title

- Close the file and switch back to the **Recruitment** presentation

- On the **Standard** toolbar, click **Paste** 🖼️

The graphic is pasted onto the slide in the same position as on the original slide.

To copy a graphic onto the master slide

- Select the logo and the graphic you just pasted then from the **Edit** menu, select **Copy**

- From the **View** menu, select **Master** then **Title Master**

- From the **Edit** menu, select **Paste**

- Move the string of chillies under the title placeholder and resize it to fit

> **Tip** The **Insert, Object...** command lets you create a wide variety of data objects using any of the software applications installed on your PC. You can also use this command to insert data from any kind of file.

To use the Picture toolbar

When you select a picture (this applies to Word and Excel too), the **Picture** toolbar is displayed.

You can use this toolbar to adjust the appearance of most types of picture.

ECDL   Use of the Picture toolbar is not a syllabus requirement.

- Select the logo
- If the **Picture** toolbar does not appear, right-click a toolbar and select the **Picture** option from the shortcut menu

Click	To
Insert Picture from File	Display the **Insert Picture** dialogue box.
Image Control	Display settings that allow you to change the selected graphic object to **Greyscale**, **Black and White**, **Watermark** or **Automatic**.
More and Less Contrast	Add or reduce the contrast between the different colours used in the graphic object.
More and Less Brightness	Lighten or darken the colours used in the graphic object.
Crop	Enable the cropping tool to display only part of the picture.
Line Style	Display the **Line Style** menu for adding a border to the selected graphic object.
Recolor Picture	Display the **Recolor Picture** dialogue box, where you can change the fill colours and outline colours used in the graphic.
Format Picture	Display the **Format Picture** dialogue box, where you can change the fill colour, line style, size of the graphic, position of the graphic, crop the graphic and change the image control.
Set Transparent Color	Set one colour in a picture to transparent.
Reset Picture	Return the graphic to its original settings.

- With the logo selected then on the **Picture** toolbar, click **Set Transparent Color**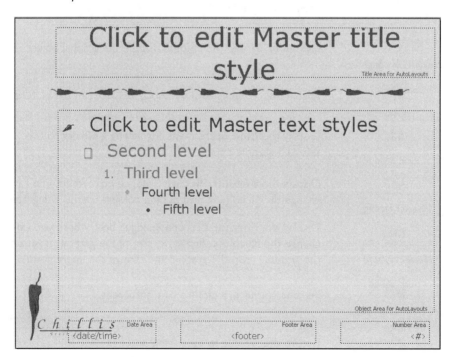

- Click a white area of the logo

The white areas of the image are made transparent.

- Close the Title Master and save the presentation

Note Some tools, such as **Set Transparent Color**, will only work with **Bitmap**-type images.

Practice

- *Select the graphics left on the title slide itself then on the **Standard** toolbar, click **Cut***

- *Open the **Slide Master** and paste the graphics*

The graphics are pasted onto the Title Master. They will now appear on every slide in the presentation (except the title slide).

- *Make the background of the logo transparent then resize it and move it into the position shown below*

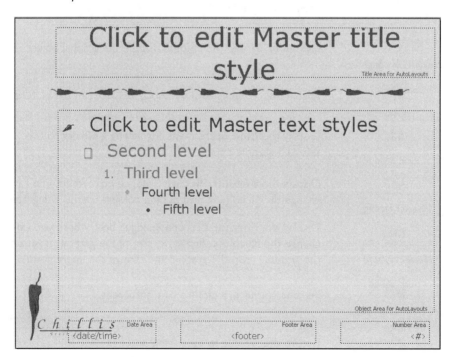

- *Close the Slide Master and save the presentation*

Charts and Graphs

As with Excel, you can use graphs to make trends and results in a set of numeric data more obvious and easy to understand.

If you do not have a chart setup in Excel, you can use **Microsoft Graph** to create and edit a data chart in PowerPoint. MS Graph is actually the same tool as the Chart editor in Excel, but with some subtle differences.

In PowerPoint, Graph uses **Object Linking and Embedding** (OLE) to place charts on a slide. When you double-click on a chart to edit it, MS Graph "takes over" the PowerPoint screen, giving you different menu and toolbar options.

There is a full discussion of what charts are and how to select different types in the Excel module on page 376.

To insert a new chart

In PowerPoint, there are three ways to insert a Graph.

- Create a new slide after slide **3 About Chillis**, selecting the **Chart AutoLayout** and switch to **Slide** view

- Add the title Departments to the placeholder

- Double-click the chart placeholder on the slide

Microsoft Graph is started.

Tip   You can insert a chart on any type of slide. On the **Standard** toolbar, click **Insert Chart** OR from the **Insert** menu, select **Chart...**

In Excel, chart data is taken directly from the worksheet. In PowerPoint, MS Graph provides a **datasheet** with some sample data as the basis for each new chart.

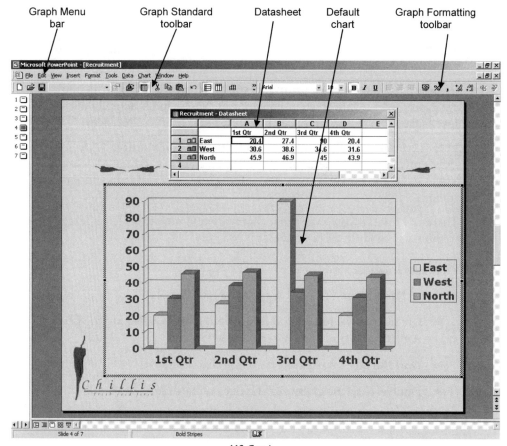

MS Graph

To enter and edit data in the datasheet window

The process of editing the datasheet is the same as editing a worksheet (refer back to page 310 for a list of mouse actions and key commands to use).

The cells in the **top** row of the datasheet hold text to label the **X-axis** (horizontal axis). These are the categories of data.

The cells in the far-left column of the datasheet hold text that is used to label each **series** of bars on the chart. The rest of the cells provide the data values to plot.

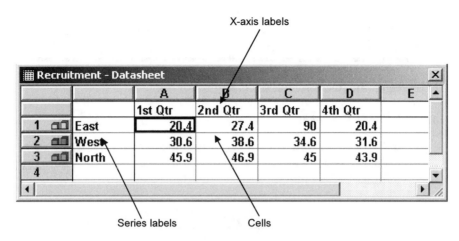

An example datasheet

- If the datasheet is not displayed, on the **Standard** toolbar, click **View Datasheet** ▦

Note Click the **View Datasheet** button again to hide the datasheet.

To delete rows and columns

- In the datasheet, select the rows or columns you want to delete – select all the columns in the datasheet, including the column of series labels

You can select several rows or columns by dragging across several row or column headings.

- From the **Edit** menu, select **Delete**

Note If you do not select entire columns or rows before choosing **Delete**, a dialogue box appears. Specify whether you want cells shifted left or up, or whether you want to delete entire rows or entire columns.

To insert rows and columns ⓘ

o Select the number of rows or columns you want to insert

For example, if you want to insert one column, select one column; if you want to insert three rows, select three rows.

> **Tip** You can select several rows or columns by dragging across several row or column headings.

 o From the **Insert** menu, select **Cells**

To add data to the sheet

- Either type the data shown below into the worksheet OR open the Excel workbook **Employees** then copy and paste the data from the **Summary** sheet into the PowerPoint datasheet

Department	Total Salaries	Total Staff
Accounts	£174,500	9
Fulfilment	£59,800	4
Kitchens	£170,400	11
Management	£96,500	3
Marketing	£46,500	2
Sales	£210,000	11

- Close Excel without saving any changes to the workbook

To include/exclude rows and columns

All rows and columns containing data are included in the chart by default. When you **exclude** data, Graph redraws the chart without the excluded data. Excluded rows and columns appear dimmed in the datasheet, and their row and column headers appear flat instead of 3D.

- Double-click the headings of the rows or columns you want to exclude from the chart – exclude the **Total Salaries** column

> **Tip** Double-click the headings of the excluded rows or columns to include them again.

Create Different Types of Chart

When you start Microsoft Graph, a three-dimensional column chart is created from the sample data in the datasheet. A column chart is not the only type of chart you can create. There are fourteen main graph types to choose from in PowerPoint.

Some of the most commonly used types are:

- **Bar** - to compare values.

♦ **Column** or **line** - to compare values (often over a period of time).

♦ **Area** - to compare values over time and show how the total value breaks down.

♦ **Pie** - to show how a total breaks down (Unlike other types, a pie chart only uses one data series).

Each main chart type also has several sub-types or variations, such as adding a 3-D effect.

To choose a chart type

• From the **Chart** menu, select **Chart Type...** then if it is not already displayed, click the **Standard Types** tab

The **Standard Types** tab in the **Chart Type** dialogue box is displayed.

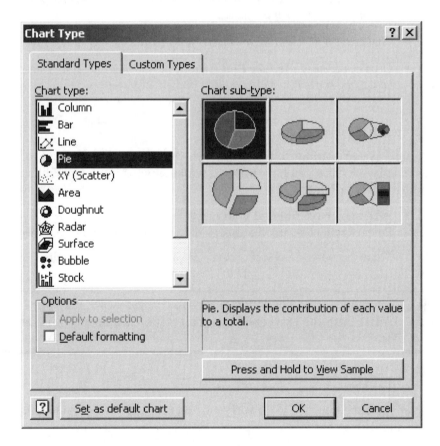

• Select a standard pie chart and click **OK**

> **Tip** If you change the chart type to a pie chart, you will need to **exclude** the data series not required.

Modify a Chart

To modify chart elements

Refer back to page 383 for a description of the tools used to edit a chart.

Practice

- *On the **Chart** toolbar, click **By Column*** ⊞
- *Use **Chart Options** to add data labels as percentages and put the chart legend at the bottom of the chart*
- *Change the font size of the data labels to **12 pt** and the legend to **14 pt***
- *Use the toolbar to select the **Plot Area** element then format it to remove the border and resize it to make the chart itself as large as possible*

To update the chart slide

As long as you continue to work in Graph, the Graph Menu bar and toolbar are displayed. Once you have finished working with Graph you will want to return to PowerPoint.

- When you have finished your graph and want to return to PowerPoint, click any blank area of the slide outside the chart area

The chart becomes an object on the slide and PowerPoint's toolbars return.

> **Tip** You can (and should) continue to save changes while working in Graph. Both the chart and your presentation are saved in the same file.

To edit a chart

After you have returned to PowerPoint, you may want to return to Graph to edit an existing chart.

- To start **Graph** again, double-click the chart

The Graph Menu bar and toolbar replace the PowerPoint menus and toolbar.

- Click away from the chart object to exit **Graph**

To move, resize and delete the chart object

- Click the chart **once** to select it - you can now move and resize it using the selection handles or press [Delete] to remove the chart – move the chart placeholder to the left

- Save the presentation

Tip   You can use copy and paste to add charts from Excel onto a PowerPoint slide.

Create an Organisation Chart

An **organisation** chart is a diagram showing how objects are related in a hierarchy. They are typically used to show levels of responsibility in a company or to show the hierarchy of personnel.

As with graphs, an organisation chart is created and edited using a separate application: **Microsoft Organization Chart**. Unlike Graph, **Organization Chart** opens in a **separate window** to PowerPoint. However the chart is still saved as an **object** in the presentation file.

To create an organisation chart

- Create a new slide before the **Departments** slide, selecting **Organisation Chart** as the chart type

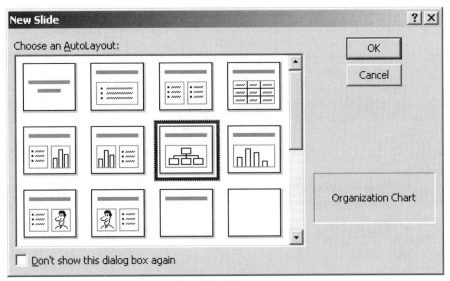

New Slide dialogue box

- Add the title Company Structure to the slide

- Double-click the icon to add an organisation chart

Note You may be asked to install Organization Chart. If so, you will need your Office 2000 Setup disk. Refer to page 687 for more information.

The **Microsoft Organization Chart** window is displayed.

- If necessary, click in the top box to select it

- Enter Joe Chilli as the Managing Director - you do not have to complete any other fields

- Enter the subordinates (**Pattinson** and **Douglas**)

- Click the extra box on the right and press Delete

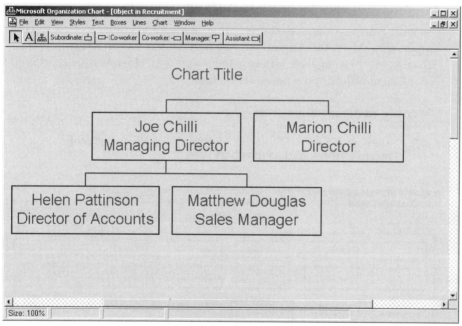

Microsoft Organization Chart

- To add further entries at a particular level, click the **Right Co-Worker** button and then click the **Managing Director** box

- Add Marion Chilli as a Director as shown above

- To add a **subordinate**, click the **Subordinate** button and then click in the **Director of Accounts** box

The subordinate is displayed in the next level of the hierarchy.

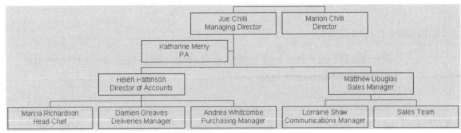

Completed layout

- Add the five subordinates shown above

- To add an **assistant**, such as a PA, click the **Assistant** button and then click in the **Managing Director** box

The assistant is displayed in an **intermediate** level in the hierarchy, attached to the downward line

- Enter Katharine Merry as a PA

You can create further levels in the hierarchy by adding subordinates to a subordinate box.

- When you have finished, from the **File** menu, select **Close and Return to Presentation**

- Click **Yes** to update the object in the presentation

- Save the presentation file

Modify the Structure of an Organisation Chart

You can make changes to the boxes, lines, or text in an organisation chart. Before doing so you need to switch to **edit mode** as follows.

To add boxes

- Double-click the organisation chart to edit it

- Click the subordinate button and add Craig Parnham as a Fulfilment Manager as a subordinate to the **Director of Accounts**

To edit text

- Click the **Fulfilment Manager** box - the centre turns black

- To edit the text in a box, click-and-drag across the name and type
  `Larry Achike`

To move boxes

- Click the **Head Chef** box to select it then click-and-drag it over the
  Fulfilment Manager box

Tip You must click-and-drag the *border* of a box to move it (this can be
quite fiddly). You cannot make minor adjustments to the screen
position of a box; you can only change its place in the hierarchy.

- Repeat the above step to make the **Deliveries Manager** and the
  Purchasing Manager subordinates of the **Fulfilment Manager**

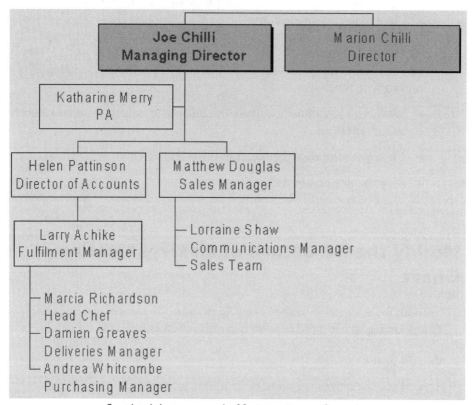

Completed chart - see overleaf for instructions on formatting

To format an organisation chart

There are a wide variety of options for formatting the chart, including changing the style of boxes, lines, fills and fonts.

Practice

- *Double-click in the **Managing Director** box to select the entire row*

- *Use the **Boxes** menu to change the fill colour to orange and apply a drop shadow*

- *Select the **Managing Director** box only and use the **Text** menu to change the font to **bold***

- *Click away from the box to deselect it*

- *Hold down the* **Shift** *key while you click all the boxes at the lowest level of the hierarchy*

- *Use the **Styles** menu to select the option highlighted below*

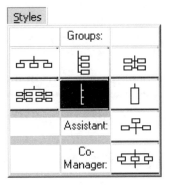

- *From the **File** menu, select **Close and Return to Recruitment***

A message box prompts you to update the presentation slide with the changes made.

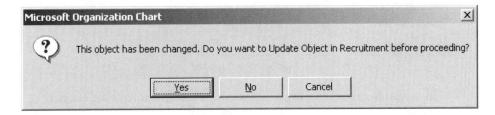

- *Click **Yes***

- *Save and close the presentation*

Setting Up a Presentation

Prepare a presentation for viewing or printing

Lesson 43

Select an appropriate **output format** for a presentation ☐
Change slide **orientation** ☐
Add slide **numbering** in headers and footers ☐
Move, copy, re-order and **delete** slides in a presentation ☐
Add **speaker notes** to a slide ☐
Use the **Spelling Checker** ☐

Select an Output Format for the Presentation

By default, the presentation area is setup for display on-screen. You can change this to a more suitable size for printing on A4 paper or to be output on 35 mm slides.

To change the page setup

- Open the **Recruitment** presentation **OR** if you have not been following the lesson, use **Recruitment (Setup)**

- From the **File** menu, select **Page Setup...**

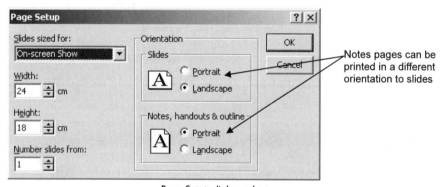

Page Setup dialogue box

In the **Slides sized for:** list box you can select an appropriate output format (for example, **A4 Paper**) and change the page orientation.

Notes pages are setup for the paper size of the default printer.

- Leave the options set as they are and click **Cancel**

When you change the slide size, objects on each slide should be resized and repositioned for the new slide size automatically, though it is as well to browse through the slides just in case something no longer fits or looks wrong. If you change the orientation you will need to adjust the slide master.

Add a Footer and Slide Numbering

You can use footers to add information you want to see on all of your slides - such as the date and time of the presentation, slide numbers, or other important text. The footers you select are added to the placeholders at the bottom of the **Slide Master**.

To insert footers

- From the **View** menu, select **Header and Footer...** and click the **Slide** tab

- In the **Date and time** panel, select the **Fixed** option and type the current month and year

- Check the **Slide number** box to add slide numbers

- Click into the **Footer** box and type the footer text Joe Chilli Ltd.

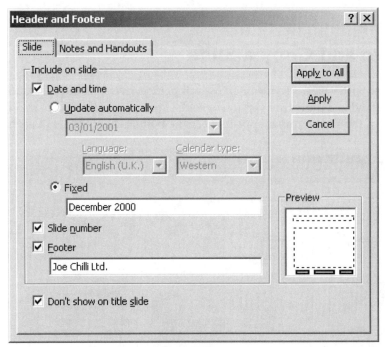

These options...

- Make sure that **Don't show on title slide** is checked

- Click **Apply to All** to apply the footer to all slides (except the title slide)

- View the Slide Master and adjust the position of the footer placeholders as shown below

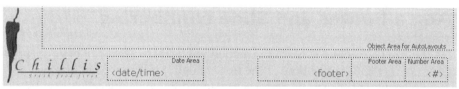

...look like this in the Slide Master

...and give these results in Slide view

- To prevent the title slide from being included in the numbering, from the **File** menu, select **Page Setup** and in the **Number slides from** box enter 0 (zero)

Move and Copy a Slide

Slide Sorter view gives you an overall perspective of your presentation by displaying a miniature version of each slide on a single screen. In Slide Sorter view, the slide number appears near the bottom-right corner of each slide.

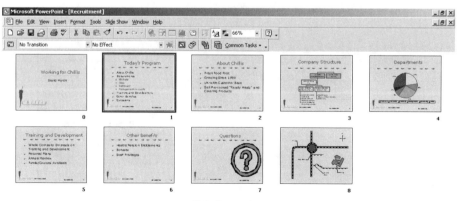

Slide Sorter view

Note You cannot edit slides in **Slide Sorter** view, you must return to **Normal, Slide** or **Outline** view to change the contents of your slides.

To select a slide ①

 o Use the arrow keys to highlight the slide

OR

 o Click the slide you want to select

OR

 o To select multiple slides in a block, press and hold down the `Shift` key while clicking on all the slides you want to select

OR

 o To select various slides, press and hold down the `Ctrl` key while clicking on all the slides you want to select

Tip Double-click a slide to open it in **Normal** view or **Slide** view.

To delete a slide ①

 o Select the slide or slides you want to delete

 o From the **Edit** menu, click **Delete Slide** (*SpeedKey:* `Delete`)

To move or copy a slide using drag-and-drop, cut, copy and paste

 • In Slide Sorter view, select the **Questions** slide then click-and-drag it to the **About Chillis** slide

When you move the pointer between two slides, a vertical bar appears to mark the location where the slide will be inserted if you release the mouse button.

 • Point to the right of the **About Chillis** slide and release the mouse button

 • Holding down `Ctrl` click-and-drag the **Questions** slide to **copy** it back to before the map

To move or copy a slide from one presentation to another

- Open the **Department Overviews** presentation in Slide Sorter view

- Select all four slides then cut ✂ or copy 📋 the slides

- Close the presentation without saving changes

- Back in **Recruitment**, click to the right of the **Departments** slide and select **Paste** 📋

- De-select all the slides

Tip   You can also move or copy slides using drag-and-drop if you arrange the windows on-screen. Also, you can cut/copy the slides, *then* open another presentation, and still use paste. You can also use exactly the same technique to copy a slide into another type of file (a Word document or Excel workbook for example).

- Drag the **Management** slide before the **Kitchens** slide

- Cut the **Sales** slide then click between the **Management** and **Kitchen** slides and select **Paste**

- Save the presentation

Use the Spelling Checker

As with Word and Excel, PowerPoint has a **Spelling Checker** to help you correct any spelling errors in your presentation.

To check for spelling mistakes

- The Spelling Checker works just like the one in Word (except that it does not check grammar)

- You can run a full spell check or correct spellings as you work - see page 252 if you need reminding

- Save and close the presentation when you have completed the spell check

---

Tip   You can also use **Find and Replace** in PowerPoint (as with Word - see page 245).

Slide Shows

Setup and run a slide show with transitions and animations

Lesson 44

Setup a presentation to run as a slide show ☐
Run a **slide show** and use **on-screen** navigation tools ☐
Add slide **transition** effects ☐
Add and customise **animation** effects ☐
Hide and **unhide** slides from a slide show ☐

Slide Show View

A **Slide Show** is a way of presenting slides electronically on your computer screen. When you use this view, the PowerPoint window is not visible; each slide occupies the complete screen area.

To setup a slide show

- Open the **Recruitment** presentation **OR** if you have not been following the lessons in sequence, open **Recruitment (Slide Shows)**

- From the **Slide Show** menu, select **Set Up Show...**

The **Set Up Show** dialogue box is displayed.

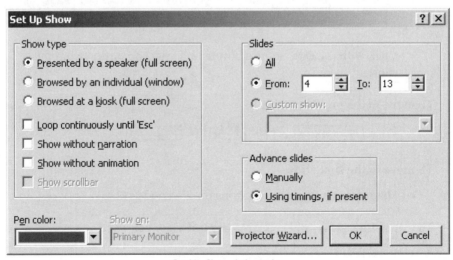

Set Up Show dialogue box

You can use this dialogue box to start a show on any slide.

- From the **Slides** panel, select the **From** option and enter 4 to 13
- From the **Show type** panel, select **Presented by a speaker**
- From the **Advance slides** panel, select the **Manually** option button
- Click **OK**

Deliver a Slide Show

You can move around between slides in a show in a variety of ways. No one way is better than the other ways - experiment and you will find the best way of navigating for you.

To start the slide show

- Click the **Slide Show** button 🖳

OR

- From the **Slide Show** menu, select **View Show** (*SpeedKey:* F5)

To move to the next slide

- Click the left mouse button

OR

- Press the Space Bar , the ➡ or ⬇ arrow, Enter or Page Down

OR

- Click with the right mouse button and select an option from the shortcut menu

To move to the previous slide

- Press Backspace , ⬅ or ⬆ arrow, Page Up

To move to the first slide

- Hold down both mouse buttons for 2 seconds

To exit a slide show and return to the last view you used

- Press Esc

Use On-screen Navigation Tools

The slide show shortcut menu lets you jump from slide-to-slide during a show.

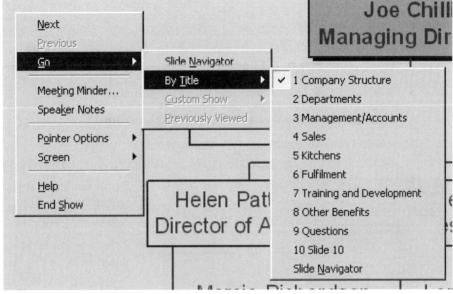

Slide Show shortcut menu

To use the shortcut menu

- Start the slide show again

- After displaying the first slide, right-click to display the menu

Tip	Alternatively, to display the menu if you do not have access to a mouse, press ⎡Shift⎤+⎡F10⎤ or (on a Windows keyboard) press the **Shortcut Menu** key (below the right-hand ⎡Shift⎤ key). Use the arrow keys to navigate the menu.

- Select **Go** then **By Title** and select the **Training and Development** slide

To get help during a slide show

- You cannot access the full help system during a slide show , but you can display a list of navigation keys by pressing ⎡F1⎤

- Press ⎡Esc⎤ to close the help box then exit the show

Add Slide Transition Effects

A **transition** is a special effect applied when one slide moves off the screen and the next slide appears. Transitions can be set in either **Slide/Normal** view or **Slide Sorter** view.

To add slide transitions

- From the **Slide Show** menu, select **Set Up Show...** and change the slides to use back to **All**

- Switch to **Slide Sorter** view and select the title slide

- From the **Slide Show** menu, select **Slide Transition...**

The **Slide Transition** dialogue box is displayed.

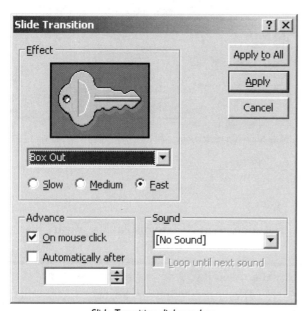

- From the **Effect** list, select the **Box Out** transition effect

- From the **Speed** box, select how quickly you want the transition to take place – select **Fast**)

- In the **Advance** box, select **On mouse click**

- Click **Apply** to apply the transition to the selected slide only

Slide Transition dialogue box

Tip   In **Slide Sorter** view, you can select multiple slides to apply the same transition to them.

Practice

- *Run the slide show to view the transition effect*

- *Add transition effects to the other slides – for example, apply one effect to all the odd numbered slides and a complementary effect to the even ones*

Add Preset Animation Effects to a Slide

Animation effects allow you to control the way an object appears on the screen. For example, text could fly in from the right-hand side of the screen. You can also choose to have an object dim or change colour when new objects are animated.

The purpose of animation effects is to draw the audience's attention to important points in the presentation, and focus their attention on that point whilst it is being discussed. Consequently, you should not use pointless effects or an excessive number of effects, which will simply *distract* your audience.

To setup basic animation

- In **Normal** view or **Slide** view, select the subtitle placeholder on the title slide

- From the **Slide Show** menu, select **Preset Animation**

- From the submenu, select the **Drop-In** effect

Preset Animation effects

> **Note** To apply the same animation effect to **all** objects on a slide, use **Slide Sorter** view, and select the effect from the **Slide Sorter** toolbar.

To preview animations in Normal view or Slide view

- From the **Slide Show** menu, click **Animation Preview...**

The animation plays in a slide miniature.

- To replay the animation, click the slide miniature

Change Preset Animation Effects

The basic animation effects can be customised to create more sophisticated slide animations. You can animate several objects on a slide, change the order in which the animations run and set options for making text appear.

To create or edit a custom animation effect

- Display the title slide in **Normal** view or **Slide** view

- From the **Slide Show** menu, select **Custom Animation...**

The **Custom Animation** dialogue box is displayed.

- Select the **Effects** tab

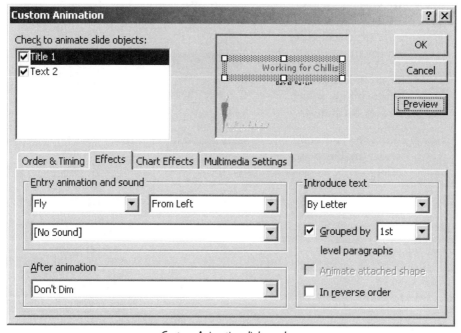

Custom Animation dialogue box

- In the **Check to animate slide objects:** panel, select the **Title 1** element

- In the **Entry animation and sound** panel, select the animation effects that you want to apply (select **Fly - From Left**)

- In the **Introduce text** panel, select how you want the text to appear on the screen (select **By Letter**)

> **Tip** If you are animating bulleted lists, you can group the paragraphs by outline level to control how each line of text appears on the screen. For example, if you have used level 1 and level 2 paragraphs in the same placeholder and want them to animate each line, you will need to group them by level 2.

> **Tip** If you are animating bullet points, to dim the previous point when the next bullet point is displayed, in the **After animation** section, select the colour you want the text to dim to.

- To change the order of the animation effects, click the **Order and Timing** tab

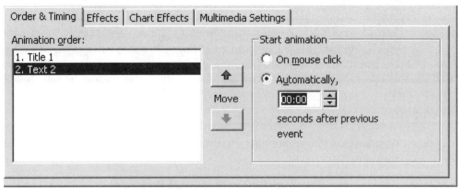

Custom Animation – Order & Timing dialogue box

- In the **Animation order:** panel, select the **Text 2** object and use the **Move** arrow to move it below **Title 1**

- With the **Text 2** object still selected, set the **Start animation** option to **Automatically** after 0 (zero) seconds; **Title 1** should be set to **On mouse click**

- To preview the animations you have set, click the **Preview** button

- Click **OK**

> **Note** To remove an animation effect, de-select the check box in the **Check to animate slide objects** panel.

To use animation effects during a Slide Show

- Run the slide show

- Click the mouse button to play the next animation effect (unless the effect plays automatically)

- End the show after viewing the animations on the title slide

---

Note If the animation takes a long time, do not become impatient and click the mouse repeatedly. PowerPoint remembers each time you click, and will advance through that number of animation effects or slides, often very quickly after the initial delay. Always test your slide shows before delivering them, and if animation or transition effects are too slow, do not use them.

Tip Do not overload a presentation with animation and transition effects. Animation can draw attention to changes in topic or important points but will distract and irritate your audience if used poorly.

Practice

- *Optionally, work through the presentation adding more animation effects to each slide*

- *Experiment with different effects to learn what they do*

Hide a Slide

There may be occasions when you want to give a presentation to several different audiences. There may well be slides in your presentation that are only relevant for one audience. To avoid duplicating work by creating several presentations to meet each audience's needs, simply hide the slides you do not require.

To hide a slide

Slides can be hidden in Normal, Slide or Slide Sorter view. In **Normal** or **Slide** view, display the slide you want to hide then from the **Slide Show** menu, select **Hide Slide**.

- For this exercise, in **Slide Sorter** view, select the **Management**, **Sales** and **Fulfilment** slides then on the **Slide Sorter** toolbar, click **Hide Slide** 🔲

A "null" sign appears over the slide number to indicate a hidden slide.

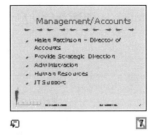

A hidden slide

To display a hidden slide during a slide show

- Start the slide show, then right-click and from the shortcut menu, select **G̲o** then **Slide N̲avigator**

The **Slide Navigator** dialogue box is displayed.

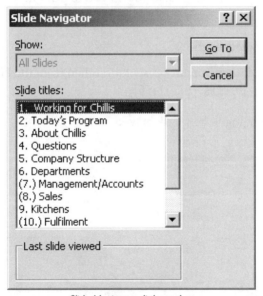

Slide Navigator dialogue box

- Double-click on the slide you want to display (Numbers in parentheses () indicate hidden slides)

To unhide a slide

- In **Slide Sorter** view, select the hidden slides

- On the **Slide Sorter** toolbar, click **Hide Slide**

- Save and close the presentation

Exchanging a Presentation

Print slides and save a presentation in different file formats

Lesson 45

Print slides in different views and formats ☐
Save a presentation in a different **file format** ☐
Save a presentation as a **web page** ☐

Print a Presentation

You may not want to print all the slides in the presentation. The **Print** dialogue box lets you determine whether to print the current slide, selected slides or a range of slides. It also allows you to print notes pages and handouts.

To print presentation slides

- Open the **Recruitment** presentation then from the **File** menu, select **Print...** (*SpeedKey:* $\boxed{\texttt{Ctrl}}$ + $\boxed{\texttt{P}}$)

The **Print** dialogue box is displayed.

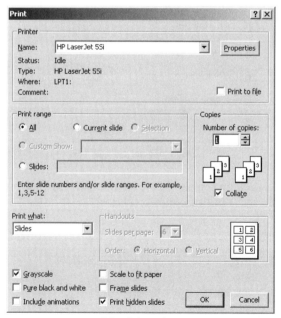

Print dialogue box

The usual options are available here. Click **Current Slide** to print the current slide. Click **Selection** to print slides selected in **Slide Sorter** view.

- Click the **Slides:** option then in the box, enter 4-6,13

Note   Use the slide numbers set in the Page Setup dialogue box (for example, in this presentation you need to enter 0 to print the first slide).

- Click **OK** - the specified slides are printed

To print the presentation outline

- In **Normal** or **Outline** view, arrange the outline to show just the slide titles

Click to expand or collapse text for the selected slide

Click to expand or collapse the whole presentation

- From the **File** menu, select **Print...** (*SpeedKey:* `Ctrl`+`P`)

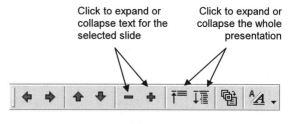

Outlining toolbar

- From the **Print what:** box, select **Outline View**

- Click **OK**

To print notes pages ①

o   Follow the same steps as for printing slides but in the **Print what:** box, select the **Notes Pages** option

To print handouts

Handouts contain miniature versions of the slides you have created. They can be used to give to your audience either as your presentation is running or to take away as a reminder of what they have seen.

PowerPoint lets you print handouts using one of five different layout styles. You can have two, three, four, six or nine slides per page.

- Follow the basic steps as for printing slides, but in the **Print what:** box, select **Handouts**

- In the **Handouts** panel, select the number of slides per page and whether the order should be horizontal or vertical across the page

- Click **OK**

Tip   You can also use Notes Pages as handouts, if you want to supply additional information to the slides.

Save a Presentation for Use in Another Application

If you want to share presentations with colleagues using a different business graphics application to PowerPoint (or an earlier version of MS PowerPoint), you can use the **Save as type** box to save a presentation in a different **file format**. The table below describes some of the different formats you can choose.

Select	To
PowerPoint 95/ PowerPoint 4.0	Save the presentation so that it can be opened and edited in a previous version of PowerPoint or in an older version of another presentation graphics application (for example, Lotus Freelance or Corel Presentations).
Design Template	Save the presentation in the Office Templates folder. You can then use the presentation as the basis of new presentations, by selecting it from the New dialogue box.
Outline/RTF	Save the text only in a format that can be opened by most word processor or presentation graphics programs.
Graphics (GIF, JPEG, TIFF, BMP)	Save the current slide (or all slides) as a graphics file so that it can be imported into different applications. You will not be able to edit objects on the slide.
Windows Metafile	Save the current slide (or all slides) as a graphic. You should be able to continue editing the objects on the slide in drawing applications.

Note Applications such as Lotus Freelance and Corel Presentations have **file converters** that let you open a Microsoft presentation in its original format. Not all PowerPoint features will convert exactly to other file formats though.

To convert a PowerPoint presentation to a different file format

- Select the map slide at the end of the presentation then from the **File** menu, select **Save As...**

- In the **Save as type** box, select **GIF** then click **Save**

When you pick a graphics format (such as **JPEG**, **GIF** or **TIFF**) you can save either just the **current** slide or **all** slides in the presentation. If you export all slides, each slide is saved as a separate file in a new subfolder.

- Click **No** to save the current slide only

Save a Presentation as a Web Page

You can save a presentation as a series of **web pages**, so that people can view it in a web browser over the internet or on a company intranet.

When you create a web presentation, PowerPoint saves it as a series of Hypertext Markup Language (HTML) documents plus graphics. It also creates **hyperlinks** automatically, to allow users to move between slides in the web browser.

To save a presentation as a web page

- Save the **Recruitment** presentation normally (otherwise any changes you have made would only be saved to the web page file)

- From the **File** menu, select **Save As Web Page...**

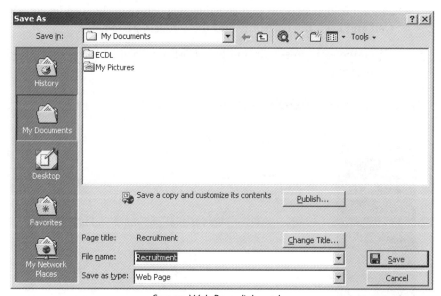

Save as Web Page dialogue box

- In the **File name:** box, enter a name for the HTML file (leave this as **Recruitment**)

- Click **Save**

PowerPoint will create an HTML version of your presentation in the folder selected. If this folder is viewed in Windows Explorer or My Computer, you will find the .HTM file for the web presentation and its supporting files stored in a subfolder called *PresentationName*_**files**.

- Close PowerPoint then view the **My Documents** folder in **Windows Explorer**

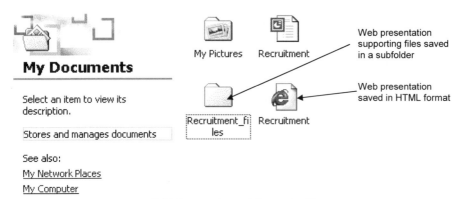

My Pictures   Recruitment

Web presentation
supporting files saved
in a subfolder

My Documents

Web presentation
saved in HTML format

Select an item to view its
description.

Recruitment_fi   Recruitment
les

Stores and manages documents

See also:

My Network Places

My Computer

Web Presentation and Supporting Files

The supporting subfolder contains items such as graphic files, bullets, background textures, pictures and navigation bars. It is essential to the web presentation. If you need to move the web presentation (.HTM file) to another folder, be sure to move the supporting folder and its contents as well and keep the HTM file and the folder together.

- Open the web presentation file (.HTM file) to view the presentation in your web browser

Viewing a web presentation in Internet Explorer

- Use the arrow buttons at the bottom of the window or the **hyperlinks** on the left-hand side to move through the presentation

- Close any open windows when you have finished

Review of Presentation

Review the topics covered during the module and identify areas for further practice and goals for the future

---

Review

(Check **objectives**) ☐
(Complete **consolidation** exercise) ☐
(Identify topics for **further** study) ☐

Check Objectives

Congratulations on completing the lessons for ECDL Module 6 "Presentation".

You have learned to:

♦ **Open** a presentation and recognise elements of the **screen**.

♦ **Create** a basic presentation and work with views.

♦ Use the **formatting** tools to customise slides and presentations.

♦ Add and format **lines** and **shapes**.

♦ Import data **objects** and create **charts**.

♦ Prepare a presentation for **viewing** or **printing**.

♦ Setup and run a **slide show** with **transitions** and **animations**.

♦ **Print** slides and save a presentation in different **file formats**.

Make sure you have checked off each syllabus item and identified any topics you do not fully understand or remember.

Consolidation and Going Further

Tests for Module 6 can either be practice-based or question-based. Practical tests will ask you to create and format a slide show.

There are further test-style exercises for you to try on the CD in the folder **ECDL Tests\6 Presentation**

Print the document **Presentation Questions** and try to complete the test unaided, using the data files from the folder.

> **Note** These questions are provided as a consolidation exercise. They do not make up an approved ECDL test. See page **689** for more information about the extra tests.

Going further

There are more tools in PowerPoint for formatting and fine-tuning slide layout and design. You can also add multimedia, such as sound and video, to a slide show and learn to record a voice narration. There are also a variety of options for printing and distributing slides to learn about, including broadcasting a presentation over the internet and using presenter tools.

PowerPoint can also be used in several other ways. You can create interactive presentations, allowing users to navigate through the show themselves. You can also use PowerPoint to manage meetings.

Many of these topics can be studied under the **ECDL Advanced Syllabus**.

Refer to page 744 for more details about further courses in gtslearning's range of **Learn** training books.

Information and Communication

Getting Started with Internet Explorer

Connect to the internet and open a web page and use the browser tools

Lesson 46

Start Internet Explorer and **recognise** elements of the screen ☐
Connect to the internet ☐
(Use basic browser buttons - **Forward**, **Back**, **Stop** and **Refresh**) ☐
Change the browser **home page** ☐
Get **Help** using Internet Explorer ☐
Close the web browser ☐

The first part of this module describes how to use the **web browser** Internet Explorer to view web pages published on the internet.

You will need to be connected to the internet to complete the practice exercises, but if you do not have an internet connection, you can still read the material to prepare yourself for tests in this module.

> **Note** To minimise the time spent on the internet (and any call charges that might apply), you may want to read through each lesson first and then complete the exercises in one go.

Open Internet Explorer and Connect to the Internet

To start Internet Explorer

- On the **Windows Taskbar**, click **Start** [Start], select the **Programs** menu item then from the submenu displayed, select the **Internet Explorer** item [Internet Explorer]

OR

- Click the **Launch Internet Explorer Browser** icon on the **Taskbar** or the **Desktop**

You may be required to make a connection and logon to your **Internet Service Provider**.

To connect to the internet

You are likely to connect to the internet in one of two ways. You might connect through your company's computer network, in which case simply starting Internet Explorer connects you.

Alternatively, you may use a **modem** to connect. If this is the case, the **Dial-up Connection** dialogue box is displayed when you start Internet Explorer.

Dial-up Connection dialogue box

- In the **Connect to:** box, select the **Internet Service Provider** (ISP) you want to use to connect to the internet

- Type in your **Password:**

- Click **Connect** to access the internet

Your modem will make the telephone call to your ISP, which connects you to the internet. From this point you will be paying any telephone call charges that may apply.

Tip   Click **Work Offline** to browse HTML files on your PC's hard disk or company intranet.

ECDL with MS Office 2000   © CWC (90) 2001

The Internet Explorer Window

When the Internet Explorer web browser program is launched, a window similar to the one below is displayed.

Like most Windows applications Internet Explorer has been designed to be easy to use. The Internet Explorer **application window** contains a number of features that let you browse the web.

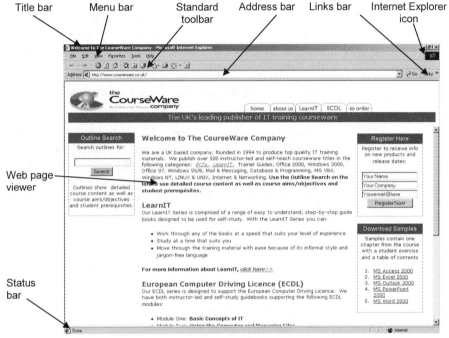

Internet Explorer window

The main part of the window will show your **home page**. This is the web page that is displayed when Internet Explorer starts.

The Title Bar

The **Title** bar contains the standard window control icons. The name in the bar is the **Title** of the web page, which usually identifies the subject of the web page or the organisation owning it or both.

The Internet Explorer Standard Toolbar

The most common actions can be carried out using the buttons on the **Standard** toolbar.

Click	To
Back Forward	Navigate forward or backward through web pages you have visited. If you point to a button without clicking, a **ScreenTip** is displayed, showing which page the button will take you to. To see a list of the last few pages you visited, click the arrow to the right of each button.
Stop	Stop loading a page (for example, if the web page is taking a long time to load).
Refresh	Reload the current web page - this can be used if a page has not loaded properly or to check that the information you are viewing is up-to-date. If you are working **offline**, clicking **Refresh** prompts you to connect to the internet and download the latest version of the page.
Home	Go directly to the page that is set as your default **Home Page**.
Search	Load the **Search Assistant** to look for a particular web page.
Favorites	View a list of web pages you have stored for quick access or add a web page to this list.
Mail	Send or read email and connect to newsgroups.
Print	Print a copy of the web page in the web page viewer to your default printer.

The Address Bar

The **Address** bar shows the location of the web page you are currently browsing. You can also type a location and click the **Go** button to access a particular website.

Address bar and Go button

- Click in the **Address** bar to select the existing text

- Type www.courseware.co.uk then click **Go**  (*SpeedKey:* [Enter])

Internet Explorer **downloads** the files used in a web page from the internet and displays them on the screen. This often involves a delay. The **Internet Explorer** icon will animate while the web page is loaded.

The Links Bar

The **Links** bar contains shortcuts to useful internet sites. These sites can be accessed quickly by clicking these links.

| Links | Best of the Web | Channel Guide | Customize Links | Free HotMail | » |

Links bar

If there are more links than will fit on the screen, the **More Links** button » is displayed. Click the **More Links** button to see the rest of your links.

- Click the **Channel Guide** link (OR if there is no such link on your own bar, choose any of the links)

The **Windows Media** website is loaded, advertising various services that you can subscribe to.

The Status Bar

The **Status** bar displays helpful information while you work. If you position the mouse pointer over a **hyperlink** to a web page, the actual address of the web page on the internet is displayed.

While a web page is being opened, the Status bar displays details of its location and how much of the page has been **downloaded** (displayed in the browser window).

The Status bar also shows you whether you are connected to the internet or working offline and gives you information about how **secure** the current website is.

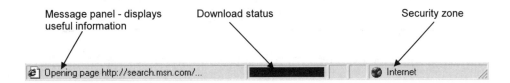

Message panel - displays useful information

Download status

Security zone

The Explorer Bar

When you click the **Search** Search , **Favorites** Favorites or **History** History buttons, the **Explorer** bar is displayed on the left-hand side of the screen.

Explorer bar   Split bar

- To resize the Explorer bar, click-and-drag the split bar left or right

- To change the contents of the **Explorer** bar, click **Search** Search , **Favorites** Favorites and **History** History in turn - you will learn to use these features in later lessons

---

Tip   To browse folders on your PC/PC Network, from the **View** menu, select **Explorer** bar then from the submenu, select **Folders**. You can now use the **Explorer** bar like **Windows Explorer**.

- Close the **Explorer** bar by clicking the **Close** button   Search   ✕

The Back and Forward Buttons

Internet Explorer remembers where you have visited since starting the program. You can use the **Back** ⇐ Back ▾ and **Forward** ⇨ ▾ buttons to move between these pages.

To go back and forward between web pages

- On the **Standard** toolbar, position the mouse pointer over the **Back** button ⇐ Back ▾

A **ScreenTip** is displayed showing the name of the web page you just left.

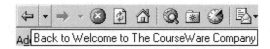

- Click the **Back** button

The web page you just left (CourseWare Company) is displayed in the web page viewer. When you use the **Back** button, the **Forward** button is activated.

- On the **Standard** toolbar, position the mouse pointer over the **Forward** button ⇨ ▾

A **ScreenTip** is displayed showing the name of the web page you just left.

- Click the **Forward** button

The web page you went back from (Windows Media) is redisplayed in the web page viewer. Note that the **Forward** button is now greyed out, because you are back where you started.

You can click the down arrow beside the **Back** and **Forward** buttons to see a list of pages you have visited. You can click any page on the list to move directly to it.

The Stop and Refresh Buttons

Some sites have complex graphics, sound and video which, if you are trying to access them with a slow modem or when the internet is busy, can take several minutes to load. The **Stop** button (*SpeedKey:* Esc) allows you to halt downloads.

If you interrupt a loading page by clicking the **Stop** button as much of the web page as has currently loaded will be displayed. You may still be able to read much of the text and click on any hyperlinks that are present.

- Click one of the links on the **Links** bar then when you see the page start to change quickly click **Stop**

Depending on how quickly you clicked, you may see part of the site only.

If you have visited a site before, the files used for the site will still be **cached** on your hard disk. This means that the site can **load** more quickly. In some circumstances though, the page that appears may not be up-to-date.

- To update the page, use the **Refresh** button (*SpeedKey:* F5)

The current page is redisplayed. If the page had only partially loaded before, you can now see all of it.

The Home Page

The web browser's **home page** (or **your** home page) is the web page loaded when Internet Explorer is first started.

> **Note** Do not confuse **your** home page with the home page of the websites you visit. Your home page is set through Internet Explorer. The home page of a website is the introductory page for the site.
> If you click a hyperlink such as **Home** on a web page, you will jump to the **website's** home page, not yours.

To go to your home page

- Return to your **Home** page by clicking the **Home** button (*SpeedKey:* Alt + Home)

To set your home page

You can set your home page to whatever web page you like, either on the internet, on an intranet or on your PC's hard drive.

- Use the drop-down arrow on the **Back** button to return to **The CourseWare Company** page

After a few moments, the web page for The CourseWare Company will be displayed.

- When the page has loaded, from the **Tools** menu, select **Internet Options...**

The **Internet Options** dialogue box is displayed.

Internet Options dialogue box

- If it is not already displayed, click the **General** tab

- From the **Home page** panel, copy the text in the **Address:** box to the space below (so that you can restore your original home page when you have completed this course)

_____

- Click the **Use Current** button

The current web page (http://www.courseware.co.uk) is displayed in the **Address:** box.

- Click **OK**

Tip   Click the **Use Blank** button to start Internet Explorer with a blank home page. This means you will not be prompted to connect to the internet when Internet Explorer starts.

Close Internet Explorer

When you have finished browsing, you can exit Internet Explorer in several ways.

To exit Internet Explorer

- On the **Internet Explorer Title** bar, click **Close** ⊠

OR

- On the **Internet Explorer Title** bar, click the **Program Icon** and select **Close**

OR

- From the **File** menu, select **Close** (*SpeedKey:* Alt + F4)

If you use a modem to connect to the internet, the **AutoDisconnect** dialogue box will be displayed, prompting you to close your connection to the internet.

Disconnect from the Internet

If you pay telephone charges to connect to the internet, you should close Internet Explorer and disconnect the telephone connection when you have finished browsing.

To close Internet Explorer and disconnect from the internet

When you close Internet Explorer, the **AutoDisconnect** dialogue box is displayed prompting you to close the connection.

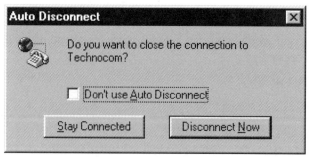

AutoDisconnect dialogue box

- Click **Disconnect Now**

Get Help with Internet Explorer

The Help system in Internet Explorer is the same as the one in Windows. Refer back to page 115 if you do not remember how it works.

To browse for help

- Start Internet Explorer again - if you are prompted to connect to the internet, click the **Work Offline** button

- From the **Help** menu, select **Contents and Index** (*SpeedKey*: F1)

The **Internet Explorer Help** window is displayed.

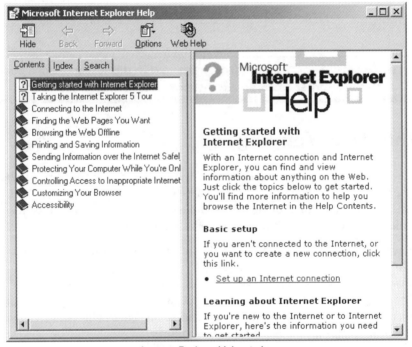

Internet Explorer Help window

- Use the **Index** and **Search** tabs to look for help on the following topics

    Changing your home page

    Using the Links bar

    Favorite pages

- Close the Help window and Internet Explorer when you have finished

Web Addresses

Browse web pages on the internet and open hyperlinks

Lesson 47

Understand the make-up and structure of a **web address** ☐
Display a given web page ☐
Open a **URL** and collect data ☐
Open a **hyperlink** or an image link ☐
Browse a specified site ☐
(Recognise different **navigation tools** on web pages) ☐
(**Download** files) ☐

Note You may want to read through the text in this lesson before connecting to the internet to complete the exercises on pages 613 to 615.

What is a Web Page?

The **world wide web** is a collection of **hyperlinked** web pages **published** on the internet. Web pages are published by organisations and individuals interested in putting themselves on the web. A collection of web pages belonging to one organisation is called a **website**.

Each web page has an **address** on the internet. This address is called a **Uniform Resource Locator** (URL). A **hyperlink** is a piece of text or a graphic that provides a link to something's URL. The "something" could be a heading on the same web page, the next page in a website, a page in another website, a sound file or digital video and so on. When you click a hyperlink, the link's **target** is opened in Internet Explorer.

The size of each page can vary considerably. Internet Explorer can only show you the size of the page that fits in its current view window. To view the rest of the page you can use the scroll bars at the bottom and right of the view window to scroll the page. This is exactly the same as any other Windows application.

The web browser interprets web pages. Different browsers made available at different times may or may not be able to present all of the features available on a particular site. However, as Internet Explorer is a very popular browser, most websites are designed with it in mind.

Uniform Resource Locators

Every resource (email service, web page, internet chat room and so on) on the internet has an address that allows other computers to connect to it. Each resource is **hosted** by a **server**, which is identified to other computers by its **IP address** number and the service's **port** number. An IP address number consists of four decimal **bytes** (a number ranging from 0 to 255) separated by dots (for example, **194.36.18.194**). A port number is like a broadcast channel for particular types of service (web pages, email, ftp and so on).

The numerical internet address understood by computers is quite incomprehensible to most people. For this reason a system of identifying servers using a **domain name** was developed. An internet domain name consists of the name itself (usually the name of the company or organisation) and one or more suffixes (such as **.COM** or **.CO.UK**) used as categories.

A website can be accessed by typing a domain name (such as www.courseware.co.uk) into the Address bar. This will open the website's default page (or **home page**).

This is a shorthand way of accessing a website however. Every single document and service on the internet has a **unique address**, called a **Uniform Resource Locator** (URL). The domain name is only part of this address.

A URL contains all the information needed by a web browser to get a specific document from a server. The information required is as follows:

♦ The type of **service** that should be used to get the data and consequently the **port** number of the service.

♦ The name and location of the host computer (**server**) storing the document - the **domain name**.

♦ The location of the **file** on the host computer.

Make up of a web address

For example, consider the following URL:

Service

The above URL begins with the letters **http**. This means that the documents
are **served** by a HyperText Transfer Protocol (HTTP) server. The URLs for
web pages usually start with this (though you will also see **HTTPS(ecure)**,
which indicates a secure web server, used for e-commerce). Most URLs do
not specify the port number of the service, as common services are always
found on the same port number (for example, HTTP is always on port
number 80).

:// - means that the next part of the URL is the name and location of the
server. This group of characters is called a **separator**. Separators are used to
indicate to the computer processing the URL that one part of the URL has
ended and the next part is coming.

Domain name

www.courseware.co.uk is the **domain name** of the server. When a web
browser requests a URL, the domain name gets translated into an **IP
number**, which is then used to find the server on the internet, by looking up
the domain name on a **database**. Domain names make it easier for people to
remember URLs. They also make it easier to move a website from one server
to another without having to tell everyone that the address has changed -
you only have to change the number in the database.

Domain names contain some standard notations. For example, **www** identifies
the service as being on the world wide web. **.co** identifies the website as a
commercial organisation. It is convention that commercial sites use **co** or **com**,
academic URLs have **ac** or **edu** (for academic or education) and governmental
or non-profit organisations use **org**. **.uk** indicates that the site is based in the
UK. These suffixes are created and controlled by internet organisations.

Note that a company can register itself with any domain name (provided it is
still available). For example, the **.com** extension does not necessarily indicate
a US company. It is easier to type in (it is more **visible**) and so more highly
prized by companies. The Scotsman newspaper demonstrates its
independence in its domain name **www.scotsman.com** whereas the Daily
Telegraph is happy to be **www.telegraph.co.uk**

Path

The URL up to now has identified where to look for the web page on the
internet. The rest of the URL describes where on the **server** the page is located.
This part of the URL is like the path and file names you see in Microsoft
Windows, except that forward slashes (**/**) are used to separate folder and file
names rather than backslashes (****) and there is no need to identify the disk
drive.

about/contact.htm indicates that the **Contact** web page (HTML page) is
located in the **About** subfolder of the server's web folder.

Practice

Q1. Answer the following questions on web addresses:

a) What three parts make up a URL?

_____

_____

_____

b) What does HTTP stand for?

_____

c) What is a domain name?

_____

_____

_____

d) If Joe Chillis is a company registered in the UK, what might its domain name be?

_____

_____

_____

Answers on page 679

Jump Directly to URLs

If you know the URL of a web page or website you can type it directly into the **Address** bar and jump directly to that page.

To enter a URL to browse a page

- Start Internet Explorer and choose to **Connect** to the internet

If you use a **modem** to connect, there will be a delay while the modem **dials-up** to connect to your **Internet Service Provider**. After some time, your **home** page (set to The CourseWare Company if you completed the previous lesson) will be displayed.

- On the **Address** bar, click into the text box

The text of the current URL is selected.

- Type `www.ecdlcourseware.eu.com`

> **Tip** When entering a URL, you can usually omit the **http://** part. Internet Explorer will recognise the type of server from the **www** part of the URL.

- Click **Go** 🔗 Go (*SpeedKey:* Enter)

The Internet Explorer icon ▓ at the end of the Menu bar will animate while the page loads. If you look at the **Status** bar, Internet Explorer displays messages showing the progress of the connection.

- Once the ECDL courseware page is displayed, try visiting another site, such as www.microsoft.com

URLs that you type into the Address bar are saved for future use.

- On the **Address** bar, click the down arrow

- Select the www.courseware.co.uk URL

- Click **Go** 🔗 Go (*SpeedKey:* Enter)

> **Tip** If you enter a URL that Internet Explorer recognises, the **AutoComplete** drop-down list box is displayed. Select a link from the box with the mouse (or press ⬇) to select the URL quickly.

AutoComplete

Practice

The next few topics describe some of the ways that web pages can appear when you open them. Read the text first, then to see some of these features on the web, either browse sites that you have been planning to visit, or try out some of the suggestions below.

- *Visit www.bbc.co.uk and identify the range of different devices used for navigation and interaction*

- *Visit the ECDL Foundation's website www.ecdl.com*

- *Visit the Internet Explorer home page www.microsoft.com/windows/ie/default.htm*

- *Visit the BBC's webguide to find interesting entertainment and leisure sites www.bbc.co.uk/webguide/servlet/start*

- *Visit www.shockwave.com to see examples of multimedia on the web*

- *Close the browser and disconnect from the internet OR go on to the next internet practice exercise on page 622*

Browse the Web

Moving around and between web pages is known as **browsing** (or navigating, or sometimes "Surfing the Web"). You can browse web pages in several different ways.

Hyperlinks

Almost all web pages have hyperlinks. These links connect:

- One page to another part of the same page (useful if it is a really large page).

- One page to another page somewhere on the web.

- A page to a file, such as a sound clip, video, a spreadsheet or a Word document.

- To an email address.

Hypertext links are indicated by underlined text highlighted in blue (usually). Hyperlinks are also frequently in the form of buttons, graphics or pictures.

To find hyperlinks on a page, move your mouse pointer over the page and where there is a hyperlink the pointer will turn into a hand with a pointing finger .

Mortgage mirth or misery?
Will that dream mansion break your bank? Try our mortgage calculator to find out what it costs per month.

Example of hyperlinks from BBC Online

In the example above, both the graphic and the underlined text link to the same page. You could click either to follow the link.

As you surf around the web, Internet Explorer remembers where you have been. You will notice that hypertext links you previously selected are now coloured purple. Internet Explorer does this to remind you that you have already visited the page identified by this link.

Note Sometimes website designers prevent Internet Explorer from recolouring links in this way in order to preserve the colour scheme they have created for their website. In the example above for instance, the hypertext link **Mortgage mirth or misery?** is always black.

Using the keyboard ①

As well as using the mouse, you can use the keyboard to explore a website.

o Press the `Tab` key to select the next link on the page

o Press `Shift`+`Tab` to select the previous link

o Press `Enter` to open the link in the viewer

Navigation controls

The designer of a website should have put a lot of thought into creating ways for you to move around the site. There is no set way for **navigation controls** to appear on web pages. However, as you browse websites, you will notice that some of the following controls are used regularly.

♦ **Navigation panels**

Often hyperlinks to the main sections of a website will be grouped into panels at the top or left-hand side of the web page. When you click links from these panels, the main body of the web page changes but the panel remains.

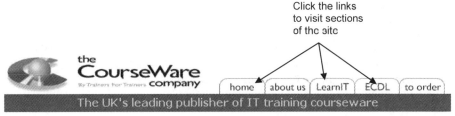

Click the links to visit sections of the site

Site navigation panel

♦ **List boxes**

Another commonly used device is the list box. You can select an area of the site to visit by clicking the down arrow on the list box and scrolling through the hyperlinks to the available areas. When you have selected an area, click the **Go** button next to the box (*SpeedKey:* Enter).

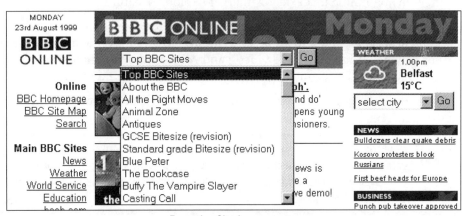

Example of list box navigation

Note In the example above, you can also use a list box to change which city the weather is displayed for. In this case, only that part of the web page would be affected. The rest would look the same.

♦ **Forms (text boxes and buttons)**

A **form** is a web page where you can enter information. Forms are used to collect information to enable you to search databases, send messages to the website owner, play games and so on.

Some forms may be very simple. For example, most websites have search engines, consisting of a text box for you to type search text into and a **Search** button for you to submit the request. Objects such as text boxes and buttons are called **controls**.

Other forms may be more complex, using several text boxes, list boxes, option buttons and so on, but they all work on the same principle: type the information into the boxes and press the button to send it.

    o   To move between controls use the mouse or press `Tab`

    o   To submit the form, click the button or press `Enter`

♦ **Multimedia content**

Some websites may contain hyperlinks to sections with sound, video and animation. Depending on how the website is designed, you may be prompted to download a **plug-in** file to browse this kind of content. A plug-in is an application that extends Internet Explorer's features.

Popular plug-ins include **Flash** and **Shockwave** for animation and dynamic content such as games; **RealPlayer**, **Windows Media Player** and **QuickTime** for playing sound, music and videos; and **Adobe Acrobat Reader** for presenting longer documents so that you can save and print them.

If you want to download the plug-in, follow the instructions on the website.

> **Note** Plug-ins could possibly carry **viruses**, which can damage your PC or gain access to private information. Only download plug-ins from trustworthy sites, and check any plug-in you want to use with an up-to-date virus scanner.

Links and the Browser

Certain types of links can affect the way web pages display in your browser window.

Links that open a new browser window ①

Often when a website provides links to a **different** website, following the link will open a new browser window. This will leave you with two versions of Internet Explorer running.

    o Close the original browser window if you do not need it any more

Links that open within a frame ①

Some websites use **frames** to display navigational controls in a panel. You may find that when you follow a hyperlink to a new site, the navigation panels from the old site remain.

    o To get rid of the frames, **right-click** a hyperlink

A **shortcut** menu is displayed.

Open
Open in New Window
Save Target As...
Print Target

Cut
Copy
Copy Shortcut
Paste

Add to Favorites...

Properties

Hyperlink shortcut menu

    o Select **Open in New Window**

The web page the hyperlink connects to is opened in a new browser window.

    o Close the old browser window

Dealing with advertising banners ①

Some sites carry advertising banners that open within a small dialogue box.

    o To get rid of the advert, on the banner's **Title** bar, click the **Close** button ☒

Error 404

If you visit a web page and see the message **Error 404** it means that Internet Explorer cannot find the page. This is usually either because the URL you entered is wrong or because the page has been moved or removed.

However, the error may occur simply because the website's server is **not responding** (undergoing technical difficulties). If you are sure the page exists, try again later.

Downloading files ⓓ

When a web page makes a program available for download, there will be a hyperlink to start downloading it.

Click **Get It Here** to start
downloading the file

Click **Read the details** for
instructions on how to use
the file

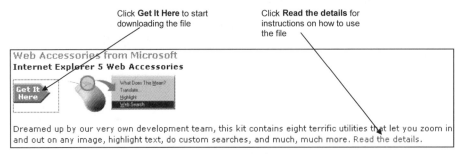

Microsoft's Internet Explorer website

o Read (and print a copy) of the instructions for using the file and take note of any licence/copyright restrictions on its use

When you follow the link, the **File Download** dialogue box is displayed.

This means that the link does not go to a web page, but to a file. You can either open the file from the internet or save it to disk.

In most cases, it is better to save the file to disk. It is important to scan files for **viruses** before opening them. Also, the file will be much quicker to respond if you are opening it from a local hard disk.

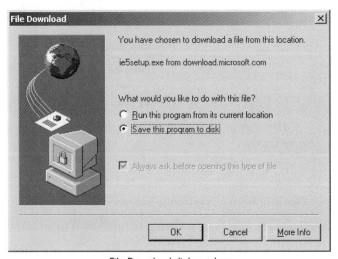

File Download dialogue box

Searching the Web

Make use of search engines and directories to locate information on the world wide web

---

Lesson 48

Understand what a **search engine** is ☐
Create a **keyword** search using **logical operators** ☐
Locate and select an appropriate **search engine** ☐

How Search Engines Work

There is no single, definitive index or table of contents of the internet. To find information, you need to use a search engine.

Search engines use programs - called agents, robots, spiders and crawlers - to trawl through the web reporting on what they find. Starting with the sites they know, they snoop out all the links embedded in those pages, follow them, then repeat the process for all the new sites they come across.

Indexing software then compiles the information into an enormous database of keywords, text and URLs. When you query a search engine, it is actually this database you are searching, not the world wide web. URLs are returned in response to your query based on how relevant the web page is to the text in your query. Different search engines use different rules to determine the relevance of a page.

The owners of search engines are in competition with each other to get you to use their service. You do not have to pay to use a search engine, but the owners generate revenue from advertising they put on their website. Therefore they want their sites to be as easy-to-use, up-to-date and relevant as possible.

Also, the owners of websites are in competition with one another to get their sites noticed. The most astute sites use various tricks to get their web pages to the top of the lists of URLs returned by search engines.

Smart search engines

New search engines appear all the time, often in response to demand for more specialist information. There are search engines that can return the URL of just sound, picture or video files. You can search by document date, geographical region or domain name.

Many of these new search engines are **meta-engines**. A meta-engine queries the databases of other search engines.

Directory sites

An internet **directory** is an indexed collection of websites. Each site is put into one or more categories. Sites may be submitted manually or discovered by search engines.

Website specific search tools

You will also find search tools on many websites. These usually let you search just that website for the page you are looking for.

Use the Search Assistant

Continuing with the Joe Chilli example, for the exercises in this section, you will be doing some market research, looking for information about online food retailers.

You can use the Internet Explorer **Search Assistant** to find sites quickly.

To search for information using the Search Assistant

- Start Internet Explorer and connect to the internet

- When your home page has loaded, on the **Standard** toolbar, click **Search** `Search` **OR** from the **View** menu, select **Explorer Bar** then click **Search** (`Ctrl`+`E`)

The **Explorer** bar is displayed with the **Search Assistant** loaded.

Search Assistant

You can enter the search text (or **criteria**) into the box. You can type as many words as you like.

- In the **Find a Web page containing:** box, type `chilli`

- Click the **Search** button (*SpeedKey:* `Enter`)

The Search Assistant will perform your search and display the results in the Search pane. The sites that most closely match your query are listed first. The list will probably contain a wonderful mixture of different types of sites: food retailers, clothing retailers, bands and films.

- If you do not see what you want, click the **Next** link in the search pane (not the button on the **Explorer** bar) to move down the list of matches

- Click any link to a food retailer - the page is displayed in the main window

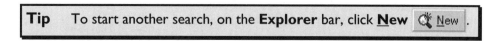

Tip To start another search, on the **Explorer** bar, click **New**

Tip If you want to find similar pages to the one currently displayed, from the **Tools** menu, select **Show Related Links**.

- Close the **Explorer** bar

To search for a website from the Address bar

You can also type search text directly into the **Address** bar rather than typing a URL. Internet Explorer will try to find the site that best matches your query and display it in the web page viewer. Other matches are displayed in the **Search** bar.

Search Operators and Syntax

When you simply type in text to locate what you want, you may quickly become frustrated at the number of links returned by the search engine.

To get better results, it is worth understanding what factors influence the search results and to know the correct use of search **syntax** (similar to using criteria operators in a database query).

The following factors influence search results in a typical search engine:

♦ The query terms are found near the start of the document or in the title.

♦ The document contains more of the query terms.

♦ The document contains query terms that have a high weight (words that are relatively uncommon in the database will have a high weight).

Searches can be made more effective using the correct **syntax** and **operators**.

Syntax	Usage	Example
CAPS	Using upper case makes the search case sensitive.	Rock Hudson
"	Use quotation marks (") around phrases.	"stupid pet tricks"
-	Use hyphens (-) between words that must appear next to one another.	stupid-pet-tricks
+	Put a plus sign (+) in front of a word that **must** be found in the results.	city guides +London
-	Put a minus sign (-) in front of a word that should **not** appear in the results.	python -monty
		Use a pipe (|) to search within a certain set of results.	dogs	dalmatians
*	Use * for partial word matches.	quilt*

Tip This syntax should work with most search engines, but click the **Advanced** button on the search engine's home page to check whether there are any special instructions or features.

Use Different Search Engines

Through the Search Assistant, you can get quick access to several powerful search engines to perform quick searches. However the results displayed in the **Explorer** bar are generally not as detailed as those found on the search engine's actual website. Also, for some searches you may want to use a particular search engine.

You can use a different search engine by going to the relevant website.

To use Excite from its home page

- In the **Address** bar, type www.excite.co.uk

- Click **Go**   🖰 **Go**   (*SpeedKey:* [**Enter**]) - the Excite home page is loaded

- In the **Search** box, type `chilli food -bands`

- Leave the list box set to **UK Sites** and click **Search** (*SpeedKey:* [**Enter**])

The results of your search are displayed on a new web page.

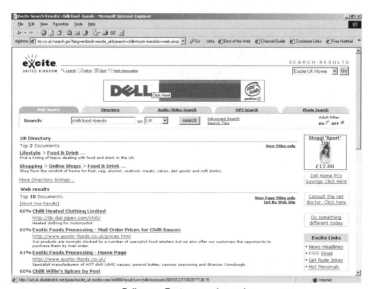

Full page Excite search results

Notice that there is a short extract from the web page to help you decide whether it is relevant. Also, there are two sets of results. The top of the web page shows matches to **categories** in Excite's website **directory**. The bottom of the page shows matches to actual **websites** (in the UK).

Tip   Other popular search engines include: www.lycos.co.uk, www.ukplus.co.uk, www.altavista.com, www.go2net.com and www.google.com.

Use a Web Directory

Yahoo is an example of a **web directory**. Yahoo receives submissions from website designers and adds the pages to the relevant subject headings. You can either follow the hyperlinks to browse a specific category for pages, or use the search tool to locate a web page in its database.

- In the **Address** bar, enter the URL www.yahoo.co.uk and click **Go** Go (*SpeedKey:* Enter)

You will be presented with a page similar to this:

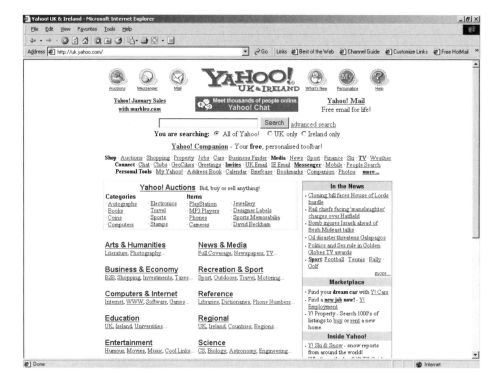

- Click the **Business & Economy** hyperlink to browse that category

- In the search box, enter chilli and select **This category only** from the list box

- Click the **Search** button

- Keep the results page open to complete the next lesson

Note You can use the same search syntax in Yahoo as you would for other search engines.

Saving and Printing Web Pages

Collect and print data from a web page

Modify **page setup** options ☐
Print a web page using basic options ☐
Print **search results** ☐
Save a web page as a file ☐
Collect data from a web page for use in another application ☐

Modify Page Setup Options

You can use **Print** to create a printed list of search results for future reference and print a copy of any web page if required.

Page Setup options determine the paper size and orientation, margins and the header and footer.

To change the page setup

- If you are not continuing from the previous lesson, search **www.yahoo.co.uk** for information about `chilli`

- When you have a page of search results, from the **File** menu, select **Page Setup...**

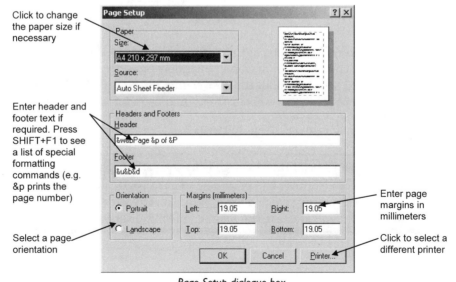

Click to change the paper size if necessary

Enter header and footer text if required. Press SHIFT+F1 to see a list of special formatting commands (e.g. &p prints the page number)

Select a page orientation

Enter page margins in millimeters

Click to select a different printer

Page Setup dialogue box

- Add the following text to the end of the existing footer &bPrepared by your name

This will add the text "Prepared by..." on the right-hand side of the footer (in addition to what is already setup).

- Click **OK**

Print a Web Page

To print a web page

- On the **Standard** toolbar, click **Print** 🖶

The page will print out to your default printer.

If you need to set more advanced print options, or change your printer, follow the steps below.

- From the **File** menu, select **Print...** (*SpeedKey*: Ctrl + P)

The **Print** dialogue box is displayed.

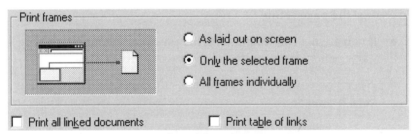

Print dialogue box

If you are browsing a web page with frames, you have the option of printing the contents of each frame separately or as they appear on the screen. If you select **Print all linked documents**, Internet Explorer will print all the pages in that website (this could use a lot of paper).

- Click **OK** to print a copy of the search results

Tip If you need to print more search links than are displayed on one page, you can either display and print each results page one by one or alternatively, most search engines have an **Advanced Search** page that will let you increase the number of links displayed on one page.

Save a Web Page

You can download an individual web page by saving it as a file on your PC.

To save a web page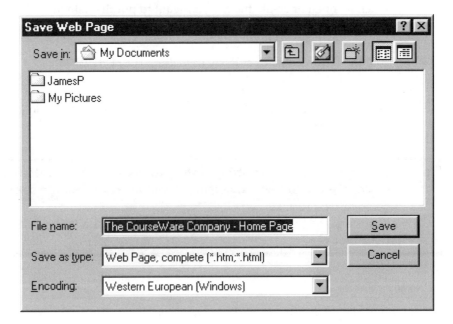

- o Browse to the page you want to save
- o From the **File** menu, select **Save As...**

The **Save Web Page** dialogue box is displayed.

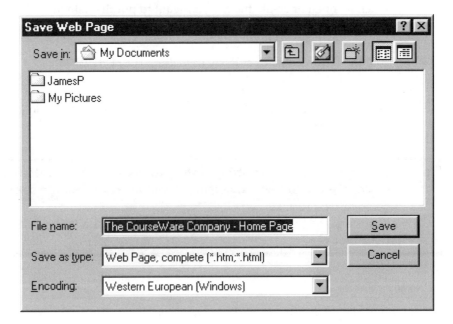

- o Enter a file name and select a folder
- o In the **Save as type** box, select **Web page, complete** to save the page and any associated graphics or **Web page, HTML only** to save the page's underlying code only
- o Click **Save**

Collect Data from a Web Page

You can use the Windows Clipboard to copy text and/or graphics from a page to another file, such as a word processed document or a spreadsheet.

To copy data from a page ①

o   Click-and-drag across the text and graphics to select the data

o   From the **Edit** menu, select **Copy** (*SpeedKey:* `Ctrl`+`C`)

o   Switch to, open or create the file you want to put the data in

o   Position the insertion point where you want to insert the data

o   From the **Edit** menu, select **Paste** (*SpeedKey:* `Ctrl`+`V`)

The data is pasted at the insertion point. This may take some time to complete. The formatting of the data will depend on the type of file you are pasting it into.

> **Tip**   If you do not like the formatting of the pasted data, select **Undo** then try using the **Paste Special** command (on the **Edit** menu) to select a different data format.
> If you are pasting data into a worksheet, try to select a table of data for the best results.

Practice

- *Open the web page results for the chilli search*

- *Click-and-drag to select just the links to pages then copy the data*

- *Start Excel and paste the data into the new workbook*

You should find that each paragraph is pasted into a separate cell.

- *Save the workbook as ChilliLinks then close it and exit Excel*

- *In Internet Explorer, save the page of search results as ChilliLinks*

- *Close Internet Explorer and disconnect from the internet, unless you are starting the next lesson straightaway*

Favourites

Create and manage a list of favourite web pages

Lesson 50

Open a favourite web page ☐
Add a web page to the favourites list ☐
Add web pages to a favourites **folder** ☐
(**Move** and **delete** favourites) ☐

The world wide web contains millions of web pages. Despite the domain name system, remembering lots of URLs is quite difficult, which makes it hard to revisit web pages.

While browsing the web, Internet Explorer remembers the last few locations you visited and allows you to retrace your steps using the Forward and Backward buttons. However, when you exit from Internet Explorer this information is lost.

The **Favourites** feature allows you to keep an address book of URLs. You can sort and organise the links so that they are easy to find.

Note Favourite links are also known as **bookmarks**.

Open a Favourite Web Page

To browse the Favourites list

- On the **Standard** toolbar, click **Favorites** `[*] Favorites`

OR

- From the **View** menu, select **Explorer Bar** then **Favorites**
  (*SpeedKey:* `Ctrl`+`I`)

The **Explorer** bar is displayed with the **Favourites** list loaded. Links are either organised into folders or appear on their own.

Explorer bar displaying the Favourites list

- Click the **Links** folder to open it 🗀 Links

This folder contains links that appear on your **Links** bar.

- Click a web page or document icon to browse it

Tip   You can also select links from the **F<u>a</u>vorites** menu.

Add a Web Page to the Favourites List

To add a link to the Favourites list

- Go to www.ecdlcourseware.eu.com

- When the page has loaded, on the **Standard** toolbar, click **Favorites** 🖈 Favorites then on the **Explorer** bar, click **Add...** 🖼️Add... **OR** from the **F<u>a</u>vorites** menu, select **<u>A</u>dd to Favorites...**

The **Add Favorite** dialogue box is displayed.

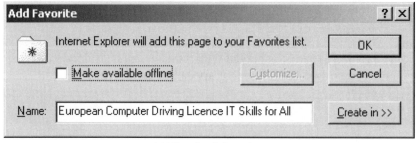

Add Favorite dialogue box

You will notice that it is not the URL that you see listed in the **Name:** text box, but the title of the page you are viewing.

If necessary, you can edit or change the name so that you will remember what is on this page.

- Click **OK**

Add Web Pages to a Favourites Folder

As with most other things in computing, your favourites list will be easier to use if you organise it with subfolders. This allows you to keep links relating to a particular topic or category together.

To create a Favourites folder

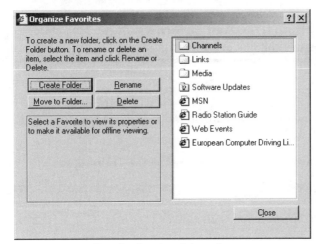

- On the **Explorer** bar, click **Organize...** [Organize...]

OR

- From the **Favorites** menu, select **Organize Favorites...**

The **Organize Favorites** dialogue box is displayed.

Organize Favorites dialogue box

- Click **Create Folder**

A new folder is created in the list box on the right-hand side of the dialogue box.

- Type a name (Training) and press Enter

- Click **Close**

You have now created a new folder heading under which favourite places can be stored.

> **Note** In the **Favorites** menu, subfolders appear as submenus.

To move a link to a folder

- Open the **Organize Favorites** dialogue box

- From the list, select the **ECDL CourseWare** link then click **Move to Folder...**

The **Browse for Folder** dialogue box is displayed.

- Select a destination folder and click **OK**

The link is moved.

> **Note** Favourite links can also be moved between folders using the **Explorer** bar by dragging and dropping them onto the required folder.

> **Tip** When you add a link, from the **Add Favorite** dialogue box, click **Create in >>** to store the link in a folder.

To delete favourite links

As you add more and more links, there are bound to be ones you no longer want to keep.

- In the **Organize Favorites** dialogue box, select the **Training** folder

- Click **Delete** (*SpeedKey:* [Delete])

You will be asked to confirm deleting the link.

- Click **Yes**

- Click **Close**

- Close Internet Explorer and disconnect from the internet

Customising the Browser

Customise Internet Explorer to suit your requirements

Lesson 51

Change **view/display** modes ☐
Customise the **toolbars** ☐
Display or **hide** images on web pages ☐

Change View/Display Modes

If you want to get the full impact of some websites, you may want to browse them in **full-screen** mode. In full-screen mode, most of Internet Explorer's toolbars are hidden, leaving more space on-screen for the web page itself.

To browse a web page full screen

- Start Internet Explorer and choose to work offline

- From the **View** menu, select **Full Screen** (*SpeedKey:* F11)

- To use the toolbar, move the mouse to the top of the screen

- Return to normal view by clicking the **Restore** button 🔲 (*SpeedKey:* F11)

To change the text size ①

You can make basic text on a web page larger or smaller.

- o From the **View** menu, select **Text Size**

- o Pick an option from the submenu

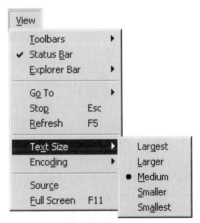

Text Size menu

Note If the web page designer has used a special way of formatting the page this option may not have any effect.

Customise the Toolbars

You can change the size and position of toolbars and the Menu bar on the screen and change which buttons are displayed on the **Standard** toolbar.

You can also display smaller icons on the **Standard** toolbar or turn off any of the toolbars to give you more room to see page content.

To show/hide toolbars

- From the **View** menu, select the **Links** toolbar to hide it

A tick next to the toolbar name indicates that it is displayed.

- Display the **Links** toolbar again

To customise the Standard toolbar

- From the **View** menu, select **Toolbars** then **Customize...**

The **Customize Toolbar** dialogue box is displayed.

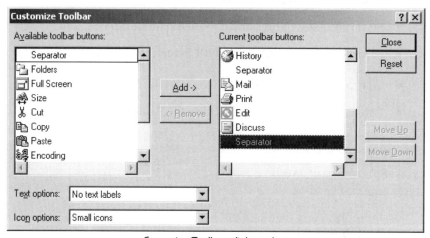

Customize Toolbars dialogue box

- From the **Available toolbar buttons:** box, select the **Full Screen** button

- Click **Add ->**

- From the **Current toolbar buttons:** box, select the **Edit** button

- Click **<- Remove**

- To use a larger toolbar, from the **Text options:** box, select **Selective text on right** and from the **Icon options:** box, select **Large icons**

- Click **Close**

To move/resize toolbars

- On the toolbar, click the **Move/Resize** handle next to the **Links** label and hold down the mouse button

Move/Resize
handle

- Drag the toolbar left or right to resize it

- Click-and-drag the **Address** bar up and to the right of the **Standard** toolbar

- Arrange the toolbars in whichever way you prefer

Display and Hide Images

Moving from site to site can be slow if the internet is busy, if the site you are trying to access is busy or if you are using a slow modem. Although site providers are always trying to make their pages quicker to access, the volume of traffic on the internet is growing more quickly.

If a site contains graphics (or other multimedia content) you can prevent the graphics from downloading and so speed up browsing.

Note A well-designed site will not rely on graphic hyperlinks for you to navigate it. However, be aware that many sites will be confusing to move around with only the text displayed.

To disable multimedia content

- From the **Tools** menu, select **Internet Options...**

- Click the **Advanced** tab

- In the **Settings:** box, scroll down to the **Multimedia** section

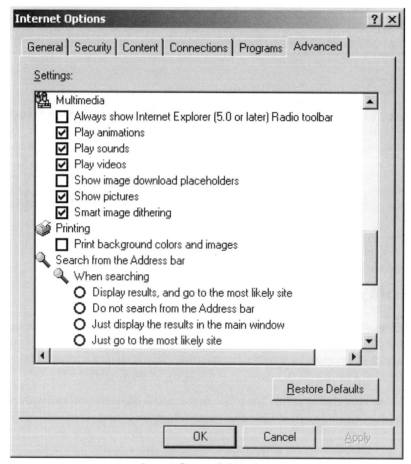

Internet Options dialogue box

- De-select the content you want to turn off

Note If the **Show pictures** check box is cleared, you can still view an individual picture on a web page by right-clicking its icon and then clicking **Show Picture**.

- Close Internet Explorer

Getting Started with Outlook

Open your mail inbox and recognise parts of the screen

Lesson 52

Understand the difference between **workgroup** and **internet** email ☐
Open your mail inbox ☐
Open **Outlook** and **recognise** parts of the screen ☐
Exit Outlook ☐

Email is a very important part of modern business communications. Internet email especially allows companies to transmit data very quickly and cheaply all over the world.

This part of the module shows you how to send and receive email and keep email contacts using the application Microsoft Outlook.

> **Note** You may prefer to use **Microsoft Outlook Express 5**, which is installed along with Internet Explorer, for email. The appendix on page 685 gives you a quick reference to the main screens and commands.

MS Outlook and Messaging Systems

MS Outlook is a **Desktop Information Manager** for managing all your personal information, just like a personal organiser. Outlook is made up of different **components** for storing different types of information. In this course we will look at just the **email** and **contacts** components.

Inbox

The **Inbox** is used to send and receive email messages. You can use Outlook for **workgroup** email and for **internet** email.

Contacts

The **Contacts List** lets you store contact information for friends and associates. You can store telephone, email and address details as well as keeping general contact notes.

Outlook is designed to work as a **universal inbox** for all your data communications. You can use Outlook to create, send and receive email messages and faxes. Outlook is a mail **client**. It displays and manages mail, but the actual mail delivery is handled by one or more **servers**.

Outlook can be setup in one of two ways. If you are using Outlook at work, you will probably have support for a **workgroup**. A workgroup allows you to send email internally to your colleagues using a workgroup server such as **Microsoft Exchange**. You may **also** be able to send email over the internet, depending on the services your company have provided.

If you are using Outlook at home, you will probably only require support for internet email, as provided by your Internet Service Provider. In this case, you connect to the ISP's mail server through your **dial-up internet** connection.

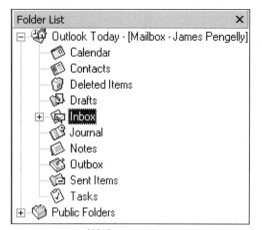

Workgroup support

Internet mail only

As you can see from the screenshots above, mail is stored differently depending on how Outlook is setup. Generally speaking, if the folder list indicates that mail is stored in a **Mailbox**, you have access to workgroup services. If mail is stored in a **Personal Folder**, you will probably only have internet email setup.

Open a Mail Inbox

If you are part of a **workgroup**, you will use a logon name and password to start Windows. When you start Outlook, the application automatically opens your own mailbox based on the logon name you use to start Windows. Data in a **mailbox** is stored on a **server** computer. This means that you can access all your items (mail, contacts, appointments and so on) from **any PC** in the workgroup, when you **logon** with your user name and password.

If you use a **personal folder**, your inbox is stored on the hard disk of your PC.

Workgroup and Internet Email Addresses

To send someone an email, you usually need to know his or her email address.

With workgroup mail, you only need to know someone's name to send him or her email. Also, it is likely that each person in the workgroup has several **aliases**. This means that the email server will recognise several names as belonging to the same user: for example, **davidm**, **dmartin**, **davidmartin** and **david martin**.

With internet mail, you need to know their internet email address. Internet email addresses usually comprise the name of the person to whom you are sending the mail, plus their location, which is given by the **domain name**.

An example of an internet email address is: **james@courseware.co.uk**

james is the name of the recipient.

@courseware.co.uk is the domain name, or location of James.

Open Outlook

Outlook is part of the Office 2000 suite. You will find that many features in Outlook are similar to those in other Office programs. The Outlook application can be started from the Office 2000 Shortcut bar, from the Desktop and from the Start menu by clicking its shortcut icon ▣.

To start Outlook

- Click the **Start** [Start] button and display the **Programs** menu

- Select the **Microsoft Outlook** program item [Microsoft Outlook]

The **Outlook** window is opened.

The Outlook Window

The layout of the Outlook application window is similar in some respects to other Office applications. It has a Title and Menu bar, several toolbars and a Status bar.

The main part of the window is divided into several frames (or **panes**). The pane(s) on the left are used to navigate the window. The rest of the screen (the **Information Viewer**) shows the **component** selected.

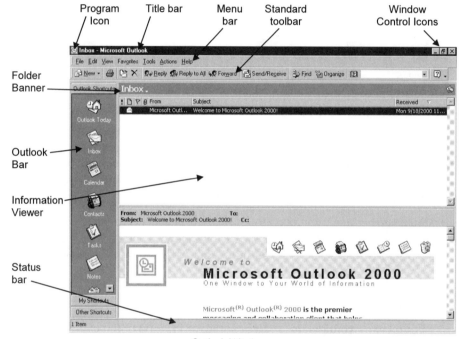

Outlook Window

Note Your Outlook screen may look quite different to the above with more or fewer panels and toolbars. You will learn how to change the display later.

The **Title** bar, **Menu** bar, scroll bars and **Status** bar work as they do for other Office programs (see page 183 for details). The **Help** system is also the same (see page 194).

The Outlook Toolbar

When you first start Outlook the **Standard** toolbar is displayed. The buttons
on the Standard toolbar change depending on which Outlook component is
selected.

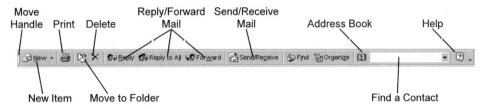

Standard toolbar with Inbox selected

Otherwise, working with toolbars is the same as for Microsoft Word. Refer
back to page 185 for notes on changing the display of toolbars.

The Information Viewer

This part of the Outlook screen changes depending on the Outlook
component (or **folder**) in use. Below is the **Information Viewer** for the
Inbox folder, which displays mail items.

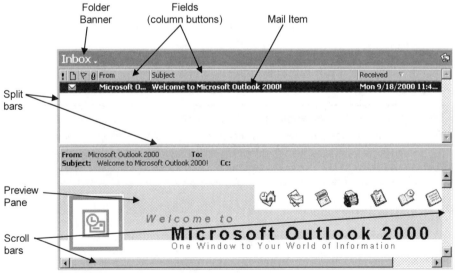

Information Viewer Window

- To make panes larger or smaller, click-and-drag on the **split bar**

The Folder List

The **Folder Banner** shows the name of the **folder** displayed in the **Information Viewer**.

By clicking the arrow on the **Folder Banner**, you can view a list of all the components and folders available in Outlook. This list resembles the Explorer pane in Windows. You can use it to open different components in the Information Viewer.

- On the **Folder Banner**, click the arrow to the right of "Inbox" - the **folder list** is revealed

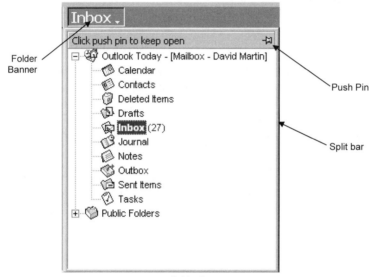

Folder List

- Click the **Push Pin** to keep the folder list open

Tip If you have a large monitor, keeping the folder list open makes it easier to navigate between components. On a smaller monitor though you may find it takes up too much space to keep on-screen all the time.

- Click on **Contacts**

The **Contacts** folder is displayed in the Information Viewer.

- Now click back on **Inbox**

- Close the folder list by clicking the **Close** ⊠ button to the right of the words **Folder List**

The Outlook Bar and Group Buttons

Group button

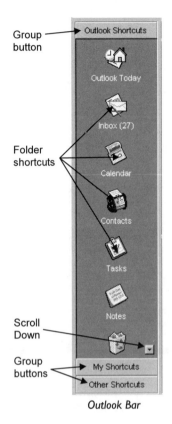

Folder shortcuts

Scroll Down

Group buttons

Outlook Bar

The **Outlook Bar** is the group of icons on the left-hand side of the screen.

The Outlook Bar is the easiest way of selecting the Outlook component or folder you want displayed in the **Information Viewer**

For ease of use the various components of Outlook are split into three groups by default: **Outlook Shortcuts**, **My Shortcuts** and **Other Shortcuts**.

Clicking on a group button will reveal other Outlook components.

Change Display Modes

Special toolbars are normally displayed automatically when you select the relevant component. However, you can also change the display of toolbars, and other elements of the screen, using the View menu.

To show and hide elements of the screen

- From the **Menu** bar, select the **View** menu

- Select an option (**Outlook Bar**, **Folder List**, **Preview Pane**, **AutoPreview**, **Status Bar** and so on) to toggle that element on and off

Inbox View menu

- Click **Toolbars** and select the **Advanced** toolbar

- Arrange the screen display to best suit your monitor, but try to keep the **Folder List** and **Advanced** toolbar displayed

Close Outlook

You will probably want to leave Outlook running in the background while you are working at your computer, so that you can receive email and view task reminders.

However, you may want to exit Outlook at some point in order to free up more resources on your PC.

To exit Outlook

- From the **File** menu, select **Exit** (*SpeedKey:* [Alt]+[F4])

OR

- At the top right-hand corner of the Outlook window, click the **Close** button [X]

OR

- At the top left-hand corner of the Outlook window, double-click the **Program** Icon [icon]

Composing Mail Messages

Create, format and send mail

Create a **new message** ☐
Address a message to one or more **recipients** ☐
Enter a message **subject** ☐
Enter and delete message **text** ☐
Attach a file to a message ☐
Create and insert an **AutoSignature** ☐
Set the message **priority** ☐
Use the **Spelling Checker** ☐
Send a message ☐

Mail Messages

An email message is created rather like a document in a word processor, such as MS Word. At its simplest, you can create a mail message simply by typing some text.

However, you do not have to restrict your messages to plain text. You can send messages that include **formatted** text, inserted **files** and **objects** (attachments) and a **signature**. You can even use other Microsoft Office applications, such as Word itself, or PowerPoint or Excel, to create the mail.

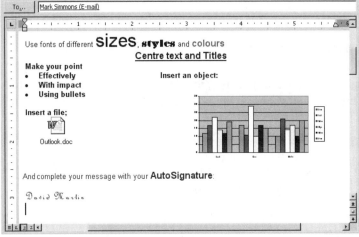

Rich text email

If you are creating mail for sending over the internet, it is usually best to create simple text messages.

Messages containing formatted text, attachments and graphics cannot be read by all mail systems, so the person receiving your message may not be able to make sense of it.

Also, using graphics and attachments increases the size of the message and therefore the time it takes for you to send it and for the recipient to receive it.

Steps to Sending a Mail Message

Creating an email in Outlook itself can include up to eight steps, as shown below:

♦   **Address** the message to the recipient and copy to others (if required).

♦   Enter a **subject**.

♦   Type in the body of the **message**.

♦   Add **attachments** (optional).

♦   Add a **signature** (optional).

♦   Set any **send options** (optional).

♦   Check the **spelling** (optional).

♦   **Send** the message.

You will also want to set **default** options to use, so that you can create most of your emails with a minimum of effort.

Message Formats and Editors

A message can be almost any size. However, it is good practice to keep the mail message short and to the point and to use **attachments** for more complex documents.

You can use the following formats for email:

♦   **Plain text** - use to send mail to people with older mail systems or to keep the message size as small as possible.

♦   **Rich text** - use to include formatted text.

♦   **HTML** - similar to rich text but can include backgrounds and web pages.

You also have the choice of using the Outlook mail editor or MS Word to edit messages. Using Word gives you access to a far greater range of formatting and editing tools.

The Outlook rich text editor is the default setting. It gives you the ability to enhance your message for visual impact, whilst allowing it to be read easily by most other email systems. Also it reduces the risk of spreading virus infections that can attach themselves to Word documents (See the topic on page 85).

To set the default message format

- If necessary, start Outlook

- From the **Outlook** window select the **Tools** menu, then **Options...** and click the **Mail Format** tab

The **Mail Format** options are displayed.

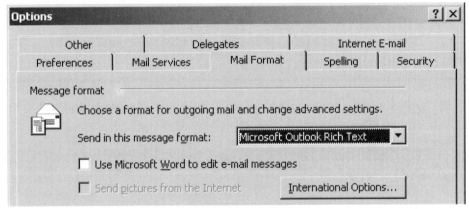

Options dialogue box

- If necessary, from the **Send in this message format:** drop-down list select **Microsoft Outlook Rich Text**

This option is probably already selected.

- Click **OK**

Note If you choose the **Plain Text** option and use Word as your mail editor, you will find that you are able to *create* rich text messages, but be warned that these will be sent and seen as plain text. Any formatting you add will be discarded.

Start a New Email Message

The first step in creating a message is to create the mail item itself.

To create the mail item

- On the **Outlook Bar** or from the **Folder List**, select the **Inbox**

The **Inbox Information Viewer** is displayed.

- On the **Standard** toolbar, click **New Mail Message** 📄 New ▾

OR

- From the **File** menu, select **New** and then **Mail Message**
  (*SpeedKey:* Ctrl + N)

Tip Ctrl + N creates a new item relevant to the current component.
You can create a new message from within any component by
pressing Ctrl + Shift + M .

Outlook opens a new window for the mail item. The Mail window has its
own menu, toolbars and window control icons.

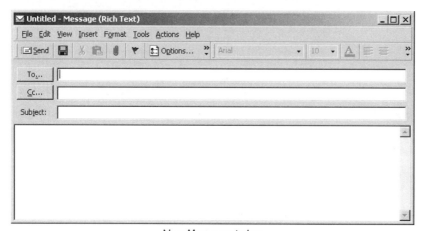

New Message window

The mail item also appears as an icon on the Taskbar, so that you can switch
between it and other Windows programs.

Mail item's Taskbar icon

Address a Mail Message

You can complete this exercise in one of two ways, depending on whether you can create mail for a workgroup recipient or for an internet mail recipient (or both if you prefer).

To address the message to a workgroup recipient

To do this, you can simply type the name of the recipient in the **To...** box. Outlook also contains a feature to help you lookup ambiguous names.

Note If you do not have access to workgroup mail, go to the next topic on the page following.

- In the **To...** box, type the name of the recipient - for this exercise, type just the **first** letter of your own name

- On the **Message** toolbar, click the **Check Names** button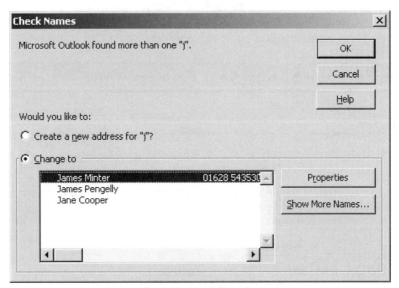

If the name typed is ambiguous (and with just one letter entered it hopefully will be) the **Check Names** dialogue box is displayed.

Check Names dialogue box

- In the **Change to** list box, select your name

- Click **OK**

Your name now appears in the **To...** box. Note that the name is underlined, indicating that Outlook recognises it as a valid recipient of email.

To address mail to an internet mail recipient

Internet mail does not use people's proper names, because too many people in the world have the same name. Instead people can have one or more internet email addresses. If you type the internet email address into an address line, the mail will be delivered to that address.

To copy mail to several recipients ①

You can also address the same mail item to as many recipients as you like. There are several ways to do this:

o Enter all the recipients in the **To...** box, separating each name with a semi-colon (for example, `James Pengelly;Jane Cooper;James Minter;development@courseware.co.uk`)

OR

o Enter the main recipient in the **To...** box and copy the message to one or more recipients using the **Cc...** box (**Cc** stands for **Carbon Copy**)

Using either of the above methods means that all recipients will be able to see who else has received the mail. If you prefer, any (or all) recipient's names to be hidden, use the **Bcc...** box (**Bcc** stands for **Blind Carbon Copy**).

o If the **Bcc...** box is not displayed, from the **View** menu, select **Bcc Field**

o Enter recipients you want to be hidden from other addressees

Note You can use either the **Cc** or **Bcc** boxes without using the **To** box.

Practice

- *Type the following internet mail address in the **Cc...** box:*
  `development@courseware.co.uk`

If you completed the first exercise, the message is now addressed to two recipients.

- *If necessary, display the **Bcc...** box and enter the address* `nobody@nowhere.com`

- *Click in the **Subject:** box*

Outlook checks each address and underlines it if it is valid.

Note If the address or name is not underlined, check the spelling carefully. Note that in the case of internet mail, Outlook only checks that the address is in the correct format - this does not guarantee that it exists.

Enter a Subject Heading

You will receive very many mail messages, which you will want to deal with quickly.

The main way of identifying the topic of a mail item is the **subject**, which, along with the sender, is often the only part of the mail item displayed when it is first received.

You will come to appreciate mail that includes a clear and meaningful subject heading. The recipients of your mail messages will feel the same.

To enter a subject heading

The cursor should be in the **Subject:** box.

*   Type: `Using Microsoft Outlook`

This is the title that will appear in the recipient's Inbox.

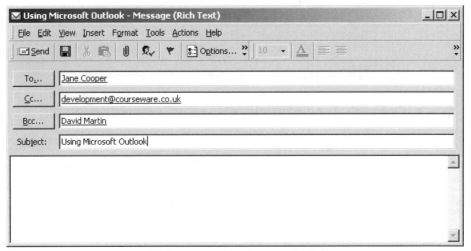

Mail item correctly addressed and titled

Tip   As well as clicking in the boxes to select them, you can also use `Tab` to move to the next field or `Shift`+`Tab` to move to the previous field.

Create the Message

As discussed above, you can make your message text as simple or complex as you like. The formatting tools used work in the same way as other word processors.

To enter the message text

- `Tab` to or click in the main message area

The cursor is positioned in the main body of the message.

- Type the following message, pressing the `Enter` key after each paragraph (¶)

```
Outlook provides several features
to help you to enhance your
messages, including:¶
Bold, Underlining and Italics¶
Different fonts and font sizes¶
Different font colours¶
Paragraph alignment¶
Bulleted lists¶
```

- Optionally, use the formatting tools to style the text

To delete text ①

o Press `Backspace` to delete text to the left of the insertion point

o Click-and-drag across text and press `Delete` to delete selected text

Add a File Attachment

You can include one or more data files with your email message. Any type of file can be attached to a message, including documents, spreadsheets, graphics and so on.

You need to take several points into consideration when using file attachments though:

♦ Most, but not *all*, email systems can receive file attachments.

♦ The recipient can only open and edit the attachment if they have the correct software - they cannot open the attachment in their email editor.

♦ Large file attachments can be very slow to send and receive.

♦ Some email systems will reject messages if they exceed a certain size (often 1 MB).

♦ File attachments can contain computer viruses.

To attach a file to a message

- On the **Message** toolbar, click the **Insert File** button 📎 **OR** from the **Insert** menu, select **File...**

The **Insert File** dialogue box is displayed.

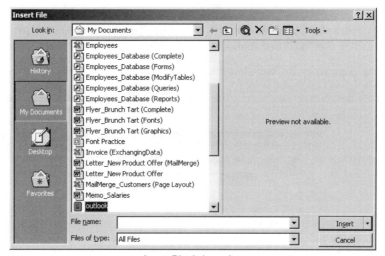

Insert File dialogue box

- Select the file called **outlook** and click the **Insert** button

The file is inserted into the message at the insertion point.

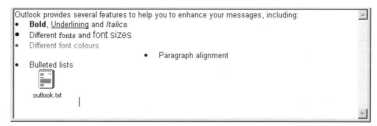

File attachment

Tip   If you change your mind about including an attachment, click the attachment icon and press `Delete`.

Add a Signature

A **signature** (or **auto-signature**) is text that can be added to messages. You can use a default signature on all messages and/or insert a signature manually.

A typical signature might include your name, job title, and telephone and fax number. However you can create signatures with any text you like. They can be useful for creating "form" email, such as an acknowledgement of receipt or to add a legal disclaimer to a message.

To create a default signature

- Minimise the message window

- From the **Outlook** window, select the **Tools** menu, then **Options** and click the **Mail Format** tab then click the **Signature Picker...** button

The **Signature Picker** dialogue box is displayed.

- Click **New...** to display the **Create New Signature** dialogue box.

Create New Signature dialogue box

- In the **Enter a name for your new signature** box, type: Personal

A name for the signature is entered.

- Under **Choose how to create your Signature**, select **Start with a blank signature**

- Click **Next >**

The **Edit Signature** box is displayed.

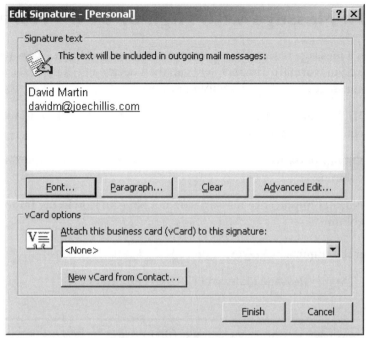

Edit Signature dialogue box

- In the **Signature text box**, type your name and press `Enter`

- Type your email address

- Select the email address and use the **Font...** button to format it as underlined text

Your email address is entered.

- Click **Finish** then **OK** twice

The signature is added to the picker and should appear as your default signature in the next message you create.

To insert a signature manually

You may want to create a range of signatures for different purposes. Signatures do not always have to go at the end of the email. They can be used like AutoText to create standard messages quickly.

- Switch back to the mail message and create a new paragraph at the end of the message text

- From the **Insert** menu, select **Signature** - a submenu displays a list of signatures available

- Select **Personal** - the text is inserted into your message

Send a Message with High or Low Priority

When a message is sent, its importance can be set to **High** or **Low** (as opposed to **Normal**). The recipient can then decide in which order to deal with messages based upon their importance.

♦ **High importance** messages have a red icon ⁞ in the **Importance** column ! of mail folders.

♦ **Low importance** messages have a blue icon ↓ in the **Importance** column.

♦ **Normal importance** messages do not have an icon in the **Importance** column.

To set the importance level

- On the **Message** toolbar, click **High Importance** !

Tip Click the button again to reset the message to Normal importance.

Use the Spelling Checker

It is a good idea to check your spelling before sending a message. Outlook uses the same spelling checker as the other Office applications.

To check spelling

- From the **Message** window, select the **Tools** menu, then **Spelling** (*SpeedKey:* F7)

Unless you have selected text, the spelling check will begin at the insertion point.

When an incorrect word is found, the **Spelling** dialogue box is displayed.

Spelling dialogue box

- Select one of the following

Select	To
Ignore or **Ignore All**	Skip only the current instance of the word or all instances of the word.
Change or **Change All**	Correct a word or all instances of the same word with the spelling in the **Suggestions:** box.
Add	Add a new spelling to the custom dictionary.

- When the spell check is complete, click **OK**

Send a Message

You are now ready to send your message.

- On the **Message** toolbar, click the **Send** button 📧 Send
  (*SpeedKey:* Ctrl + Enter)

The message is sent to the **Outbox**.

Delivering Mail

Workgroup mail is sent and received almost instantaneously - it only appears in the **Outbox** for a few seconds before being delivered.

However, if you are sending an email message via the internet, the message will remain in the Outbox until you next connect.

All sent messages are moved to your **Sent Items** folder, allowing you to keep or discard them.

To send and receive mail

You can setup Outlook to check dial-up internet connections for mail regularly.

- From the **Tools** menu, select **Options** then click the **Internet E-mail** tab

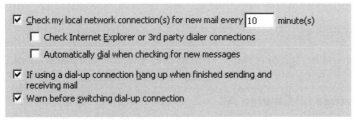

Options dialogue box - Internet E-mail tab

Note If you are using Outlook in internet only mode, these options appear on the **Mail Delivery** tab.

- Check the **Check my local network** box to have Outlook check for mail automatically

- Enter the checking interval in minutes into the text box

OR

- Clear the check box if you do not want Outlook to check automatically

- If you use a dial-up connection to the internet, check the **Automatically dial** box

- Click **OK**

If you do not want Outlook to dial-up automatically, or if you just want to check for mail at a particular time, you can force the delivery of mail by clicking the **Send/Receive** button ![Send/Receive] on the **Inbox** toolbar.

Use Cut, Copy and Paste in Outlook

You can use the Windows Clipboard to move and copy text within a message, between one or more open messages or to/from an open message from/to another file, such as a word processed document or a spreadsheet.

To move or copy text ①

o   Click-and-drag across the text to select it

o   From the **Edit** menu, select **Cut** (*SpeedKey:* Ctrl + X) or **Copy** (*SpeedKey:* Ctrl + C)

o   Position the insertion point where you want to move the text

For example, you could click somewhere else in the message or use the Windows Taskbar to switch to another message or other document and click there.

o   From the **Edit** menu, select **Paste** (*SpeedKey:* Ctrl + V)

The text is pasted at the insertion point. You can paste the same text again as often as you like until you use Cut or Copy again.

Tip   If the message is in rich text or HTML format, you can also move or copy graphics, tables, charts and other objects.

Practice

- *Open the **Flyer_Brunch Tart (Complete)** document in Word*

- *Press* Ctrl + A *to select all the text then copy it*

- *Close Word*

- *In Outlook, create a new mail message addressed to yourself with the subject* Training

- *Paste the text into the mail message*

- *On the **Message** toolbar, click the **Send** button* ⟦Send⟧ *(SpeedKey:* Ctrl + Enter *)*

- *Click **Send/Receive** ⟦Send/Receive⟧ now to deliver your mail*

Reading and Replying to Mail

Open mail to read it and reply to or forward a message

Lesson 54

Collect and **open** new mail ☐
Reply to and **forward** a message ☐
Use different Reply/Forward **options** ☐
Open and **save** a file attachment ☐

Open a Mail Message

Messages that are sent to you appear in your **Inbox**. When new mail arrives in your **Inbox**, the header appears in bold, indicating that you have not read it.

To preview a message

Outlook may already be setup to preview messages in the Inbox. There are two ways to preview messages:

◆ **AutoPreview** displays the first few lines of the message under the mail header.

◆ **Preview Pane** displays the full message in a panel below the Inbox.

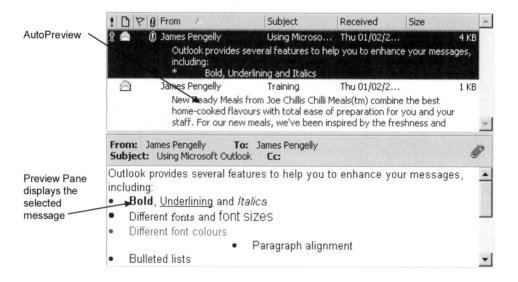

AutoPreview

Preview Pane
displays the
selected
message

- If the **Advanced** toolbar is not displayed, from the **View** menu, select **Toolbars** then **Advanced**

Buttons on the Advanced toolbar let you toggle AutoPreview and the Preview Pane on and off.

- On the **Advanced** toolbar, click **Preview Pane** and **AutoPreview**

To open a message

If you didn't complete the previous lesson, get your colleagues to send you some emails (with a file attachment) or send a message to yourself.

- If necessary, click the Send/Receive button so that the message you sent to yourself appears in the **Inbox**

The message is displayed in the Inbox.

- Double-click the message to open it

Reply To and Forward a Message

There are several options for replying to and forwarding messages.

Click	To
Reply	Send a response only to the original sender.
Reply to All	Send a response to the sender and recipients in the **Cc** and **Bcc** boxes.
Forward	Forward the message to a new person whose name/address you type in the **To** line

Each of these buttons opens a new message containing the original message.

- Click the Reply button

- Type in a response, confirming receipt of the message

A new mail message is created with the text from the original message at the bottom.

- Click the **Send** button Send

The message is sent for delivery.

- Close the original message

By default, when you reply to a message, the original message is included in the reply.

You can change the default options to exclude the original message or to include it in a different format. If you do not want to include the original message in a specific reply, you can simply delete the text.

To remove the original message from one reply

- Click-and-drag to select the text of the original message

- Press `Delete`

To change the default options

- In Outlook, from the **Tools** menu, select **Options...**

- From the **Preferences** tab, click **E-mail Options...**

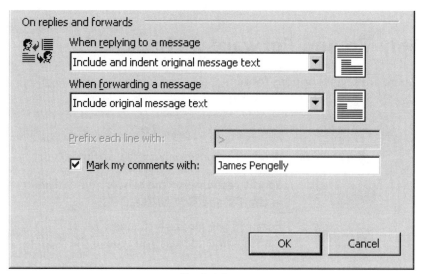

Email options

- From the **When replying** list box, select an option to apply to all future emails

The effect of the option is previewed in the graphic.

- Click **OK** to exit both dialogue boxes

Open and Save a File Attachment

An attached file appears as an icon in a message.

> **Warning** File attachments can contain viruses that can damage your computer. The virus will be activated when you **open** the attachment.
> Do not open file attachments that you were not expecting to receive. It is also wise to install an up-to-date virus scanner capable of checking incoming email.

To open an attached file

- Open your message again

- Double-click on the attached file's icon

  outlook.txt

The **Opening Mail Attachment** dialogue box is displayed.

Opening Mail Attachment dialogue box

This dialogue box warns you that attachments may contain viruses or malicious scripts. If you have any doubts about the source of the attachment, click **Cancel** now.

You are also given the option of opening the attachment directly from the message or to save it as a new file on disk. In most cases it is wise to use the **Save it to disk** option so that you can check the file for viruses before opening it. Use Windows Explorer to open the file after saving it into a folder on your PC.

If you open the attachment, you can save it as a file using the application's **Save As** command anyway.

- .TXT type files cannot contain viruses, so for this exercise, select the **Open it** option button

- Click **OK**

The file is opened in your default text editor (probably MS Notepad).

- Click the **Close** button ⊠ to exit Notepad

Tip   If a message contains several attachments that you want to save to disk, from the **File** menu, select **Save Attachments...** This opens a dialogue box allowing you to pick one or more attachments to save.

Contacts

Create and manage a list of email addresses in the Contacts folder

---

Lesson 55

Add and delete a **mail address** from the **Contacts** list ☐
Update the Contacts list from **new mail** ☐
Create a mail **distribution list** ☐
Address messages using a distribution list ☐

Create a New Contact

The **Contacts List** lets you store contact information, such as telephone, email and address details, for friends and associates.

To create a new contact

- On the **Outlook** Bar, click the **Contacts List**

The **Contacts Information Viewer** is displayed.

- On the **Standard** toolbar, click the down arrow on the **New** button and select **Contact OR** from the **File** menu, select **New** then **Contact** (*SpeedKey:* Ctrl + Shift + C) **OR** double-click a clear area in the **Contacts Information Viewer**

Click to enter data using a standard form

Select or type a name to file the contact by

Type or paste text and graphics to create notes on the contact

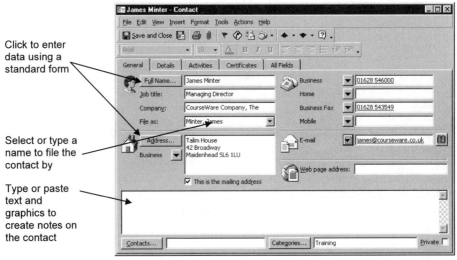

New Contact window

- Enter the details shown in the screenshot
- Click **Save and Close** ![Save and Close] to add the name to your contacts

Practice

- *Add yourself as a contact - you will use this to create an email calling card*

To create a contact from incoming mail ⏱

o You can create a contact from new mail messages simply by dragging the message onto the **Contacts** icon ![icon] on the Outlook Bar

A new **Contact** form is opened with several fields (email address, name and so on) filled in automatically.

Browse Contacts

By default, contacts are displayed as **Address Cards**. The contacts are organised by the **File as** field, which defaults to the contact's last name. Each address card shows the File As field plus address, telephone and email details.

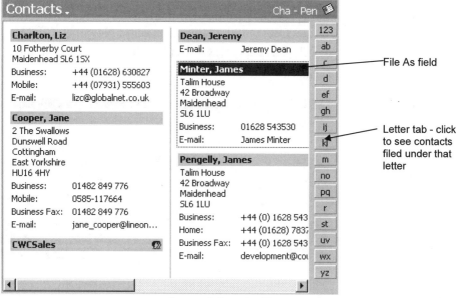

Contacts Information Viewer

o Click the **File As** field to select the contact

o Double-click to open the contact form for editing

To delete a contact

- Click the **File As** field for the **James Minter** contact then on the **Standard** toolbar, click **Delete** ✕ (*SpeedKey*: `Delete`)

Create a Personal Distribution List

If you frequently send mail to the same group of people, you can create a **Personal Distribution List** (PDL) for that group. When you address a message to that group, each individual in the group receives it. You can add both workgroup and internet email addresses to the PDL.

You can store PDLs in your Contacts list.

To create a PDL

- From the **Contacts** screen, on the **Standard** toolbar, click the drop-down arrow on the **New** button and select **Distribution List**

A new window is opened to allow you to enter the addresses of recipients in the list.

- Click in the **Name:** box

- Type Outlook Training Mail List

This name will be used to identify the list in the Contacts folder.

- Click the **Select Members...** button

The **Select Members** dialogue box is displayed.

- Select the name of a colleague

- Click **Add ->** to add the name to the PDL

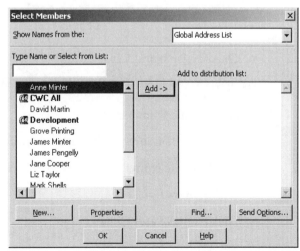

Select Members dialogue box

- Select further names as required and add them to the list

Additional names are separated by semi-colons (;).

Note If a recipient does not appear in the list shown, select another list (the **Contacts** list for example) from the **Show Names from the:** drop-down list box. You can address the same message from multiple address lists.

- Click **OK**

The **Select Members** dialogue box is closed and the PDL is updated to show the names you picked.

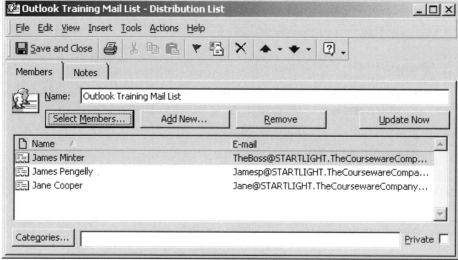

Distribution list

- Click the **Save and Close** button

The list is saved to the Contacts folder.

To remove a name from a PDL

- Locate the PDL in your Contacts List and double-click its **File As** field

- Select a name from the list

- Click **Remove**

- Click the **Save and Close** button

Use Contact Data in Mail Messages

There are many ways in which contact information can be used in conjunction with mail messages.

To use contact data in email

- Select the PDL contact you just created

- From the **Actions** menu, select **New Message to Contact**

A new mail message is opened with the contact(s) - in this case the name of the distribution list - added to the **To...** address field

---

Tip   You can also use the name of the contact to address mail manually by typing the contact name into an address field. If the name has been recognised it will be underlined.

- Enter a subject and message along the lines of `I'm learning to use Outlook`

- Arrange the Outlook application window and the message window together on-screen

- Drag-and-drop the contact card you created for yourself into the message

When you receive a contact card, you can drag-and-drop it onto the **Contacts** icon in the Outlook Bar to add the card to your own contacts list (The recipient will require Outlook to use the data).

- Close the message window

Outlook prompts you to save a copy of the unsent message to the **Drafts** folder.

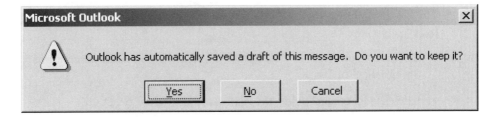

- Click **No** to discard the message

- Delete the PDL contact you created (unless you want to keep it)

Organising Mail

Use the Find and Sort tools to locate mail and use folders to organise messages

Lesson 56

Sort messages by name, subject and date ☐
Search for text in your messages ☐
Highlight mail items ☐
Create a **mail folder** ☐
Move messages to a mail folder ☐
Delete and **recycle** messages ☐

Sort and Find Messages

As you receive more and more messages, finding a particular item of mail can become difficult.

There are two simple ways to locate a message. You can sort messages by any of the field headings on the Inbox Information Viewer (**Importance**, **From**, **Subject**, **Received** and so on). Alternatively, use the **Find** feature to look for messages containing particular text.

To sort messages

- If you do not have very many messages in your Inbox, get your colleagues to send you some mail before starting this exercise

- Select the Inbox

- In the Inbox Information Viewer, click the **From** field header

  `From`

The list of mail messages is sorted by sender in ascending alphabetical order.

- Click the **From** field header again - the list is resorted in descending alphabetical order

- Click the **Received** field - the list is sorted by date received

- Click the **Subject** field - the list is sorted by subject again

To find a message

- On the **Standard** toolbar, click **Find**

The following panel opens above the **Inbox**.

Find Panel

- Ensure that the **Search all text in the message** check box is selected

- In the **Look for:** text box, type in some text that appears in the message you are trying to find - type `Outlook`

- Click **Find Now**

The search takes place and the results are displayed.

- To return all the other messages to the Inbox, click the **Clear Search** option in the **Find** box

- Close the **Find** box by clicking the **Close** ✕ button to the right of **Advanced Find**

Highlight Messages

If a message requires some sort of response in the future, or if you want to keep track of it, you can mark the item for follow up.

To mark a mail item for follow up

- Select the **Using Microsoft Outlook** message that you sent to yourself

- From the **Actions** menu, select **Flag for Follow Up...**
  (*SpeedKey:* `Ctrl`+`Shift`+`G`)

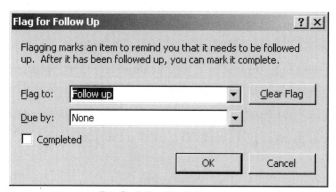

Flag for Follow Up dialogue box

Optionally, you can change the type of flag by selecting from the **Flag to:** box (containing options such as **Forward** or **Call**). You can also set a date to follow up by using the **Due by:** box.

- For this exercise, click **OK**

The message is marked with a red flag in the **Flag** column.

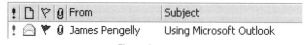

Flagged message

To remove a message flag

- Select the message again and press `Ctrl`+`Shift`+`G`

- Click the **Clear Flag** button

Create a New Mail Folder

You can use folders and subfolders to store and organise information.

Once you begin receiving messages, you will want to organise them so that they will be easy to find at a later date.

To create a folder

For this exercise, we will create a subfolder of the **Inbox**, in which to store the mail generated by this training course.

- In the Inbox Information Viewer, from the **File** menu, select **New** then **Folder...** (*SpeedKey:* [Ctrl]+[Shift]+[E])

The **Create New Folder** dialogue box is displayed.

Create New Folder dialogue box

- In the **Name:** box, type Training

- In the **Select where to place the folder:** window, select the **Inbox** icon

- Click **OK**

- When Outlook prompts you to add a shortcut to the folder to the **Outlook Bar**, click **No**

The **Training** folder is created as a subfolder of the Inbox.

To expand and collapse folders

You can expand and collapse the view of folders in the Folder List in the same way as you use Windows Explorer.

- If the **Folder List** is not displayed, on the **Advanced** toolbar, click **Folder List** ▦

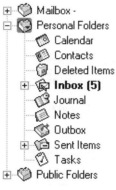

Folder List

- To expand a folder, click the plus sign (⊞) next to the parent folder name

- To collapse a folder, click the minus sign (⊟) next to the parent folder name

Move a Message to a New Mail Folder

Once you have created one or more folders, you can move your messages into the folder(s) as required. The easiest way to move messages to folders is by dragging them.

To move a message using drag-and-drop

- If necessary, expand the **Inbox** icon so that the **Training** subfolder is visible

- Select the **Inbox** itself so that its contents are displayed in the Information Viewer

- Select the mail messages you have received during the course then click-and-drag them over the **Training** folder icon

> **Tip**   Select several items together by holding `Shift` when selecting.
>
>   Select several separate items by holding `Ctrl` when selecting.

- Release the mouse button

The messages are moved to the subfolder.

> **Note** You can also use **Cut, Copy** and **Paste** (**Edit** menu) to move or
>   copy mail items or **Move/Copy to Folder** (also **Edit** menu).

Delete a Message

You can delete a message, file, or other item you are reading, or you can select and delete one or more items in the folder contents list.

To delete an item

- Select or open the item(s) you want to delete - select the **Training** folder

- On the **Standard** toolbar, click the **Delete** button ✕ OR from the **Edit** menu, select **Delete** (*SpeedKey:* `Delete`)

The folder is moved to the **Deleted Items** folder.

Use the Mail Bin

Deleted items are moved to the **Deleted Items** folder, which works like the Windows **Recycle Bin**. By default, items stay in this folder for **2 months** (at which point they are deleted automatically).

To retrieve an item ①

o Select items from the **Deleted Items** folder and move them to another **Outlook** folder (for example, the **Inbox**)

To permanently delete mail items ①

o Select items in the **Deleted Items** folder and press `Delete`

Review of Information and Communication

Review the topics covered during the module and identify areas for further practice and goals for the future

---

Review

(Check **objectives**) ☐
(Complete **consolidation** exercise) ☐
(Identify topics for **further** study) ☐
(**Answers** to practice questions) ☐

Check Objectives

Congratulations on completing the lessons for ECDL Module 7 "Information and Communication".

You have learned to:

♦   **Browse** web pages on the internet and open **hyperlinks**

♦   Make use of **Search Engines** and **Directories** to locate information on the world wide web

♦   **Print** from a web page

♦   Create and manage a list of **favourite** web pages

♦   **Customise** Internet Explorer to suit your requirements

♦   Create, format and send **mail**

♦   **Open** mail to read it and **reply** or **forward** a message

♦   Create and manage a list of email addresses in the **Contacts** folder

♦   Use the **Find** and **Sort** tools to locate mail and use **folders** to organise messages

Make sure you have checked off each syllabus item and identified any topics you do not fully understand or remember.

Consolidation and Going Further

Tests for Module 7 can either be practice-based or question-based. Practical tests will ask you to open web pages and use the browser tools and to create and manage email.

There are further test-style questions for you to try on the CD in the folder **ECDL Tests\7 Information&Communication**

Print the document **Information & Communication Questions** and try to complete the questions unaided. Mark your own work using the **Answers** document.

> **Note** These questions are provided as a consolidation exercise. They do not make up an approved ECDL test. See page 689 for more information about the extra tests.

Going further

There are several internet topics that are not covered in the syllabus. The most important is to understand security on the web. You can find information about this in the online help and in other CourseWare training books.

There are a variety of other services available on the internet, such as FTP, newsgroups and chat. You should be able to use these confidently however, by applying what you have learned already.

Outlook contains a very large number of features, which have not been covered by this course. As well as advanced options for managing email, you can learn to use Outlook to manage all kinds of information, such as meetings, appointments and tasks.

Refer to page 744 for more details about further courses in gtslearning's range of **Learn IT** training books.

Practice Answers

Q1. Answer the following questions on web addresses:

a)   Type of service, Server location, File location
    b). Hypertext Transfer Protocol
    c) A name representing a server computer
    d) Examples could include: www.joechillis.co.uk, www.joechillis.com, www.joe-chillis.co.uk, www.joe_chillis.co.uk and so on

Notes

Appendices

Windows *Me* Quick Reference

Use the Microsoft Windows Me operating system

Appendix

Use **Windows Me** for the **Using Computers** component of ECDL ☐

This appendix is intended to supplement the information given in **Module 2** for people using **Windows *Me*** in preference to **Windows 2000**.

Even though they are completely different "beneath the hood", Windows 2000 and Windows *Me* look very similar to you, the user.

You should be able to work through most of the exercises in the course. Note that some dialogue boxes are different in Windows *Me* so you will not be able to complete every instruction. Also, you will not be able to locate some of the files or folders referred to in the **Search** topic.

To logon to Windows *Me*

o   There is no need to press $\boxed{\texttt{Ctrl}}$+$\boxed{\texttt{Alt}}$+$\boxed{\texttt{Delete}}$ to display the logon dialogue box with Windows *Me*

To get help with Windows *Me*

The **Help** system has a completely different interface to the one in Windows 2000, but it actually works in much the same way using content headings plus index and search tools.

o   From the **Start Menu**, select **Help**

The **Help and Support** window is displayed.

o   Select one of the main topic headings from the left-hand side of the screen

A list of subtopics is displayed.

o   Follow the links to locate help topics, indicated by the question mark icon ⍰ Using the desktop

o   Click a help topic to display the topic in the right-hand pane

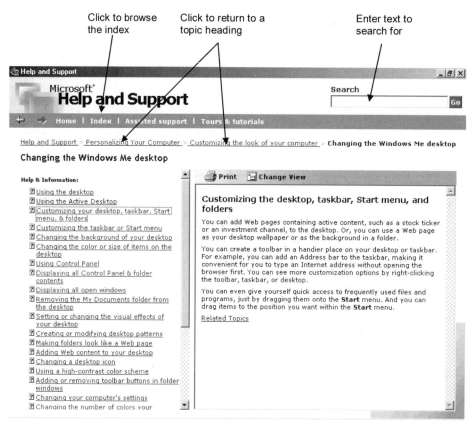

Help topics

Some topics link to the internet 🖻 <u>Active Desktop Troubleshooter</u>. Clicking the link will prompt you to connect. Other topics link to a multimedia tour 🖵 <u>Take the Desktop tour</u>.

o   Click the **Close** button ⊠ on the **Title** bar to exit Help

Outlook Express Quick Reference

Use Outlook Express to manage email and contacts

Appendix

Use **Outlook Express** for the **Communication** component of ECDL □

This appendix is intended to supplement the information given in **Module 7** for people using **Outlook Express** in preference to **Outlook**.

You will need to read through the lessons on Outlook before using this appendix.

To get started with Outlook Express

Outlook Express is used to send and receive mail over the internet. Mail is stored in **Inbox**, **Outbox** and **Sent Items** folders, just like Outlook.

> o   Open the **Outlook Express** icon ⬛ from the **Start Menu**, **Desktop** or **Taskbar**

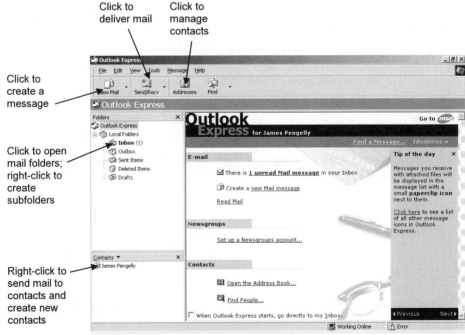

Outlook Express window

To send mail with Outlook Express

The message form is very similar to Outlook.

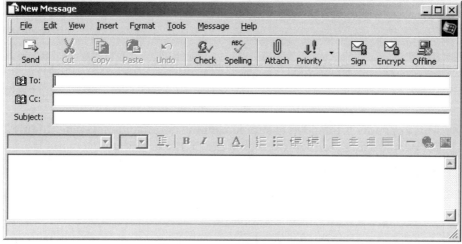

Mail message in Outlook Express

The main differences from Outlook are:

o Use **View**, **All Headers** to display the **Bcc:** field

o Signatures are setup from the main window - select **Tools**, **Options...** then click the **Signatures** tab

To manage mail

The mail folders are much the same as in Outlook.

o Use the column headers to sort mail

o Right-click in the **Folder List** to create a subfolder

o Click-and-drag messages between folders

o Click-and-drag a message to the Contacts pane to create a contact from incoming mail

To create a distribution list

Distribution lists are referred to as **Groups** in Outlook Express.

o Click the **Addresses** button

o From the **File** menu, select **New Group...** (*SpeedKey:* Ctrl + G)

o Enter a **Group Name** and **Select Members** as with Outlook

Office Setup Quick Reference

Install and configure MS Office

Appendix

(Install and **configure** MS Office) □

MS Office does not install every feature referred to in this course by default. This appendix is intended as a brief guide to using the Office Setup program.

> **Note** Please do not change the setup of applications on a computer in your workplace without first gaining the permission of your IT Administrator.

To install or upgrade MS Office

- **Make a backup of any important data files**

- Close any open software applications, including any applications running in the background, such as virus checkers (right-click the icon in the System Tray on the right-hand side of the Taskbar)

- Put the MS Office Setup CD in your computer's CD-ROM drive

- After 30 seconds, if the **Setup** program has not started, from the **Start Menu** select **Run** and type D:\setup (where **D** is the letter of your CD-ROM drive)

- Enter your user information and the product key then click **Next >**

- Read the licence agreement then select **I accept** and click **Next >**

- Click the **Install Now** button

- Remove the CD when installation is complete

To install features on-demand

Some features are not installed be default. When you try to use the feature, Office attempts to install it.

- When the **Configuring Office** dialogue box is displayed, put the Office Setup disk into you CD-ROM drive

- If you do not have access to the Setup disk, click **Cancel** then **OK** to exit the dialogue boxes and get help from your IT Administrator

---

To configure Office

- Make a backup of any important data files
- Start the Office Setup application as described above
- Click the **Add or Remove Features** button

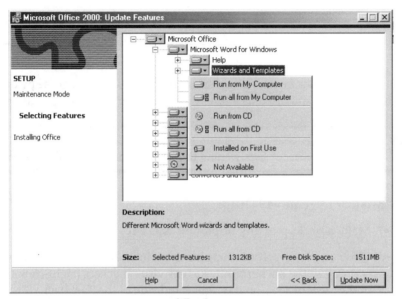

Office Setup

- Use the plus icons to expand the program groups to find the feature to install
- Click the feature and select an option from the menu

Select	To
Run from My Computer	Install the feature on your hard disk.
Run all from My Computer	Run all features below the one selected on your hard disk.
Run (all) from CD	Leave data for the feature on the CD to save disk space.
Installed on First Use	Install the feature if it is selected.
Not Available	Remove the feature

- Repeat to install other features
- Make sure there is enough disk space to install the selected features
- Click **Update Now**

Consolidation Exercises

Get further practice in all seven modules

The Data CD contains exercises for all seven modules for you to get further practice and to prepare for tests in ECDL.

These exercises are stored in the **ECDL Tests** folder.

There are two sets of exercises:

♦ **CWC Test Exercises** - these are a set of consolidation exercises testing your ability to complete tasks from the ECDL syllabus.

♦ **ECDL-F Test Samples**- these are mock tests published by the **ECDL Foundation** and are publicly available from the **British Computer Society** (www.ecdl.co.uk).

Both sets of exercises consist of a **Question Document** in Adobe Acrobat format plus exercise data, where relevant. The CourseWare exercises also include an **Answer** document for question-based exercises.

• Copy the tests to your PC and make the data files editable (see page 150)

• Print a copy of the question paper to refer to

You will need the **Adobe Acrobat Reader** to view and print the questions. If the Reader is installed, the question documents will appear with a red icon.

Adobe Acrobat document

If the reader is not installed, there is a copy on the CD (the reader is **freeware**). If you are using your computer at work, please get permission to install the software first.

To install Adobe Acrobat Reader

- Close any open application windows and disable any background programs (right-click the icon on the right-hand side of the Taskbar)

- In the root folder of the CD, open the **ar40eng** icon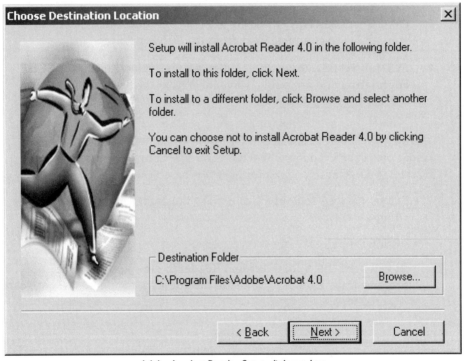
  ar40eng

The **Adobe Acrobat Reader Setup** program will start.

- Click **Next >** to continue

- Read the licence agreement then click **Accept**

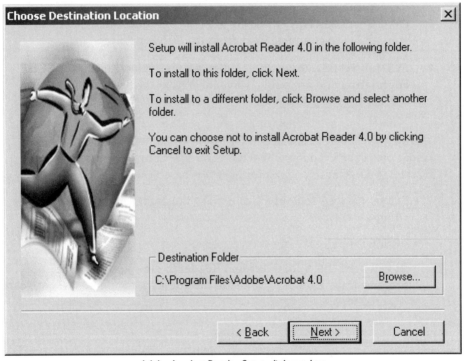

Adobe Acrobat Reader Setup dialogue box

- Click **Next >** to install the software to the default folder

ECDL Syllabus

Track your progress against the ECDL Syllabus

Use the following tables to track your progress against the ECDL syllabus.

- Put a tick in the **1** column when you have completed a topic for the first time

- Put a tick in the **X** column when you are confident that you know about/can complete the task unaided

> **Note** There is an Adobe Acrobat copy of this form in the course's data folder on the CD. Refer to page **689** for instructions on printing it.

1. Basic Concepts of Information Technology (IT)

Ref.	Task Item	Page	1	X
1.1.	**Getting Started**			
1.1.1.	*Hardware/Software/ Information Technology*			
1.1.1.1.	Understand the Basic Concepts of Hardware, Software and Information Technology (IT).	15-16		
1.1.2.	*Types of Computer*			
1.1.2.1.	Understand and distinguish between mainframe computer, minicomputer, network computer, personal computer, and laptop computer in terms of capacity, speed, cost, and typical users. Understand the terms intelligent and dumb terminal.	16-20		
1.1.3.	*Main Parts of a Personal Computer*			
1.1.3.1.	Know the main parts of a personal computer: the central processing unit (CPU), the hard disk, common input/output devices, types of memory, removable storage devices such as diskette, zip disc, CD-ROM etc. Understand the term peripheral device.	21-42		
1.2.	**Hardware**			
1.2.1.	*Central Processing Unit*			
1.2.1.1.	Understand the term central processing unit (CPU) and know what the CPU does - calculations, logic control, immediate access memory etc. Know that the speed of the CPU is measured in Megahertz (MHz).	23-24		

Ref.	Task Item	Page	I	X
1.2.2.	*Input Devices*			
1.2.2.1.	Know the various devices for inputting data into a computer such as mice, keyboards, trackballs, touchpads, light pens, etc	24-27		
1.2.3.	*Output Devices*			
1.2.3.1.	Know the most common output devices for displaying the results of processing carried out by a computer, e.g. visual display unit (VDU) or screen, liquid crystal displays (LCD) and light emitting diode displays (LED), printers such as those currently available, plotters, microfilm, speech synthesisers etc. Know where and how these devices are used.	28-31		

1.3. Storage

Ref.	Task Item	Page	I	X
1.3.1.	*Memory Storage Devices*			
1.3.1.1.	Compare the main types of memory storage device in terms of speed, cost and capacity e.g. internal/ external hard disk, zip disk, data cartridges, CD-ROM, diskette etc.	33-42		
1.3.2.	*Types of Memory*			
1.3.2.1.	Understand different types of computer memory: e.g. RAM (random-access memory), ROM (read-only memory). Say when they are used.	34-35		
1.3.3.	*Measuring Memory*			
1.3.3.1.	Know how computer memory is measured; (bit, byte, KB, MB, GB). Relate computer memory measurements to characters, fields, records, files and directories/ folders.	33, (144)		
1.3.4.	*Computer Performance*			
1.3.4.1.	Know some of the factors that impact on a computer's performance, e.g. CPU speed, RAM size, hard disk speed and capacity.	39-42		

1.4. Software

Ref.	Task Item	Page	I	X
1.4.1.	*Types of Software*			
1.4.1.1.	Know the meaning of the terms: operating systems software and applications software, and understand the distinction between them.	43		
1.4.2.	*Operating System Software*			
1.4.2.1.	Understand the main functions of an operating system. Understand the term Graphical User Interface (GUI) and give examples. Be aware of the main advantages of using a GUI interface.	43-46		
1.4.3.	*Applications Software*			
1.4.3.1.	List some common applications together with their uses, e.g. word processing, spreadsheets, database, payroll, presentation tools, desktop publishing and multimedia applications.	46-47		
1.4.4.	*Systems Development*			
1.4.4.1.	Understand how computer-based systems are developed. Know about the process of research, analysis, programming, and testing often used in developing computer-based systems.	48-50		

Ref.	Task Item	Page	I	X

1.5. Information Networks

1.5.1. LAN and WAN

1.5.1.1.	Know the definitions of local area networks (LAN) and wide area networks (WAN). Know about the advantages of group working and sharing resources over a network.	51-55		

1.5.2. The Telephone Network in computing

1.5.2.1.	Understand the use of the telephone network in computing. Understand the terms Public Switched Data Network (PSDN), Integrated Service Digital Network (ISDN), satellite communications. Understand the terms fax, telex, modem, digital, analogue, baud, (measured in bps – bits per second).	56-58		

1.5.3. Electronic Mail

1.5.3.1.	Understand the term Electronic Mail and know the uses of e-mail. Understand what is needed to send and receive e-mail. Detail some of the information and communications technology (ICT) equipment needed to use e-mail.	59		

1.5.4. The Internet

1.5.4.1.	Know what the Internet is. Understand the concept of the Internet and its main uses. Understand the economics of Internet mail systems relative to other mail delivery methods. Know what a search engine is. Understand the distinction between the Internet and the World Wide Web (WWW).	60-63		

1.6. Computers in Everyday Life

1.6.1. Computers in the Home

1.6.1.1.	Know some of the uses of the PC at home e.g. hobbies, household accounts, working from home, projects and homework, using e-mail and the Internet.	64-65		

1.6.2. Computers at Work or in Education

1.6.2.1.	Know the uses of office applications; give examples of the types of computer based systems used in business, industry, government and education. Be aware of where a computer might be more appropriate than a person for carrying out a task and where not.	65-66, 69-71		

1.6.3. Computers in Daily Life

1.6.3.1.	Be aware of the uses of computers in everyday life (in supermarkets or libraries, at the doctor's surgery, the use of smart cards etc).	67-68		

Ref.	Task Item	Page	I	X
1.7.	**IT and Society**			
1.7.1.	*A Changing World*			
1.7.1.1.	Understand the terms Information Society, Information Superhighway. Know some of the implications of the Year 2000 issue (Y2K). Understand the concept of Electronic Commerce.	72-76		
1.7.2.	*A Good Workspace*			
1.7.2.1.	Understand what elements and practices can help create a good working environment e.g. frequent breaks away from the computer, appropriate positioning of screens, chairs and keyboards, provision of adequate lighting and ventilation.	76-77		
1.7.3.	*Health and Safety*			
1.7.3.1.	Be aware of Health and Safety precautions when using a computer like ensuring that power cables are safely secured, and that power points are not overloaded. Know about injuries common in a bad working environment e.g. repetitive strain injury (RSI), eye strain caused by screen glare, problems associated with bad posture.	78		
1.8.	**Security, Copyright and the Law**			
1.8.1.	*Security*			
1.8.1.1.	Know about the purpose and value of backing store of computer files to removable storage devices. Know how to protect a personal computer against intrusion. Know about privacy issues associated with personal computers, e.g. protecting the computer, adopting good password policies. Know what happens to your data and files if there is a power cut.	81-84		
1.8.2.	*Computer Viruses*			
1.8.2.1.	Understand the term virus when used in computing. Be aware how viruses can enter a computer system. Understand the dangers of downloading files onto files onto your computer. Know about some anti–virus measures.	85-87		
1.8.3.	*Copyright*			
1.8.3.1.	Understand software copyright and the security and legal issues associated with copying, sharing and lending diskettes. Understand some of the implications of transferring files across a networks. Understand the terms shareware, freeware, and user licences.	88-89		
1.8.4.	*Data Protection Act*			
1.8.4.1.	Know the Data Protection Act in your country. Understand the implications of the Data Protection Act. Describe some of the uses of personal data.	89-90		

2. Using the Computer and Managing Files

Ref. Task Item	Page	I	X
2.1. Getting Started			
2.1.1. First Steps with the Computer			
2.1.1.1. Start the Computer.	102-103		
2.1.1.2. Shut down the computer properly.	118		
2.1.1.3. Restart the computer.	118		
2.1.1.4. View the computer's basic system information e.g. the operating system, processor type, installed RAM (random-access memory) etc.	166		
2.1.1.5. View the computer's desktop configuration: date & time, volume settings, desktop display options (e.g. background options, screen settings, screen saver options etc.).	165-167		
2.1.1.6. Be able to format a diskette.	152		
2.1.1.7. Use Application Help functions.	115		
2.2. Desktop Environment			
2.2.1. Work with Icons			
2.2.1.1. Select and move desktop icons. Recognise basic desktop icons such as hard disk, directory tree, directories/folders and files, recycle bin/wastebasket. Create a desktop shortcut icon or a desktop menu alias.	104-108, 134, 176		
2.2.2. Work with Windows			
2.2.2.1. Recognise the different parts of a desktop window: title bar, toolbar, menu bar, status bar, scroll bar etc.	109		
2.2.2.2. Understand how to reduce a desktop window, how to enlarge a desktop window, how to re-size and scale a desktop window, how to close a desktop window.	110-111, 117		
2.2.2.3. Recognise the different parts of an applications window: title bar, toolbar, menu bar, status bar, scroll bar etc. Move windows on the desktop.	110-111, 114, 117, 119		
2.2.2.4. Understand how to reduce an applications window, how to enlarge an applications window, how to re-size and scale an applications window, how to close an applications window. Move between open windows.	110-111, 114 117, 119, 129		

Ref.	Task Item	Page	I	X
2.3.	**Organising Files**			
2.3.1.	*Directories/Folders*			
2.3.1.1.	Understand the basic directory and folder structure on the computer.	130-134		
2.3.1.2.	Create a directory/folder and a further subdirectory and sub-folder.	140		
2.3.1.3.	Examine a directory/folder. View some of the directory/folder attributes: name, size, date when last updated etc.	135-139		
2.3.1.4.	View the computer's desktop configuration; date & time, volume settings, processor type, installed RAM (random access memory) etc.	165-176		
2.3.1.5.	View file attributes e.g. name, size, file type, date last modified etc.	135-139		
2.3.1.6.	Re-name files and directories/folders.	145, 150		
2.3.2.	*Copy, Move, Delete*			
2.3.2.1.	Select a file individually or as part of an adjacent or non-adjacent group.	146, 150		
2.3.2.2.	Copy and Paste files within directories/folders to make a duplicate copy.	147-149, 150		
2.3.2.3.	Take backup copies of data onto a diskette.	153-154		
2.3.2.4.	Use Cut and Paste functions to move files within directories/folders.	147-149, 150		
2.3.2.5.	Delete files from one or more directories/folders.	154-155		
2.3.2.6.	Delete selected directories/folders.	154-155		
2.3.3.	*Searching*			
2.3.3.1.	Use the Find tool to locate a file or a directory/folder.	156-158		
2.3.3.2.	Search by name, date created, file or directory/folder type etc.	158-160		
2.4.	**Simple Editing**			
2.4.1.	*Use a Text Editing Application*			
2.4.1.1.	Launch an editing application or a word processing program and create a file.	119-128		
2.4.1.2.	Save the file to a directory/folder.	127-128		
2.4.1.3.	Save the file onto a diskette.	129		
2.4.1.4.	Close the editing application.	129		
2.5.	**Print Management**			
2.5.1.	*Printing*			
2.5.1.1.	Be able to print from an installed printer.	161-163		
2.5.1.2.	Change the default printer from an installed printer list.	162		
2.5.1.3.	View a print job's progress from a desktop print manager.	163-164		

3. Word Processing

Ref. Task Item	Page	I	X
3.1. Getting Started			
3.1.1. First Steps with Word Processing			
3.1.1.1. Open a word processing application.	181-182		
3.1.1.2. Open an existing document - make some modifications and save.	200-217		
3.1.1.3. Open several documents.	217-218		
3.1.1.4. Create a new document and save.	192-193		
3.1.1.5. Save an existing document onto the hard disk or diskette.	216-217		
3.1.1.6. Close the document.	199		
3.1.1.7. Use Application Help functions.	194-198		
3.1.1.8. Close the word processing application	199		
3.1.2. Adjust Basic Settings			
3.1.2.1. Change page display modes.	190-191		
3.1.2.2. Use the page view magnification tool/zoom tool.	202-203		
3.1.2.3. Modify the toolbar display.	185-186		
3.1.3. Document Exchange			
3.1.3.1. Save an existing document under another file format: txt file, Rich Text Format (rtf), document template, software type or version number etc.	297-298		
3.1.3.2. Save a document in a format appropriate for posting to a Web Site.	298-299		
3.2. Basic Operations			
3.2.1. Insert Data			
3.2.1.1. Insert a character, word, sentence, or small amount of text.	192		
3.2.1.2. Use undo command.	210		
3.2.1.3. Insert a new paragraph.	192, 204-206		
3.2.1.4. Insert special characters/symbols.	211-212		
3.2.1.5. Insert a page break into a document.	255-256		
3.2.2. Select Data			
3.2.2.1. Select character, word, sentence, paragraph or entire document.	207-209		
3.2.3. Copy, Move, Delete			
3.2.3.1. Use Copy and Paste tools to duplicate text within a document. Use Cut and Paste tools to move text within a document.	213-215		
3.2.3.2. Copy and move text between active documents.	217-219		
3.2.3.3. Delete text.	210		
3.2.4. Search & Replace			
3.2.4.1. Use the search command for a word or phrase within a document.	245-246		
3.2.4.2. Use the replace command for a word or phrase within a document.	245-246		

Ref. Task Item	Page	I	X
3.3. Formatting			
3.3.1. Text Formatting			
3.3.1.1. Change fonts: sizes and types.	223-224		
3.3.1.2. Use italics, emboldening, underlining.	226		
3.3.1.3. Apply different colours to text.	225		
3.3.1.4. Use alignment and justification options.	228-229		
3.3.1.5. Use hyphenation where appropriate.	256-258		
3.3.1.6. Indent text.	231-232		
3.3.1.7. Change line spacing.	229-230		
3.3.1.8. Copy the formatting from a selected piece of text.	241		
3.3.2. General Formatting			
3.3.2.1. Use and set tabs: left, right, centre, decimal.	233-235		
3.3.2.2. Add borders to a document.	238-240		
3.3.2.3. Use lists (bulleted and numbered).	237		
3.3.3. Templates			
3.3.3.1. Choose an appropriate document template for use in a specified task.	264-265		
3.3.3.2. Work within a template on a specified task.	266		
3.4. Finishing a Document			
3.4.1. Styles and Pagination			
3.4.1.1. Apply existing styles to a document.	247-249		
3.4.1.2. Insert page numbering in a document.	250		
3.4.2. Headers & Footers			
3.4.2.1. Add Headers and Footers to a document.	249-251		
3.4.2.2. Insert date, author, page numbers etc. in Headers and Footers.	251		
3.4.2.3. Apply basic text format options in Headers and Footers.	251		
3.4.3. Spelling & Grammar			
3.4.3.1. Use a spell-check program and make changes where necessary.	252-254		
3.4.3.2. Use grammar tool and make changes where necessary.	252-254		
3.4.4. Document Setup			
3.4.4.1. Modify document setup: page orientation, page size etc.	242-243		
3.4.4.2. Modify document margins.	244-245		
3.5. Printing			
3.5.1. Prepare to Print			
3.5.1.1. Preview a document.	259-260		
3.5.1.2. Use basic print options.	261-262		
3.5.1.3. Print a document from an installed printer.	261		

Ref. Task Item	Page	I	X
3.6. More Advanced Features			
3.6.1. Tables			
3.6.1.1. Create standard tables.	267-268		
3.6.1.2. Change cell attributes: formatting, cell size, colour etc.	271-275		
3.6.1.3. Insert and delete columns and rows.	270		
3.6.1.4. Add borders to a table.	274-275		
3.6.1.5. Use the automatic table formatting tool.	275		
3.6.2. Pictures & Images			
3.6.2.1. Add an image or graphics file to a document.	276-278		
3.6.2.2. Add AutoShapes to a document: change line colours, change AutoShape fill colours.	281-284		
3.6.2.3. Move images or drawn objects within a document.	279-280		
3.6.2.4. Re-size a graphic.	281		
3.6.3. Importing Objects			
3.6.3.1. Import a spreadsheet into a document.	285-287		
3.6.3.2. Import an image file, chart or graph into a document.	278, 287		
3.6.4. Mail Merge			
3.6.4.1. Create a mailing list or other data file for use in a Mail Merge.	292-293, 294-296		
3.6.4.2. Merge a mailing list with a letter document or a label document.	290-296		

4. Spreadsheets

    ECDL with MS Office 2000

Ref.	Task Item	Page	I	X

4.2.3. Copy, Move, Delete

4.2.3.1.	Use the Copy and Paste tools to duplicate cell contents in another part of a worksheet.	354-55, 358-60		
4.2.3.2.	Use the Cut and Paste tools to move cell contents within worksheet.	354-55, 358-60		
4.2.3.3.	Move cell contents between active worksheets.	354-55, 358-60		
4.2.3.4.	Move cell contents between active spreadsheets.	354-55, 358-60		
4.2.3.5.	Delete cell contents in a selected cell range.	322, 352		

4.2.4. Search and Replace

4.2.4.1.	Use the search command for specified cell content.	363-364		
4.2.4.2.	Use the replace command for specified cell content.	363-364		

4.2.5. Rows and Columns

4.2.5.1.	Insert rows and columns.	356, 360		
4.2.5.2.	Modify column width and row height.	346-347		
4.2.5.3.	Delete selected rows or columns.	356, 360		

4.2.6. Sort Data

4.2.6.1.	Sort selected data in ascending or descending numeric order.	361-362		
4.2.6.2.	Sort selected data in ascending or descending alphabetic order.	361-362		

4.3. Formulas and Functions

4.3.1. Arithmetic and Logical Formulas

4.3.1.1.	Use basic arithmetic and logical formulas in a spreadsheet addition, subtraction, multiplication, division.	321, 325		
4.3.1.2.	Recognise standard error messages associated with formulas.	328-331		
4.3.1.3.	Use the AutoFill tool/copy handle tool to copy or increment data entries.	337-339		
4.3.1.4.	Understand and use relative cell referencing in formulas or functions.	323-324		
4.3.1.5.	Understand and use absolute cell referencing in formulas or functions.	336-337		

4.3.2. Working with Functions

4.3.2.1.	Use the sum function.	326-327		
4.3.2.2.	Use the average function.	332-333		

4.4. Formatting

4.4.1. Format Cells – Numbers

4.4.1.1.	Format cells to display different number styles: number of decimal places, number of zeros after the decimal point, with or without commas for 000's.	341-342		
4.4.1.2.	Format cells to display different date styles.	343		
4.4.1.3.	Format cells to display different currency symbols.	344		
4.4.1.4.	Format cells to display numbers as percentages.	341-342		

5. Database

6. Presentation

Ref.	Task Item	Page	I	X
6.5.	**Printing and Distribution**			
6.5.1.	*Slide Setup*			
6.5.1.1.	Select appropriate output format for slide presentation; overhead, handout, 35 mm slides, on-screen show.	576-577		
6.5.1.2.	Change slide orientation landscape or portrait.	576-577		
6.5.2.	*Prepare for Distribution*			
6.5.2.1.	Add notes for the presenter to slides.	528		
6.5.2.2.	Number the slides.	577-578		
6.5.2.3.	Use spell-check program and make changes where necessary.	580		
6.5.3.	*Printing*			
6.5.3.1.	Preview the presentation document in slide, outline, slide sorter or notes view.	525-28, 578-79		
6.5.3.2.	Print slides in various views and output formats.	590-591		
6.6.	**Slide Show Effects**			
6.6.1.	*Preset Animation*			
6.6.1.1.	Add preset animation effects to slides.	585		
6.6.1.2.	Change preset animation effects.	586-587		
6.6.2.	*Transitions*			
6.6.2.1.	Add slide transition effects.	584		
6.7.	**View a Slide Show**			
6.7.1.	*Delivering a Presentation*			
6.7.1.1.	Start a slide show on any slide.	581-582		
6.7.1.2.	Use on-screen navigation tools.	583		
6.7.1.3.	Hide slides.	588-589		

7. Information and Communication

Ref.	Task Item	Page	I	X
7.1.	**Getting Started**			
7.1.1.	*First Steps with the Internet*			
7.1.1.1.	Open a Web browsing application.	599		
7.1.1.2.	Understand the make-up and structure of a Web address.	610-613		
7.1.1.3.	Display a given Web page.	613-614		
7.1.1.4.	Change the Web browser home page/start page.	606-607		
7.1.1.5.	Save a Web Page as a File.	629		
7.1.1.6.	Close the Web browser.	608		
7.1.1.7.	Use Application Help functions.	609		
7.1.2.	*Adjust Basic Settings*			
7.1.2.1.	Change view/display modes.	635		
7.1.2.2.	Modify toolbar display.	636-637		
7.1.2.3.	Display images on Web page.	637-638		
7.1.2.4.	Do not load image files onto Web page.	637-638		
7.2.	**Web Navigation**			
7.2.1.	*Accessing a Web Address*			
7.2.1.1.	Open a URL (Uniform Resource Locator) and collect data.	613-615, 630		
7.2.1.2.	Open a hyperlink or an image link and return to original page.	605, 615-620		
7.2.1.3.	Browse a specified site and collect data.	615-620, 630		
7.3.	**Web Searching**			
7.3.1.	*Using a Search Engine*			
7.3.1.1.	Define search requirements.	621-622		
7.3.1.2.	Use a key word in a search.	622-623		
7.3.1.3.	Use common logical operators in a search.	624-626		
7.3.2.	*Printing*			
7.3.2.1.	Modify page setup options.	627-628		
7.3.2.2.	Print a Web page using basic print options.	628		
7.3.2.3.	Present a search report as a printed document.	628		
7.4.	**Bookmarks**			
7.4.1.	*Create a Bookmark*			
7.4.1.1.	Open a bookmarked Web page.	631-632		
7.4.1.2.	Bookmark a Web page.	632-633		
7.4.1.3.	Add Web pages to bookmark folder.	632-633		

Ref. Task Item	Page	I	X
7.5. Getting Started			
7.5.1. First Steps with Electronic Mail			
7.5.1.1. Open an electronic mail application.	641		
7.5.1.2. Open a mail inbox for a specified user.	641		
7.5.1.3. Open a mail message.	662-663		
7.5.1.4. Close the electronic mail application.	646		
7.5.1.5. Use Application Help functions.	642		
7.5.2. Adjust Basic Settings			
7.5.2.1. Change display modes.	645-646		
7.5.2.2. Modify toolbar display.	643, 646		
7.6. Messaging			
7.6.1. Send a Message			
7.6.1.1. Create a new message.	650, 654		
7.6.1.2. Insert a mail address in the 'mailto' field.	651-652		
7.6.1.3. Insert a title in the subject field.	653		
7.6.1.4. Add an auto-signature to a message.	656-657		
7.6.1.5. Use a spell checking tool if available.	658-659		
7.6.1.6. Attach a file to a message.	654-655		
7.6.1.7. Send a message with high/low priority.	656-660		
7.6.2. Copy, Move, Delete			
7.6.2.1. Use Copy and Paste tools to duplicate text within a message or to another active message.	661		
7.6.2.2. Use Cut and Paste tools to move text within a message or to another active message.	661		
7.6.2.3. Use Cut and Paste tools to insert text from another source into a message.	661		
7.6.2.4. Delete text in a message.	654		
7.6.2.5. Delete a file attachment from a message.	655		
7.6.3. Read a Message			
7.6.3.1. Collect or open mail.	660, 662-663		
7.6.3.2. Mark/highlight a message in a mail folder.	674		
7.6.3.3. Use the mail bin.	677		
7.6.3.4. Open and save a file attachment.	665-666		
7.6.4. Reply to a Message			
7.6.4.1. Use reply to sender function.	663		
7.6.4.2. Use reply to all function.	663		
7.6.4.3. Reply with original message insertion.	664		
7.6.4.4. Reply without original message insertion.	664		
7.6.4.5. Forward a message.	663		

ECDL with MS Office 2000

Glossary

Recognise technical terms and jargon

Term	Definition
Absolute Reference	Cells in a formula refer to specific cells on a worksheet. If the formula is moved or copied the cell references remain the same. Absolute and relative references can be mixed, for example to refer to a column absolutely but a row relatively.
AC	A domain name suffix indicating that the website owner is an academic organisation - a university, school, college and so on.
Active Cell	The cell selected on a worksheet. Any data typed appears in the active cell.
ActiveX	In terms of website design, a way to provide interactive content, such as a connection to a database.
Address Book	A list of names and email addresses.
ADSL	Asynchronous Digital Subscriber Line - a method of providing a fast connection to the internet over the normal telephone network.
Alignment	The horizontal and/or vertical position of an object relative to its background. For example, text can be centred between the document margins or a picture can be placed in the middle of a slide.
Analogue	Using length (for example, a wave) to represent data. The telephone network is an analogue system.
Application	A software program such as a spreadsheet, word processor or database.
Apply	A button allowing you to apply changes without closing a dialogue box.
Appointment	An Outlook item that schedules a particular date and time for something to happen.
Archiving	Removing old items from Outlook folders by either deleting them or storing them in a compressed file.
ATM	Automatic Teller Machine - a cash machine.
Attachment	A file sent by email.
Authentication	Identifying electronically that a user, application or file is who or what it says it is. Authentication is usually established through an encrypted digital certificate. For example, Microsoft Internet Explorer displays a warning message when you try to open any file without an authentication certificate from Microsoft.
AutoFill	A feature of Excel that allows you to automatically enter a series of values or text.

Term	Definition
AutoForm	An Access tool that automatically generates a form from a table or a query.
AutoLayout	A PowerPoint feature for adding new slides. AutoLayout contains 24 default slide layouts with different placeholders and arrangements.
AutoReport	An Access tool that automatically generates a report from a table or a query.
AutoShapes	A series of predefined shapes available from the Drawing toolbar.
AutoSignature	An Outlook tool for inserting text into a message. An AutoSignature can be a line or block of text and can be added to all new messages by default.
AutoSum	In Excel, a toolbar shortcut to using the SUM function to add up a series of cells.
B2B and B2C	Business to Business and Business to Consumer - two modes of ecommerce.
Backbone	A high-speed line or series of connections forming the main communication channel within a network.
Backup	Making copies of data files. Backups are often made according to a schedule. Regular backups are essential to maintain data securely.
Bandwidth	A measure of how much data can be sent in a given amount of time. For internet connections, bandwidth is usually measured in kilobits per second (kbps, or sometimes just K) or bits per second (bps). For example, a 56K modem can transfer up to 56,700bps.
Best Fit	A tool to change column width so that it accommodates the widest cell entry.
BIOS	A software program stored in ROM that checks the computer's hardware when it is booted and makes sure that the basic components (CPU, memory, graphics adapter, disk drives and so on) are functioning.
Bit	The fundamental unit of data storage, representing a 1 or a 0.
Boolean	A data type - a Boolean value is either 1 or 0, usually expressed as True or False, or Yes or No.
Boot	The process of starting the computer, identifying essential hardware components and starting the operating system.
Bound Control	An object on a form or report that is tied to underlying data.
Bullet	A symbol that precedes a paragraph, usually used to format a list.
Bus	The circuits on the motherboard connecting different components.
Byte	A group of eight bits.
Cache	Immediate access memory used to streamline instructions sent to PC components. Cache is commonly used on the CPU, motherboard, hard disk and graphics card.
CAD	Computer Aided Design - using software applications to create technical plans, drawings and models.

Term	Definition
Calculated Field/Control	A query field or unbound control containing an expression that calculates the data it displays.
Calendar	The diary component of Outlook.
Cancel	A button allowing you to exit a dialogue box without applying any changes you have selected.
Capacity	A measure of how much data a disk can store.
Cascade	A means of displaying windows back-to-back rather like a set of index cards.
Categories	A tool for grouping related items together.
CBT	Computer Based Training - using computer applications to provided child and adult learning. Most CBT applications use multimedia.
Cc and Bcc	Carbon Copy and Blind Carbon Copy - for addressing mail to more than one recipient.
CD-ROM	Compact Disc Read-Only Memory - holds large amounts of data (approximately 650MB). Used for transferring large amounts of data and for installing applications. CDs are also used as backup media in the form of CD-R(ecordable) and CD-R(ead)W(rite).
Cell	The intersection of a row and column in a table.
Cell Reference	A label for a cell, made up of the column letter and row number. For example, D5 means column D, row 5.
CGI	Common Gateway Interface. A set of commands used to program HTTP web servers. A CGI script can automate or customise parts of a web page based on options chosen or information typed into forms.
Character Map	A Windows tool allowing you to paste symbols into a document.
Chart	A way of representing data graphically.
Check Box	A control in a dialogue box that allows you to turn an option on or off.
Child Table	The table on the "many" side in a one-to-many relationship.
Click	Point to the item you want to click on then press and release the left mouse button.
Click-and-drag	Point to the item or area you want, then press the left mouse button and hold it down whilst pointing to another area of the screen. Release the mouse button.
Click-and-Type	A feature that allows you to type anywhere on the page without setting format options first.
Client	A software program that is used to contact and obtain data from a Server software program on another computer, often across a great distance. Each client program is designed to work with one or more types of server programs.
Clip Art	A library of graphics for use in Office programs.
Clipboard	A temporary storage area for text that is being cut or copied.

Term	Definition
Clock Speed	The CPU's activities are co-ordinated by a clock, which is used to synchronise all the internal processes within it.
Cold Boot	The system is shut down and switched off by the user. The user then switches the system back on. A cold boot is sometimes required to remove a virus.
COM/CO	A domain name suffix indicating that the name is owned and operated by a commercial (or for-profit) business. .CO suffixes are also followed by the company's home country (so .CO.UK indicates that the company is located in the United Kingdom). .COM companies are often (but not always) located in the United States.
Command Button	A button in a dialogue box that executes a command, such as opening a dialogue box or printing a document.
Computer	A device capable of making calculations very quickly based on instructions from a software program and user input.
Computer Programs	Applications software such as word processing packages, desktop publishing, spreadsheets, graphics, databases and so on.
Contacts	A folder for keeping contact details about friends and associates.
Context Sensitive Help	Help specific to a particular element of the screen.
Control	In an Access database, an object on a form or report. Bound controls display data from the underlying table or query. Unbound controls can be used to add labels, lines, boxes and graphics to a report or to add a calculated control.
Control	An object in a dialogue box allowing data entry.
Cookie	Small text files, which download automatically to your computer when you browse a site, to provide personalised features on the website.
Copy	Copy a selection to the Clipboard, leaving the original data in place. Any type of data can be copied, including text, pictures, charts, tables, records, files and folders.
Copyright	Intellectual property, such as a software application or computer design, is owned by the designer or producer, who holds the copyright (that is the sole right to authorise distribution of the property).
CPU	Central Processing Unit. The "brains" of a PC.
Crash	When a software application stops working due to internal errors (bugs). When a program crashes, any unsaved data is usually lost. If the operating system crashes, any unsaved data in all open files may be lost. If a program crashes it is usually best to restart your PC.
Criteria	Conditions that control what is selected in a Search or Query.
CSS	Cascading Style Sheets - an extension to HTML allowing physical formatting of web page text and graphics and absolute positioning of objects on the page.

Term	Definition
Custom List	A user created list that can be used in conjunction with the AutoFill feature.
Cut	Remove a selection to the Clipboard. Any type of data can be cut, including text, pictures, charts, tables, records, files and folders.
Cyberspace	A science fiction term for the internet.
Data Protection Act	Regulates how personal data is collected, stored and used.
Data Type	All data is of a certain type (text, number, date, Boolean, object). Most databases require the data type of a field to be declared in the field definition. The data type of a field affects any calculations in which it is used.
Data Validation	Checking that data entered by the user meets the criteria set for the field.
Database	An organised collection of records.
Datasheet	A simple way of viewing data in columns and rows. Each column in the datasheet is a field. Each row is a record.
Date Format	The way a date is represented. D stands for days, M for months and Y for years. For example, d/mmm/yyyy would appear 1/Jan/1999 and dd mmmm yyyy would appear 01 January 1999.
Default	The way something appears or is setup without any modifications.
Design View	The view used to make structural or formatting changes to database objects, including tables, queries, forms and reports. You cannot enter data in design view.
Desktop	The area you work on in MS Windows. The Desktop contains icons to start programs, the Start button and Menu and the Taskbar.
Desktop Publishing	Using PCs and software to create documents with sophisticated page layout. Word contains many desktop publishing features (such as tables, drawing tools and clip art).
Desktop Shortcut	An icon that is added to the Desktop to start a software application or open a folder or file.
DHTML	Dynamic HTML - an extension to HTML allowing for active graphics and animations on a web page.
Dialogue Box	A box that appears after executing certain menu commands. It is used for setting the options required by the menu command.
Digital	Using 1 and 0 to represent data. Series of 1s and 0s are combined to form bits and bytes. Computers store and process data digitally.
Directory	An internet directory is an indexed collection of websites. Each site is put into one or more categories. Sites may be submitted manually or discovered by search engines.
Directory	A directory stores files. In Windows, directories are referred to as folders.
Disk	A component used to store data when the computer is switched off. There are many different types of disk and tape drives. All PCs need a fixed hard disk drive to run software applications.

Term	Definition
Distribution List	A list of email addresses that can be selected quickly as one recipient.
Document	Often used as another word for a file, but more specifically a file created in a word processor containing formatted text.
Domain Name	A unique name that identifies an internet resource to human internet users. Computers identify resources on the internet using the TPC/IP protocol, which assigns an IP number to each resource. Domain names map an English name onto these resources to make them more recognisable. A domain name consists of the name itself ("courseware" for example) and a suffix, such as .COM identifying the type of service (commercial, educational and so on). On the internet, suffixes are ultimately controlled by ICANN, who licence operation of suffixes to various businesses. Domain names must be unique. A company wanting to use its own name as a domain name must make sure that it has registered it to claim the name before anyone else. Domain names are used in URLs, for example to identify websites and email addresses.
Double-click	Point to the item then press and release the mouse button twice in quick succession.
Download	Saving files from the internet on your PC. Your web browser downloads files all the time, but most of these are only kept temporarily. You can also choose to download files and save them permanently on your PC.
Drag-and-Drop	The process of clicking and dragging text or objects from one location to another.
Drop-Down List Box	A control in a dialogue box. A drop-down list box is a text box with an arrow on the end. Clicking the arrow displays a menu of values to enter in the box.
Dumb Terminal	A thin client with almost no processing power or storage capacity used to access services on a server.
DVD	Digital Versatile Disc (or Digital Video Disc) - a sort of high-capacity CD-ROM.
Ecommerce	Use of the internet to market and sell goods and services.
EDI	Electronic Data Interchange.
EDU	A domain name suffix indicating that the host is operated by an educational institution, usually in the US.
EFT	Electronic Funds Transfer - a computer system for processing financial transactions.
EFTPOS	Electronic Funds Transfer at Point of Sale.
Email	A system for sending electronic messages and data between computers.
Embed	Storing a data object created and edited using a different application to the file the object is stored in.

Term	Definition
Encryption	A system for preventing unauthorised access to data, In public key encryption, encrypted data is scrambled using a public key, sent to the person encrypting the data by the recipient. On receiving the data, the recipient can decrypt it using their private key. If the method of encryption is strong enough, decrypting the data is impossible without access to the private key. Weaker encryption can be cracked by a hacker.
EPOS	Electronic Point of Sale.
Ergonomics	The study of factors affecting the performance of people at work.
Event	An item that schedules a particular date for something to happen.
Exchange	A Microsoft server application providing workgroup services such as email and public folders.
Export	Transferring data from the current database to another database or a different file format.
Expression	A formula used to make a calculation. An expression consists of data (either constant values or data from a table or query), operators and functions.
FAQ	Frequently Asked Questions. An information resource for new users of a bulletin board, newsgroup, software application...
Field	In a database, fields define the information stored as part of a record (the columns of data). In a document, fields are used to include automatically updated information, such as the date or page number.
Field Selector	In a worksheet or datasheet, the heading at the top of a column. This contains the column label and allows selection of the entire column.
File	Electronic data stored on a hard disk, floppy disk or network folder. Each software application creates different kinds of files, which can be recognised by their icon and file extension.
File Extension	A way of identifying the file type. A file extension consists of a period and three letters after the file name. File extensions are not always visible in Windows - refer to the online help if you want to see them.
Fill Handle	A small black cross in the bottom right-hand corner of a worksheet cell allowing you to AutoFill the cell contents using the mouse.
Filter	A filter restricts the number of records selected according to criteria you set.
Filter by Form	Filter by form lets you enter criteria in a form.
Filter by Selection	Creates filter criteria according to data you select.
Firewall	A filter for data. An internet server is open to access from anywhere else on the internet (using programs such as Telnet and FTP), but the computer running the internet server is also likely to be connected to the company's internal network (containing private and confidential data). A firewall prevents unauthorised access to the internal network from the internet.
Flame	An email composed and sent in some degree of annoyance.

Term	Definition
Floppy Disk	A storage disk for transferring files between computers. Also known as the A:\ drive.
Folder	A directory for storing and organising files. You can create folders on a hard disk and on a floppy disk. You may also be able to store files in a network folder.
Font	The typeface style of text. Font is shorthand for font family in Office. For example, strictly speaking, Arial, Arial Bold, Arial Italic and Arial Bold Italic are all different fonts.
Foreign Key	One or more fields in a child table that match values in the primary key field(s) in a parent table. The primary and foreign keys are set by creating a relationship between two tables.
Form	A more user-friendly method of displaying data than a table or query. A form usually displays just one record at a time.
Format	The appearance of text or objects.
Format Painter	A tool that allows you to copy formats from one selection to another.
Formula	An expression combining mathematical operators, functions and values to calculate a result, which is displayed in the cell. Values can be numerical constants, text literals or cell references.
Formula Bar	In Excel, the toolbar where formulae and cell contents are displayed and where cells are edited.
Forum	An internet chat room dedicated to a particular topic.
Freeware	Software that is available for use at no charge. The software developer may have put restrictions on the use to which the software is put however.
FTP	File Transfer Protocol - a protocol for transferring files from computer to computer over a network (including the internet).
Function	A built-in formula that is used to perform a special calculation, such as finding the lowest number in a range.
Gateway	A computer that connects one network with another when the two networks use different protocols.
GB	Gigabyte. A unit of data storage, equivalent to 1,024MB.
General Format	The default cell value format in the worksheet.
GOV	A domain name suffix indicating that the website belongs to a governmental organisation.
Grammar Checker	The Word Spelling Checker can also test grammar in a document.
Graph	A type of chart. A graph is a diagram representing the relationship between variables. Graphs are created and edited using MS Graph and can be inserted (as objects) into most files.
Graphic	A picture file or object. There are two types of graphics: bitmaps (such as pictures created using Paint) store information about each pixel in the picture; vector graphics (such as AutoShape pictures) store information about the lines and fills used.

Term	Definition
GUI	A user interface is a method by which the user of the computer system interacts with it. A Graphical User Interface uses icons and windows to represent commands, files and applications.
Hacking	An attempt to overcome security and gain access to unauthorised information held on a computer system.
Handouts	Printed pages with each slide in a presentation represented as a miniature.
Hard Disk/Hard Drive	The main data storage area on a PC. Also known as the C:\ drive.
Hard Page Break	A page break that is inserted by the user.
Hardware	Actual pieces of equipment in a computer.
Header/Footer	An area reserved for text and graphics that appear at the top/bottom of every page.
Help	Most software applications have a help file. The help is usually divided into a series of topics, which can be accessed using a contents page, index and search tool. Microsoft Help systems also have a "natural language" search tool, such as the Office Assistant, to allow you to ask questions in plain English.
Hidden Text	Characters used by the application to format the document. These marks can be hidden or viewed in the screen display, but do not print. For example, the paragraph mark (¶) indicates the end of a paragraph.
Home Page	For a website, the first page browsers come to. For world wide web users, the page that is loaded first when they start their web browser.
Horizontal Scroll Bar	The bar that appears above the Status bar. It is used for moving to the left or right of a window.
Hosting	As most companies cannot afford a permanent internet connection, they use Internet Service Providers to host their websites and email. The website is stored on a computer in the ISP's offices and updated using FTP. Email is also received on the ISP's computer and then delivered to the company when they make a dial-up connection.
HTML	HyperText Markup Language - the codes (or tags) used to create web pages. HTML tags provide information about layout and text structure (Headings, body text, lists and so on) that can be interpreted by web browsers. HTML is still the basis for web pages, but most websites also make use of advanced features such as Dynamic HTML (DHTML), Cascading Style Sheets, XML, Java, ActiveX and server extensions.
HTTP	HyperText Transfer Protocol - the protocol for hosting web pages. HTTP is the "language" web browsers use when requesting web pages from an internet server. HTTPS (HTTP Secure) is an enhanced version of HTTP for conducting online transactions. Most online shopping sites use a HTTPS server to take credit card and other payment details.
Hyperlink	A shortcut linking one document or file to another.

Term	Definition
ICANN	Internet Corporation for Assigned Names and Numbers - the not-for-profit organisation responsible for technical management of domain name space and internet addressing.
Icon	A pictorial representation of a command or file.
Immediate Access Memory	Another term for cache.
Import	Transferring or copying data stored in one file to another. Data can be imported using the cut, copy and paste, drag-and-drop or Insert/Import commands.
Inbox	A folder for receiving and storing email. Your inbox may be on a server or on your PC depending on how your email application is setup.
Indent	The distance between the margin and the text.
Indexed	A field property that determines whether the field is indexed or not. Indexing a field speeds up searches performed on the field. An index can be set to No Duplicates, in which case the user cannot enter identical values in the field. A primary key field is automatically set to Indexed (No duplicates).
Information Superhighway	Another phrase coined to describe the internet. This emphasises the internet's ability to transport huge quantities of information all around the world almost instantaneously.
Information Technology	Use of computing and telecommunications devices to manage and exchange data.
Input Device	Any device used to provide information to a computer.
Input Mask	A property that defines a data input format for a field.
Insert Mode	The normal typing mode. New characters are inserted before existing characters.
Insertion Point	The typing (or cursor) position in a text area.
Installation	Software usually needs to be installed onto a hard disk to run. When you install software on a PC, it copies its files and folders to the hard disk and registers itself with the operating system. Some software also requires the CD to be put in the drive when it is run, so that it can access large files.
Intelligent Terminal	A client computer designed to access services on a computer. The client may or may not be able to function independently of the server.
Internet	A global network of computers hosting services such as the world wide web and email.
Intranet	A private network using the TCP/IP protocol to carry data around and identify resources. This also allows the company to use an internal website.

ECDL with MS Office 2000 © CWC (90) 2001

Term	Definition
IP Number	A four-part number separated by dots (e.g. 165.113.245.2) which uniquely identifies a resource on the internet. Every resource on the internet has a unique IP number. Most resources are identified to the user by a URL using a domain name rather than the IP number.
IRC	Internet Relay Chat. A system for users to communicate in "real-time" over the internet. Using special chat software, users log in to a chat room and exchange messages.
ISDN	Integrated Services Digital Network. A high-speed telecommunications system.
Java	A programming language allowing interactive web page content.
Javascript	Another programming language, much simpler than Java, but also allowing interactive web page content.
Join	A line between a field in one table or query and a field of the same data type in another table or query. There are different join types, which affect how records are selected in a query.
Journal	An Outlook component for recording the time spent on an activity (such as editing a file).
Joystick	An input device used to move a cursor on the screen.
KB	Kilobyte. A standard unit used to measure the size of a file. A kilobyte is 1,024 bytes.
Keyboard	Input device for text-based information.
LAN	Local Area Network. A computer network based at a single site.
Landscape	Page orientation where the page is wider than it is tall.
Laptop Computer	A portable computer with the same functionality as a Personal Computer.
LCD	Liquid Crystal Display. A flat-panel display screen commonly used on portable computers.
Leader Characters	Characters that appear before a leader tab.
LED	Light Emitting Diode. LEDs light up in response to electrical signals. They are used on computer hardware to indicate that a device is turned on. They are also used to indicate data activity. For example, most PCs have a red LED which flickers when the hard disk is being accessed.
Licence	Use of software is usually governed by a licence. The licence usually restricts you to installing the software on one PC. Multi-user licences enable an organisation to install applications on multiple PCs or to allow a set number of users to access the software from a server.
Light Pen	An input device operated by pointing a pen to a screen.
Link	Storing a link to a file (or part of a file) within another file.
List Box	A control in a dialogue box from which an item can be selected. A list box often has scroll bars.

Term	Definition
Log on	Access computer resources with a user name and password. Most network resources require the user to log on. On a network, a user's logon is maintained by the system administrator. A user can be given permissions to access and edit certain folders and resources.
Logic Control	Obtain alternative results depending on the data entered. Complex instructions from software are converted into a series of basic logical operations (AND, OR and NOT) and calculations for the CPU to perform on data.
Lookup Field	A field where a list of values is stored in a table, query or as part of the field definition. The user can select a value for the field from this list and/or type in a value, depending on the properties set for the lookup. Lookups are usually used to select a foreign key value from a list of primary key field values.
Lowercase	Text that is not in capital letters.
Macro	A series of commands saved so that they can be initiated with one action. Macros can also be created using a programming language, such as Visual Basic for Applications (VBA).
Macro Virus	A virus created using a macro programming language.
Mail Folder	A storage area for mail messages in an email application, such as Inbox or Sent Items. You can only access mail folders through the email application, not through My Computer.
Mail Merge	Combining text in a standard document with text from a database or data document.
Mainframe	A very powerful computer capable of serving very many users at the same time.
Margins	The white areas between the paper edges and the text boundaries on the page.
Master Slide	The Slide Master or Title Master.
Maximise	To expand a window so that it fills the whole screen.
MB	Megabyte. A standard unit used to measure the storage capacity of a disk. A megabyte is 1,048,576 bytes (1024KB).
Meeting	An appointment created in conjunction with Outlook email to invite meeting participants.
Megahertz	A measure of frequency. CPU clock speeds are measured in megahertz (though the latest models reach gigahertz speeds).
Memory	Component used to store data for computer operations.
Menu	A list of related commands, such as File or Edit operations. When the menu heading is clicked, a drop-down menu is displayed.
Microfilm	Miniaturised reproductions of documents on photographic film. Microfilm is usually used with a special viewer. Modern microfilm technology allows films to be viewed using a PC.
MIME	Multipurpose Internet Mail Extensions. Used to encode email attachments as plain text for sending over the internet.

ECDL with MS Office 2000

Term	Definition
Minicomputer	A powerful computer capable of serving many users at the same time.
Minimise	To reduce a window to a button on the Taskbar.
Mirror Site	A website duplicated on two or more servers (possibly in different countries). This makes the site more reliable and quicker (If there is a problem with one server, the site will still be available at the other).
MIS	Management Information Systems - a term often used by the IT department to describe itself.
Modem	Modulator/Demodulator. A device that sends and receives signals from your PC to your ISP over a telephone line. You usually need a modem designed for the type of line: analogue, ISDN, cable or ADSL.
Monitor	A screen that presents visual information about the PC's activity. The monitor is the most important output device for a PC.
Motherboard	A circuit board housing and connecting the components of a PC.
Mouse	An input device used to select items on the screen or carry out commands.
Mouse Pointer	The appearance of the mouse when it is pointing to an element on the screen.
Multimedia	An application using a combination of different data formats (text, pictures, sound and video).
My Computer	An application used for organising files and folders.
Name Box	A list box that displays the current cell reference and allows you to select named ranges in the worksheet.
Name Resolution	The process of mapping a domain name onto its corresponding IP number.
NC	Network Computer. A thin client computer designed to access applications and files stored on a server. A network computer may have a fair amount of processing power but almost no storage capacity.
Network	A way of connecting several PCs so that they can share data files, folders and printers. Networks are usually controlled by computers called servers.
NNTP	Network News Transfer Protocol - a protocol for distribution, inquiry, retrieval and posting of news articles.
Node	In terms of the internet, a server connected to one or more other servers. A server connected to the internet allows anyone's data to pass through it on the way to its final destination.
Normal View	In PowerPoint, a combined view showing the slide, outline and notes pages together.
Normal View	In Word, the view used to edit text, especially in a long document.
Notepad	A mini application that allows you to create and print plain text documents.
Notes Page View	In PowerPoint, the view used to edit and format notes text.

Term	Definition
Number Format	The way a number appears (for example, with currency symbols, commas before 1000s and decimal places).
Object	A unit of data that can be copied between different files and applications. Examples of objects include pictures, charts and tables. Object is also used to refer to components within a file (for example, tables, forms and reports in Access).
Office Assistant	An on-screen helper that allows you to ask questions and provides tips while working.
Office Clipboard	An extension to the Windows Clipboard allowing multiple items to be collected and pasted in MS Office 2000 applications.
OK	A button allowing you to apply changes and close a dialogue box.
OLE	Object Linking and Embedding. OLE allows different applications to share data. You can insert an OLE object or file in any other file created in an OLE-compliant application. The object can be edited from the destination file using the original application. An embedded object is saved as part of the destination file. A linked object is saved in the original file and can be edited from either file.
Open Source	A method of developing computer software. Open source means that the code used to create a program is made freely available for others to develop and improve, so long as they re-publish these improvements for others to use. Many applications used to run the internet are open source.
Operating System	A software application that controls the operations of a computer system and/or computer network. Systems software runs in the background and is installed on all PCs. The operating system is often referred to as the platform.
Operator	One of the mathematical operations: add, subtract, greater than, equals...
Option Button	A control that allows you to select one from a group of options.
ORG	A domain name suffix indicating that the website is owned by a non-profit organisation.
Organisation Chart	A type of chart designed to display a hierarchy, often of personnel or levels of responsibility within an organisation. Office applications share the MS Organisation Chart tool, which is used to create organisation charts as linked objects.
Orientation	The direction of an object, usually used to refer to the dimensions of a page (portrait or landscape) but also of the direction of text.
Outline View	Used to edit and organise a document.
Output Device	Devices that (dis)play information from the computer, such as monitors, speakers, printers and so on.

Term	Definition
Packet	A chunk of information sent over a network. Data is sent over a network in very small pieces. Each piece is wrapped up in a packet, containing information about the data, where it has come from and where it is going. A packet may in turn be wrapped up in another packet, depending on which protocols are used on the network.
Pages	HTML web documents.
Paint	A mini application that allows you to create and print pictures
Palmtop Computer	A hand-held device with limited functionality, such as messaging, contact and diary management and internet access.
Paragraph	A block of text ended by a carriage return. The paragraph mark (¶) indicates the end of a paragraph.
Parent Table	The table on the "one" side in a one-to-many relationship.
Password	A series of characters required to gain entry to a system (for example, a network or file). The ideal password is 7-10 characters long with a mix of letters and numbers. Some passwords are case-sensitive, that is lower-case letters cannot be exchanged for upper-case letters.
Paste	Put the current Clipboard contents into the object or area selected. If the original selection was copied, it can be pasted any number of times to different places until the Cut or Copy command is used again. Paste does not work if the destination cannot use or display the type of data on the Clipboard.
Paste Special	A way of pasting specific elements of copied data (such as just formatting or values).
PC	Personal Computer - a desktop computer capable of storing and running software applications.
Performance	The performance of a computer system is governed by the performance of its components (principally the CPU, memory, motherboard, hard disk and graphics card). However, several very fast components may not be able to compensate for one very slow component. A computer system needs to be well balanced to obtain the best results for the least amount of money.
Peripheral Device	A component attached to a PC via a port, usually an input or output device or a disk drive.
PGP	Pretty Good Privacy. A third party program for encrypting email messages and other data transmissions on the internet.
Piracy	Using a non-shareware/freeware computer application without a licence.
Placeholder	A holder for a type of object such as text, clip art or charts. Placeholders appear as faint dotted lines on the slide and contain identifying text, such as "Click to add text"
Plotter	A type of printer for printing the output from charts, graphs and diagrams.

Term	Definition
Point	Move the mouse so that the pointer is over the object or item required.
POP	Post Office Protocol. A system for storing and downloading email sent to you over the internet on your mail server. When you Send/Receive mail, the mail client checks the server for any mail that you have not downloaded to your Inbox. Depending on how the system is setup, mail on the server may be deleted after download, or may persist there for several days.
Port	A device for connecting peripheral components to a PC. Also, on the internet, as the same computer can host a number of servers, different servers are accessed via ports. A server is usually found on the same port on different machines. For example, HTTP servers usually use port 80.
Portrait	Page orientation where the page is taller than it is wide.
Presentation Graphics	An application for creating overhead slides.
Preview	To view a document as it will print.
Primary Key	A field that uniquely identifies a record in a database table. Values in a primary key field cannot be null or duplicated.
Print Layout View	Used to edit and format document pages, which are displayed much as they will print.
Printer	An output device allowing a document to be printed onto paper. Most printers can print text and graphics. Many applications can match the screen display with printed output.
Program	A software application.
Program Icon	The icon on the left-hand side of the Title bar allowing control of the window.
Programming	Writing a software application using a programming language, such as C++, Java or Visual Basic. Most programming languages are software applications themselves, offering visual tools for Rapid Application Development (RAD).
Properties	In Access, the characteristics of an object, such as a field or control.
Protocol	A protocol is a definition for sending data over a network. The definition standardises the way data is wrapped in packets.
Public Folder	A mail folder accessible to several (or all) members of a workgroup.
Query	A query selects records from a data source, such as table(s) or other queries. A query often includes criteria, to restrict the number of records returned and a sort, to change the order of records. Special types of query can also summarise data or change records (action queries).
RAM	Random Access Memory. Used to store software and data files as they are being used. Any data in RAM is lost when the computer is switched off.
Range	A rectangular area in a worksheet. A range can be one cell, for example, A1:A1 or several cells, for example, D3:D19.

Term	Definition
Record	A collection of fields with values comprising one entry (row) in a database.
Recycle Bin	A folder storing deleted files.
Relationship	In a database, matching values stored in one table with values stored in another table. Storing related records in several tables is more efficient than trying to create a table with fields for every bit of information required.
	The most common type of relationship identifies a field in a child table (a foreign key) where each value corresponds to one unique value in the parent table (a primary key). This type of relationship is called a one-to-many relationship.
	Defining a relationship creates a join between the two tables, which is used in queries.
Relative Reference	Cell references in a formula refer to cells in a position relative to the cell containing the formula. The references are updated to maintain the same relative position if the formula is moved or copied.
Removable Storage	Disks used to store data files away from the PC, usually as a backup.
Report	A method of formatting and displaying data for printing or summary.
Required Property	Determines whether an entry in the field must be made. If set to Yes, the field cannot be left blank.
Requirements Analysis	The first stage of systems design, where the capabilities of the new system are set.
Restore	To return a maximised window to its original size and position.
Right-click	Point to the item you want to click on then press and release the right mouse button.
Robot	A software program that searches the internet cataloguing new websites for a search engine's database. Robots are also known as spiders or crawlers.
Robust	A software application with relatively few errors that cause it to crash. Almost all programs have at least some errors in them. Robustness is particularly important in an operating system.
ROM	Read-Only Memory. Used to store the instructions necessary for starting the PC.
Router	A special-purpose computer (or software package) that handles the connection between two or more networks. Routers look at the destination address of the packets passing through them and decide which route to send them.
Row Selector	In a worksheet or datasheet, the box to the left of a row. In a worksheet, this also contains the row label. In a datasheet it displays the record status. You can click the row selector to select the entire row.
RSI	Repetitive Strain Injury - a complaint caused by performing the same hand/arm movements for a long time.

Term	Definition
Saving	Creating a file on disk. Data typed into an application must be saved as a file or else it is lost when you exit.
Scalability	The ability of a software application (typically a database or network operating system) to support a larger number of users.
Scale	On a chart, the units used to represent data.
ScreenTip	A help box that appears on screen telling you what a screen element is or does.
Scroll	To move through a window by dragging the arrows and boxes on the scroll bars.
Search Engine	Generally used to mean a website offering internet search tool(s). A search engine is specifically a software program that follows hyperlinks all over the internet to add pages (and information about the pages) to a database. The database can then be searched by entering keywords (criteria) to return a list of pages relevant to the search.
Section	Part of a document with different page formatting, headers or footers than the rest.
Security	Ensuring the integrity of an organisation's data. Data needs to be secured against theft and loss. Security is implemented using passwords, encryption and backup.
Server	Both the computer hosting a server application and the application itself. There are many different types of server, providing different services, such as web page access and email.
Shareware	Software that is available for a limited period for no cost (for evaluation purposes for example). After the evaluation period ends, a fee must be paid to continue using the software.
Shortcut/SpeedKey	A keyboard equivalent to a menu command.
Shortcut Menu	A context menu that appears when you click the right mouse button.
SIG	Special Interest Group. A collection of people dedicated to extending the sum total of human knowledge on a particular topic.
Site	The short name for a website.
Slide	The basic unit or "page" in a presentation.
Slide Master	A slide controlling the format and placement of titles and text on all slides except Title Slides.
Slide Show	A way of viewing a presentation. In this view the PowerPoint window is not visible; each slide occupies the complete screen area.
Slide Sorter View	A view where each slide in a presentation is displayed as a miniature. Slides cannot be edited in this view, but they can be deleted, moved and copied.
Slide View	View used to format and edit a slide.
Smiley	In email messages, smileys are "cute" ways of representing the author's feelings about something using typographical symbols. For example :-) means "I am happy".

Term	Definition
SMTP	Simple Mail Transfer Protocol - the protocol used to deliver mail over the internet.
Socket	A socket is the conversation your computer is having with a server. You may have one socket for web browsing, another socket for getting your mail...
Soft Page Break	A page break that is inserted by Word as soon as text reaches the bottom margin.
Software	The programs which are written to run computers or to help computer users perform tasks.
Sort	Change the order in which records or items in a list are displayed. Records can be sorted by one or more fields. Blanks always appear at the end.
Sort Ascending	Sort values and dates with the lowest value or earliest date first. In an alphanumeric sort, 0 (zero) to 9 appear first, then spaces, then typographical symbols then A to Z.
Sort Descending	Sort values and dates with the highest value or latest date first. In an alphanumeric sort, Z to A appear first, then typographical symbols, then spaces and finally 9 to 0 (zero).
SPAM	Junk email.
Speech Synthesiser	Using a sound card, speakers and a microphone, a computer can interpret speech and "speak" itself.
Spelling Checker	A tool to check spelling in the document. The Office products use the same spelling tool, though some features are not available in all applications. The checker uses a custom dictionary to keep track of words that are correct but that it does not recognise.
Spin Box	A control in a dialogue box with arrows allowing the value to be incremented/decremented.
Spreadsheet	A table of data with formulae for making calculations.
Start Menu	A menu containing shortcuts to applications, files, help and Windows tools.
Stationery	A format for HTML email.
Status Bar	The bar at the bottom of the screen that gives information about the current file or selection.
STT	Secure Transaction Technology - designed to provide a secure method for transferring data over a public network, such as the internet.
Style	A collection of formats used to maintain consistent formatting in a document.
Subform	A form within a form displaying child records related to the parent record.
Surfing the Web	Meaning to look for information. Often used in the context "I surfed the web last night and I found this really interesting site that...."

Term	Definition
Symbol	A character with no representation on the keyboard. Symbols can be inserted using a tool in the application or with the Windows feature Character Map. Special fonts are available containing a range of special symbols and pictures. Symbols are often used as bullet points.
Tab	A hidden character used to advance text to a certain position on the page. Tabs are inserted using the Tab key. The position of tabs is controlled by setting tab stops.
Table	An object in a file displaying information in a grid. Tables are divided into rows and columns; rows representing records and columns representing fields. Tables can also be used in a document for page layout.
Tape	A type of removable storage device.
Taskbar	A Windows feature allowing you to switch between applications (and in Office 2000 between documents).
TCP/IP	Transfer Control Protocol/Internet Protocol. The suite of protocols used to transmit data between computers on the internet.
Telecommunications	A variety of communications networks for transferring data, including the telephone system (PSTN), ISDN, cable, satellite and radio communications.
Telnet	A command program used to login from one internet site to another. Many computers on the internet are controlled by typing in commands rather than by selecting buttons from toolbars and menus.
Template	The basis of a document, containing formatting (such as margins and line spacing), text and/or graphics. A document template has a different file extension
Testing	Stage of systems design where components are used under different conditions to discover errors (bugs) or usability problems.
Text Box	A control in a dialogue box used for typing text.
Thesaurus	Word's thesaurus allows you to look up similar words (synonyms) and words with the opposite meaning (antonyms).
Tile	A way of displaying open windows so that they are side by side horizontally or vertically.
Title Bar	The bar at the top of a window that contains the name of the window or dialogue box.
Title Master	A slide controlling the format and placement of titles and subtitles on Title Slides.
Toolbar	A bar containing buttons that provide quick access to frequently used commands. Most applications have more than one toolbar.
Touch pad	An input device operated by moving a digit over a pad.
Trackball	An "upside-down" mouse used as an input device.
Trojan Horse	An application or file that is not what it appears to be. For example, a file may claim to be a digital video whereas in fact it sends rude messages when you logon to newsgroups or attempts to email itself to everyone in your address book.

Term	Definition
Typeover Mode	The mode used to type over existing characters in a document.
Unbound Control	Objects such as lines and graphics or calculated controls added to a form or report.
Undo	A feature that allows you to reverse changes you make to a file in sequence. The number of Undos available depends on the application.
UNIX	An operating system. The most popular HTTP web server on the internet (Apache) is primarily designed for use with UNIX. There are actually many different types of UNIX incorporating different features.
Uppercase	Text in capital letters.
UPS	Uninterruptible Power Supply. Provides enough power to shut down the computer properly in the event of a power cut.
URL	Uniform Resource Locator - a description of the location of a file or service on the internet.
Validation Rule	A property setting limits or conditions on data entry in a field.
VDU	Visual Display Unit - the main output device on a computer, a VDU displays the data being processed. VDUs can be Cathode Ray Tube (CRT) monitors or Liquid Crystal Display (LCD) screens.
Version	New versions of software (or upgrades) are released regularly. New versions of the Office applications come out every 2-3 years. A new version of software usually involves cosmetic changes to the GUI, additional features and fixed features. Some upgrades involve more fundamental changes. Usually newer versions of software will be able to open files created in older versions, but older versions will not be able to open files created in newer versions.
Vertical Scroll Bar	The bar that appears at the far right of the screen. It is used for scrolling up or down a window.
Video-conferencing	Holding a meeting over a network using video cameras and computers. Videoconferencing is possible over the internet, but the quality of picture and sound is difficult to guarantee.
Virus	A malicious program concealed within a data file designed to disrupt your PC or to steal information.
WAN	Wide Area Network. A collection of LANs and workstations based at different sites, connected using the telecommunications system.
Warm Boot	Restarting the computer without turning off the power. A warm boot is often required to complete the installation of software.
Web Page	An HTML file that can be opened in a web browser. Web pages can be published on the internet for worldwide access or on a company intranet. A collection of web pages is called a website.
Website	A website is a collection of web pages serving a common purpose. Large websites may refer to sections of the overall site as being sites themselves. Microsoft products have their own "sites" within the overall Microsoft company website.

Term	Definition
Wildcard	A character used in search criteria to represent other characters. For example, "*" means "Any number of any alphanumeric characters".
Window	All software applications run in their own window. Closing the window exits the application. Some applications can open multiple documents. Each document opens in its own window.
Window Icons	Icons on the right-hand side of the Title bar (and Menu bar) allowing control of the window.
Windows 9x	A family of operating systems, including Windows 95, Windows 98 and Window Millennium.
Windows NT	An operating system. The latest version of Windows NT is called Windows 2000. Windows NT is designed for business and is more robust and secure than Windows 9x. Many companies use Windows NT for their company networks and the MS Internet Information Server as a web server for their intranet.
Wizard	A set of dialogue boxes that allow you to perform a task using step-by-step instructions.
Word Processor	A software application for creating and editing text on-screen. Modern word processors such as Word also allow you to create documents with sophisticated page layouts.
Word Wrap	In a document, when text reaches the right margin, any new text is automatically carried down to the next line without the Return key being pressed.
WordPad	A mini application that allows you to create and print formatted text documents.
Workbook	The files created by Excel to store worksheets.
Workgroup	A computer network allowing a group of users access to shared resources, such as applications, files, email and printers.
Worksheet	The area in an Excel file in which you enter data. Worksheets are comprised of rows and columns. Worksheets are saved in a workbook.
World Wide Web	The collection of hyperlinked web pages on the internet.
Worm	A type of virus designed to copy and transmit itself between computers (for example, by email) but not to infect other files.
XML	EXtensible Markup Language - a proposed replacement to HTML, allowing greater flexibility for web page design.
Year 2000 Problem	The (in)ability of PCs and PC software to interpret dates using 2-digit year formats correctly.
Zip Disk	A type of removable storage device.
Zoom	To view the document at a different size.

 ECDL with MS Office 2000

Index

Lookup features and topics in the course

ECDL with MS Office 2000 © CWC (90) 2001

I

Icon, 45, 104, 107, 108, 131, 134, 137, 142, 162, 176
Image. See Picture
Image Library. See Clip Art
Immediate Access Memory. See Cache
Import, 278, 285, 287, 289, 390, 423, 439, 440, 441, 442, 491, 558, 559, 560
Inbox, 639, 640, 641, 643, 653, 660, 662, 663, 672, 673
Indent, 231, 232, 235, 239, 244, 249, 375
Indexed Property, 115, 432, 438, 446
Industrial Systems, 65
Information Society, 15, 73
Information Superhighway, 74
Inkjet, 30, 31
Input Device, 24, 26, 27, 33, 41
Input Mask, 434
Insert. See Clipboard; Import
Insert Mode, 209
Insertion Point, 106, 121, 122, 187, 191, 204, 205, 206
Installation, 18, 36, 88, 687
Intelligent Terminal. See Terminal
Internet, 15, 47, 56, 59, 60, 61, 62, 63, 64, 65, 66, 72, 73, 74, 75, 82, 84, 85, 88, 89, 298, 299, 300, 301, 395, 396, 593, 594, 600, 610
   Dial-up, 600, 608
   Email, 641
   Search, 621
   URL, 611
Intranet, 298, 300, 301, 395, 593, 600, 607
ISDN, 56, 57, 58, 62
ISP, 62, 600, 640
IT, 15, 51, 72, 73
   Benefits, 70
   Limitations, 70

J

Joystick, 27

K

Keyboard, 22, 24, 41, 46, 77, 78, 80, 127
   Settings, 170
Keyword Search. See Criteria; Search
Kilobyte, 33, 144

L

LAN, 52, 53, 54, 56, 59
Landscape. See Orientation
Laptop Computer, 19, 26
Laser Printer, 31
LCD, 20, 28
Leader Characters. See Tabs
LED, 29, 129, 154
Licence, 88, 620
Light Pen, 27
Link. See Hyperlink; OLE
List, 237, 361, 523, 540, 542
Logic Control, 23
Logon, 52, 56, 103, 133, 136, 140, 165, 406, 599, 641, 683
Lookup Field, 450
Lowercase. See Change Case

M

Mail Bin, 86, 677
Mail Folder. See Inbox
Mail Merge, 285, 287, 290, 291, 292, 293, 294, 295, 296, 360, 365
Mainframe, 16, 17, 18
Margin, 191, 192, 244, 366
   Guide, 228
Master Slide. See Slide Master
Maximise. See Window
Megabyte, 33, 144
Megahertz, 24, 40
Memory, 22, 24, 34, 40
Menu. See also Start Menu
Menu, 45, 46, 107, 113, 120, 123, 124, 188
Menu Bar, 184
Message. See Email
Microfilm, 27
Microprocessor. See CPU
Minicomputer, 17, 18, 53

T

U

V

Going Further

Find out about other courses in **Léarn**

Congratulations!

Having completed this training course successfully, you are now a skilled user of Windows and Office software.

If you are going to take the ECDL tests, good luck and best wishes. Please let us know how you get on, by emailing development@courseware.co.uk

Feedback

We hope that you have enjoyed this course and found it practical, informative and easy-to-use. We do appreciate feedback in order to improve our courseware further. If you have any comments to make, please email them to us at the address above.

Further study

As outlined in the **Review** topics, there are many more features to study in each application. As an experienced user, you can now go on to follow "Advanced" or "Expert" courses if you wish.

gtslearning's **Léarn** contains a large number of courses at different levels of experience. The table on the next page lists a selection of current courses, but please note that we publish new courses all the time.

Get up-to-date information about **Léarn** from our website:

www.learnitbooks.com

Further Titles in the LearnIT Series

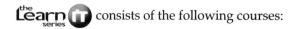 consists of the following courses:

COURSE CODE	COURSE TITLE	MOUS	ECDL
DIOF897I	ECDL with MS Office 97		√
DIOF200I	ECDL with MS Office 2000		√
CSAC597X	MS Access 97 Expert User Part 1	√	√
CSAC597Y	MS Access 97 Expert User Part 2	√	
CSAC800P	MS Access 2000	√	√
CSAC800X	MS Access 2000 Expert User	√	
CSPP597X	MS PowerPoint 97 Expert User	√	√
CSPP800P	MS PowerPoint 2000	√	√
CSPP800X	MS PowerPoint 2000 Expert User	√	
CSWD597P	MS Word 97 Proficient User	√	√
CSWD597X	MS Word 97 Expert User	√	
CSWD800P	MS Word 2000	√	√
CSWD800X	MS Word 2000 Expert User	√	
CSXL597P	MS Excel 97 Proficient User	√	√
CSXL597X	MS Excel 97 Expert User	√	
CSXL800P	MS Excel 2000	√	√
CSXL800X	MS Excel 2000 Expert User	√	
CSOL800P	MS Outlook 2000	√	
SSIEI50I	MS Internet Explorer 5.0 User Introduction		√
SSPC500I	Basic Concepts of IT		√
SSWN500I	MS Windows 95/98 User Introduction		√
SSWN200I	MS Windows 2000 User Introduction		√

Further titles are added to the range all the time- to order a course or find out more, please write or visit our Learn ꭲꭲ website www.learnitbooks.com